THE END

THE END

Everything You'll Want to Know about the Apocalypse

MARK HITCHCOCK

TYNDALE MOMENTUM®

The nonfiction imprint of
Tyndale House Publishers, Inc.

Visit Tyndale online at www.tyndale.com.

Visit Tyndale Momentum online at www.tyndalemomentum.com.

TYNDALE, *Tyndale Momentum*, and Tyndale's quill logo are registered trademarks of Tyndale House Publishers, Inc. The Tyndale Momentum logo is a trademark of Tyndale House Publishers, Inc. Tyndale Momentum is the nonfiction imprint of Tyndale House Publishers, Inc., Carol Stream, Illinois.

The End: Everything You'll Want to Know about the Apocalypse

Designed by Erik M. Peterson

Edited by Adam Graber

For information about special discounts for bulk purchases, please contact Tyndale House Publishers at csresponse@tyndale.com, or call 1-800-323-9400.

Library of Congress Cataloging-in-Publication Data

Hitchcock, Mark, date.
The end : a complete overview of Bible prophecy and the end of days / Mark Hitchcock.
p. cm.
Includes bibliographical references (p.) and indexes.
ISBN 978-1-4143-5373-9 (hc)
1. End of the world—Biblical teaching. 2. Bible—Prophecies—End of the world. I. Title.
BS649.E63H567 2012
236'.9—dc23 2012011474

ISBN 978-1-4964-3029-8 (sc)

Printed in the United States of America

24 23 22 21 20 19
7 6 5 4 3 2

Dedication

This book is humbly and gratefully dedicated to the elders, staff, and members of Faith Bible Church. No pastor and his family have ever had a more loving, encouraging, and generous flock. I have been blessed beyond words to teach you and to learn from you. "After all, what gives us hope and joy, and what will be our proud reward and crown as we stand before our Lord Jesus when he returns? It is you! Yes, you are our pride and joy" (1 Thessalonians 2:19-20).

CONTENTS

PREFACE

In 1958, Dr. J. Dwight Pentecost published his doctrinal dissertation from Dallas Theological Seminary in a monumental book titled *Things to Come*. His book is an exhaustive study of Bible prophecy and has served as the standard for end times prophecy for over fifty years. I had the great privilege of studying under Dr. Pentecost, and I hold him in the highest respect. My goal for *The End*, in some small way, is to provide for this generation what Dr. Pentecost did for his. Although no book can or should replace his work, I would like for this book to serve as a comprehensive resource for a new generation interested in biblical eschatology.

Never has it been more important for God's people to understand the prophetic word and to look for Christ's appearing. People everywhere today have sobering, searching questions about what the future holds. God's Word is the only place we can find sure answers. Yet, at the very time when serious study of and preaching about prophecy is most needed, its importance has diminished in many churches and in the lives of many Christians. I pray that this work can play some small role in sparking a renewed interest in and passion for the blessed hope.

INTRODUCTION

What We Can All Agree On

A FEW YEARS AGO I ran across "The Top Ten Ways to Know If You Are Obsessed with Prophecy."

1. You always leave the top down on your convertible in case the Rapture happens.
2. You never buy green bananas.
3. You talk your church into adapting the '60s pop song "Up, Up, and Away" as a Christian hymn.
4. Bar code scanners make you nervous.
5. You refuse a tax refund check because the amount comes to $666.
6. You can name more signs of the times than you can commandments.
7. You believe that there is an original Greek and Hebrew text with Scofield's notes.
8. You believe the term "Church Fathers" refers to Hal Lindsey and Tim LaHaye.
9. You get goose bumps when you hear a trumpet.
10. You use the Left Behind books as devotional reading.[1]

I'm not obsessed with Bible prophecy—I only scored six out of ten—but I certainly am interested in the end times. The Bible is a book of prophecy. So much of the Bible is prophecy that I say I love prophecy because I love the Bible. Studying the end times has helped me more than anything else to understand the whole Bible.

One of the primary reasons the average Christian avoids studying Bible prophecy is all the different views. A person picks up a few books to brush up on his or her knowledge of the end times, and soon he or she is hopelessly lost in lengthy explanations of long, unfamiliar words.

It reminds me of the little boy whose father was a preacher. After hearing his dad preach on justification, sanctification, and all the other "-ations," he was ready when his Sunday school teacher asked if anyone knew what *procrastination* meant. The boy immediately replied, "I'm not sure what it means, but I know our church believes in it!" That's how many people are when it comes to Bible prophecy. They're not sure what these big words mean, but they know that they must believe in it.

The Bible prophecy novice is overwhelmed by words like *premillennial*, *postmillennial*, *pretribulational*, *posttribulational*, *dispensational*, and *covenantal*. He or she has seen enough charts and time lines to last a lifetime. The novice finally adopts the position of the "panmillennial": it will all "pan out" in the end, so there's no need to worry about it anymore.

There are many different views of end times prophecy, and we'll cover the major ones in this book (except for panmillennialism). Nonetheless, it is critical to remember that there are three great nonnegotiables in Bible prophecy—three events that all Christians believe will happen: 1) the literal, physical, visible return of Jesus Christ to the earth; 2) the bodily resurrection of the dead; and 3) the final judgment of all people. These three truths are crystal clear in Scripture and have been consistently affirmed by God's people throughout history. Although we may disagree and debate other details of the end times scenario, these are the three immovable pillars in our eschatology.

Beyond these fundamentals, there is often a great deal of disagreement about end times biblical prophecy. Theories abound. I do not have all the answers, nor do I have every puzzle piece in place. To claim otherwise would be arrogant and foolish. Not every issue or event of end times prophecy will be addressed. There just is not enough space in one book to cover it all. Entire books have been written on most of the topics that are addressed in this volume, so not every subject will be as fully developed as many would like or even as much as I would like. But I will do the best I can to get to the heart of the matter and present the most important information clearly and understandably. Some will disagree with most of my conclusions, others will disagree with some of them, and probably no one will agree with me on all of them.

My overall paradigm in *The End* is a futurist, premillennial viewpoint (we will look at these categories in chapter 3). I will present alternate views in many places, especially surrounding the Millennium and the Rapture, and I hope to present them fairly and graciously. In the end, I believe one must adopt some overall system informed by Scripture. This is my best effort, using a consistent, literal method of interpretation, to put the pieces together in a way that makes sense of Scripture.

My prayer is that our Lord will use this book to stir His people to anticipate the blessed hope and motivate us to serve Him as pure vessels awaiting our glorious Bridegroom.

PART I

Foundations for the Future

Have you ever driven down a strange dark road in a blinding rainstorm? Every minute you wish you could see beyond the edge of the headlights to see what's ahead. If only you could know what was coming next—could intuitively know what's out there or predict what you'll find at the next bend in the road. We long to see ahead, to know, perhaps to avert disaster.

Can someone see what's ahead by intuition or a special gift? Can a prophet know the future because the path of our lives is part of a larger drama scripted ahead of time? This is what the prophets of the Bible claim. Can we know where we are in that pattern of events foretold by prophets, written in Scripture, or seen in apocalyptic visions of the future? . . . In the uncertain storm of the days in which we live, all of us yearn to see beyond the headlights—but can we?

JOHN F. WALVOORD, *Armageddon, Oil, and Terror*[1]

CHAPTER 1

DON'T STOP THINKING ABOUT TOMORROW

PEOPLE ARE FASCINATED with the future. Psychic hotlines, tabloid newspapers, and astrologers make a living preying upon people's innate interest in the future. Like someone once said, "I'm interested in the future because that's where I'm going to spend the rest of my life." But is this the only incentive for studying Bible prophecy? Was prophecy given just to satisfy our curiosity about the signs of the times and the end of the world? With all the different interpretations, many wonder why we should even study biblical prophecy. Others have become disillusioned by date setters and other reckless speculators. So why is it important to study biblical prophecy?

Years ago the singing group Fleetwood Mac recorded a blockbuster song titled "Don't Stop," with the well-known line "Don't stop thinking about tomorrow." The Bible tells us the same thing. God's people are to think about tomorrow. We are to never stop doing so. While many reasons could be given for thinking about tomorrow and gaining a deeper understanding of biblical prophecy, ten key reasons stand out.

1. Prophecy Is a Major Part of Divine Revelation

A seminary student who was also a pastor explained that he didn't preach on prophecy because "prophecy distracts people from the present." One of his professors observed, "Then there is certainly a lot of distraction in the Scriptures!"

In Bible study there's a principle known as the "Law of Proportion." This law simply means that you can discern the importance of a subject in Scripture by how much attention is devoted to it. Few people have any idea just how much of the Bible is prophetic in nature. The following statistics shed some light on the amount of prophecy in the Bible.

Number of Verses in the Bible	31,124
Number of Predictions in the Old Testament	1,239
Number of Old Testament Verses that Contain Predictions	6,641 out of 23,210
Percent of the Old Testament that is Prophecy	28.5%
Number of Predictions in the New Testament	578
Number of New Testament Verses that Contain Predictions	1,711 out of 7,914
Percent of the New Testament that is Prophecy	21.5%
Percent of the Whole Bible that is Prophecy	27%
Number of Separate Prophetic Topics in the Bible	737[1]

Consider these facts:

- Of the 333 prophecies concerning Christ, only 109 were fulfilled by His first coming, leaving 224 yet to be fulfilled in the Second Coming.
- There are over 300 references to the Lord's coming in the 260 chapters of the New Testament—one out of every 30 verses.
- Twenty-three of the 27 New Testament books mention the Lord's coming.
- Jesus refers to His second coming at least twenty-one times.

- [There are] 1,527 Old Testament passages [that] refer to the Second Coming.
- For every time the Bible mentions the first coming, the Second Coming is mentioned eight times.
- People are exhorted to be ready for the return of Jesus Christ over fifty times.[2]

Applying the Law of Proportion, biblical prophecy warrants serious study. To disregard this much of the Bible is foolish. To say that Bible prophecy is unimportant ignores how much prophecy the Bible contains. Entire books such as Isaiah, Ezekiel, Daniel, Zechariah, and Revelation are prophetic. Many other books contain large sections of prophecy: Jeremiah, Joel, Malachi, Matthew, and the Thessalonian epistles.

Who would study American history and leave out almost 30 percent of the textbook? Who would go to medical school and call himself or herself a doctor yet fail to understand how over one-fourth of the body functions? Likewise if we call ourselves believers in Jesus Christ and followers of Him, it is critical that we understand at least the basics of Bible prophecy.

We see the importance of prophecy reflected in the lives of godly people in Scripture. The prophet Daniel, while he was in captivity in Babylon, carefully studied the book of Jeremiah and discerned that the seventy-year exile was nearly over (see Daniel 9:1-2). In Luke 2 an old man named Simeon and an elderly woman named Anna were both in the Temple when Jesus' parents brought Him there. Simeon and Anna knew from Old Testament prophecy that the time of the Messiah's coming was near. They were "eagerly waiting for the Messiah to come and rescue Israel" (Luke 2:25). "This salvation was something even the prophets wanted to know more about when they prophesied about this gracious salvation prepared for you. They wondered what time or situation the Spirit of Christ within them was talking about when he told them in advance about Christ's suffering and his great glory afterward" (1 Peter 1:10-11). We should eagerly follow the pattern of these godly men and women. We should be compelled to study prophecy if for no other reason than to follow the example of godly saints in Scripture who recognized its importance.

2. Special Blessing Is Promised on Those Who Study Prophecy and Pay Attention to What It Says

In Revelation 1:3, the Lord promises a special blessing on those who study the book of Revelation: "God blesses the one who reads the words of this prophecy to the church, and he blesses all who listen to its message and obey what it says, for the time is near." This is the only book in the Bible that contains this specific, unique promise. For this reason the book of Revelation has often been called the "Blessing Book." The inclusion of this blessing seems to anticipate that many would be tempted to neglect the study of Bible prophecy, especially the book of Revelation.

Revelation contains seven blessings scattered throughout its pages (1:3; 14:13; 16:15; 19:9; 20:6; 22:7; 22:14). The blessing in Revelation 1:3 is the first and most comprehensive one. It is a blessing that anyone reading can enjoy.

Notice the blessing in Revelation 1:3 is threefold.

The one who reads. In the early church, few people had a personal copy of the Scriptures, so someone would read them aloud to the people. Today this blessing extends to all who read this grand climax to God's prophetic program.

All who listen. Just to hear the book of Revelation—and other prophecies of the Bible—read is a great blessing in troubled times like our modern world.

All who obey. It is not only important to read and hear Bible prophecy but also to obey what is written. We should diligently pay attention and watch for signs of the end times.

Any believer in Christ can receive the unmitigated blessing of God by simply reading, hearing, and paying attention to the things written in Revelation and in the other Scriptures that reveal the consummation of human history. Why would anyone want to miss out on this blessing?

3. Jesus Christ Is the Subject of Prophecy

Prophecy is all about Christ. It begins and ends in the person and work of the Savior. Revelation 19:10 says, "The essence of prophecy is to give a clear witness for Jesus." The truth of this verse is certainly borne out in

Scripture. The very first prophecy in the Bible in Genesis 3:15 promises a Deliverer who will crush the head of the serpent. Enoch's ancient prophecy recorded in Jude 1:14-15 prophesies the second coming of Christ. From Genesis to Revelation, the Bible is filled with prophecies that ultimately point in some way to the Savior. Look at some of the ways Jesus is revealed in prophecy.

1. the seed of the woman who will crush the serpent's head (Genesis 3:15)
2. Shiloh ("the one to whom it belongs") (Genesis 49:10)
3. the Passover Lamb (Exodus 12; John 1:29; 1 Corinthians 5:7)
4. the star from Jacob (Numbers 24:17)
5. the Great High Priest (Psalm 110)
6. the prophet (Deuteronomy 18:18)
7. the King (2 Samuel 7; Luke 1:32-33)
8. Wonderful Counselor, Mighty God, Everlasting Father, Prince of Peace (Isaiah 9:6)
9. a righteous king (Isaiah 32:1)
10. "My servant" (Isaiah 53:2)
11. a man of sorrows (Isaiah 53:3)
12. the smiting stone/the smashing rock (Daniel 2:31-35)
13. the Son of Man (Daniel 7:13)
14. the Anointed One (Daniel 9:25-26)
15. the Son who will rule the world (Psalm 2)
16. "My shepherd," "My partner" (Zechariah 13:7)
17. the Lord of the Temple (Malachi 3:1)
18. the resurrection and the life (John 11:25-27)
19. the glorified, risen Savior (Revelation 1)
20. the Lord of the church (Revelation 2–3)
21. the Lamb of God (Revelation 5:6ff)
22. the judge of the nations (Revelation 6–11)
23. the miracle-born man-child (Revelation 12)
24. the coming King (Revelation 19)
25. the Lord of heaven and earth (Revelation 20–22)

The Names and Titles of Christ in Revelation

1. Jesus Christ (1:1)
2. faithful witness (1:5)
3. firstborn of the dead (1:5, NASB)
4. ruler of the kings of the world (1:5)
5. Alpha and Omega (1:8; 22:13)
6. who is and who was and who is to come, the Almighty (1:8, NASB)
7. Son of Man (1:13)
8. the First and the Last (1:17; 2:8; 22:13)
9. the living one (1:18; 2:8)
10. the one who holds the seven stars in His right hand (2:1)
11. the one who walks among the seven gold lampstands (2:1)
12. the one with the sharp two-edged sword (2:12)
13. the Son of God (2:18)
14. the one whose eyes are like flames of fire, whose feet are like polished bronze (2:18)
15. He who has the seven Spirits of God and the seven stars (3:1, NASB)
16. the one who is holy and true (3:7)
17. the one who has the key of David (3:7)
18. the Amen (3:14)
19. the faithful and true witness (3:14)
20. the Beginning of the creation of God (3:14, NASB)
21. the Lion that is from the tribe of Judah (5:5, NASB)
22. the Root of David (5:5; 22:16, NASB)
23. the Lamb (28 times)
24. their Lord (11:8)
25. a son who is to rule all the nations with a rod of iron (12:5, NASB)
26. Faithful and True (19:11)
27. the Word of God (19:13)
28. King of kings and Lord of lords (19:16)
29. the Beginning and the End (22:13)
30. the bright morning star (22:16)

Studying Bible prophecy is vital because its very essence gives witness to Jesus.

4. Prophecy Gives Us a Proper Perspective in Life

There is a story of an airplane lost over the ocean in the middle of a hurricane. The captain decided it was time to inform the passengers of the dilemma, so he turned on the intercom. "I have some good news and some bad news," he began. "The bad news is that our guidance system has malfunctioned and we have no way of knowing where we are or which way we are going. The good news is, we're making great time!" Many people today are like the people on that plane. They are making great time, moving quickly through life, but they have no clue where they are, which way they're going, or where they are going to land. As a result they lack proper perspective about life, and their focus is only on today.

Bible prophecy is important because it tells us the end of the story. It is our guidance system and tells us where we're going. It reveals that just as our world had a definite beginning in Genesis 1:1, it will also have an ending. History is not an endless recurrence of reincarnations. This world will not continue on forever through infinite cycles of history. Bible prophecy reveals to us that there is an end. It reveals to us that there is a purpose and a goal—for this world, for creation, for humanity, and for everyday life.

Knowing this truth gives us meaning, perspective, and purpose and helps us embrace hope in life. If a person really believed that this world would continue on forever with no ultimate goal, it would lead to hopelessness and despair. It would mean there would be no existence beyond the grave, no ultimate justice, no tying up of the loose ends of human history. Bible prophecy tells us that there is a time when every wrong will be righted and every right will be rewarded. There is a consummation of human history and this present world. Bible prophecy is the vehicle God has given us to reveal his plan for history and to provide a goal in our thinking about life and its ultimate meaning and purpose.

5. Prophecy Helps Us Understand the Whole Bible

There's a story about a preacher whose parishioners said he was the best they had ever heard at taking the Bible apart, but the problem was he couldn't put it back together. Sadly, this describes far too many Christians.

Many Christians faithfully read their Bible but really have no idea what they're reading because they lack a framework for understanding the pieces and putting them in the proper place.

Understanding God's plan for the future gives a person the best framework possible for understanding the Bible from Genesis to Revelation. As Randall Price observes, "To be a student of the prophetic scriptures is to be a student of the Scriptures in their entirety."[3] While there is certainly much that we don't know about the future, prophecy reveals God's plan for the Jewish people, the Gentile nations, and the church of Jesus Christ. Bible prophecy clarifies many things in God's Word and in the world around us. A person without a basic understanding of prophecy will be lost in large sections of the Old Testament and in several books of the New Testament, and he or she has little hope of "accurately handling the word of truth" (2 Timothy 2:15, NASB).

6. Prophecy Is a Tool for Evangelism

I have listened to the testimonies of hundreds of people through the years, and I am amazed by how many people first began to think about their relationship with God as a result of Bible prophecy. The first Christian book many unbelievers read is a book on Bible prophecy. God often uses the prospect of the last days and the coming of Christ to awaken people to their need for Christ.

This phenomenon shouldn't surprise us, because Bible prophecy fascinates everyone—even unbelievers. People today have a sense that our world is getting near "closing time," that things are not "business as usual." Most people have the same basic questions about the future: What's going to happen to the world? Are these the last days of the world as we know it? Is Jesus really coming back? Will the human race survive in the future? Is there life after death? Are heaven and hell real?

The Bible answers all these questions about the future, and we can and should use this knowledge to share Christ with others as God opens the door of opportunity. I like the way Randall Price puts it: "What good is it to be able to understand the seven heads described in Revelation 13:1 if we don't use our own head? Of what profit is it to discern the ten toes of Daniel 2:41-44 if we don't move our own two feet? And what value is it to know about the great mouth that speaks lies (Daniel 7:8; Revelation 13:5), unless we open our mouth and speak the truth? In every generation where prophecy has been properly proclaimed, the results have been a harvest of souls to the glory of God."[4]

7. Prophecy Helps Protect People from Heresy

From the earliest days of Christianity, the true teachings of the church have been attacked and corrupted by false teachers. Almost every book in the New Testament contains at least one section that addresses false teaching. Some of the more notable sections are 2 Corinthians 10–12; Philippians 3; 2 Timothy 3; and Titus 1. In some cases the whole book is devoted almost entirely to combating false teaching and the corrupt lifestyle it produces (Galatians; Colossians; 1 Timothy; 2 Peter; and Jude).

In a few instances the false teaching that erupted in the early church concerned speculation about the last days and the coming of Christ. In 2 Thessalonians 2, Paul corrects a false teaching that the Day of the Lord has already come. Then in chapter 3 he commands some of the people to go back to work and quit sponging off the other believers. Apparently, they had applied the false teaching about the Tribulation period to their lives and had quit working. In 2 Peter 3 a group of scoffers took the false teaching in another direction, mocking the idea that Jesus was coming back at all.

The same kinds of speculative errors have continued throughout church history. William Miller was a date setter who gained a large following by predicting that Jesus was coming back in 1843. When Christ didn't come, he then revised the date to 1844. Since Miller's day there have been hundreds of date setters who have led throngs of people to sell their belongings and wait for Jesus in their pajamas on some mountaintop. Most recently, Harold Camping has set dates for the Rapture, in 1994 and 2011, only to be proven wrong.

The Jehovah's Witnesses often appeal to Bible prophecies to gain a listening ear. My wife told me that, when they came to our house, their opening appeal was about the Bible's predictions of future conditions of life on the earth. Mormons have a confused, corrupt, yet very appealing view of the last days and the afterlife that draws in new converts every year.

Theonomists, reconstructionists, and adherents of dominion theology use their postmillennial view of the last days to promote a proactive, even militant, agenda toward secular society.

Years ago, a charismatic charlatan named David Koresh sucked people into his outlandish brand of the Adventist movement primarily by his teachings about the last days. His tirades on the end of the world, Armageddon, and the judgment of God held his followers spellbound. At the time of his death, he was composing his own twisted view of the seven seals in Revelation 6–8.

The bizarre Heaven's Gate cult attracted its following through its wacky views on the last days, alien life, and heaven.

Taking the time to study Scripture and find out what it really says can go a long way in preventing the spread of false teachings like these. An accurate understanding of Bible prophecy protects God's people from those who misuse it.

8. Prophecy Motivates Us to Live Godly Lives in Light of Eternity

Several years ago during a question-and-answer session at a prophecy conference, I heard one of the speakers say, "I believe in the three Ps of Bible prophecy. I'm premillennial, pretrib, and prepared." I like that. That's really the key. What we believe is very important. We should never minimize it. This entire book presents what I believe the Bible teaches about the future. If what we believe about the future doesn't matter, then I've wasted my time and yours. God spent a great deal of time and ink telling us what to expect in the future. It's important. But while the doctrines we hold are key, it's equally important that our doctrines hold us. That is, they should make a practical difference for how we live each day. Prophecy was not given to just stir our imagination or capture our attention. God intends for prophecy to change our attitudes and actions so they will be more in line with His Word and His character.

Charles Dyer, a prophecy expert, emphasizes this practical purpose of

Bible prophecy: "God gave prophecy to change our hearts, not to fill our heads with knowledge. God never predicted future events just to satisfy our curiosity about the future. Every time God announces events that are future, He includes with His predictions practical applications to life. God's pronouncements about the future carry with them specific advice for the 'here and now.'"[5]

9. Prophecy Reveals the Sovereignty of God over Time and History

I read a story one time about a person who went to a psychic, but there was a sign on the door that read, "Closed due to unforeseen circumstances." There are no unforeseen circumstances with God. He rules sovereignly over His world. The God of the Bible knows everything (omniscient), is present everywhere (omnipresent), and possesses all power (omnipotent). Because He knows all things and is present at all times in all places, He has the power to fulfill all of His predictions.

The God of the Bible challenges any pretenders to His position of supremacy in the universe: only the true God can accurately predict the future. Consider what God says about His ability to disclose the future:

> "Present the case for your idols,"
>   says the LORD.
> "Let them show what they can do,"
>   says the King of Israel.
> "Let them try to tell us what happened long ago
>   so that we may consider the evidence.
> Or let them tell us what the future holds,
>   so we can know what's going to happen.
> Yes, tell us what will occur in the days ahead.
>   Then we will know you are gods.
> In fact, do anything—good or bad!
>   Do something that will amaze and frighten us.
> But no! You are less than nothing and can do nothing at all.
>   Those who choose you pollute themselves."
>
> ISAIAH 41:21-24

[The Lord says,] "Everything I prophesied has come true,
and now I will prophesy again.
I will tell you the future before it happens."

ISAIAH 42:9

This is what the LORD says—Israel's King and Redeemer, the LORD of Heaven's Armies:

"I am the First and the Last;
there is no other God.
Who is like me?
Let him step forward and prove to you his power.
Let him do as I have done since ancient times
when I established a people and explained its future.
Do not tremble; do not be afraid.
Did I not proclaim my purposes for you long ago?
You are my witnesses—is there any other God?
No! There is no other Rock—not one!"

ISAIAH 44:6-8

Do not forget this! Keep it in mind!
Remember this, you guilty ones.
Remember the things I have done in the past.
For I alone am God!
I am God, and there is none like me.
Only I can tell you the future
before it even happens.
Everything I plan will come to pass,
for I do whatever I wish.
I will call a swift bird of prey from the east—
a leader from a distant land to come and
do my bidding.
I have said what I would do,
and I will do it.

ISAIAH 46:8-11

> Praise the name of God forever and ever,
>   for he has all wisdom and power.
> He controls the course of world events;
>   he removes kings and sets up other kings.
> He gives wisdom to the wise
>   and knowledge to the scholars.
> He reveals deep and mysterious things
>   and knows what lies hidden in darkness,
>   though he is surrounded by light.
>
> DANIEL 2:20-22

My favorite word in the book of Revelation is the word *Almighty* that describes God eight times. The Greek word translated "Almighty" is *pantokrator*. It is made up of two Greek words—*pantos*, meaning "all" or "everything," and *kratein*, meaning "to hold." This compound word describes a God who holds everything in His hands. The prophecies of Revelation confirm that God has His hands on everything. He is the Almighty.

Bible prophecy proves beyond any shadow of a doubt that God is the true God who alone rules over time and history! He not only rules the ages, but He also controls the events in the life of every person. What a comfort and encouragement to know that God has His hands on every area of your life!

10. Prophecy Proves the Truth of God's Word

An old Chinese proverb says, "It is very difficult to prophesy, especially about the future." But hundreds of prophecies have come to pass exactly as the Bible has said, which is absolute proof that the Bible is the inspired Word of the Sovereign Lord. According to prophecy scholar John Walvoord, the Bible contains about one thousand prophecies of which about five hundred have already been fulfilled. The Bible has an amazing track record of 100 percent accuracy 100 percent of the time. It is batting 1.000.

Just as Bible prophecy establishes that God is the true God, it also proves that God's Word is the true Word. Here are five examples of some amazing prophecies that separate the Bible from every other book ever written and prove the divine inspiration of the Bible.

King Cyrus of Persia

The Hebrew prophet Isaiah wrote during the Golden Age of the Hebrew prophets, around 700 BC. In his writing, Isaiah identified a Medo-Persian king by name: "Cyrus." But Cyrus didn't become king for nearly 150 years. His conquests began around 550 BC and culminated when he took the city of Babylon in October 539 BC. Isaiah names Cyrus in Isaiah 44:28 and 45:1. Isaiah 45:2-6 goes on to predict Cyrus's conquests and his restoration of the Jewish people to their land. Isaiah 44:28 specifically foretells his restoration of the Jews to their land and their temple worship: "When I say of Cyrus, 'He is my shepherd,' he will certainly do as I say. He will command, 'Rebuild Jerusalem'; he will say, 'Restore the Temple.'" Isaiah not only predicted the rise of Cyrus but foresaw the destruction of the Jewish Temple, the deportation of the people to Babylon, and their return to their land. All of this was completely fulfilled about 160 years later (2 Chronicles 36:22-23; see also Ezra 1:1-11).

Four Great World Empires in Succession

Around 530 BC the prophet Daniel predicted that there would be four great Gentile powers that would rule the world in succession: Babylon, Persia, Greece, and Rome (Daniel 2 and 7). Amazingly there have been four, and only four, world empires. As much as others have tried since the fall of the Roman Empire, they have always failed in their lust to rule the world. God's Word stands as the anvil of truth.

The Fall of Nineveh

Between 650 and 640 BC God revealed an amazing prophecy to Nahum. God showed him that the great city of Nineveh, the capital of the Assyrian Empire, would be destroyed. Moreover, God detailed exactly how the devastation would occur. History records that in the year 612 BC all these predictions were fulfilled exactly. The Babylonians and Medes invaded, plundered, and utterly destroyed the powerful city of Nineveh. Consider these twelve specific predictions from the book of Nahum and their precise historical fulfillment.

PROPHECY #1 THE ASSYRIAN FORTRESSES SURROUNDING THE CITY WOULD BE EASILY CAPTURED (3:12).

Fulfilled: According to the *Babylonian Chronicle* the fortified towns surrounding Nineveh began to fall in 614 BC.

PROPHECY #2 THE BESIEGED NINEVITES WOULD PREPARE BRICKS AND MORTAR FOR EMERGENCY DEFENSE WALLS (3:14).

Fulfilled: The moat at the ruins of Nineveh is still filled with fragments of mud bricks taken from Nineveh's breached walls.

PROPHECY #3 THE CITY GATES WOULD BE DESTROYED (3:13).

Fulfilled: The brunt of the attack came against the Hatamti gate at the northwest corner of the city.

PROPHECY #4 IN THE FINAL HOURS BEFORE THE ATTACK, THE NINEVITES WOULD BE DRUNK (1:10; 3:11).

Fulfilled: Diodorus Siculus, in his *Bibliotheca historica* (ca. 20 BC), says that the Assyrian soldiers were drunk and carousing when an unexpected attack came at night.

PROPHECY #5 NINEVEH WOULD BE DESTROYED BY A FLOOD (1:8; 2:6, 8).

Fulfilled: Ancient historians (Diodorus and Xenophon) report that heavy rains in 612 BC caused a nearby river to overflow its banks, breaking part of Nineveh's walls and flooding the city.

PROPHECY #6 NINEVEH WOULD BE DESTROYED BY FIRE (1:10; 2:13; 3:15).

Fulfilled: Archaeological excavations at Nineveh have revealed charred wood, charcoal, and a two-inch layer of ash.

PROPHECY #7 THE PEOPLE OF NINEVEH WOULD BE MASSACRED (3:3).

Fulfilled: According to Diodorus, the slaughter outside the city was so great that the blood changed the color of a nearby stream for quite a distance.

PROPHECY #8 THE CITY WOULD BE PLUNDERED (2:9-10).
Fulfilled: According to the *Babylonian Chronicle*, "Great quantities of spoil from the city, beyond counting, they carried off."[6]

PROPHECY #9 THE PEOPLE OF NINEVEH WOULD TRY TO ESCAPE (2:8).
Fulfilled: The king of the city sent his three sons and two daughters away from the city with great treasure to a friendly neighboring subject.

PROPHECY #10 THE NINEVITE SOLDIERS WOULD BECOME COWARDS AND FLEE (3:17).
Fulfilled: The *Babylonian Chronicle* says that the Assyrian army deserted the king.

PROPHECY #11 THE IDOLS OF NINEVEH WOULD BE DESTROYED (1:14).
Fulfilled: The statues of the goddess Ishtar were found headless in the debris of Nineveh's ruins.

PROPHECY #12 NINEVEH'S DESTRUCTION WOULD BE FINAL. IT WOULD NEVER BE REBUILT (1:9, 14).
Fulfilled: Many ancient cities were rebuilt and reoccupied after being destroyed, some several times (Samaria, Jerusalem), but not Nineveh.[7]

The ruins of Nineveh in modern Iraq stand as a mute testimony to the sovereignty of the awesome God of prophecy.

The Seventy-Year Babylonian Captivity of Judah

The prophet Jeremiah (627–582 BC) prophesied that the wicked people of Judah would be taken captive by the Babylonians and that their captivity would last for seventy years during which time the land of Judah would rest.

> [The Lord says,] "I will take away your happy singing and laughter. The joyful voices of bridegrooms and brides will no longer be heard. Your millstones will fall silent, and the lights in your homes will go out. This entire land will become a

> desolate wasteland. Israel and her neighboring lands will serve the king of Babylon for seventy years."
>
> JEREMIAH 25:10-11

> This is what the LORD says: "You will be in Babylon for seventy years. But then I will come and do for you all the good things I have promised, and I will bring you home again."
>
> JEREMIAH 29:10

This specific prophecy was given decades before the event occurred. The people were taken into captivity in 605 BC by Nebuchadnezzar of Babylon and were allowed to return to Judea in 538 BC. Accounting for the time it would take the people to return, plant crops, and harvest them, the land rested for seventy years. The fulfillment is recorded in 2 Chronicles 36:20-21:

> The few who survived were taken as exiles to Babylon, and they became servants to the king and his sons until the kingdom of Persia came to power.
>
> So the message of the LORD spoken through Jeremiah was fulfilled. The land finally enjoyed its Sabbath rest, lying desolate until the seventy years were fulfilled, just as the prophet had said.

The Destruction of Tyre

In 585 BC, Ezekiel prophesied the ruin of the ancient city of Tyre, first by the Babylonian king, Nebuchadnezzar (Ezekiel 26:7-11), and then finally by the Greek monarch, Alexander the Great (26:12-14). In Ezekiel 26:12 the prophet switches from the singular "he" (Nebuchadnezzar) to the plural "they." This shift points back to the "many nations" of verse 3 that will come against Tyre. In this context, "they" clearly refers to Alexander the Great, who devastated and pillaged Tyre in 332 BC. Ezekiel predicted the coming of Alexander against Tyre 253 years before the attack occurred.

> They will plunder all your riches and merchandise and break down your walls. They will destroy your lovely homes and dump your

> stones and timbers and even your dust into the sea. I will stop the music of your songs. No more will the sound of harps be heard among your people. I will make your island a bare rock, a place for fishermen to spread their nets. You will never be rebuilt, for I, the LORD, have spoken. Yes, the Sovereign LORD has spoken!
>
> EZEKIEL 26:12-14

Alexander the Great overwhelmed the mainland city as well as the island stronghold in 332 BC. He did it by constructing a causeway to transport his troops from the mainland to the island city. It was constructed from stones and timber from the destruction of the old city of Tyre on the mainland. This fulfilled Ezekiel's prophecy that the very stones, timbers, and dust of the city would be cast "into the water" (Ezekiel 26:12, NASB). No Old Testament prophecy was more dramatically fulfilled. It stands as a sober reminder to every nation, including the United States, that no power can ultimately prosper apart from God.

PROPHECIES CONCERNING TYRE
Many nations would come against Tyre (Ezekiel 26:3).
The walls of Tyre would be broken down (Ezekiel 26:4).
Dust would be scraped from her, and she would be left like a bare rock (Ezekiel 26:4).
Tyre would be a place for the spreading of nets (Ezekiel 26:5).
Nebuchadnezzar, king of Babylon, would build a siege wall around Tyre (Ezekiel 26:8).
Nebuchadnezzar would plunder the city (Ezekiel 26:9-12).
Other nations would come, and the stones, timber, debris, and soil of Tyre would be cast into the sea (Ezekiel 26:12).
The city would never be rebuilt (Ezekiel 26:14).
Mathematician Peter Stoner says the probability of the fulfillment of the entire prophecy of Tyre, taking into account all the details, is one in four hundred million.[8]

Conclusion

These are just five of five hundred Bible prophecies that have been fulfilled. History and the fulfillment of prophecy have proven the Bible to be reliable and defensible.

Jesus reminded us that prophecy proves the truth of God's Word and also proves who He is: "I tell you this beforehand, so that when it happens you will believe that I Am the Messiah" (John 13:19). He repeated the same idea one chapter later: "I have told you these things before they happen so that when they do happen, you will believe" (John 14:29). Predicting events before they come to pass is the proof that the Bible is the inerrant, inspired Word of God. More than that, it's the bottom-line basis for believing in Jesus.

CHAPTER 2

WHAT IS A PROPHET?

At the time the Bible was written, 27 percent of its content was prophetic. This fact alone makes knowing Bible prophecy indispensable to anyone wanting to understand what the Bible is all about. However, this fact also presents quite an overwhelming challenge. Understanding and digesting this much material is like untangling a knot of string. Where do we start? What is Bible prophecy? Who or what is a prophet?

For many people, Bible prophecy is only the negative, cataclysmic stuff in the Bible about how God is going to destroy everything someday. And prophets? They are those strange people, wearing strange clothes, eating strange foods, preaching strange sermons, and doing strange things that no one understands. The popular image of a prophet is of some crusty old sage gazing into a crystal ball or a crazy-eyed lunatic with a bad case of bed head.

Because this book is about Bible prophecy, we should get acquainted with the men and women that the Bible calls prophets and prophetesses. Who are they? What did they say? How were they identified?

The Titles of a Prophet

The titles for any job can reveal a lot about a person and what he or she does. People call me a pastor, teacher, minister, elder, reverend, or sometimes a few names I can't repeat here. Most of these titles give insight into the ministry I fulfill. Likewise, several titles for prophet appear in the Bible and can help us to understand who the prophet was and what he or she did.

Old Testament Terms and Titles

English translations of the Old Testament use five main titles for those who spoke on behalf of God. While each of these terms is used for those who filled the office of prophet, each stresses a different aspect of the prophet's job description.

Prophet—This title, the most commonly used, emphasizes that the person was an authoritative spokesperson for God.
Seer—This word focuses on the way in which the prophet received God's message.
Man of God—This title identifies the prophet as one who knew God and who was commissioned by God to a specific mission.
Servant of the Lord—This term stresses the close relationship between God and his faithful messenger.
Messenger of the Lord—This term emphasizes the mission and message rather than the person. A prophet was *sent* as God's messenger to deliver His Word.

Three main Hebrew words in the Old Testament are translated "prophet" or "seer." The third one is the one used most.

1. *ro'eh* Twelve times
2. *hozeh* Eighteen times

These words are both "revelational" terms. They both come from words that basically mean "to see, look at, or behold." The prophet or seer, therefore, is one who can see things that others cannot see. The prophet is one to whom God directly and uniquely reveals His word and His will, usually through dreams or visions.

3. *nabbi'* Almost six hundred times (both noun and verb)

The term *nabbi'* refers primarily to one who speaks for someone else, someone who is a "mouth" for someone else (see Exodus 7:1). Whenever prophets are assigned a specific task by God, the assignment is always focused on speaking God's message. Therefore, the basic meaning of the term *nabbi'* is "to speak God's message," to be a "speaker for God," or "one who is a spokesman for God" (cf. Deuteronomy 18:18; Isaiah 1:20; Jeremiah 1:7). The *nabbi'* was a "divinely inspired preacher" who faithfully spoke the message God had revealed—the prophet spoke when God spoke.

THE RELATIONSHIP BETWEEN "PROPHET" AND "SEER"[1]

NAME	BASIC CONCEPT	FOCUS	EMPHASIS
Prophet	Spokesman	Proclamation of Divine Revelation	Output (What he does)
Seer	One who "sees"	Reception of Divine Revelation	Input (How he knows)

New Testament Terms and Titles

The primary New Testament term for a prophet or prophetess is the Greek noun *prophetes* and the verb *propheteuo*. The word, like its Old Testament counterpart, refers to one who speaks for God, one who speaks the word and will of God. The New Testament prophet brought God's Word to his fellow man.

The Traits of a Prophet

The prophets are towering individuals in the Scripture. It was a great and distinct honor to be a prophet of the living God. That's why there were so many false prophets in Israel. The prophets anointed kings, performed miracles, and predicted the future.

At the same time, a prophet's assignment could also bring great danger, difficulty, and even death. The prophet was called to speak God's uncompromising message to an often rebellious people. This frequently brought reproach, opposition, criticism, and even execution to the prophet of God. Not just anyone could be a prophet. There were at least two major qualifications required of a true prophet of God.

1. The Prophet Must Be Called

Unlike kings and priests, the son of a prophet did not automatically follow in his father's footsteps. Prophets did not inherit their jobs by being born into a prophetic tribe or family. Each prophet or prophetess was selected and called by God to a specific work that God had for him or her to accomplish. This divine call is what made a person a true prophet, and the lack of a call made a person a false prophet. Here are just a few examples of the divine call of a prophet.

- God called Moses through the burning bush (see Exodus 3:4).
- God called Isaiah through a vision of the Lord high and lifted up in the Temple (see Isaiah 6).
- God called Jeremiah while Jeremiah was still in his mother's womb (see Jeremiah 1:5).
- God called Ezekiel near the Kebar River in Babylon (see Ezekiel 1:1; 2:2-3).
- God called Amos, who remembered it like this: "I'm not a professional prophet, and I was never trained to be one. I'm just a shepherd, and I take care of sycamore-fig trees. But the LORD called me away from my flock and told me, 'Go and prophesy to my people in Israel'" (Amos 7:14-15).

2. The Prophet Must Be Courageous

The rigors and responsibilities of a prophet demanded a special kind of person. Above all, he or she had to be a bold individual. Prophets experienced both persecution and praise, both accolades and antagonism. Just think about the job assignments of some of the prophets.

Samuel's first task was to inform the high priest Eli that God had rejected Eli's family (see 1 Samuel 3:4-18).

Nathan had to confront David about his sin with Bathsheba and his murder of her husband (see 2 Samuel 12:1-12).

Gad made David choose one of three punishments for his sinful census (see 2 Samuel 24:10-17).

Elijah warned King Ahab of a terrible drought and famine (see 1 Kings 17:1).

Jonah had to call the wicked city of Nineveh to repentance (see Jonah 1:2; 3:1-2).

Old Testament scholar Leon Wood summarizes the courage needed by a prophet.

> Prophets had to be people of outstanding character, great minds, and courageous souls. They had to be this by nature and then, being dedicated to God, they became still greater because of the tasks and special provisions assigned them. Thus they became the towering giants of Israel, the formers of public opinion, the leaders through days of darkness, people distinguished from all those about them either in Israel or the other nations of the day.[2]

The Tasks of a Prophet

When most people think of a prophet, they immediately think of dramatic dreams and apocalyptic beasts. The common image of a prophet is of a predictor. This aspect of the prophet's ministry is often called foretelling. The prophet was God's mouthpiece and spokesman for predicting and previewing the future of Israel and the nations. Biblical prophets foretold the future with 100 percent accuracy and announced the coming Messiah, the coming of the Antichrist, and the end of the world.

This book is focused on the still-future Bible prophecies that have not yet come to pass. However, the prophets also had a powerful, pertinent message for the people of their own day. The prophet echoed forth God's message to his or her own generation. This aspect of the prophet's ministry is sometimes called forthtelling.

In both foretelling and forthtelling, the prophet's purpose was the same. Whether the prophet was predicting future events (foretelling) or speaking to the people of the present day (forthtelling), the goal was to call people to trust the Lord, obey His Word, and submit to His will for their lives. The ministry of the prophet was to call people to live their lives conformed to God's law.

Even in forthtelling, the element of foretelling is always present to some degree. When the prophets spoke to the people about current situations, there were always warnings and encouragements about the future included in the message. Almost every prophet first appears as a foreteller. Prediction seems to be the very heart of being a prophet (see Deuteronomy 18:20-22).

With this in mind, let's look at the kinds of messages that the prophets gave to God's people. In the Scriptures, prophets carried out at least five specific missions as they announced God's message to the people of their own day. While this part of prophecy is not the focus of this book, let's briefly consider these five aspects.

First, the prophets were reformers. They consistently called the people to obey the law of God. The prophets were ethical preachers who denounced all the moral, religious, and social evils of the day. The prophet of God was called on to fearlessly rebuke idolatry; marital infidelity; oppression of the poor and needy; injustice; and social, moral, and political corruption. The prophets called people to turn from their sinful ways back to conformity with God's Word.

Second, the prophets confronted the kings and played a statesman's role in national affairs. Interestingly, the first two kings of Israel, Saul and David, were also prophets. But the two roles even in that day were clearly separate. Samuel the prophet confronted Saul about his disobedience (see 1 Samuel 15:13-23), and Nathan the prophet confronted David when he committed murder and adultery (see 2 Samuel 12:1-15).

Third, the prophets served as watchmen among the people. God raised up the prophets to point out religious apostasy and to warn of judgment for failure to turn from it.

"Son of man, I have appointed you as a watchman for Israel. Whenever you receive a message from me, warn people immediately" (Ezekiel 3:17).

"Now, son of man, I am making you a watchman for the people of Israel. Therefore, listen to what I say and warn them for me" (Ezekiel 33:7).

Fourth, the prophets prayed for God's people. While the priests were the primary intercessors for the people in offering sacrifices, the prophets also assumed this role, but without sacrificial and ceremonial activity. We see prophets praying for the needs of people on numerous occasions.

1 Kings 13:6	An anonymous man of God prayed for King Jeroboam.
1 Kings 17:17-24	Elijah prayed for the widow's son.
2 Kings 4:18-37	Elisha prayed for the son of the woman from Shunem.
Jeremiah 7:16; 14:7	Jeremiah continuously prayed for God's mercy on the rebellious nation.
Amos 7:2	Amos asked God to forgive the people.

Fifth, the prophets comforted and encouraged God's people. Prophets are often caricatured as "doomsdayers" who spent all their time lambasting people for their sins. This was certainly a chief part of their calling, but a prophet also consoled and comforted. First Corinthians 14:3 says, "One who prophesies strengthens others, encourages them, and comforts them." God called the prophets again and again to remind the people of His faithfulness, love, mercy, and compassion. By urging the people to conform their lives to the law, the prophets were used of God to edify and encourage the Lord's people.

In Isaiah 40:1-2, the Lord tells the prophet Isaiah, "Comfort, comfort my people. . . . Speak tenderly to Jerusalem. Tell her that her sad days are gone and her sins are pardoned." The prophet Nahum, whose name means "comfort" or "consolation," was raised up by God to comfort the nation of Israel. But bringing that comfort involved predicting and previewing the savage destruction of the wicked city of Nineveh. (Nahum is often called the book Jonah would like to have written.) In the book's three chapters, judgment and comfort are clearly presented side by side. This dualism is not unique to Nahum. While almost all the prophets spoke a message involving God's judgment and wrath on the unrepentant, they also closed their messages with the promise of a glorious future in the messianic kingdom. So even in the midst of judgment, there is a beautiful message of hope, comfort, and encouragement. Hobart Freeman summarizes the task of the biblical prophet.

> The prophets boldly rebuked vice, denounced political corruption, oppression, idolatry and moral degeneracy. They were preachers of righteousness, reformers, and revivalists of spiritual religion, as well as prophets of future judgment or blessing. They were raised up in times of crisis to instruct, rebuke, warn and comfort Israel, but interwoven with their ethical and moral teaching are to be found numerous predictions of future events concerning Israel, the nations and the Messianic kingdom.[3]

The Themes of a Prophet

God used prophets and prophetesses on many occasions to deliver His message. The messages were as diverse as the situations the prophets confronted. Yet several key themes repeat throughout the prophetic messages with amazing regularity.

1. Impending Judgment

A consistent diatribe of the prophets was that God will rain His judgment on those who fail to repent of their evil ways. God's judgment will reach its climax during the coming Tribulation or Day of the Lord, of which the prophets spoke so frequently.

2. Social Justice

The prophets repeatedly called the people to practice fairness and compassion.

3. Condemnation of Idolatry

The people of Israel joined themselves to idols again and again. One of the chief themes of the prophets was to call the people to put away their false gods and turn in faith and dependence to the only true God.

4. The Coming of a Messiah and His Kingdom

The prophets consistently spoke of the coming of a Messiah and of the future deliverance and Kingdom He would bring. This message of hope and comfort weaves through all the prophets. The first prophecy announcing a coming deliverer is found in Genesis 3:15. Hundreds of years later prophecies added details about who He would be and what He would do. More than one hundred prophecies were fulfilled at the first advent of Christ, while hundreds more await fulfillment at His second coming. The following is a list of forty-five of the most significant messianic prophecies that were fulfilled during the first advent of Christ.

1. He was born of a woman (see Genesis 3:15; Galatians 4:4).
2. He was a descendant of Abraham (see Genesis 12:3, 7; Matthew 1:1; Galatians 3:16).
3. He was of the tribe of Judah (see Genesis 49:10; Hebrews 7:14; Revelation 5:5).
4. He was of the house or family of David (see 2 Samuel 7:12-13; Luke 1:31-33; Romans 1:3).
5. He was born of a virgin (see Isaiah 7:14; Matthew 1:22-23).
6. He was called Immanuel (see Isaiah 7:14; Matthew 1:23).
7. He had a forerunner (see Isaiah 40:3-5; Malachi 3:1; Matthew 3:1-3; Luke 1:76-78).
8. He was born in Bethlehem (see Micah 5:2; Matthew 2:5-6; Luke 2:4-6).

9. He was worshiped by wise men and given gifts (see Psalm 72:10-11; Isaiah 60:3, 6, 9; Matthew 2:11).
10. He was in Egypt for a season (see Hosea 11:1; Matthew 2:15).
11. His birthplace was a place where infants were slaughtered (see Jeremiah 31:15; Matthew 2:16-18).
12. He was zealous for the Father (see Psalm 69:9; John 2:17; John 6:37-40).
13. He was filled with God's Spirit (see Isaiah 11:2; Luke 4:18-19).
14. He was a mighty healer (see Isaiah 35:5-6; 61:1; Matthew 8:16-17).
15. He ministered to the Gentiles (see Isaiah 9:1-2; 42:1-3; Matthew 4:13-16; 12:17-21).
16. He spoke in parables (see Isaiah 6:9-10; Matthew 13:10-15).
17. He was rejected by the Jewish people (see Psalm 69:8; Isaiah 53:3; John 1:11; 7:5).
18. He made a triumphal entry into Jerusalem riding on a donkey (see Zechariah 9:9; Matthew 21:4-5).
19. He was praised by little children (see Psalm 8:2; Matthew 21:16).
20. He was the rejected cornerstone (see Psalm 118:22-23; Matthew 21:42).
21. His miracles were not believed (see Isaiah 53:1; John 12:37-38).
22. He was betrayed by His friend for thirty pieces of silver (see Psalm 41:9; Zechariah 11:12-13; Matthew 26:14-16, 21-25).
23. He was a Man of Sorrows (see Isaiah 53:3; Matthew 26:37-38).
24. He was forsaken by His disciples (see Zechariah 13:7; Matthew 26:31, 56).
25. He was beaten and spit upon (see Isaiah 50:6; Matthew 26:67; 27:26).
26. His betrayal money was used to purchase a potter's field (see Zechariah 11:12-13; Matthew 27:9-10).
27. He was executed by means of piercing His hands and feet (see Psalm 22:16; Zechariah 12:10; John 19:34, 37).
28. He was crucified between criminals (see Isaiah 53:12; Matthew 27:38).

29. He was given vinegar to drink (see Psalm 69:21; Matthew 27:34).
30. His garments were divided, and soldiers gambled for them (see Psalm 22:18; Luke 23:34).
31. He was surrounded and ridiculed by enemies (see Psalm 22:7-8; Matthew 27:39-44).
32. He was thirsty on the cross (see Psalm 22:15; John 19:28).
33. He commended His spirit to the Father (see Psalm 31:5; Luke 23:46).
34. He uttered a forsaken cry on the cross (see Psalm 22:1; Matthew 27:46).
35. He committed Himself to God (see Psalm 31:5; Luke 23:46).
36. He was hated without a cause (see Psalm 69:4; John 15:25).
37. People shook their heads as they saw Him on the cross (see Psalm 109:25; Matthew 27:39).
38. He was silent before His accusers (see Isaiah 53:7; Matthew 27:12).
39. His bones were not broken (see Exodus 12:46; Psalm 34:20; John 19:33-36).
40. He was stared at in death (see Zechariah 12:10; Matthew 27:36; John 19:37).
41. He was buried with the rich (see Isaiah 53:9; Matthew 27:57-60).
42. He was raised from the dead (see Psalm 16:10; Matthew 28:2-7).
43. He was and is a High Priest greater than Aaron (see Psalm 110:4; Hebrews 5:4-6).
44. He ascended to glory (see Psalm 68:18; Ephesians 4:8).
45. He was and is seated at the right hand of the Father (see Psalm 110:1; Hebrews 10:12-13).

Jesus fulfilled as many as thirty-three prophecies in a single day when he died on the cross.[4] In addition to these fulfilled messianic prophecies, hundreds of presently unfulfilled messianic prophecies are associated with the last days and the second coming of Christ. These future prophecies of Messiah, His second coming, and His Kingdom are the main subject of this book and will be outlined in the subsequent chapters.

The Test of a Prophet

The true word and way of God have always been plagued by imitators and counterfeiters. For this reason, the Lord established a clear set of test questions a person had to pass in order to be received as a true spokesman for God. Four main passages in the Old Testament deal with false prophets:

1. Deuteronomy 13
2. Deuteronomy 18:9-22
3. Jeremiah 23:9-40
4. Ezekiel 12:21–14:11

In these four passages and many others, Scripture presents at least seven key distinguishing marks of a true prophet. These marks were not always present in every case, but certainly in some cases they were. However, for any follower of God who really wanted to know, there would have been no question who was a true prophet and who was false.

The Seven Distinguishing Marks of a True Prophet[5]

1. The true prophet never used divination, sorcery, or astrology (see Deuteronomy 18:9-14; Ezekiel 12:24; Micah 3:7). The source of the prophet's message was God Himself (see 2 Peter 1:20-21).
2. The true prophet never tailored the message to cater to the desires of the people (see Jeremiah 8:11; 28:8; Ezekiel 13:10). The false prophets—or "pillow prophets" as some have described them—spoke the message that would bring them popularity and money. They were the "Fortune 500" prophets, the religious opportunists (see Micah 3:5-6, 11). The true prophet spoke God's unadulterated message regardless of personal loss, shame, and even physical harm.
3. The true prophet maintained personal integrity and character (see Isaiah 28:7; Jeremiah 23:11; Hosea 9:7-9; Micah 3:5, 11; Zephaniah 3:4). Jesus said that true and false prophets will be known by their fruits, that is, by what they do and say (see Matthew 7:15-20).

4. The true prophet was willing to suffer for the sake of the message (1 Kings 22:27-28; Jeremiah 38:4-13; Ezekiel 3:4-8).
5. The true prophet announced a message that was consistent with the Law and the messages of other true prophets (see Jeremiah 26:17-19). The true prophet's message must neither contradict nor disagree with the previous revelation of truth, but rather should confirm and build upon that body of truth (see Deuteronomy 13:1-3).
6. The true prophet, when predicting future events, had a 100 percent success rate (see Deuteronomy 18:21-22). Unlike the modern psychics, 25 percent—or even 99 percent—was not good enough! If alleged prophets were not 100 percent accurate, the people were to take them outside the city to stone them to death (see Deuteronomy 18:20).
7. The true prophet sometimes had the message authenticated by a miracle (see Exodus 5–12). This test was not conclusive evidence, however, because false prophets also produced miracles on occasion (see Exodus 7:10-12; 8:5-7; Mark 13:22; 2 Thessalonians 2:9). Therefore, Moses added further aspects to this test (Deuteronomy 13:1-5). The true test is the content of the message, not miracles. The true prophet spoke only in the name of the Lord and called people closer to God, not away from God.

Focus on the Future

As we have seen, prophets often spoke a divine message for their own day, and their message was always closely tied to a predictive element of future judgment for disobedience and future blessing for obedience. Many of the predictive prophecies in the Bible have already been fulfilled. Certainly, the hundreds of messianic prophecies associated with the first coming of Christ have already found complete fulfillment. This book will not focus on the prophecies of the Bible that have already been fulfilled. The focus of the rest of this book will be on the currently unfulfilled, predictive prophecies of what is commonly referred to as the end times.

CHAPTER 3

BRINGING THE FUTURE INTO FOCUS

One of the main criticisms of biblical prophecy is that there are so many views that it all gets too confusing. I sympathize with this sentiment, but I hope that by simplifying the various views, this common objection can be alleviated. The starting point is to get the main categories in mind. Prophecy is constructed upon three key building blocks concerning the timing of events and their fulfillment. The study of eschatology revolves around three key issues:

1. the framework concerning the timing of prophetic events
2. the nature and timing of the Millennium
3. the timing of the Rapture

Many other finer distinctions can be made, but these are the main paradigms that need to be basically understood. For each of these three key areas, a number of viewpoints can be adopted.

FOUR MAIN CATEGORIES CONCERNING THE TIMING OF EVENTS AND THEIR FULFILLMENT

1. preterist
2. historicist
3. idealist
4. futurist

THREE VIEWS OF THE NATURE AND TIMING OF THE MILLENNIUM

1. amillennial
2. postmillennial
3. premillennial

THREE VIEWS OF THE TIMING OF THE RAPTURE

1. pre-Tribulation
2. mid-Tribulation
3. post-Tribulation

After decisions have been reached on these three points, the other conclusions fall more easily into place. These issues will be discussed in detail later in the book, but here is the view from thirty thousand feet. Addressing these three big questions will guide your approach to end times prophecy. Let's take a look at the common categories for each of these three big issues.

The Big Picture

There are four main approaches to the timing of prophetic events and their fulfillment.[1]

1. Preterist View (Past)

The preterist view understands most, if not all, of key New Testament prophetic passages as having been fulfilled in the first century by the events leading up to and surrounding the fall of Jerusalem in AD 70. These include passages such as Matthew 24, 1 Thessalonians 4–5, 2 Thessalonians 2, and Revelation. There are two main strands of preterism:

full (extreme or radical) and partial (moderate). Preterists include R. C. Sproul, Kenneth Gentry, and Gary DeMar.

Extreme preterism maintains that *all* prophecies including the Second Coming and the resurrection of believers are past events. They view the Resurrection as spiritual. According to this view we are beyond the Millennium and are presently in the new heaven and new earth (that's pretty depressing). Full preterists contend that if there is an end to history, it is not recorded in the Bible. By rejecting clear biblical truths such as the second coming of Christ, the bodily resurrection, and the final judgment, full preterists stand outside the pale of orthodoxy.

R. C. Sproul, a moderate preterist, says that the preterist approach "places many or all eschatological events in the past, especially during the destruction of Jerusalem in AD 70."[2] Moderate preterists believe that the destruction of Jerusalem in AD 70 fulfilled most of Revelation's visions. They believe that Jesus actually returned in AD 70 in a "cloud coming" to destroy Jerusalem through the Roman army and that Nero was the "beast" in Revelation 13. Sproul goes on, "Preterists argue not only that the kingdom is a present reality, but also that in a real historical event the parousia [Christ's coming] has already occurred."[3]

Partial preterists believe that while the "coming" of Jesus in AD 70 was *a* coming of Christ, it was not *the* coming of Christ.[4] For them, the coming in AD 70 was a judgment for the Jews but not the final judgment coming at the end of history. Moderate preterists believe in a literal, future Second Coming, the resurrection of the dead, and a final judgment.

The strength of the partial preterist view is its desire to connect the events of Revelation to the original audience, sometimes called "reader relevance." The weakness of the preterist view is that it cannot consistently interpret the book of Revelation literally; this is because it restricts the global, catastrophic events described in Revelation to the period leading up to the fall of Jerusalem. It tends to spiritualize and allegorize the text in various places when events don't fit what happened in AD 70.

Lastly, preterists have to date the book of Revelation before AD 70 in order for Revelation to be a prediction at all. The usual date they give for the writing of Revelation is AD 65. They have to have a date before

AD 70 in order for their view to be viable. The problem for preterists is that John wrote Revelation in AD 95, twenty-five years after Jerusalem was destroyed.[5] This date was the consistent view of the early church and has been the dominant view throughout church history. The date of John's writing of Revelation is the Achilles' heel for preterism.

2. Historicist View (Present)

The historicist view interprets Revelation and many other prophecies as a panorama or overview of church history from the time of the apostles until the Second Coming. This view began with Joachim of Fiore in the twelfth century and was very common among the Reformers at the time of the Protestant Reformation, but it is not widely held today. The Reformers identified the Antichrist with the pope and Roman Catholicism.

The strength of this position is its desire to make Revelation relevant to readers in every generation. The central problem with historicism is that adherents frequently disagree on what the symbols refer to, which leads to a general lack of consensus about what the book of Revelation means. Another problem is that historicism can easily degenerate into speculation, conjecture, and "newspaper exegesis" (reading today's headlines into the Bible).

3. Idealist View (Timeless)

Idealists envision the book of Revelation not as a prophecy of future events but as a depiction of the ongoing struggle between good and evil that teaches ideal, timeless principles to inspire believers as they endure the setbacks and suffering of life. Idealism grew out of the allegorical method of interpretation used by church fathers like Origen and Clement and gained traction with the amillennial view of Augustine. The idealist view is probably the main view among scholars today.

The strength of this view is its desire to connect prophecy to the reader in every period of history. However, it fails to give concrete meaning to the symbols of the book. This is its great shortcoming. The book of Revelation is filled with symbols that refer to literal things (Revelation 1:20). We will discuss literal interpretation more in the next chapter. The bottom line is that the idealist view has no interpretive anchor to hold it together. It is very reader centered and not tied to the original meaning of the text. Meaning becomes a moving target. Moreover, what are the timeless principles we are to draw from all these prophetic passages, and are they really relevant?

4. Futurist View (Future)

Futurists interpret many New Testament prophetic texts as describing real people and events yet to appear on the world scene. These passages include Matthew 24 (at least verse 15 and following), 1 Thessalonians 4:18–5:9, 2 Thessalonians 2:1-12, and Revelation 4–22, as well as others. Many of the luminaries in the early church adopted a futurist view: Justin Martyr, Irenaeus, Hippolytus, and Victorinus. Some contemporary futurists are John Walvoord, John MacArthur, J. Dwight Pentecost, Charles Ryrie, Tim LaHaye, David Jeremiah, and Thomas Ice.

The main objection to the futurist view is that "it removes Revelation from its original setting so that the book has little meaning for the original audience."[6] After all, how can Matthew 24, Thessalonians, and Revelation have been relevant to the original readers if the events were over two thousand years in the future? There are two answers to this objection.

First, one could make the same objection about hundreds of Old Testament prophecies. The prophecies of Isaiah about the coming Messiah, such as the Virgin Birth in 7:14, were written seven hundred years before His birth. Micah's prophecy about the birthplace of the Messiah in Bethlehem in 5:2 was also written about seven hundred years before His coming. Many of Daniel's predictions weren't fulfilled for centuries, and some of Daniel's prophecies, written over 2,500 years ago, still await fulfillment. Nonetheless, these prophecies were relevant because the readers did not know when they would be fulfilled. The believers in Asia Minor who first received Revelation didn't know it would be fulfilled more than two thousand years later. They believed the prophecies could come true in their lifetime. Each subsequent generation has lived with the hope that Revelation's prophecies could be fulfilled in their time. This spirit of expectancy makes them relevant for every generation.

Second, Revelation was relevant to its original readers because knowing how history will end, whether it was in their lifetime or not, offered great comfort and hope. Prophecy teaches us that God is sovereign, that He rules from His throne in heaven, that He has a plan, and that His Kingdom will ultimately come to the earth. Vernon Grounds tells a great story about a friend of his.

> A friend told me of an incident that happened while he was in seminary. Since the school had no gymnasium, he and his friends played basketball in a nearby public school.
>
> Nearby, an elderly janitor waited patiently until they finished playing. Invariably he sat there reading his Bible. One day my friend asked him what he was reading. The man answered, "The book of Revelation." Surprised, my friend asked if he understood it. "Oh, yes," the man assured him. "I understand it!" "What does it mean?" Quietly the janitor answered, "It means that Jesus is gonna win."[7]

And it also means those of us who know him are "gonna win" too. The promises of prophecy comfort and reassure believers in every generation as we await the consummation of the ages.

I believe the futurist approach is far superior to the other views. It is the only view that consistently applies the principles of literal interpretation, which we will consider in the next chapter. Futurism was also the dominant view of the early church. Moreover, just as Genesis told us how everything began, it makes sense that the prophecies of the New Testament, especially Revelation, would tell us how everything finally comes out in the end. Overall, the futurist view provides the best explanation for the prophecies of Jesus and the apostles. It is the approach adopted in this book.

Three Views of the Millennium

After adopting an overall approach to the timing of the events of biblical prophecy, the next major issue involves the nature and timing of the

Millennium. The Millennium is a period of one thousand years when Satan is bound and Christ reigns (Revelation 20:1-6). Christ's rule brings unprecedented peace and justice to the earth.

The key questions concerning the Millennium include, Are the one thousand years literal or figurative? Is the Millennium present or future? There are three main positions.

1. Amillennial

Amillennialists maintain that there will be no future, literal, earthly, one-thousand-year reign of Christ, but that the Kingdom is spiritual in nature and is presently fulfilled as Christ reigns in heaven and in the hearts of His people. The one-thousand-year time frame is understood as symbolic of a long period of time during the current age.

2. Postmillennial

This view teaches that Christ will return to earth after the Millennium, hence "post." The millennial kingdom is not a literal thousand years but a golden age that the church will usher in by the preaching of the gospel during this present age. The golden age will arrive gradually as the gospel spreads throughout the earth, until the whole world is eventually Christianized. The Millennium will grow on earth as Christians exercise more and more influence over the affairs of this planet. Ultimately, the gospel will prevail, and the earth will become a better world, after which time Christ will appear to usher in eternity.

3. Premillennial

This view holds that Christ will return to earth at His second coming and will usher in a literal one-thousand-year earthly reign. For premillennialists, the Millennium is still to come.

These three views and their strengths and weaknesses will be presented more completely in chapters 34-35. The strongest view in my opinion is the premillennial view, and that will be the one traced throughout this book.

For more on the Millennium, see chapter 34, page 399.

Three Main Views of the Timing of the Rapture

The final, key foundational issue in establishing an approach to the end times is the timing of the Rapture. The Rapture will happen in a moment; Jesus will return, collect all living believers from earth, and transport them alive to heaven. The timing of the Rapture is usually described in relation to the Tribulation. In other words, will the Rapture happen before, during, or after the Tribulation? There are three main views of the timing of the Rapture:

1. Pre-Tribulation

As the name indicates, pretribulationists maintain that the Rapture will occur before the Tribulation. Raptured believers will escape the wrath of God poured out during the Tribulation.

2. Mid-Tribulation

This view teaches that believers will be caught up to heaven at the midpoint of the Tribulation. Most midtribulationists believe that the seventh trumpet in Revelation 11 will signal the Rapture.

3. Post-Tribulation

This view holds that the Rapture will occur at the end of the Tribulation in conjunction with the second coming of Christ to earth. Believers will be transported to meet Christ in the air as He returns and will then escort Him back to earth.

The pros and cons of each of these views, as well as a couple of less popular Rapture views, will be discussed in great detail in chapters 7–15, so we won't delve into the specifics here. But the timing of the Rapture is a third central issue that forms the prophetic template. I believe the best view is the pre-Trib position. For more on the timing of the Rapture, see chapters 10-12, page 135.

Putting It All Together

Developing a coherent view of biblical prophecy begins with the broad question of when prophetic events will be fulfilled. It then narrows like a funnel to the nature and timing of the millennial kingdom and then narrows further to the timing of the Rapture of the church. Here is how all of these parts can fit together:

Preterists are amillennial or postmillennial and equate the Rapture with the Second Coming, if they even hold to the idea of a Rapture at all.

Historicists can hold to any of the three views of the Millennium and are post-Trib.

Idealists are amillennial or postmillennial and are post-Trib.

Futurists are predominantly premillennial but can hold to any of the three views of the Rapture.

This chart will help even further.

	PRETERIST	HISTORICIST	IDEALIST	FUTURIST
MILLENNIAL VIEW	Amillennial or Postmillennial	Any of Three Views	Amillennial or Post-millennial	Pre-millennial
RAPTURE VIEW	Partial preterists are post-Trib (full preterists deny a future coming of Christ).	Post-Trib	Post-Trib	Any of the Three Views

Take a few minutes to digest this information, because it forms the basis for much of the material in the rest of this book.

A Vision of the End

Before diving into the details of what we talked about above, it will be helpful to unpack the overall prophetic scenario as I see it. This brief overview will explain where we're headed and will define a few basic terms you will see throughout the book. Let's start with where we are today—the church age—and move through some of the key end times events that lead all the way to eternity.

The Church Age

We currently live in the church age, which began suddenly on the Day of Pentecost (Acts 2) and will end dramatically with the Rapture. During the church age, Jews and Gentiles who come to faith in Christ are being formed into one body with Jesus Christ as the Head.

The church age is also setting the stage for the end times. I use the term "end times" to describe the future period of time beginning with the Rapture of the church. We do not live in the end times, but there are events foreshadowing the end times and setting the stage for their coming. These developments are what we often refer to as "signs of the times." Not every minor incident is a sign, but there are major events that point toward what lies ahead.

Signs of the times can be thought of this way: a sign is something that points beyond itself toward something else. When you see a sign above the highway, your interest is not in the sign, but in what it points toward. It alerts you to something ahead that you need to be watching for. A sign indicates what's ahead. It directs attention beyond itself to something more significant. In the same way today, some major world events are signs of the times that point beyond themselves to events that Scripture predicts will occur during the end times. Scripture helps us to see them.

A Time of Further Preparation

The next event on God's prophetic calendar is the Rapture of the church, when all living believers on earth will be suddenly snatched away to heaven. When the Rapture happens, deceased church-age believers will be resurrected and rejoined with their perfected spirits. This will be the surest sign of the times. The Rapture will shock the world and inaugurate the "end times." The world will struggle to make sense of what has happened and to recover from the vanishing of millions of people. Their absence will have ripple effects.

In the wake of the Rapture, a group of ten leaders will form a reunited Roman Empire to restore order and some semblance of normalcy. I call them the "Group of Ten," or G-10. Along with the G-10, a striking individual will appear from the shadows. He will rise out of insignificance and obscurity. He will seem to come out of nowhere, yet quickly ascend to prominence. We know him best by his biblical title—the Antichrist.

Between the Rapture and the Tribulation, other preparations will set the stage for the end times. Many of the pieces of the prophetic puzzle will begin falling into place. We don't know how soon after the Rapture the Tribulation will begin, but several months seems reasonable; however, it could be longer or shorter.

The Tribulation Begins

The seven-year Tribulation will commence when the reunited Roman Empire signs a peace treaty with Israel, guaranteeing the country safety and security, and probably solving the thorny Middle East crisis. The Antichrist, as leader of this Roman Empire, will secure this peace accord. The world will hail him as the great peacemaker. The treaty will lull Israel into a sense of security. Then, during the first half of the Tribulation, when Israel has let its guard down, a massive Russian-Islamic coalition will attack Israel. The Bible refers to this Pearl Harbor–like invasion as the War of Gog and Magog.

God will supernaturally deliver Israel by wiping out the armies of the Gog coalition. The decimation of these armies will leave a power vacuum in the East, and the Antichrist will seize control, break his pact with Israel, and swiftly begin to consolidate his power. The Antichrist will dominate the latter half of the Tribulation (3½ years) as he institutes a one-world government, economy, and religion aided by his henchman, the false prophet. During this time the Antichrist will declare himself to be God, will require universal worship, and will institute the notorious Tribulation trademark—the mark of the Beast—666.

Armageddon and the Advent of Christ

Two great events will bring the Tribulation to a close—the War of Armageddon and the second coming of Christ. As the Antichrist leads the armies of the world against Israel with genocidal intent, Jesus Christ will return to earth, accompanied by the armies of heaven. The Antichrist's military forces will turn to fight the Lord Jesus as He comes, but He will decimate them by simply speaking. He will only have to say a word and the War of Armageddon will be over. Jesus will seize the Antichrist and the false prophet and cast them alive into the lake of fire. At the Second Coming, Old Testament saints and believers who died during the Tribulation will be resurrected.

The One-Thousand-Year Reign of Christ

The second coming of Christ will usher in the messianic age on the earth. This is also called the millennial kingdom of Christ, or simply the Millennium. During these one thousand years, Christ will reign in peace and prosperity, fulfilling God's original plan for creation. Believers who survive the Tribulation, both Jews and Gentiles, will enter the messianic kingdom in their natural human bodies and will have children and populate the kingdom. Those on earth when Christ returns who do not trust in Him will be cast into hell. Meanwhile, Satan and his minions will be bound in the abyss.

At the end of the Millennium, Satan will be released for a brief period of time to lead a final rebellion against Christ. Then he will be defeated and cast into the lake of fire for eternity.

The Final Judgment

After the Millennium and Satan's final rebellion, Christ will sit upon a great white throne, and all unbelievers from every age will be resurrected and assembled before Him to be judged. This will be the final resurrection.

Those who refused to trust in the Lord will be judged according to their deeds. Since their names will not be found written in the Book of Life, which contains the names of the redeemed, they will be consigned to the lake of fire forever.

The Eternal State

The millennial reign of Christ will serve as the front porch to eternity. It will be the initial phase of God's eternal Kingdom. When the Millennium culminates, the final state of God's prophetic program will be ushered in with the destruction of the present heaven and earth and the creation of a new heaven and new earth. The heavenly city, the new Jerusalem, a 1,500-mile cube the size of a continent, will come down out of heaven and sit upon the new earth as the capital city of the new universe. The Lord will reign forever, and His people will serve Him and reign with Him for eternity.

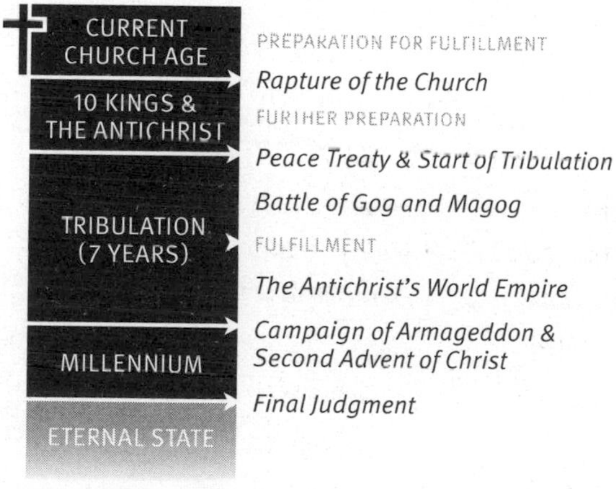

With this overall template in mind, the next step is to address the method of interpretation of prophecy. After all, the principles of interpretation are the essential factor that determines which of these views one adopts. It all ultimately boils down to how prophetic Scriptures are interpreted.

CHAPTER 4

IT'S ALL A MATTER OF INTERPRETATION

THE WATERSHED ISSUE in understanding all Scripture, including Bible prophecy, is the method of interpretation one adopts. Scholars call this "hermeneutics." The basic principles of interpretation that one uses will necessarily lead to certain conclusions about what a specific text or even an entire book of the Bible means. Since more than one in four verses of the Bible are prophetic, every reader of Scripture will eventually ask, "How should I interpret prophecy?"

Biblical prophecy is heavily symbolic, which often makes interpreting it seem difficult, if not impossible. Remember—prophecy was given to be understood. The first verse of the book of Revelation declares that this book is a "revelation from Jesus Christ." The word *revelation* (*apokalupsis*) means "to unveil, reveal, or remove the cover from something." This presupposes that prophetic truth can be understood. The Lord has given prophecy not to confuse us or hide the truth but to help us understand it and be transformed by it.

Unfortunately, many today assume that prophetic passages are to be spiritualized or interpreted in a purely figurative manner. All too often, preachers and teachers adopt different principles of interpretation depending on whether the passage is prophetic or not. This inconsistency has resulted in a great deal of confusion. Roy Zuck highlights the danger of employing a different hermeneutic for prophecy: "Nowhere does Scripture indicate that when we come to prophetic portions of Scripture we should ignore the normal sense of the words and overlook the meanings of words and sentences. The norms of grammatical interpretation should be applied to prophetic as well as to nonprophetic literature."[1]

We must thoughtfully adopt a consistent method of interpreting biblical prophecy. While this is not a book about biblical interpretation or hermeneutics, it is imperative to lay out some key, guiding principles for interpreting prophecy to shape our thinking. Let's consider five basic guidelines for accurately unpacking the meaning of prophetic texts.

1. Interpret Prophecy Literally

Of all the rules, a literal interpretation is the crux. Yet it is very often misunderstood or misstated. Thus, when speaking of literal or normal interpretation, it is important to carefully clarify and define both what is *not* meant as well as what *is* meant. Literal interpretation does not refer to "wooden literalism," that is, failing to take into account figures of speech and symbols that are common to all language and communication. For instance, if I were to tell someone that my dog "kicked the bucket," no one familiar with the idiom would take that to mean that my dog actually used his leg to kick a plastic bucket. Everyone knows it's a figurative way of saying that my dog died. Literal interpretation is not wooden literalism. It's an umbrella term that encompasses both "plain literal" and "figurative literal" language. Speaking of literal interpretation, this is what Charles C. Ryrie says:

> It is sometimes called the principle of *grammatical-historical* interpretation since the meaning of each word is determined by grammatical and historical considerations. The principle might also be called *normal* interpretation since the literal meaning of words is the normal approach to their understanding in all

> languages. It might also be designated *plain* interpretation so that no one receives the mistaken notion that the literal principle rules out figures of speech. . . . Symbols, figures of speech and types are all interpreted plainly in this method and they are in no way contrary to literal interpretation. After all, the very existence of any meaning for a figure of speech depends on the reality of the literal meaning of the terms involved. Figures often make the meaning plainer, but it is the literal, normal, or plain meaning that they convey to the reader.[2]

LITERAL INTERPRETATION		
	ONE MEANING	
Plain-Literal	or	Figurative-Literal

Dr. David L. Cooper states what has come to be known as the "Golden Rule of Interpretation": "When the plain sense of Scripture makes common sense, seek no other sense; therefore, take every word at its primary, ordinary, usual, literal meaning, unless the facts of the immediate context, studied in the light of related passages and axiomatic and fundamental truths, indicate clearly otherwise."[3] This is excellent advice for interpretation.

The dictionary defines *literal* as "belonging to letters."[4] It also says literal interpretation involves an approach "based on the actual words in their ordinary meaning, . . . not going beyond the facts."[5] "Literal interpretation of the Bible simply means to explain the original sense of the Bible according to the normal and customary usages of its language."[6] How is this done? It can only be accomplished through the *grammatical* (according to the rules of grammar), *historical* (consistent with the historical setting of the passage), *contextual* (in accord with its context) method of interpretation.

Examining how past prophecies were fulfilled can show us how to interpret unfulfilled prophecy. Paul Lee Tan says that at "the first coming of Christ, over 300 prophecies were completely fulfilled" and "every prophecy that has been fulfilled has been fulfilled literally. On the basis of New Testament attestations and the record of history, the fulfillment of Bible prophecy has always been literal."[7] Charles C. Ryrie also argues that the literal fulfillment of past prophecy means that we should interpret future prophecy to be fulfilled literally. He says, "The prophecies in the Old Testament concerning the first coming of Christ—His birth, His rearing, His ministry, His death, His resurrection—were all fulfilled literally. That argues strongly for the literal method."[8] The great bishop of Liverpool J. C. Ryle said it well: "It is high time for Christians to interpret unfulfilled prophecy by the light of prophecies already fulfilled. . . . At His first advent the least predictions were fulfilled to the very letter: so also will they be at His second."[9]

The prophet Micah foretold, seven hundred years in advance, that the Messiah would be born in Bethlehem (Micah 5:2). The Messiah was born in Bethlehem. Zechariah 14:4 says that Jesus will return to the Mount of Olives. John says that when Jesus comes, armies will be gathered at Armageddon in northern Israel (Revelation 16:16). We should learn from fulfilled prophecies as we consider what is still to come. We have no more license to spiritualize Scripture's clear words about the end times than we do to say that Bethlehem was only figurative. The first essential key to accurately interpreting biblical prophecy is to consistently use a literal system of interpretation.

2. When Interpreting Symbols, Look for the "Built-In" Interpretations

The most difficult aspect of interpreting prophecy is understanding the meaning of all the symbols. Bible prophecy uses a broad assortment of symbols to communicate its meaning—horns, beasts, stars, and various colored horses. It's critical at the outset to remember that, when symbols are employed, they refer to something that is literal.

For instance, in Revelation 1, Jesus stands in the middle of seven golden lampstands holding seven stars in His right hand (1:13, 16). At the end of the chapter Jesus identifies the seven lampstands as the seven churches of Asia and the seven stars as seven angels (1:20). Jesus Himself provides a key to unlock the meaning of symbols. In other words, when we see a symbol in prophecy, we are to look for the literal referent.

Jesus also teaches us in Revelation 1 that numbers in Revelation are to be interpreted literally unless specified otherwise. There are seven lampstands and seven stars, and these correspond to seven literal churches that existed in Asia and seven literal messengers of these churches. Seven means seven both times it is used in Revelation 1 by Jesus.

When interpreting symbols, no interpreter has the freedom to make a symbol mean whatever he or she wants. Scripture sets the parameters for our interpretation of symbols. There are two important steps in understanding what the symbols mean.

First, the immediate context of a symbol in Scripture may offer a "built-in" interpretation. The example of Jesus in Revelation 1 is an apt illustration of this. Jesus tells the reader the meaning of the seven lampstands and the seven stars in the same chapter (1:20). Another "built-in" interpretation is found in Daniel 2. King Nebuchadnezzar had a dream of a metallic man with a head of gold, chest and arms of silver, belly and thighs of brass, legs of iron, and feet of iron and clay mixed. God gives Daniel the meaning of the image beginning with the head of gold. Daniel tells Nebuchadnezzar, "You are the head of gold" (Daniel 2:38). The metals represent Gentile kingdoms, and the first one is Babylon. Daniel then tells the king that the other metals represent the Gentile kingdoms that will follow Babylon in succession.

This kind of "built-in" interpretation occurs often in Revelation. Frequently, John explains the meaning of a symbol. Here are a few examples.[10]

SYMBOL	MEANING
the seven stars (1:16)	seven angels (1:20)
the seven lampstands (1:13)	seven churches (1:20)
the morning star (2:28)	Christ (22:16)
the seven lamps of fire (4:5)	the sevenfold Spirit of God (4:5)
the seven eyes (5:6)	the sevenfold Spirit of God (5:6)
the incense (5:8)	the prayers of God's people (5:8)
the fallen star (9:1)	the angel of the abyss (9:11)

the great city, Sodom and Egypt (11:8)	Jerusalem (11:8)
the stars in the sky (12:4)	fallen angels (12:9)
the woman and the child (12:1-2)	Israel and Christ (12:5-6)
the large red dragon (12:3)	Satan (12:9)
the ancient serpent (12:9)	Satan (12:9)
the time, times, and half a time (12:14)	1,260 days (12:6)
the beast out of the sea (13:1-10)	future world ruler and his empire (13:1-10)
the beast out of the earth (13:11-17)	the false prophet (19:20)
the great prostitute (17:1)	the great city, Babylon (17:18)
the many waters over which the woman rules (17:1)	the peoples of the world (17:15)
the ten horns (17:12)	ten kings associated with the Beast (13:1; 17:3, 7-8, 11-13, 16-17)
the fine linen (19:8)	the righteous deeds of the saints (19:8)
the rider on the white horse (19:11-16, 19)	Jesus Christ, the King of kings (19:11-16, 19)

So, the first key to discerning the meaning of a symbol is to look at the immediate context for explanations of its meaning.

Second, if a symbol has no clear interpretation in the immediate context, consider the larger context of the entire book where the symbol is found. Sometimes you may even need to consider another portion of Scripture. Many of the symbols used in prophetic passages appear elsewhere in Scripture and have an established meaning. For instance, in Revelation 12:14 the woman is given "two wings like those of a great eagle" to escape from the serpent. In the immediate context, the woman represents the nation of Israel, and the serpent represents Satan. But the wings of the eagle remain unidentified. What are they? Do they symbolize the United States Air Force, who will airlift the Jews to safety in the end times? Some people believe this, but Scripture points us in another direction. The imagery of eagles' wings is found in Exodus 19:4 and Isaiah 40:28-31 and pictures the loving care and deliverance of God for His people.

Symbols are not meaningless, but neither are they an open invitation to let our imaginations run wild. They do not give the interpreter free rein to make the symbol mean whatever he or she wants it to mean. In most cases the immediate context or the use of that same symbol by other biblical writers will establish the boundaries for proper interpretation.

3. Compare Parallel Passages

Since so much of the Bible was prophetic when it was written, and since it all originates from the same divine author, many passages throughout the Bible discuss the same persons and events, and there are no contradictions among those passages. As we interpret Scripture with Scripture, the prophetic picture becomes more and more developed and complete. Rarely does one Scripture contain all that the Bible says about a given topic. This is especially true with Bible prophecy. Our understanding is widened and deepened by tying parallel prophetic passages together.

Of course, in comparing Scripture with Scripture it's important to avoid what is commonly called "proof texting," that is, coming to a conclusion about what a particular passage is saying and then searching for other scriptural texts to support that view. Often this happens by finding a few common words or ideas but ignoring the intended purpose and meaning of the text as determined by context, grammar, and historical background. Each passage of Scripture must first be interpreted in its own context to make sure that it is understood properly before comparing it with others.

Many prophetic passages describe the final world ruler (Daniel 7:8-25; 9:27; 11:36-39; 2 Thessalonians 2:8-12; Revelation 13:1-10), the Tribulation (Isaiah 24; Revelation 6–18), the second advent of Christ (Daniel 7:13; Zechariah 14:4; Matthew 25:31; Revelation 19), and the Millennium (Isaiah 2; 9; 35; Zechariah 14:9-21; Revelation 20:1-6). All of these passages need to be studied, compared, contrasted, and put together in a coherent outline of what the future holds. As we interpret

Scripture with Scripture, we gain a clearer, more comprehensive picture of what God is doing, what He will do, how He will do it, and sometimes even why He will do it.[11]

4. Be Aware of Time Intervals

As the Old Testament prophets peered into the future, they were only able to see the "mountain peaks" of the two comings of the Messiah, but they could not see the valley in between. The current church age was a mystery that had not yet been revealed (Ephesians 3). For this reason the Old Testament prophets often blended the two comings of Christ, sometimes even in one verse. The long time gaps between two events have often been referred to as "prophetic skips." The Old Testament has several examples of this.

One clear illustration is Zechariah 9:9, which refers to the Triumphal Entry of Jesus into the city of Jerusalem riding on a donkey and then catapults in the very next verse to the second coming of Christ to establish His global Kingdom. Some other examples of "prophetic skips" are found in Isaiah 9:6-7; Isaiah 61:1-2; Joel 2:28-32; and Malachi 3:1-2.

Today, with further divine revelation in the New Testament, we can discern the time gap between the two advents. Keeping this feature of prophecy in mind prevents us from mixing and confusing events that are separated by long periods of time.

5. Distinguish between Fulfilled and Unfulfilled Prophecies

Carefully distinguishing between what has been fulfilled and what remains unfulfilled is a final key to accurately interpreting prophecy and putting together a prophetic outline. Doing this might seem to be obvious and fairly simple, and normally is, but sometimes it is difficult to know if a certain event occurred in the past or the future.

The first step is to read the passage in its context and determine if the specifics of the prophecy actually occurred at some point in the past. This will require some investigation into the historical events from the relevant time period of history. If the entire prophecy or some elements of it have not been literally fulfilled, then, based on the biblical pattern of literal fulfillment, we should expect it to be literally accomplished in the future.

Conclusion

As we follow these five guidelines for interpreting prophecy, we can arrive at clear, consistent interpretations of future events predicted in Scripture. But serious study also requires diligence and dependence on the Holy Spirit, the author of the Word of God. When we do these things, our minds become settled, and we come to firmly held convictions and beliefs about what the future holds. It is good to hold strong convictions and views about various aspects of prophecy. The Lord wants us to study, understand, and experience transformation. He wouldn't have told us so much about the future if He didn't want us to know about it and come to some conviction about it. But we all have to carefully avoid getting angry or demeaning fellow believers who hold differing interpretations on various points of prophecy. Justin Martyr, an early church father and premillennialist, wrote, "I admitted to you formerly, that I and many others are of this opinion [premillennialism], and [believe] that such will take place, as you assuredly are aware; but on the other hand, I signified to you that many who belong to the pure and pious faith, and are true Christians, think otherwise."[12] We should imitate his attitude. Healthy, constructive discussion, debate, and give-and-take are helpful and should be encouraged, but attacking, mocking, and questioning the intelligence or spirituality of those who disagree with us are always wrong. We must not allow our egos and pride to get the best of us. We must hold to our prophetic views with the spirit of the Lord Jesus, who is Himself the heart of prophecy.

CHAPTER 5

KEY PROPHETIC PASSAGES

WHILE ALL BIBLICAL prophetic passages make a unique contribution, there are three main sections of the Bible that contain the essential keys to understanding the future. These three sections are (1) the book of Daniel, (2) the Olivet discourse (Matthew 24), and (3) the book of Revelation. To gain a basic understanding of Bible prophecy, one must have a general grasp of these three passages.

Daniel—The Handwriting on the Wall

The book of Daniel is one of the most beloved and beneficial books in the Bible. The stories in this book are unparalleled in their drama and suspense. Every child who has ever been to Sunday school knows about the three Hebrew young men in the fiery furnace and Daniel in the lions' den. However, there is much more to this precious book than just children's Bible stories. It is one of the strategic passages in the Bible that describes the events of the end times.

PURPOSE

The purpose of Daniel can be summarized in two words: *prophecy* and *piety*. Daniel reveals God's prophetic program for the future of our world and how God's people are to live in the present. The Bible always links prophecy with living a godly life. The book of Daniel is no exception. It contains many of the greatest prophecies in the Bible as well as some of the greatest examples of godly living. Prophecy and piety are the twin pillars of Daniel.

In terms of prophecy, five sections reveal God's prophetic program for this world. Each section contains information about the future that God gave to Daniel either in a vision or through a heavenly visitor or in some cases both. These prophecies were still in the future in Daniel's day. Today, some have already been fulfilled, such as the prophecies about Babylon, Medo-Persia, Greece, the evil king Antiochus Epiphanes (Daniel 8:9-14, 23-26; 11:21-35), and the domination of the Roman Empire. But much is still future even for us.

1. Chapter 2	Nebuchadnezzar's Nightmare (the great statue)
2. Chapter 7	The Jungle Book (the four beasts out of the sea)
3. Chapter 8	East Meets West (Persia v. Greece)
4. Chapter 9:24-27	God's Prophetic Clock (the seventy weeks prophecy)
5. Chapters 10–12	All's Well That Ends Well (the final vision of Daniel)

In terms of piety, five sections in Daniel reveal how we are to live our lives among unbelievers as we anticipate the end times. Daniel 1, 3, and 6 provide us with the positive examples of Daniel and his three friends who refused to compromise their standards under the pressure of the world. Daniel 4 and 5 warn against pride and rebellion against God.

1. Daniel 1	Daniel refuses to compromise and defile himself with the king's food
2. Daniel 3	The three Hebrew men refuse to bow to the king's image

3. Daniel 4	Nebuchadnezzar, the proud king, is humbled by God
4. Daniel 5	Belshazzar's drunken orgy is dramatically ended by the finger of God
6. Daniel 6	Daniel continues to pray to God even in the face of death

Three Key Prophetic Sections of Daniel

Three sections in Daniel are indispensable to properly understanding the end times. The first two are Daniel 2 and 7. Together these two chapters form the heart of the book. These two chapters outline an era that Jesus called the "times of the Gentiles." During this era, there is no king in Israel and Jerusalem is under Gentile control (see Luke 21:24). This era commenced when King Nebuchadnezzar besieged Jerusalem (605 BC). That was when Jerusalem first fell into the hands of Gentiles. The era continues to this present day and will persist until the second coming of the Messiah.

Some argue that the times of the Gentiles have ended since Israel today is not under Gentile domination, but what we see today is only a brief interruption of Gentile rule over Israel, and Israel currently has no Davidic king ruling. Israel is still enduring the times of the Gentiles. It will close with the second advent of Christ when He returns to rule as King.

DANIEL 2—THE STATUE AND THE STONE

Daniel 2 is often called the ABCs of prophecy. It contains the first and most basic prophetic outline of the times of the Gentiles. In this chapter the Babylonian king, Nebuchadnezzar, dreams of a great statue of a man made up of four different metals. The head is gold, the chest and arms are silver, the belly and thighs are bronze, the legs are iron, and the feet are iron and clay mixed. Then a great stone cut out of a mountain crashes into the image, smashing it to pieces. A wind blows the pieces away, and the stone that shattered the image becomes a great mountain, filling the whole earth.

Daniel interpreted this dream for Nebuchadnezzar. He said that the four different metals in the image represented Gentile world empires that would rule over Israel in succession.

THE METALLIC MAN	
Head of Gold	Babylon
Chest and Arms of Silver	Medo-Persia
Belly and Thighs of Bronze	Greece
Legs of Iron	Rome
Feet and Toes of Iron and Clay	Rome II (final form of the Roman Empire in a ten-nation confederacy symbolized by the ten toes)

The stone that destroyed the statue represents the second coming of Christ when He will destroy Gentile rule. The stone's becoming a mountain and filling the earth is a picture of the Messiah's worldwide kingdom that will forever replace the kingdoms of man.

DANIEL 7—THE FOUR BEASTS

In Daniel 7, the prophet has a night vision in which four great beasts emerge from the sea: a winged lion, a bear, a four-winged leopard, and a terrible beast with iron teeth and ten horns. Another smaller horn appears among these ten horns, replacing three of them. Meanwhile, "the Ancient One" sits down to judge, attended by millions of angels. The fourth beast is then killed, and the small horn along with it. Then "someone like a son of man coming with the clouds of heaven" (v. 13) appears and approaches the Ancient One and is given authority over the world.

Comparing these beasts to the statue in Daniel 2 reveals that Daniel 7 covers basically the same ground yet from a different perspective. As J. Dwight Pentecost notes, "Whereas in Daniel 2 the course of world empire is viewed from man's perspective, in Daniel 7 the same course of empire is viewed from the Divine viewpoint, where the empires are seen, not as an attractive glorious image, but as four wild voracious beasts, which devour and destroy all before them and, consequently, are worthy of judgment."[1]

THE FOUR BEASTS OF DANIEL 7	
Lion	Babylon
Bear	Medo-Persia
Leopard	Greece
Terrible Beast	Rome

PARALLELS BETWEEN DANIEL 2 AND 7

WORLD EMPIRE	DANIEL 2	DANIEL 7
Babylon	Head of Gold	Lion
Medo-Persia	Chest and Arms of Silver	Bear
Greece	Belly and Thighs of Bronze	Leopard
Rome I (Historical Rome)	Iron	Terrible Beast
Rome II (Future, final Roman Empire)	Ten Toes	Ten Horns
Antichrist		Little Horn
Christ's Kingdom	The Smiting Stone destroys the image.	The Son of Man receives the Kingdom.

After putting Daniel 2 and 7 together, the picture becomes clear. The times of the Gentiles began with the Babylonian Empire in 605 BC, followed by the Persian Empire, which replaced Babylon in 539 BC. The Persians in turn were overthrown by Alexander the Great in 334–331 BC, and Greece was succeeded by Rome, which lasted until AD 476.

Daniel 2 and Daniel 7 clearly refer to the Roman Empire. But the ten horns of Daniel 7 do not seem to match the historic Roman Empire. Daniel says, "Its ten horns are ten kings" (7:24), but those ten leaders have never existed. This absence indicates that the Roman Empire will be revived or reunited in the end times and will ultimately be headed by the "little horn," which is another title for the final Antichrist. His rule, and the times of the Gentiles, will be terminated when Christ, the smiting stone, the Son of Man, comes to establish His Kingdom. "His rule is eternal—it will never end. His kingdom will never be destroyed" (Daniel 7:14).

Daniel 9:24-27—The Seventy Weeks

Daniel 9:24-27 has often been called the "Backbone of Bible Prophecy" and "God's Prophetic Clock." This prophecy tells us that God has put Israel's future on a time clock. The setting for this prophecy is found in Daniel 9:1-23. The prophet Daniel is in Babylon, where the Jewish people have been in exile for almost seventy years. Daniel knows from reading the prophecies of Jeremiah (Jeremiah 25:11-12; 29:10) that the Captivity will only last seventy years. In Daniel 9:1-23, Daniel confesses the sins of the Jewish people and prays about the restoration of the people from Babylon. He knows that the seventy years of captivity are over (9:1-2), so he begins to intercede for his people. While Daniel is still praying, God sends Daniel an immediate answer by the angel Gabriel (9:21). Daniel 9:24-27 is God's answer to Daniel's prayer, but in this response God goes far beyond the restoration of the people from Babylon to Israel's ultimate and final restoration under the Messiah.

> A period of seventy sets of seven has been decreed for your people and your holy city to finish their rebellion, to put an end to their sin, to atone for their guilt, to bring in everlasting righteousness, to confirm the prophetic vision, and to anoint the Most Holy Place. Now listen and understand! Seven sets of seven plus sixty-two sets of seven will pass from the time the command is given to rebuild Jerusalem until a ruler—the Anointed One—comes. Jerusalem will be rebuilt with streets and strong defenses, despite the perilous times.
>
> After this period of sixty-two sets of seven, the Anointed One will be killed, appearing to have accomplished nothing, and a ruler will arise whose armies will destroy the city and the Temple. The

> end will come with a flood, and war and its miseries are decreed from that time to the very end. The ruler will make a treaty with the people for a period of one set of seven, but after half this time, he will put an end to the sacrifices and offerings. And as a climax to all his terrible deeds, he will set up a sacrilegious object that causes desecration, until the fate decreed for this defiler is finally poured out on him.
>
> DANIEL 9:24-27

As you can see, this passage is quite detailed. So, to help us better understand its astounding accuracy and significance, we will break it down into ten basic keys.

TEN KEYS TO UNDERSTANDING THE SEVENTY WEEKS OF DANIEL

1. It's about weeks of years

The term "week," or "sets of seven," refers to sets of seven. It could refer to sets of days, weeks, months, or years. The context determines its meaning. We know in the context of Daniel 9:24-27 (NASB) that this refers to sets of years because Daniel had already been thinking in terms of years in Daniel 9:1-2.

2. The total time is 490 years

The entire period involved, therefore, is a time period of 490 years (seventy sets of seven-year periods using a 360-day prophetic year).

3. It's about the Jewish people and the city of Jerusalem

The 490 years concerns the Jewish people and the city of Jerusalem, not the church. Gabriel tells Daniel this time period is "for your people [Israel] and your holy city [Jerusalem]" (9:24).

4. The purpose of the seventy weeks

The purpose of these 490 years is to accomplish six divine goals. The first three have to do with man's sin, and the last three have to do with God's righteousness:

to finish the transgression
to make an end of sin

to make atonement for iniquity
to bring in everlasting righteousness
to seal up vision and prophecy
to anoint the Most Holy Place

Christ's death on the cross made provision for sin, but Israel's acceptance of this sacrifice will not be realized until they repent at the end of the seventy weeks, in conjunction with Christ's second coming.

The last three of these goals look ahead to the coming Kingdom Age. As Harold Hoehner says, "To view the six things in Daniel 9:24 . . . as having been fulfilled in Christ's death at His first advent is impossible. All these have reference to the nation of Israel and none of these has been fulfilled to that nation."[2]

5. When the clock starts ticking

The divine prophetic clock for the seventy weeks or 490-year period began ticking on March 5, 444 BC, when the Persian king Artaxerxes issued a decree allowing the Jews to return to rebuild Jerusalem (Nehemiah 2:1-8).

6. The first sixty-nine weeks (483 years)

Sixty-nine sets of seven (7 x 69) or 483 years would transpire between the beginning of the countdown and the coming of the Messiah. This exact period of time—173,880 days—is elapsed from March 5, 444 BC, until March 30, AD 33—the day that Jesus rode into Jerusalem for the Triumphal Entry (Luke 19:28-44).[3] The precision of this prophecy is staggering! I call it the greatest prophecy ever given. It stands as a monumental proof of the inspiration of the Bible.

7. The gap called grace

The first sixty-nine weeks have already run their course. But what about the final period of seven years or what is commonly called the "seventieth week"? When Israel rejected Jesus Christ as its Messiah, God suspended His plan for Israel. There is a gap, therefore, or parenthesis of unspecified duration between the sixty-ninth and seventieth set of seven.[4] During this parenthesis two specific events are prophesied in Daniel 9:26:

The Messiah will be killed (this was fulfilled on April 3, AD 33).
Jerusalem and the Temple will be destroyed (this was fulfilled on August 6, AD 70).

God's prophetic clock for Israel stopped at the end of the sixty-ninth set of seven. We are living in this gap between week sixty-nine and week seventy—it's called the church age. The church age will end when Christ raptures His bride, the church. After all, since the church was not around for the first sixty-nine weeks from 444 BC to AD 33, it makes sense the church will not be here for the final week of years either. The seventy weeks have to do with Israel, not the church. This rationale supports the pre-Tribulation Rapture view that we will discuss later in this book.

8. The Antichrist's treaty and the final seven years

God's prophetic clock for Israel will begin again after the church has been raptured, when the Antichrist comes onto the scene and ratifies a seven-year treaty with Israel (Daniel 9:27).[5] This is the seventieth set of seven years, which awaits fulfillment. Because the first sixty-nine weeks of years were literally fulfilled down to the very day, it stands to reason that this future time of seven years will be just as literally fulfilled in the future.

9. The Antichrist breaks the treaty

In one of the greatest double crosses of all time, the Antichrist will break his covenant with Israel at its midpoint (after 3½ years) and set an abominable, sacrilegious statue or image of himself in the rebuilt Temple of God in Jerusalem (Matthew 24:21; Revelation 13:14-15). The final 3½ years will be the "great tribulation" Jesus talked about in Matthew 24:21 (NASB).

10. The end of the seventy weeks

At the end of the seven years, God will slay the Antichrist (see Daniel 9:27; 2 Thessalonians 2:8; Revelation 19:20). This event will mark the end of the seventy sets of seven and the beginning of the one-thousand-year reign of Christ when the six divine goals in Daniel 9:24 will be completely fulfilled (see Revelation 20:1-6). To help you understand this incredible prophecy even better, here are a couple of visual aids.

OVERVIEW OF THE SEVENTY WEEKS	
Daniel 9:24	The entire seventy weeks (490 years)
Daniel 9:25	The first sixty-nine weeks: 7 weeks + 62 weeks (483 years or 173,880 days)
Daniel 9:26	The time between the sixty-ninth and seventieth weeks (? years, the current age)
Daniel 9:27	The seventieth week (seven years)

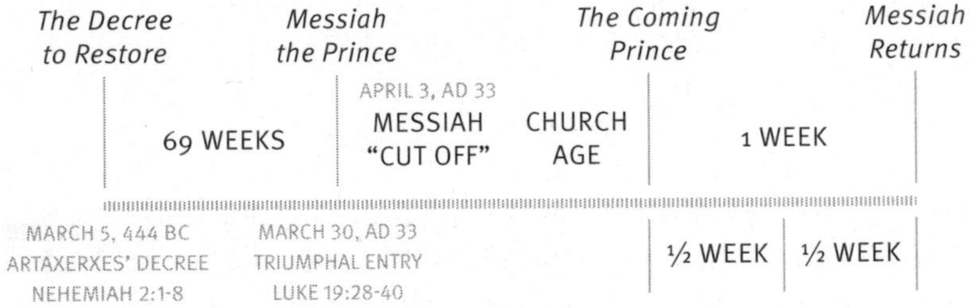

Predicting a time period of 173,880 days to the very day is the greatest prophecy ever given. When Jesus rode into Jerusalem on March 30, AD 33, the first sixty-nine weeks of years (483 years) were fulfilled to the very day. Jesus knew the significance of it when He said to the people, "If you had known in *this day*, even you, the things which make for peace" (Luke 19:42, NASB, italics added). He added these sobering words, "because you did not recognize *the time* of your visitation" (Luke 19:44, NASB, italics added). Jesus emphasized "this day" and "the time" to the Jewish people because He stood before them fulfilling this astonishing prophecy. The time of visitation had come on the exact day prophesied, but they had missed it due to their unbelief.

Jesus is coming again someday, maybe very soon. There is a final, future "time of visitation" that will also occur right on time according to God's timetable.

The Antichrist in Daniel

One of the key topics in Daniel 7–12 is the person and work of the coming world ruler, the Antichrist. He is the dominant human character in these chapters. He holds a prominent place in each of the final four great prophetic sections of Daniel.

THE ANTICHRIST IN DANIEL 7–12	
Daniel 7	The little horn (7:8, 11)
Daniel 8	A king, insolent and skilled in intrigue (8:23)
Daniel 9	The prince, or ruler, who is to come (9:26) The one who causes desecration (9:27)
Daniel 11	The king (11:36)

TWENTY KEY PREDICTIVE PROPHECIES OF DANIEL[6]
1. The successive rule of four great world empires: Babylon, Medo-Persia, Greece, and Rome (chapters 2 and 7)
2. The reuniting of the Roman Empire in the last days under the rule of ten kings or leaders (2:41-44; 7:24)
3. The appearance of the Messiah to rule 483 years after the decree is given to rebuild Jerusalem (9:25). This prophecy was fulfilled to the day when Christ rode into Jerusalem at the Triumphal Entry.
4. The violent death of the Messiah (9:26)
5. The destruction of Jerusalem in AD 70 (9:26)
6. The rise of the Antichrist to power (7:8, 20; 8:23)
7. The beginning of the seventieth week: the Antichrist's seven-year covenant with Israel (9:27)
8. The Antichrist's breaking of the covenant at its midpoint (9:27)
9. The Antichrist's claim that he is God (11:36)
10. The Antichrist's persecution of God's people (7:21)

11. The setting up of the abomination of desolation in the last days' Temple by the Antichrist (9:27; 12:11)
12. The Northern-Southern invasion of Israel and the Antichrist (11:40-45; Ezekiel 38–39)
13. The Antichrist's military conquest and consolidation of his empire (11:38-44)
14. The final doom of the Antichrist (7:11, 26; 9:27)
15. The second coming of Christ (2:44-45; 7:13)
16. The resurrection of the dead (12:2)
17. The rewarding of the righteous (12:3, 13)
18. The judgment of the wicked (7:9; 12:2)
19. The establishment of Christ's Kingdom (2:44-45; 7:14, 22, 27)
20. A great increase in the knowledge of Bible prophecy in the last days (12:4)

The Olivet Discourse—Blueprint of the End Times

The Olivet discourse is a sermon that Jesus preached from the Mount of Olives, just east of Jerusalem, three days before He died on the cross. The Olivet discourse is found in three places in the Gospels: (1) Matthew 24–25, (2) Mark 13, and (3) Luke 21. Jesus preached this sermon to a select group of His disciples. The Olivet discourse was Jesus' response to His disciples' question about the destruction of the Temple and the end of the age. Mark 13:3 says that Jesus' audience consisted of only four men: Peter, James, John, and Andrew. Imagine what it must have been like to hear the Savior outline the blueprint of the end times in such an intimate setting!

Matthew tells us that before this sermon, Jesus and His disciples had been in Jerusalem on the Temple grounds. "As Jesus was leaving the Temple grounds, his disciples pointed out to him the various Temple buildings. But he responded, 'Do you see all these buildings? I tell you the truth, they will be completely demolished. Not one stone will be left on top of another!'" (Matthew 24:1-2). As Jesus and the disciples crossed the Kidron Valley to the Mount of Olives, Jesus' words must have been seared into the minds of the disciples. They must have wondered how this could be. When would this happen? When would the end come?

When Jesus and His disciples finally arrived at the Mount of Olives, the four men came to Him for some clarification: "Later, Jesus sat on the Mount of Olives. His disciples came to him privately and said, 'Tell us, when will all this happen? What sign will signal your return and the end of the world?'" (Matthew 24:3). The disciples were asking one big question with three parts. Clearly, the disciples' question focuses on Christ's return and the end of the age. The disciples could not fathom the destruction of the Temple apart from the end of the age. For them, the destruction of the Temple, the coming of the Messiah, and the end of the world were tied together (Zechariah 14:1-11). This sermon, therefore, addresses the seven-year Tribulation period that will occur just before Christ returns.

The Olivet discourse of Jesus is often called "The Mini Apocalypse" because it provides a concise yet comprehensive overview of the end times. Jesus gives us the basic blueprint for the end—a checklist of the signs of the times for Christ's second advent. In twenty-seven verses, Matthew 24:4-31 moves from the beginning of the future Tribulation to the second coming of Christ.

In Matthew 24:4-14 Jesus lists eight key signs that He likens to birth pains that will portend His coming: false Christs (v. 5); wars (vv. 6-7); famines (v. 7); earthquakes (v. 7); persecution (vv. 9-10); false prophets (v. 11); lawlessness (v. 12); and worldwide preaching of the gospel (v. 14). The comparison with birth pains indicates that as the time of Christ's coming draws near, the judgments will increase immensely in frequency and intensity.

Then, in Matthew 24:15, Jesus says, "The day is coming when you will see what Daniel the prophet spoke about." Jesus directly appeals to the prophecies of Daniel and specifically to Daniel 9:27. Jesus goes on to describe the terrors of that time. Matthew 24:15-20 marks the midpoint of the Tribulation when the Antichrist breaks his treaty with Israel, invades the nation, and desecrates the Temple (cf. Daniel 9:27).

Beginning in Matthew 24:21, the final 3½ years of this age are graphically outlined. The terrors will be so great that God will abbreviate that time for the sake of His people. There will be people pointing here and there, claiming to have identified the Messiah, but Jesus warns against believing such claims.

After the Tribulation, in verse 29, the second coming of Christ is presented. He describes the signs in the heavens that will indicate that the Son of Man is coming, and finally His coming and gathering of His chosen ones from around the world. He describes it as being "like it was in Noah's day" (v. 37). Jesus encourages the disciples to look for the signs, like leaves on a fig tree, even though the day of His return is unknown. Nonetheless, He encourages them to keep watch and remain faithful.

WHAT ABOUT "THIS GENERATION"?

Some scholars argue that the destruction of Jerusalem in AD 70 fulfilled Jesus' predictions in Matthew 24. This view is based primarily on Matthew 24:34, which says, "I tell you the truth, this generation will not pass from the scene until all these things take place." Proponents maintain that "this generation" must refer to the generation that originally heard the words of Jesus. The chief problem with this view is that the destruction of Jerusalem did not fulfill the events described in Matthew 24, so Jesus could not have been referring to that time period.

In the context, "this generation" probably refers to those living during the Tribulation who will personally witness the events described in Matthew 24:4-31. Jesus is emphasizing that those who see the signs that He listed, and experience the Great Tribulation, will also witness the Second Coming.[7] Jesus is saying that those who are alive to see the beginning of the birth pangs will also witness the birth.

MATTHEW 24 IS FUTURE

I believe the best view is to see all the conditions and characteristics in Matthew 24:4-28 as future events that will occur during the Tribulation, immediately preceding the return of Christ. Two key points from the surrounding context lead me to this view.

First, Jesus established the time frame for this sermon in Matthew 23:39. "I tell you this, you will never see me again until you say, 'Blessings on the one who comes in the name of the LORD!'" Jesus was telling His disciples that He was going to leave this world but that He would come again only when the Jewish people would repent and receive Him as their Messiah. This statement is very significant; it forms the backdrop and context for what Jesus says in Matthew 24. Jewish repentance, which has never occurred and certainly didn't occur in AD 70, is the ultimate event that will trigger His return. At the end of the Tribulation, the Jewish people will repent, and their Messiah will return to rescue them from the Antichrist (Zechariah 12:10).

Second, when the disciples asked Jesus about the end of the world, they were thinking of when the Messiah would come to establish His glorious Kingdom in Israel. In fact, Jesus Himself used this exact terminology, "the end of the world," twice before to refer to the final judgment (Matthew 13:39, 49). I agree wholeheartedly with this concise summary by John MacArthur.

> It seems more sensible and more consistent, therefore, to take a futurist approach with respect to the Olivet Discourse—to interpret the entire discourse as a prophetic picture of a "generation" and events that would take place long after the destruction of Jerusalem in AD 70. These are events that will immediately precede Christ's coming to establish His kingdom, and therefore they are events that are yet future even today.[8]

Therefore, I believe that Jesus used this prophetic sermon to outline the events that will lead up to the return of Israel's Messiah to establish His Kingdom on earth and to call his people to faithfulness in view of that coming.

TIMELINE OF THE OLIVET DISCOURSE			
THE SEVEN-YEAR TRIBULATION PERIOD			THE SECOND COMING
24:4-14	vv. 15-20	vv. 21-28	vv. 29-31
The Beginning Birth Pangs	The Abomination of Desolation (The Antichrist Defiles the Temple)	The Great Tribulation	Jesus Returns
First 3½ Years of the Tribulation	Middle of the Tribulation	Last 3½ Years of the Tribulation	After the Tribulation

The Book of Revelation—Apocalypse Wow!

Revelation holds a special place in the hearts of God's people. It is God's final inspired message to the church. Revelation is particularly important for two key reasons.

Revelation Looks Back

It is perfectly fitting and necessary that the sixty-sixth book in the Bible ties up the loose ends from the previous sixty-five books. Revelation not only looks forward to the future consummation of all things under Christ, but it also looks back and weaves together all the threads from the first sixty-five books of the Bible. Revelation contains 404 verses, and at least 278 allude to the Old Testament Scriptures. There may be up to 550 total allusions back to the Old Testament in Revelation. Proportionally, Revelation alludes to Daniel most frequently, followed by Isaiah, Ezekiel, and Psalms. Revelation has been called the "Grand Central Station of the Bible" because it's the place where all the trains of thought throughout the whole Bible come in!

Revelation Looks Ahead

It is also fitting and necessary that the last book in the Bible reveals God's prophetic program for the future and tells us how everything is going to come out in the end. And this is exactly what Revelation does. The word *revelation* in Greek is *apocalupsis*, which means "to unveil, uncover, or disclose something that was hidden." The purpose of this book is to reveal, uncover, or take the lid off the future. Revelation is an exciting, breathtaking account of the future of this world.

OUTLINE

Many different outlines have been proposed for Revelation, but the best one is the inspired three-fold outline contained in Revelation 1:19: "Therefore write the things which you have seen, and the things which are, and the things which will take place after these things" (NASB).

I. "The things which you have seen" (chapter 1)
II. "The things which are" (chapters 2–3)
III. "The things which will take place after these things" (chapters 4–22)

Another simple way to survey Revelation is by using this simple framework that divides Revelation into the four different ages that are found in the book.

THE FOUR AGES IN REVELATION		
CHAPTERS	AGE	YEARS
Chapters 1–3	Church Age	? Years
Chapters 4–19	Tribulation	7 Years
Chapter 20	Kingdom Age	1,000 Years
Chapters 21–22	Eternal Age	Endless Years

What's It All About?

The primary purpose of the book of Revelation is to give the advanced history of how Jesus Christ receives the Kingdom and takes the throne by means of judgment. The book of Revelation can be supremely confusing. It contains its share of interpretive challenges, but there is a clear, overarching goal that the book builds toward. Revelation crescendos in chapters 19–20. These two chapters can help us understand its central purpose and theme—the authority of Jesus over the whole universe.

The key to the book in many ways is the heavenly scene in Revelation 5. After presenting the "Lordship of Christ" in Revelation 1 and the "Letters of Christ" in chapters 2–3, the book shifts from earth to heaven in Revelation 4, where the focus is on God's throne. Then, in chapter 5, Jesus—the Lamb who is a Lion—takes the seven-sealed scroll from the hand of the Father. He is the only one found worthy to open it. There are many interpretations of the contents of the seven-sealed scroll, but the only document that was sealed in this way in the first-century Roman world was a last will and testament.[9] When a will was executed, seven witnesses were present to seal it. The will would become a seven-sealed document. That's what we have in Revelation 5.

The seven-sealed scroll represents the messianic kingdom that was promised in the Old Testament (Psalm 2:8; Daniel 7:14). By receiving the scroll, Jesus is receiving His inheritance—to be King over His Kingdom. This is the ultimate goal and meaning of history. "If the scroll is not opened, then [there is] no protection for God's children in the hours of bitter trial; no judgment upon a persecuting world; no ultimate triumph for believers; no new heaven and earth; no future inheritance."[10] When Jesus opens the scroll, He unrolls history and begins to reign as King.

Chuck Swindoll describes the scene: "Only one Person in heaven and earth was found worthy to take that scroll, to open its seals, and to begin the step-by-step process of snatching control of the world from evil and forever vanquishing sin and death: Jesus Christ. The steps necessary for preparing the world for His kingdom on earth, however, involve a period of unparalleled judgment."[11]

With Revelation 6, the main action of the book begins. Jesus, the Lord of the future, begins to open the seals one by one—each one a judgment. The first six seals are ominously opened. These judgments pave the way for the inheritance of the Kingdom. When the seventh seal is opened in Revelation 8, it appears that the scroll will be fully opened, but the seventh seal contains seven more judgments—called the seven trumpets. Each succeeding trumpet is blown, and more dire judgment falls. Finally in Revelation 11, the seventh trumpet sounds, containing seven bowls of God's wrath. These are poured out in rapid succession just before the second coming of Christ to earth (Revelation 16). When He comes to earth, Jesus defeats the armies of the Antichrist gathered at Armageddon, judges the living on earth, and takes the throne.

At this point, the seven seals have been broken, the scroll is fully opened, and Jesus' inheritance is fully realized. David J. MacLeod says, "Only when they are all broken, that is, only after the judgments have taken place, is the scroll opened, and the will read. The will contains the inheritance of God's people. . . . The breaking of the seals is preparatory to God's people entering the promised inheritance, namely, the future one-thousand-year rule of Christ on earth."[12] Jesus takes rightful possession as King. The Kingdom He was promised by the Father has come, but it comes only after the world under its final leader, the Antichrist, has been defeated and judged. The Kingdom comes, but it is attained by means of severe judgment upon the earth.

All of history is moving toward this grand climax—the Kingdom of God on earth. That's what Revelation is all about: Christ coming to inherit the Kingdom. Revelation shows us that all of history is under God's control, that history is headed somewhere, and that it is all tied to the person and work of Jesus Christ. There "is a simple but profound biblical truth here which cannot be overemphasized: apart from the person and redeeming work of Jesus Christ, history is an enigma. . . . Christ, and Christ alone, has the key to the meaning of human history. . . . Apart from the victorious return of Christ, history is going nowhere."[13]

Two Patterns in Revelation

There are two key patterns to pay attention to in Revelation. John structures the book to alternate back and forth. First, like a long play, Revelation progresses and then pauses for an intermission, progresses some more, and then pauses for another intermission. Second, also like a play, Revelation switches scenes, alternating between heaven and earth. Understanding this alternating pattern will help you read and follow John's Revelation much better.

INTERMISSIONS

The three series of judgments—the seals (Revelation 6), trumpets (Revelation 8–9), and bowls (Revelation 16)—follow one another in sequence and move the action forward in the book of Revelation toward its culmination in the Kingdom. Those judgments form the "chronological backbone" of Revelation.[14] Yet, between them there is a great deal of information provided about key events and players who will emerge as the drama unfolds. These interludes are like intermissions in the progression of the book. Sometimes the interlude runs ahead of the story and sometimes backs up to add or emphasize key information.[15]

For this reason, Revelation 6–18 has been likened to a telephone conversation between two people: Revelation 6 starts telling the story in order as the seals are opened, but soon there is an interruption between the sixth and seventh seals to fill in some information (Revelation 7).

The main order of events resumes in Revelation 8–9 with the first six trumpets. Then there is another interlude between the sixth and seventh trumpets with more fill-in information in chapters 10–15. This section introduces the two witnesses and the two beasts (Revelation 11, 13).

The main progression returns in Revelation 16 with the seven bowls and concludes with one final intermission that gives more detail in chapters 17–18, where the destruction of Babylon is highlighted.[16]

It may be helpful to put this in the form of a chart.

SEQUENCE OF EVENTS IN REVELATION 6–20
Main Action: Revelation 6 (six seals)
Intermission between the sixth and seventh seals—Revelation 7
Main Action Returns: Revelation 8–9 (seventh seal, which contains the seven trumpets)
Intermission between the sixth and seventh trumpets—Revelation 10–15
Main Action Resumes: Revelation 16 (seven bowls)
Intermission describing the destruction of Babylon the Great—Revelation 17–18
Main Action Restarts: Revelation 19–20 (Second Coming and Millennial Kingdom)

HEAVEN AND EARTH

One final feature of Revelation that is helpful to understand is the way the scenes alternate back and forth from heaven to earth in Revelation 4–20. This alternating pattern reassures readers that the chaos on earth is being controlled by heaven. God is on His throne and superintends all that transpires on earth. This should be a supreme comfort in uncertain, troubled times.

IN HEAVEN	ON EARTH
The heavenly throne (ch. 4) The Lamb on the throne (ch. 5)	The first four seal judgments (6:1-8)
The fifth seal judgment (6:9-11)	The sixth seal judgment (6:12-17) The sealing of the 144,000 (7:1-8)
The great multitude (7:9-17) Preparations for the trumpet judgments (8:1-5)	The first six trumpet judgments (8:6–9:21) The little book (ch. 10) The ministry of the two witnesses (11:1-14)
The announcement of the seventh trumpet (11:15-19) The expulsion of Satan (12:1-12)	The activity of Satan (12:13-17) The activity of the two beasts (ch. 13) Judgment at the end of the Great Tribulation (ch. 14)
The announcement of the seven last judgments (ch. 15)	The seven bowl judgments (ch. 16) Babylon's destruction (ch. 17–18)
Praise for judging (19:1-10)	The second coming of Christ (19:11-21) The millennial reign of Christ (ch. 20)

Conclusion

Daniel, the Olivet discourse, and the book of Revelation are three solid legs of the prophetic stool. Other passages include Ezekiel 38–39, 1 Thessalonians 4–5, and 2 Thessalonians 2. Together they form the stable base to construct a consistent, clear prophetic paradigm. You will see these passages referred to again and again in this book, so it's important to be familiar with them. I hope the background from this chapter will serve you well as we continue our exploration of the end.

CHAPTER 6

BACK TO THE FUTURE

The End Times Fulfill God's Covenants

THERE ARE SEVERAL BASIC issues in developing a consistent view of the end times. One of the key building blocks is an understanding of the biblical covenants God made with Abraham and his descendants. How one interprets the covenants determines the overall timing and understanding of end times events and answers questions that are still significant today: Who owns the land of Israel? Is there a future for the Jewish people in God's plan for the world? What is that future?

God made four great unconditional, unilateral, eternal covenants with Abraham and his descendants that established a permanent relationship between God and His people. These covenants are critical to understanding the end times because Israel will ultimately fulfill them in the millennial kingdom. In that day, Israel will be in right relationship with God forever, just as these covenants had promised.

The first of these covenants was the Abrahamic Covenant. It frames the other covenants that follow.

The Abrahamic Covenant (Genesis 12:1-3; 15:18-21)

The Abrahamic Covenant is the foundation of the history of Israel and God's dealings with Abraham's descendants. John Walvoord observes:

> The covenant of God with Abraham is one of the important and determinative revelations of Scripture. It furnishes the key to the entire Old Testament and reaches for its fulfillment into the New. . . . The analysis of its provisions and the character of their fulfillment set the mold for the entire body of Scriptural truth.[1]

J. Dwight Pentecost also sees this covenant as laying the groundwork for the rest of Scripture: "The eternal aspects of this covenant, which guarantee Israel a permanent national existence, perpetual title to the land of promise, and the certainty of material and spiritual blessing through Christ, and guarantee Gentile nations a share in these blessings, determine the whole eschatological program of the Word of God."[2] Due to its importance, the Abrahamic Covenant must be carefully examined.

The Provisions of the Covenant

God's promise to Abraham is first made in Genesis 12:1-3. The promise is formalized into a covenant in Genesis 15:1-21 and then is amplified in Genesis 17:1-18. God's promises to Abraham had three dimensions—personal, universal, and national. God's *personal* promise to Abraham himself was that he would make Abraham's name great (Genesis 12:2). This promise was made to Abraham alone and was literally fulfilled in his life. Abraham owned vast herds and had the resources to defeat five kings (Genesis 14; 24:35). Beyond that, he has been venerated by the Jews and by Christians since his death nearly four thousand years ago.

The promise was not only personal, though; it was also *universal*. God promised Abraham, "In you all the families of the earth will be blessed" (Genesis 12:3, NASB). Certainly, this prophecy has been partially fulfilled in the blessing that has come to the entire world through Abraham's greatest descendant, Jesus Christ. However, the final blessing from Abraham through Christ will come during the wonderful conditions that will exist on this earth during the Millennium.

God also made two *national* promises to Abraham: (1) the promise of descendants who would become a great nation (Genesis 12:1-3; 13:16; 15:5; 17:7; 22:17-18) and (2) the promise of the land of Israel as an eternal inheritance (Genesis 12:1; 13:14-17; 15:18-21). The land God promised includes the modern-day nation of Israel and parts of modern-day Egypt, Syria, Lebanon, and Iraq (Genesis 15:18-21). The promise of God is Israel's title deed to the land. Israel is the only nation God ever promised a particular piece of real estate. The Promised Land belongs to Israel. This unconditional promise of the land has never been completely fulfilled in history, but it will be fulfilled in the Millennium when Christ gives the Jewish people the land He promised (Isaiah 60:21; Ezekiel 34:11-16).

The Nature of the Covenant

The nature of the Abrahamic Covenant is critical to understand. The basic question is this: Is it conditional or unconditional? Is the covenant dependent on the fidelity of God and Israel (conditional), or is it dependent only on God's faithfulness (unconditional)? In other words, is it a mutual covenant (bilateral) or is it one way (unilateral)?

Your view of the nature and timing of the Millennium will guide how you answer these questions. Most amillennialists and postmillennialists believe this covenant was conditional; they argue that Israel failed to uphold their end of the covenant, so the covenant need not be literally fulfilled. However, some amillennialists and postmillennialists do believe that the covenant is unconditional, but they spiritualize God's promised blessing and transfer it from Israel to the church. Premillennialists maintain that the Abrahamic Covenant is literal and unconditional and will be fulfilled in the future reign of Christ on earth. This is the view I hold.

The Abrahamic Covenant should be interpreted literally, not spiritually, because the parts of it that have already been fulfilled have been literally fulfilled. Abraham literally had many descendants who became a great nation, the whole world has been blessed through him, and God made his name great. The parts of the covenant that have been fulfilled in history have followed this literal pattern, so we should expect the unfulfilled parts—such as the promise of the land—to be literally fulfilled as well. It is inconsistent to shift in midstream from literal to spiritual fulfillment without some clear indication that such a change is to be expected.

The covenant should be understood as an unconditional covenant for five basic reasons.[3] First, the Abrahamic Covenant was a blood covenant that bound the parties unconditionally to fulfill their pledge. In a blood covenant, animals would be cut in half, and the divided carcasses would be placed apart from one another with enough room for both parties to walk between. In doing this, each party was pledging with his own blood to keep his end of the bargain until the pledge was fulfilled.

Abraham, in keeping with covenant custom, sacrificed the animals, divided the carcasses of the three large animals, and laid them all on the ground. Then, a most significant thing took place: "Abram fell into a deep sleep" (Genesis 15:12). He never walked between the animals; only God did. On this unique occasion Abraham (at that time called Abram) was not a *participant* in the covenant; rather, he was a *recipient of* a covenant. God's covenant ceremony with Abraham shows that it is unconditional and one way. Abraham never walked between the pieces of the slain animals. He made no promises. Only God did. The fulfillment of the Abrahamic Covenant "rests squarely on the faithfulness of God."[4] He alone is responsible to fulfill it.

A second reason for interpreting this covenant as unconditional is that the original promises were given to Abraham without any conditions whatsoever. It is true that God later added circumcision as a sign of the covenant (Genesis 17:9-14), but later conditions cannot alter the original agreement. In the original statement of the covenant, God tells Abraham what He will do for him without any conditions stated (Genesis 12:1-3; 15:18). Furthermore, when God reiterated the covenant to Abraham's son Isaac and grandson Jacob, there were no human conditions (Genesis 26:2-4, 24; 28:13-15). The covenant is all about what God will do.

A third reason the Abrahamic Covenant is unconditional is that Scripture repeatedly states that the covenant is eternal (Genesis 13:15; 17:7,

13, 19; 1 Chronicles 16:16-17; Psalm 105:9-10; Jeremiah 31:35-36). "The Scriptures clearly teach that this is an eternal covenant based on the gracious promises of God. There may be delays, postponements, and chastisements, but an eternal covenant cannot, if God cannot deny Himself, be abrogated."[5] The eternal duration of the covenant supports its unconditionality.

Fourth, the New Testament expressly affirms the unchangeable nature of the covenant (Romans 11:1-2, 11, 28-29; Hebrews 6:13-18).

Fifth, Scripture states many times that the Abrahamic Covenant is still in effect even though the Jewish people were unfaithful. Their failure, no matter how grievous or prolonged, did not set aside the covenant (Genesis 50:24; Exodus 2:24; Deuteronomy 9:5-6; 2 Kings 13:23; Micah 7:18, 20; Malachi 3:6; Luke 1:67-75; Acts 3:25-26). Even during the apostasy in the days of Jeremiah, God reaffirmed His unwavering commitment to His covenant people.

> It is the LORD who provides the sun to light the day
>   and the moon and stars to light the night,
>   and who stirs the sea into roaring waves.
> His name is the LORD of Heaven's Armies,
>   and this is what he says:
> "I am as likely to reject my people Israel
>   as I am to abolish the laws of nature!"
> This is what the LORD says:
> "Just as the heavens cannot be measured
>   and the foundations of the earth cannot be explored,
> so I will not consider casting them away
>   for the evil they have done.
>   I, the LORD, have spoken!"
>
> JEREMIAH 31:35-37

Ronald Diprose says it well: "Israel's sin can no more thwart God's future purposes for the nation than can the heavens be measured and all the secrets of the earth be known. Thus it is clear that God will not reject the descendants of Israel because of the nation's unfaithfulness. But there is more: only in the case of the collapse of God's sovereign control over the physical universe would Israel cease to exist as a nation."[6]

What more could God have done to reaffirm the unconditional, eternal nature of His covenant with Abraham?

Conclusion

The Abrahamic Covenant contains three great unconditional, eternal promises that affect Israel and ultimately the nations. The three promises are *seed*, *soil*, and *salvation*—or descendants, land, and blessing. As Ryrie says, "Since the covenant has never been fulfilled in history, if language means anything at all, it must have a literal fulfillment."[7] This fulfillment will come when Christ returns to reign on earth.

The other three unconditional covenants each amplify one of the key elements of the Abrahamic promises—soil (the Land Covenant), seed (the Davidic Covenant), and salvation (the New Covenant).

THE UNCONDITIONAL BIBLICAL COVENANTS

ABRAHAMIC COVENANT

Soil	Seed	Salvation
Land Covenant	Davidic Covenant	New Covenant

The Land Covenant (Deuteronomy 30:1-10)

The Land Covenant, sometimes also called the Palestinian Covenant, amplifies the soil promise to Abraham. Since it is rooted in the Abrahamic Covenant and is a subset of it, then it, too, must be unconditional and eternal. The Land Covenant reiterates that Abraham's descendants possess the land. J. Dwight Pentecost summarizes the features of the Land Covenant from Deuteronomy 30:1-10:

> There are seven main features in the program there unfolded: (1) The nation will be plucked off the land for its unfaithfulness

> (Deuteronomy 28:63-68; 30:1-3); (2) there will be a future repentance of Israel (Deuteronomy 28:63-68; 30:1-3); (3) their Messiah will return (Deuteronomy 30:3-6); (4) Israel will be restored to the land (Deuteronomy 30:5); (5) Israel will be converted as a nation (Deuteronomy 30:4-8; cf. Rom. 11:26-27); (6) Israel's enemies will be judged (Deuteronomy 30:7); (7) the nation will then receive her full blessing (Deuteronomy 30:9).[8]

The only conditional feature in this covenant is the time element. Israel's repentance and their restoration to the land and to the Lord are certain; only the time is unknown. This covenant was not literally, completely fulfilled at any time in the Old Testament, so its realization must be future.[9]

It is important to distinguish between Israel's *ownership* of the Promised Land and their *occupation* of it. Scripture asserts their *ownership* of the land—God gave Abraham and his descendants the title deed to the land forever (Genesis 13:15). However, their *occupation* of the land has been broken repeatedly throughout history. Their exile from the land may happen because of their disobedience to God, which was the case with the Babylonian deportation. These consequences were part of the Land Covenant in Deuteronomy 28:63-68. Nonetheless, God promised to bring the Jewish people to salvation and to fulfill His good promise that they will one day have ownership of the land forever.

The Davidic Covenant (2 Samuel 7:12-16)

King David, the man after God's own heart, carried a deep desire to build a house for God, a place of worship worthy of the one true God, but David was not allowed to build God's house because he had been a man of bloodshed and war. In 2 Samuel 7, God told David that he would not be allowed to build God's house but that God would build him a house—a royal dynasty that would never end.

God's promise to David extends the Abrahamic Covenant for Abraham's descendants. God promised Abraham that, through his wife Sarah, "kings of peoples will come" (Genesis 17:16, NASB). This covenant, since it builds on the Abrahamic Covenant, is also unconditional and is specifically stated to be eternal (2 Samuel 7:13; Psalm 89:3-4, 28-29). The Davidic Covenant contains three basic elements.

1. House—this refers to David's dynasty or the royal family.
2. Throne—this refers to David's authority or right to rule.
3. Kingdom—this refers to David's realm, which is the earthly, political kingdom of Israel.

In this covenant, God promised David that someone from his house or dynasty would sit on his throne and rule over his kingdom forever. All believers agree that Jesus fulfilled this promise, being David's greater son (Luke 1:32-33). But will it also be fulfilled literally with Israel? Or will Jesus' throne in heaven be David's throne? Does the current church qualify as David's kingdom? Here there are differences of opinion.

Amillennialists believe that Jesus is the Son of David who fulfills this covenant, but they contend that Jesus fulfills it today by sitting on the throne in heaven and ruling over the church. This view has several problems, but for the sake of space I will only address the most serious one.

When God promised that one of David's descendants would sit on his throne and rule over his kingdom, David thought of his earthly throne, not a throne in heaven, and he understood this promise to refer to his kingdom, which was the nation of Israel (2 Samuel 23:5; 1 Kings 1:30-37). He had no concept of the New Testament church as his kingdom. An essential element of any binding, valid contract is that the parties must have a meeting of the minds. God certainly knew that David was thinking about an earthly throne and political kingdom. He could not have been thinking of anything else. That was all he knew. If God, knowing David's expectations, fulfilled the covenant in a way contrary to David's understanding, then there was never a valid covenant in the first place.

The agreement was for David's Son to sit on David's earthly throne and rule over David's kingdom on earth forever. This must be literally fulfilled for the covenant to be valid and for God to keep His solemn promise to David. This promise will be fulfilled only when Jesus Christ, from the line of David, sits on David's throne in Jerusalem, ruling over Israel in the coming Millennium and on into eternity (Ezekiel 37:22-25; Amos 9:11-15; Zephaniah 3:14-17; Luke 1:30-33, 69). The covenant does not require that the throne be occupied continuously. In fact, it anticipates that there will be interruptions in the reign of the Davidic kings (2 Samuel 7:14). "The only necessary feature is that the lineage cannot be lost, not that the throne be occupied continuously."[10]

PROPHETIC IMPLICATIONS OF THE DAVIDIC COVENANT[11]
Israel must be preserved as a nation.
Israel must have a national existence and be brought back into the land.
David's Son, the Lord Jesus Christ, must return to earth, bodily and literally, in order to reign over David's covenanted kingdom.
A literal earthly kingdom must exist over which the returned Messiah will reign.
This kingdom must become an eternal Kingdom.

The New Covenant (Jeremiah 31:31-34)

The New Covenant amplifies God's original salvation promise to Abraham. Paul Benware states its significance: "There would be a certain sense of emptiness and lack of success if the Messiah came to reign on David's throne and ruled over the designated land area, but governed an unregenerate, rebellious people. This would be absolutely unacceptable to the Lord."[12] The New Covenant is God's promise to bring the Jewish people into right relationship with Himself.

> "The day is coming," says the Lord, "when I will make a new covenant with the people of Israel and Judah. This covenant will not be like the one I made with their ancestors when I took them by the hand and brought them out of the land of Egypt. They broke that covenant, though I loved them as a husband loves his wife," says the Lord.
>
> "But this is the new covenant I will make with the people of

> Israel on that day," says the LORD. "I will put my instructions deep within them, and I will write them on their hearts. I will be their God, and they will be my people. And they will not need to teach their neighbors, nor will they need to teach their relatives, saying, 'You should know the LORD.' For everyone, from the least to the greatest, will know me already," says the LORD. "And I will forgive their wickedness, and I will never again remember their sins."
>
> JEREMIAH 31:31-34

This covenant is confirmed elsewhere in the Old Testament and is stated to be eternal (Isaiah 61:8-9; Ezekiel 16:62; 37:24-28). Like the promises to Abraham and David, God's promise to Israel in this covenant also contains three central elements.

1. The forgiveness of sins—God will forgive the people of Israel for their sins.
2. The indwelling Spirit—God will place His Spirit in the hearts of the people to personally instruct them in His way (Ezekiel 36:24-26).
3. A new heart—God will give His people a new, clean heart with His law inscribed upon it.

While believers today enjoy all of these promises as a result of the New Covenant in Christ's blood (Matthew 26:28) and are ministers of the New Covenant (2 Corinthians 3:6), the specific promises in Jeremiah 31:31-34 are to the "house of Israel and with the house of Judah" (Jeremiah 31:31, NASB) and will find their ultimate fulfillment for Israel in the millennial kingdom when they are restored to the land with Christ as their king. (Notice the context of this covenant in Jeremiah 31:35-40 is the future Kingdom.)

Even though the church participates in the blessing of the New Covenant, this does not set aside God's clear promises to Israel. These promises have never been fulfilled with Israel but will be fulfilled when Israel is restored to its land, undergoes a national conversion and regeneration, receives forgiveness and a new heart, and experiences the Holy Spirit who produces righteousness and full knowledge of God. "The Messiah who came and shed His blood as the foundation of this covenant must personally come back to the earth to effect the salvation, restoration and blessing of the national Israel."[13]

Conclusion on the Covenants

These four unconditional, one-way, eternal covenants with Israel will be fulfilled in the future because of the faithfulness of the One who made them. God will keep His word to Abraham and his descendants, not because of their worthiness, but because of His own word and reputation. The key features of these covenants can be crystallized into seven main headings.

SEVEN KEY FEATURES OF THE BIBLICAL COVENANTS[14]
A Nation Forever
A Land Forever
A King Forever
A Throne Forever
A Kingdom Forever
A New Covenant
Abiding Blessings

As you can see, these covenants, in many ways, determine the course of future events. God's promises to Israel are unconditional and eternal, yet they have not been completely fulfilled. Thus, it stands to reason that those promises will be fulfilled in the future, in the end times. Because of God's long-standing relationship with Israel, it also makes sense that the literal Israel will see God fulfill these promises and will receive those benefits. It will not be some spiritual version of Israel; it will be literal Israel. Israel has a clear part yet to play in God's plans for the whole world. These include the future events we will discuss throughout the remainder of this book.

CHAPTER 7

ARE WE LIVING IN THE "END TIMES"?

The End is about eschatology. Eschatology means "the study of the last things." In this book, we'll use a few different phrases to refer to these last things—end times, last days, the Day of the Lord. These words are somewhat interchangeable, although some have more technical definitions too. Let's take a look at some of these terms. They will help us grab hold of the ideas in the rest of this book.

The "Last Days"

Are we living in the last days? Are these the end times? Someone asks those questions at just about every prophecy conference I attend. What they usually mean is, "Are we living in the final days before the coming of the Lord?" Because there is so much talk about the "last days," it is very important for us to understand what the Scriptures mean when they refer to this period of time.

When talking about the last days and end times, we have to distinguish between the "last days" for the church, which we are in now, and the last days for Israel, which is still in the future.

> Sometimes Christians read in the Bible about the "last days," "end times," etc. and tend to think that all of these phrases all of the time refer to the same thing. This is not the case, just as in our own lives there are many endings: there is the end of the work day, the end of the day according to the clock, the end of the week, the end of the month, and the end of the year. Just because the word "end" is used does not mean that it always refers to the same thing. The word "end" is restricted and precisely defined when it is modified by "day," "week," "year," etc. So it is in the Bible that "end times" may refer to the end of the current church age or it may refer to other times. . . . The Bible clearly speaks of a last days or end time, but it does not always refer to the same period of time. The contextual referent enables the reader to know whether the Bible is speaking of the last days relating to Israel or the end times in reference to the church.[1]

So "end times" is a broad umbrella term, and "last days" is more specific. When we talk about the end times, we are referring to all the events beginning with the Rapture all the way to eternity. Thus, the end times include the Rapture, which ends the last days for the church, and the last days for Israel, which follow the Rapture.

In the Old Testament, last days refer to the time leading up to and including the coming of the Messiah and the establishment of His millennial kingdom on earth (Deuteronomy 4:30; Isaiah 2:2; Jeremiah 30:24; Ezekiel 38:8, 16; Micah 4:1). These terms refer to the last days for Israel, not the church. For the Old Testament prophets, the church and the church age were mysteries that they did not see (Ephesians 3:3-9). So, in the Old Testament, the last days refer to the last days for Israel, which are the seven years of Tribulation culminating with the second coming of Christ and the setting up of His Kingdom.

Moving into the New Testament, the term "last days" refers most often to the last days of the church and the church age (1 Timothy 4:1; 2 Timothy 3:1; James 5:3; 1 Peter 1:20; 2 Peter 3:3).

The apostle Peter said all the way back in the AD 60s that "the end of the world is coming soon" (1 Peter 4:7). Even in New Testament times the apostles "sensed that they had moved dramatically closer to the consummation of God's plan for this world."[2] The Old Testament age had ended; they were now living in a brand-new era. For the apostles, the end of the age was already a present reality. The Scriptures indicate that the first coming of Jesus Christ inaugurated the "last days" for the church. According to the New Testament, we are living right now in the last days of the church.

Hebrews 1:2 says, "Now in these final [last] days, he has spoken to us through his Son. God promised everything to the Son as an inheritance, and through the Son he created the universe." This current age is also called the "last hour" by the apostle John. "Dear children, the last hour is here. You have heard that the Antichrist is coming, and already many such antichrists have appeared. From this we know that the last hour has come" (1 John 2:18).

The last days for the church commenced with Christ's first advent and will close with the Rapture. Therefore, the entire current church age can be called the last days.

Referring to this age as the "last days" (or the "last hour") is a vivid reminder that Christ could come at any time. Every generation since the coming of Christ has lived with the hope that it could be the final generation and that Christ could break in at any moment. No prophecies must be fulfilled before Christ can come. We are living in the last days of the church age. When the Rapture takes place, the end times will begin.

LAST DAYS FOR THE CHURCH	LAST DAYS FOR ISRAEL
Began at the first coming of Christ	Begins at the start of the Tribulation
Ends with the Rapture	Ends with the millennial kingdom
End times include the Rapture, the Tribulation, the second coming of Christ, the Millennium, and eternity	

What Is the "Day of the Lord"?

Another key eschatological term to understand is the "Day of the Lord." The Old Testament refers to the Day of the Lord nineteen specific times,[3] but dozens of other places refer to "the day" or "that day."

The New Testament mentions the Day of the Lord four times (Acts 2:20; 1 Thessalonians 5:2; 2 Thessalonians 2:2; 2 Peter 3:10).

What is the "Day of the Lord"? The first thing we must do is define what we mean by "day." That may seem fairly obvious; however, the word *day* is used in the Bible in three main ways. All three uses are illustrated in the first two chapters of Genesis. First, sometimes it is used to refer to daylight—the hours between dawn and sunset (Genesis 1:5). Second, it is also used to refer to a twenty-four-hour day (Genesis 1:5). The Jewish day began at sunset and continued to the next day at sunset. Third, the word *day* is used in the Bible as a period of time (Genesis 2:4, NASB), just as we use it in English. We speak of the day of our youth. We do not mean that we were young only one day, but we mean the extended period of time in which we were young. The Day of the Lord falls into this final category. It is an extended period of time, not just a twelve-hour or twenty-four-hour period.

In 1 Thessalonians 5, the Day of the Lord refers to an extended period of time but is given characteristics like a twenty-four-hour day. It is a day that begins at midnight or in the darkness, advancing to dawn and then to daylight. That is the symbolism involved in the Day of the Lord. A few sample passages give a general overview of this period.

> See, the day of the LORD is coming—
> the terrible day of his fury and
> fierce anger.
> The land will be made desolate,
> and all the sinners destroyed with it.
> The heavens will be black above them;
> the stars will give no light.
> The sun will be dark when it rises,
> and the moon will provide no light.

"I, the LORD, will punish the world for its evil
and the wicked for their sin.
I will crush the arrogance of the proud
and humble the pride of the mighty."

ISAIAH 13:9-11

Isaiah 13 describes a dramatic judgment manifest in the physical world, which will interfere with the light of the sun, moon, and stars. God will put down the proud and deal with sinners in judgment (see also Zephaniah 1:14-16).

However, Scripture also portrays the Day of the Lord as a time of deliverance and blessing for Israel. The Day of the Lord includes the Millennium—the whole kingdom reign of Christ on earth—in which Christ personally directs the government of the world. Zephaniah 3:14-17 pictures Israel's blessing in that day, obviously following the time of judgment:

Sing, O daughter of Zion;
shout aloud, O Israel!
Be glad and rejoice with all your heart,
O daughter of Jerusalem!
For the LORD will remove his hand of judgment
and will disperse the armies of your enemy.
And the LORD himself, the King of Israel,
will live among you!
At last your troubles will be over,
and you will never again fear disaster.
On that day the announcement to Jerusalem will be,
"Cheer up, Zion! Don't be afraid!
For the LORD your God is living among you.
He is a mighty savior.
He will take delight in you with gladness.
With his love, he will calm all your fears.
He will rejoice over you with joyful songs."

This passage prophesies the praising and rejoicing of Israel during the Millennium on the earth. Joel 3 sheds additional light on the blessing phase of the Day of the Lord. Joel 3:14 refers to the "day of the LORD," and Joel later continues, "In that day [the day of the Lord] the mountains will drip with sweet wine, and the hills will flow with milk. Water will fill the streambeds of Judah, and a fountain will burst forth from the LORD's Temple, watering the arid valley of acacias" (3:18). This description looks beyond Israel's trouble in Joel's day to the time of future blessing when the land of Israel will be restored during the reign of the Messiah on earth. This indicates that the Day of the Lord extends all the way into the millennial, messianic kingdom. Finally, 2 Peter 3:10-13 indicates that the Day of the Lord will include the destruction of the present heavens and earth and the creation of the new heavens and new earth.

Putting these passages together, the day of the Lord is any time God intervenes directly and dramatically in history either to judge or to bless. God has intervened in this way in the past, and he will do so again in the future. There have been specific, past "days of the Lord" when God intervened dramatically to judge. For instance, the destruction of Egypt was called the "day of the LORD" (Ezekiel 30:1-4). The locust plague in Joel was a day of the Lord when God intervened directly to judge Israel (Joel 1:15). Yet, it is important to remember that all these past, historical days of the Lord prefigure the final, future Day of the Lord.

J. Dwight Pentecost pinpoints the timing for this future day: "The day of the Lord is that extended period of time beginning with God's dealings with Israel after the rapture at the beginning of the tribulation period and extending through the second advent and the millennial age unto the creation of the new heavens and new earth after the millennium."[4]

As revealed in Scripture, the future Day of the Lord is a period of time that will begin with the seven-year Tribulation, which we could call the *judgment phase*, and will continue throughout the entire one-thousand-year reign of Christ and the creation of the new heavens and new earth, which we could call the *blessing phase*. The future Day of the Lord will stretch all the way from the Rapture to the creation of the new heavens and new earth—from the Rapture to the re-creation. It will commence with a time of wrath and judgment upon a wicked and Christ-rejecting world and will culminate in a time of peace and prosperity; Christ will be in the midst of the earth, will rule over the earth, and will bless the nation of Israel.

Much like a twenty-four-hour day, the Day of the Lord will begin with the dark night of the Tribulation, continuing with the dawn bursting forth when Christ returns, and then the world will bask in the full sun of daylight during the Kingdom of Christ.

TWO PHASES OF THE FUTURE DAY OF THE LORD	
PHASE 1—JUDGMENT	PHASE 2—BLESSING
Tribulation	Millennium
Darkness	Light
Seven Years	One Thousand Years

We are not currently in the Day of the Lord. Our present time, this current church age, is often referred to as the day of grace. We do not mean that God never displayed grace in the previous dispensations. Obviously, many of God's dealings with humankind from the Garden of Eden to the present day have manifested His grace. People have always been saved by God's grace alone through faith. The salvation of every person, no matter when he or she lived, is a work of God's sovereign grace. But God, during this present age, has uniquely displayed His grace, highlighting it as the basis for salvation and for our Christian life.

Another feature of this day of grace is that for the most part God is not dealing openly and directly with human sin. He may impose swift judgment in some cases, but evil people often flourish, enjoy health and wealth, and succeed in their endeavors, even though they are not Christians and do not honor the Lord. A person today may even arrogantly blaspheme God, angrily declare to be an atheist, or openly denounce God and teach destructive ideas. Yet, seemingly God does nothing about it. The Lord is not attempting to straighten that out in this day of grace. The overriding purpose of God in this age is to proclaim His grace—that people may be saved by trusting in Christ and receiving God's gift of grace. However, after this day of grace has run its course and the church has been raptured to be with Christ, the Day of the Lord will begin when God will punish human sin directly in wrath and judgment.

In short, Scripture clearly portrays the Day of the Lord as a day of divine judgment upon the world followed by a time of unparalleled blessing. In the Day of the Lord, Christ will rule with a rod of iron over the entire earth (Psalm 2:9; Revelation 2:27). He will administer absolute justice (Isaiah 11:1-9). In that day Israel will also be regathered (Isaiah 11:10-12) and brought into the perfect peace of the millennial kingdom (Zephaniah 3:14-20) and on to the creation of the new heavens and new earth.

PART 2

Setting the Stage in the Current Age

The countdown seems to have begun.

When we launch a satellite into space, NASA has an impressive checklist of things to be tested before the vehicle finally lifts off from its pad. There are sometimes delays in checking off the items on the list, but once the countdown has begun, it usually continues to the end. It is only a matter of time. We are all familiar with the impressive final seconds—ten, nine, eight . . . three, two, one, blast off!

To those of us who look at today's world and then look at the variety of Scriptures that focus on the end times, it seems that the countdown to the coming of Christ has begun. Neither "the day nor the hour" nor "the times or the seasons" are ours to know (Matthew 25:13; Acts 1:7). But what we see appears to be a rapid movement of events toward the final seconds before the church is launched into space—and the subsequent judgments descend on the world.

JOHN PHILLIPS, *Exploring the Future*

CHAPTER 8

WHAT TO LOOK FOR

Discerning the Signs of the Times

One evening a man stayed up late reading an enthralling novel after his wife had gone to bed. Since he didn't have his watch on, the man listened each time the grandfather clock chimed so he wouldn't stay up too late. At 10:00 p.m. it chimed ten times, and at 11:00 it chimed eleven times. As the man was about to finish the book, he heard the clock begin to chime the midnight hour. Just to make sure he hadn't missed an hour in his focus on the book, he began to count the chimes. Ten, eleven, twelve . . . thirteen. Startled, the man ran upstairs, awakened his sleeping wife, and excitedly said, "Honey, wake up! It's later than it's ever been."

As planet earth approaches the midnight hour, there's one thing we know for sure—it's later than it's ever been. But is it possible to be any more specific than this? Is it possible to see specific signs of the times to indicate that the end times are near? Whenever dramatic, world-shaking events shock the world, we naturally want answers. We want to know what's happening. We want to make sense out of what often seems chaotic, disconnected, and frightening.

Sign, Sign, Everywhere a Sign

The April 2009 cover of *Newsmax* pictures Jesus with outstretched arms under the heading—"The Jesus Question: Will He Ever Return?" The article notes that one in five Americans "believe that Christ will return in the present generation" and that "20 percent say the global life expectancy is just a couple of decades." After laying out all the polling of Americans' end times views, *Newsmax* concludes, "So the idea that creation's clock could strike midnight at any time turns out to be as American as apple pie, pink slips, and debt collectors. If you mix the morning headlines into the average American's eschatology, you stir up quite a powerful, angst-inducing brew."

The headlines do seem to parallel the biblical end times template more and more every day. World events are unfolding exactly as the Bible predicted thousands of years ago. Yet, in our attempt to understand world news and current events in light of Bible prophecy, we need to carefully avoid two extremes.

The first extreme is *sensationalism*. Sometimes in our desperation to make sense out of what is happening in the world, we are susceptible to sensationalist claims. Date setters are among the most egregious sensationalists, people who are always trying to identify the Antichrist, and who try to make every earthquake, disease, disaster, or international feud a sign of the times. For too many prophecy buffs, virtually everything that happens is a sign that the Lord's coming is near.

The problem is that when everything becomes a sign, then nothing is a sign. This extreme position of "newspaper exegesis" is unproductive at best and unbiblical at worst and highlights how careful we need to be in times like these when people are searching for answers. There are always those who offer sensational ideas that people desperately grab onto without really knowing all the facts. We must vigilantly avoid sensationalism.

When considering signs of the times, we must make sure that we view current events in light of the Bible and not the other way around. We must also reject the reckless practice of date setting for the Lord's coming or the end of the world. Never speculate about the time of the Lord's coming or listen to others who do. If date setters have taught us anything, they have taught us that if someone sets a date for the coming of the Lord, you can be sure that's not the date. Jesus can come at any time, and He is coming on the Father's schedule, not on a date set by any person (see Matthew 24:33-34; Acts 1:7). As prophecy teacher Ed Hindson reminds us, "God's clock, the clock of history, is ticking away. It never speeds up and never slows down. It just keeps on ticking, continually and relentlessly, moving us closer and closer to the end of the age. How close we are to the end will only be revealed by time itself."[1]

The other extreme we must avoid is *scoffing* at the signs of the times. Many today react negatively to any mention of signs of the end times. They say it is foolish and unwarranted to look for or even talk about trends and developments that point toward the end times scenario portrayed in Scripture. But is this negative outlook justified? Are signs of the times important? What did Jesus say? In Matthew 16:1-3, Jesus sternly rebuked the religious leaders of His day for their blindness to the signs of the times of His first coming:

> One day the Pharisees and Sadducees came to test Jesus, demanding that he show them a miraculous sign from heaven to prove his authority. He replied, "You know the saying, 'Red sky at night means fair weather tomorrow; red sky in the morning means foul weather all day.' You know how to interpret the weather signs in the sky, but you don't know how to interpret the *signs of the times*!" (italics added)

What Are "Signs of the Times"?

"Signs of the times" are visible events, sometimes miraculous or otherwise unexplainable, that point to something beyond themselves. Many signs were predicted by Jesus and the prophets throughout Scripture. Signs help us know what to look for, what to pay attention to. When we read prophecy, we can look for these "signs of the times." They show us what to be on the lookout for, much like a road sign points to what's coming.

Jesus used the term "signs of the times" to verify His first coming. Jesus fulfilled Old Testament prophecies and performed the miracles of the Messiah right before the eyes of many people, yet they were blind to the clear confirmation of His identity (Matthew 16:1-3). Despite being shown signs to look for, the people didn't pay attention. Jesus fulfilled 109 prophecies during His life on earth, and He indicted the Jewish leaders for missing these signs of His first coming. Most people of that day missed the clear signs—Jesus' visible miracles confirmed the invisible truth that He was God. Those were the signs that verified His first coming, but what about the Second Coming? Have we been given any signs? What can we be looking for and paying attention to?

As recorded in Luke 21:25, Jesus said, "There will be strange signs in the sun, moon, and stars. And here on earth the nations will be in turmoil, perplexed by the roaring seas and strange tides." Jesus clearly referred to "signs" that will portend His second coming back to earth. In Matthew 24:3, when Jesus' disciples asked Him, "What sign will signal your return and the end of the world?" Jesus didn't say, "Don't worry about signs of the end of the age." Or He didn't say, "I'm not going to tell you, it's none of your business." No, in Matthew 24:4-31 he outlined several general and specific signs of the end of the age. Since Jesus gave us signs like these, we should be careful not to ignore them and scoff at them. We need to listen to what Jesus was saying.

After listing some of the main signs, Jesus concluded with the parable of the fig tree in Matthew 24:32-33. "Now learn a lesson from the fig tree. When its branches bud and its leaves begin to sprout, you know that summer is near. In the same way, when you see all these things, you can know his return is very near, right at the door."

Many believe that the fig tree refers to the nation of Israel since fig trees represented Israel in the Old Testament. However, Jesus was probably using a natural illustration that anyone could relate to. Just as the blossoming of the fig tree indicates that summer is near, so the fulfillment of the signs predicted in Matthew 24:4-31 will show that His second coming is near. We do not scoff at the signs of spring but look for them with anticipation. It should be the same with Jesus' return. We should look forward to it.

Another New Testament passage that emphasizes the importance of signs of the Lord's coming is Hebrews 10:24-25: "Let us think of ways to motivate one another to acts of love and good works. And let us not neglect our meeting together, as some people do, but encourage *one another*, especially now that the day of his return is drawing near" (italics added). Some believe this verse refers to the approaching judgment of AD 70 and the destruction of Jerusalem. However, the book of Hebrews repeatedly refers to the Lord's coming and the events associated with it (Hebrews 2:5; 9:28; 10:37; 12:26-28). If Hebrews 10:25 is referring to the Lord's coming, and I believe it is, then the passage only makes sense if such discernment is actually possible. No person knows the time, but according to Hebrews 10:24-25 we are to see the day of His return drawing near by discerning the signs of the times.

A Key Distinction

The signs we are seeing in the world today anticipate events that will occur *after* the Rapture in anticipation of Jesus' return. The Bible's end times prophecies refer to the seven-year Tribulation period and portend the second coming of Christ to rule and reign. But no sign presages the Rapture. Signs are for Christ's *return*, not the church's *rapture*. The Rapture is an imminent, sign-less event. It's an event that could occur at any moment without warning

Dr. John Walvoord used to share an apt illustration of how signs of the times relate to the Rapture and the Second Coming. He pointed out how there are all kinds of signs for Christmas. There are lights everywhere, decorations, Christmas trees, music, and even Santa in the mall. But Thanksgiving can sneak up on you. There are no reals signs for Thanksgiving. Dr. Walvoord noted that the second coming of Christ is like Christmas. It will be preceded by many very specific signs that Scripture outlines. The Rapture, however, is like Thanksgiving. There are no specific signs for its coming. Yet, if it's fall and you already begin to see the signs of Christmas everywhere, and Thanksgiving has not yet arrived, then you know that Thanksgiving must be very near. The signs of "Christmas" seem to be appearing all around us today. The coming of Christ to rapture His church could be very near.

Setting the Stage

My wife and I enjoy going for long walks. Often as we walk along, I notice my shadow being cast on the concrete in front of me. My shadow is not me, it's not the substance, but it signals that I am not far behind. It's a sign that I am coming. In the same way, coming events often cast their shadows upon this world before they arrive, functioning as signs of the times.

Another way to picture this is to imagine that you're at a play. You have taken your seat in the audience, and before the curtain goes up for Act One you can hear sounds behind the curtain. The stage is being set for the beginning of the play. The props are put in place, and the actors take their positions. These events are not the play itself but are a natural, necessary preparation for it. The setting of the stage creates anticipation for the raising of the curtain.

In the same way, God is preparing the world stage for His drama of the ages. The curtain is still down. But God is allowing world events to take place and players to assume their roles for the drama to begin. Before the curtain goes up, the church will rise in the air to meet the Lord at the Rapture. Sometime after the Rapture, the Antichrist will arrive on the world scene. At that point all the pieces and players will be in place ready to play their roles in the final drama of the ages.

This approach to understanding the signs of the times has often been referred to as "stage setting." Thomas Ice and Timothy Demy summarize this approach.

> Bible prophecy relates to a time after the rapture (the seven-year tribulation period). However, this does not mean that God is not preparing the world for that future time during the present church age—in fact, He is. But this is not "fulfillment" of Bible prophecy. So while prophecy is not being fulfilled in our day, it does not follow that we cannot track "general trends" in current preparation for the coming tribulation, especially since it immediately follows the rapture. We call this approach "stage setting." Just as many people set their clothes out the night before they wear them the following day, so in the same sense is

> God preparing the world for the certain fulfillment of prophecy in a future time.
>
> The Bible provides detailed prophecy about the seven-year tribulation. In fact, Revelation 4–19 gives a detailed, sequential outline of the major players and events. Using Revelation as a framework, a Bible student is able to harmonize the hundreds of other passages that speak of the seven-year tribulation into a clear model of the next time period for planet earth. With such a template to guide us, we can see that already God is preparing or setting the stage of the world in which the great drama of the tribulation will unfold. In this way this future time casts shadows of expectation in our own day so that current events provide discernible signs of the times.[2]

Biblical prophecy doesn't predict every insignificant ripple in our world today, but it does reveal the main currents and trends. Several key signs appear to be flashing in today's headlines. While many signs could be listed, some of which will be addressed in subsequent chapters, here are five significant signs of the times.

Five Signs of the End Times

The Regathering of the Jewish People

Sign number one is the regathering of the Jewish people to their ancient homeland. The Bible predicts over and over again that the Jews must be back in their homeland for the events of the end times to unfold (Jeremiah 30:1-5; Ezekiel 34:11-24; Ezekiel 37; Zechariah 10:6-10). It is the most prophesied event in end times passages in the Bible, and for that reason it is often called the "supersign" of the end times. Almost all the key events of the end times hinge on the existence of the nation of Israel. Israel is the battleground for all the great end times conflicts. The people of Israel must be preserved and regathered to their ancient homeland to set the stage for end times biblical prophecy to be fulfilled. As Adrian Rogers says, "These are dangerous days in which we live! The storm clouds are gathering. The lightning is flashing—and the lightening rod is Israel.

Christians cannot deny or ignore the significance of the nation of Israel. . . . Israel is God's yardstick. Israel is God's measuring rod. Israel is God's blueprint. Israel is God's program for what He is doing in the world."[3]

The end times Tribulation officially begins when the Antichrist makes a seven-year treaty with Israel (Daniel 9:27). Obviously, for this to happen Israel must exist. The Jews must be back in their land. Ezekiel 38 and Zechariah 12 describe armed invasions of the nation of Israel. Again, for these prophecies to be literally fulfilled the Jewish people must be back in their land.

Scripture further indicates that this regathering will occur in stages. It is portrayed as a process. Of course, this assumes that it will take some time for the returning exiles to regather and resettle the land. In the famous "valley of dry bones" vision of Ezekiel 37:1-14, Ezekiel's graveyard vision symbolizes the national return, restoration, and regeneration of "the whole house of Israel" (37:11, NASB). Israel is first restored physically, pictured by the bones, sinew, and flesh coming together. The complete skeleton comes together bone by bone, piece by piece, but it is still a lifeless corpse (37:8). Then, Ezekiel witnesses Israel's spiritual regeneration when the breath of the Spirit breathes spiritual life into the dead nation (37:9).

Of course, this spiritual regeneration won't occur until the Messiah returns. But I believe the process of physical regathering to the land has begun. The worldwide regathering of Israel has been going on now for about 130 years. A pile of bones is beginning to come together and take shape in the land of Israel. Randall Price highlights the modern miracle of the Jewish people.

> The modern return of the Jewish People to the Land of Israel has been called the "Miracle on the Mediterranean." Such a return by a people group that had been scattered among the nations is unprecedented in history. Indeed, the Jewish People are the only exiled people to remain a distinct people despite being dispersed to more than 70 different countries for more than 20 centuries. The mighty empires of Egypt, Assyria, Babylon, Persia, Greece, and Rome all ravaged their land, took their people captive,

> and scattered them throughout the earth. Even after this, they suffered persecution, pogrom, and Holocaust in the lands to which they were exiled. Yet, all of these ancient kingdoms have turned to dust and their former glories remain only as museum relics and many of the nations that opposed the Jews have suffered economic, political, or religious decline. But the Jewish people whom they enslaved and tried to eradicate live free and have again become a strong nation![4]

The modern-day return to the Holy Land began as early as 1871 when a few Jews began to trickle back into the land. By 1881, about twenty-five thousand Jews had settled there. At the first Zionist Congress in 1897, led by Theodor Herzl, the Jewish people officially adopted the goal of reclaiming the land. The regathering was very slow. By 1914, the Jewish population in the land was only eighty thousand.

During World War I, the British sought support from the Jews for the war effort. So the British foreign secretary, Arthur J. Balfour, issued what has become known as the Balfour Declaration on November 2, 1917. The declaration was stated in a letter from Balfour to Lord Rothschild, who was a wealthy Jewish entrepreneur. In the letter, Secretary Balfour gave approval to the Jewish goal of reclamation. "His Majesty's Government views with favor the establishment in Palestine of a national home for the Jewish people. . . ." The declaration stirred Jewish hopes for establishing a homeland in the Holy Land and encouraged more Jews to return. By 1939, when World War II broke out, about 450,000 Jews had returned.

The Second World War and Nazi Germany's heinous treatment of the Jewish people created worldwide sympathy and a favorable environment for the Jewish people. Hitler's atrocities actually provided the greatest momentum for the establishment of a national homeland for the Jews. The United Nations approved a national homeland for the Jews, and British control of the land ended on May 14, 1948. The new nation was given five thousand square miles and had a population of 650,000 Jews and several hundred thousand Arabs. Further waves of immigrants have poured into Israel from all over the world, most notably from Ethiopia and the former Soviet Union.

In 2009, for the first time since AD 135, there were more Jews in Israel than in any other place on earth; 5.4 million Jews now live in Israel, compared to 5.2 million in the United States.[5] According to Haaretz.com, "The data indicates the closure of an historical circle: For the first time since the destruction of the Second Temple, Israel has once again become the largest concentration of Jews in the world."[6] To put this in perspective, in 1948 only 6 percent of the Jews in the world were in Israel. Today, the statistic stands at almost 40 percent. By the year 2030 it is estimated that half of the Jews worldwide will live in the land. Prophetically, the preparations over the last 130 years are staggering. For the first time in two thousand years the Jews have returned and continue to come home to their land—just as the ancient prophets predicted. This sign should be like a flashing red light to all who know the prophetic Scriptures.

Surging Apostasy

A second sign of the end times is surging apostasy, that is, a departure from the truth, both doctrinally and morally (1 Timothy 4:1-3; 2 Timothy 3:1-9, 13; Jude 1:1-16). Writing in 1964, John Walvoord said, "The Scriptures predict that there will be a growing apostasy or departure from the Lord as the church age progresses, and its increase can be understood as a general indication that the rapture itself is near."[7] In 1971, J. Dwight Pentecost wrote, "Abundant evidence on every hand shows that men are departing from the faith. Not only do they doubt the Word; they openly reject it. This phenomenon has never been as prevalent as today. In the period of church history known as the Dark Ages, men were ignorant of the truth; but never was there an age when men openly denied and repudiated the truth. This open, deliberate, willful repudiation of the truth of the Bible is described in Scripture as one of the major characteristics of the last days of the church on earth."[8]

This apostasy foreshadows the final falling away that will break out as the end times begin to unfold (2 Thessalonians 2:2-3). John Phillips says it well:

> Some think we can look for a worldwide spiritual awaker
> before the Rapture, but the passage in 2 Thessalonians
> indicates the opposite; a worldwide departure from the f
> can be expected. God might indeed send a revival before the Rapture but the Scriptures do not prophesy one.[9]

This current age will climax with a monumental falling away, both doctrinally and morally. While the church today may not be experiencing the full-blown apostasy of 2 Thessalonians, many within the church appear to be on the leading edge of it. The book of Jude, which describes and denounces apostasy, also describes our modern world to a tee. Jude is the final book before Revelation. Some have even called it the preface to the book of Revelation. It portrays the conditions that will prevail before the events of Revelation are unleashed. Deepening apostasy is a sign of the times.

The Coming Middle East Peace

Sign number three is the worldwide clamoring for peace in the Middle East. What is the one issue in our world today that often overshadows all others? What is the one problem that has festered in the world's side for decades? What is the one issue that finds its way into the world's newspapers and television news reports every day? The ongoing hostilities in the Middle East. The Mideastern peace process. The "Roadmap to Peace." This one continuing crisis often monopolizes world attention.

Have you ever wondered why? Certainly, there are political and humanitarian reasons for the world's interest in this ongoing struggle. But I believe there is more to it than that. The Middle East peace process is a key sign of the times. The event that signals the beginning of the seven-year Tribulation is the signing of a peace treaty between the leader of the Western Confederacy (the Antichrist) and the nation of Israel (Daniel 9:27; see also 1 Thessalonians 5:1-2). The current yearning for peace in the Middle East is setting the stage for the final covenant of peace between the Antichrist and Israel predicted in the Bible.

Reuniting of the Roman Empire

Sign number four is the rebirth of the Roman Empire. As the end times begin to unfold, global alliances will emerge as nations scramble for political power and dwindling economic resources. Out of this quickly shifting situation, a coalition of nations, headed by ten leaders, will emerge to protect the interests of the West. This alliance will reconstitute the Roman Empire. This "Group of Ten" is first mentioned in Daniel 2:41-44, where it is symbolized as ten toes on a great statue. In Daniel 7:7 and 7:24 this same ruling oligarchy of ten leaders is symbolized by ten horns on a beast that represents the last world empire—the Roman Empire in its final form. Many interpreters of biblical prophecy believe that the European Union will fulfill this predicted alliance of nations. The European Union's connection to this ten-leader group is uncertain, but it appears to be a seed of what the Bible predicts. No one knows how long it will take to reach the final stage, but when it is fully developed, this Western power bloc will constitute the revived Roman Empire and will have the economic and political power necessary to control the Mediterranean. Its final leader, the Antichrist, will eventually be able to seize control of the ten leaders and consolidate power very much like the Roman Empire did in the past (Daniel 7:8).

Globalism

A fifth key sign of the times is globalism. Ever since Genesis 10–11 when Satan ruled the world through one man named Nimrod, Satan's goal has been to get the world together again so he can rule it all. World history bears out this pattern. It's the record of one person after another trying to rule the world. Many of the power-hungry rulers who have cruelly subjugated nations under their feet have been energized by Satan to foster his goal of globalization.

Now for the first time in history since Genesis 11 and the tower of Babel, globalization is within man's (and Satan's) reach. It is most significant that in the twenty-first century not only does a need for a world government exist, but the technology for establishing such a government is now in our hands. Today the electronic media, especially use of television via satellite, is a tremendous tool that allows instant communication around the world. Cable news now covers almost every corner of the planet. Access to the Internet and satellite cell phones reach around the globe. The capacity for missile warfare also makes world rule possible. Missiles can be fired and guided by GPS to almost any spot in the world in less than thirty minutes. A ruler with nuclear submarines and missiles at his disposal could threaten any portion of the world—blackmailing it into submission with the threat of extinction. No ruler in history has had such fearful weapons to enforce his rule.

In terms of economics, the Bible predicts that the world ruler will have absolute control of the economy, and no one will buy or sell without his permission (Revelation 13:17). Today, electronic funds transfers, electronic banking, and debit and credit cards make this literally possible for the first time in world history. Large monetary transfers are already controlled by the government. Electronic banking, credit and debit cards, and the use of the Internet for financial transactions have already reduced the use of cash currency. Hundreds of millions of dollars move electronically every day.

Both the need and the tools for world control exist today. The increasing availability of nuclear weapons, the propaganda power of the world media, and the blackmail power of international economic agreements and embargoes will make it possible for a world dictator to seize control that would have been impossible in any previous generation.

The necessary ingredients for a world government are present for the first time in the history of civilization. The time may not be far away when such a government—foretold in Scripture long before one was possible—will have its accurate and complete fulfillment.

The Last Act?

Sometimes life feels like entering a dark theater and realizing you are coming in near the end of a play with several acts. We didn't write it. We didn't ask to be thrust into the play. Yet we can be certain this drama is nearing the last act. Even though we didn't see the beginning of the play, we can look back and see its plot and direction. But even then, how can we be sure when the next act will start?

The biblical prophets talked a lot about the last act. What we can do is look for the events that set it up. If those events occur, we can be fairly certain the last act is just ahead. When the curtain comes down on the current scene, will the next act be the last? What are the events, the characters, and the plot that will bring the play of world history to its predicted climax? Will we be wise enough to see it coming? Will we be ready? The only way we can be ready is if we know something about the last act. In the coming chapters, we will examine some of the events that we know will occur based on biblical prophecy.

PART 3

When Will the Believing Be Leaving?

The Rapture is not only a turning point for the saints, it is a turning point for the world. The world will never be the same after the Rapture.

ARTHUR BLOOMFIELD, *How to Recognize the Antichrist*[1]

CHAPTER 9

THE MYSTERY OF THE RAPTURE

CURRENT EVENTS have drawn attention like never before to questions about the future of the world, the church, and Israel. In this explosive, ever-changing atmosphere, it's only natural for people to wonder about Christ's return, and with it the Rapture. There's an expectation that Jesus will come, possibly very soon, to rapture His people to heaven. According to a *Newsweek* poll, 55 percent of Americans "think that the faithful will be taken up to heaven in the Rapture."[1] Over half of Americans believe in the event commonly called "the Rapture."

I'm sure many of the people who responded are somewhat unclear about the details of the Rapture. Others know something about it, but hear about all the different views and get confused. So, to help cut through some of the confusion, let's begin by defining the word *Rapture*, considering some important issues, and answering some key questions. The Rapture is the next great event on God's prophetic calendar.

Three Main Rapture Passages

What does the Bible say about the Rapture? While the Rapture is referred to many times in the New Testament, three main passages describe the Rapture of the church.

> [Jesus said,] "Don't let your hearts be troubled. Trust in God, and trust also in me. There is more than enough room in my Father's home. If this were not so, would I have told you that I am going to prepare a place for you? When everything is ready, I will come and get you, so that you will always be with me where I am."
>
> JOHN 14:1-3

> What I am saying, dear brothers and sisters, is that our physical bodies cannot inherit the Kingdom of God. These dying bodies cannot inherit what will last forever.
>
> But let me reveal to you a wonderful secret. We will not all die, but we will all be transformed! It will happen in a moment, in the blink of an eye, when the last trumpet is blown. For when the trumpet sounds, those who have died will be raised to live forever. And we who are living will also be transformed. For our dying bodies must be transformed into bodies that will never die; our mortal bodies must be transformed into immortal bodies.
>
> Then, when our dying bodies have been transformed into bodies that will never die, this Scripture will be fulfilled:
>
> "Death is swallowed up in victory.
> O death, where is your victory?
> O death, where is your sting?"
>
> For sin is the sting that results in death, and the law gives sin its power. But thank God! He gives us victory over sin and death through our Lord Jesus Christ.
>
> 1 CORINTHIANS 15:50-57

> Dear brothers and sisters, we want you to know what will happen to the believers who have died so you will not grieve like people who have no hope. For since we believe that Jesus died and was raised to life again, we also believe that when Jesus returns, God will bring back with him the believers who have died.
>
> We tell you this directly from the Lord: We who are still living when the Lord returns will not meet him ahead of those who have died. For the Lord himself will come down from heaven with a commanding shout, with the voice of the archangel, and with the trumpet call of God. First, the Christians who have died will rise from their graves. Then, together with them, we who are still alive and remain on the earth will be caught up in the clouds to meet the Lord in the air. Then we will be with the Lord forever. So encourage each other with these words.
>
> 1 THESSALONIANS 4:13-18

Jesus briefly introduced the doctrine of the Rapture in John 14:1-3. Paul explained it more fully in 1 Corinthians and 1 Thessalonians. John 14:1-3 has striking parallels with 1 Thessalonians 4:13-18 that indicate they refer to the same event. J. B. Smith notes the numerous linguistic similarities.

JOHN 14:1-3 (NASB)	1 THESSALONIANS 4:13-18 (NASB)[2]
trouble (v. 1)	sorrow (v. 13)
believe (v. 1)	believe (v. 14)
God, me (v. 1)	Jesus, God (v. 14)
told you (v. 2)	say to you (v. 15)
come again (v. 3)	coming of the Lord (v. 15)
receive you (v. 3)	caught up (v. 17)
to myself (v. 3)	to meet the Lord (v. 17)
be where I am (v. 3)	ever be with the Lord (v. 17)

Now, let's turn to some of the key issues and questions related to this next great event in God's prophetic program.

Why Isn't the Word *Rapture* Found in the Bible?

Those who object to the Rapture often point out that the word *Rapture* is not in the Bible. It's a fair concern. However, the word *Trinity* is not in the Bible, or even the word *Bible* for that matter, yet we believe that these things are very real. So where does the concept of the Rapture come from?[3]

The term *Rapture* is derived from 1 Thessalonians 4:17: "We who are still alive and remain on the earth will be *caught up* in the clouds to meet the Lord in the air. Then we will be with the Lord forever" (italics added). The phrase "caught up" is in Greek *harpazo*, which means "to snatch, to seize, or to take suddenly and vehemently."

Harpazo appears thirteen times in the New Testament: Matthew 11:12; 13:19; John 6:15; 10:12, 28, 29; Acts 8:39; 23:10; 2 Corinthians 12:2, 4; 1 Thessalonians 4:17; Jude 1:23; Revelation 12:5. In those passages, *harpazo* is variously translated as "take by force," "snatch," or "caught up" (NASB). In Acts 8, the Spirit "snatches," or transports, Philip from one place to another that was twenty miles away. In 2 Corinthians 12, Paul describes being "caught up" to heaven in the presence of the Lord. This was a thrilling experience he wanted others to share. In Revelation 12:5, *harpazo* refers back to the Ascension of Jesus to heaven (Acts 1:9-11).

Our English word *Rapture* is derived from Latin. In the fourth century AD, the great scholar Jerome translated the Greek New Testament into Latin. In 1 Thessalonians 4:17, Jerome translated the Greek word *harpazo* into the Latin word *raeptius*. The Latin word *rapio* means "to seize, snatch, or seize away." This word was eventually brought into English as *Rapture*.

So, while it is true that the word *Rapture* does not occur in most English translations, 1 Corinthians 15:51-55 and 1 Thessalonians 4:17 clearly contain the concept of a catching away of living believers to meet the Lord. The Rapture could just as well be called the "catching away of the church," "the snatching away of the church," the "translation of the church," or the "*harpazo* of the church." But "Rapture of the church" is an excellent description and has become the most common title for this event.

What Is the Rapture?

Simply stated, the Rapture of the church, which is the first phase of Christ's coming, is the intersection of two events: the resurrection of the dead, specifically only believers, and the transformation of living believers. They will all be immediately together in Jesus' glorious presence, and He will escort them to heaven to live with Him forever.

Now, let me clarify a few points. First, Jesus' second coming will happen in two phases; the Rapture is the first phase. The second phase will occur after the Tribulation—Jesus will return, defeat the Antichrist at Armageddon, and set up his millennial kingdom.

Second, throughout this book, when we refer to the Rapture, we are also referring to the resurrection of the righteous. Technically, the "catching away" in 1 Thessalonians 4:17 refers specifically to transporting living believers from earth to heaven, but according to 1 Thessalonians 4:16, the righteous will be resurrected at the same time, so the Rapture is nearly synonymous with the resurrection of the righteous.

Finally, the resurrection of the righteous is one of a number of resurrections that will occur; the others will involve Old Testament believers (Isaiah 26:19; Daniel 12:1-3), the unrighteous (Acts 24:15; Revelation 20:12-13), and believers who die during the Tribulation (Revelation 20:4-6). We'll talk more about all these details later.

When the Rapture occurs, Jesus will descend from heaven, accompanied by the perfected spirits of believers who have died. He will resurrect their bodies, now glorified, and the spirits of believers will be clothed with their new bodies.

At the Rapture the soul and body, which "falls asleep" at death, will be reunited. The separation of body from spirit will be forever reversed. According to 1 Thessalonians 4:14-16, the Lord will bring the perfected spirit of each believer from heaven when He comes, and the body of each believer will be raised up incorruptible, immortal, and imperishable to meet his or her spirit in the air and be united forever.

TO UNDERSTAND THIS REJOINING of the body and the spirit, we need to understand what physical death does to our bodies and spirits. Death in the Bible always means separation, never annihilation. People will not cease to exist; their spirits will still go on. So we need to distinguish between physical and spiritual death.

When Adam and Eve sinned in the Garden of Eden, they died spiritually. That is, they were suddenly separated from God.

From that point on, every person was born into this world spiritually dead or separated from God (Ephesians 2:1). Applying this understanding to physical death means that when a person dies physically, there is a separation between the material body and the immaterial spirit of the person. When this separation takes place, the body "falls asleep" and is buried. But the spirit goes immediately to heaven if the person is a believer in Christ (2 Corinthians 5:8; Philippians 1:23). Between a believer's death and the resurrection of the righteous, the believer lives in a disembodied state that Paul likens to being "naked" (2 Corinthians 5:3, NASB).[4]

First Thessalonians 4:13-15 (NASB) uses the words "fallen asleep" or "asleep" three times. This is a common biblical euphemism for death (Matthew 27:52, NASB; John 11:11; Acts 7:60, NASB; 13:36, NASB). The Bible is clear that when a believer dies, his or her soul goes immediately into the conscious presence of the Lord (Luke 16:19-31; 23:39-43; Acts 7:56-60; 2 Corinthians 5:8; Philippians 1:23). The "sleep" in 1 Thessalonians 4:13-15 (NASB) refers to the sleep of the body, not the soul as some believe.

The Greek word for "fall asleep" is *koimao*. In ancient times it referred to natural sleep or the sleep of physical death. In the Scripture when this word is used for death, it is only used for the death of a Christian. Just as we wake up from natural sleep, the body will one day be awakened at the resurrection. A related Greek word, *koimeteria*, refers to a bedroom or a graveyard. We get our English word *cemetery* from this word. A cemetery is a place where bodies sleep until the resurrection of the dead when they will be rejoined with the spirit.

I read somewhere about a gravestone in London for a man named Solomon Peas. It reads as follows:

Here lies the body of Solomon Peas
Under the grass and under the trees
But Peas is not here only the pod
Peas shelled out and went to God

This epitaph captures the truth of physical death for a believer. The "peas" shell out and go to God, while the "pod" stays behind and is buried. A separation occurs.

During the Civil War a group of soldiers had to spend a winter night without tents in an open field. Through the night it snowed several inches, and at dawn the chaplain reported a strange sight. The snow-covered soldiers looked like the mounds of new graves, and when the bugle sounded reveille, a man immediately rose from each mound of snow, picturing for the chaplain the coming resurrection of the dead.[5] When Christ comes down from heaven, the bodies of deceased believers will be resurrected first and reunited to their perfected spirits that have returned with the Lord. The dead in Christ will rise first (1 Thessalonians 4:16).

When the dead have been raised, living believers will immediately be transformed and transported into the presence of Christ without ever tasting physical death. They will not sleep. They will be snatched up from the earth and united with Christ and other believers in the air.

Who Will Participate in the Rapture?

Only church-age believers will be resurrected when the Rapture occurs. First Thessalonians 4:16 (NASB) says that "the dead *in Christ* will rise first" (italics added). "In Christ" is a key phrase that tells us who will participate in the Rapture. Who is "in Christ"? Believers before the Day of Pentecost, described in Acts 2, were not "in Christ." The Holy Spirit came on the Day of Pentecost like "tongues of fire" and settled on believers (Acts 2:3). This event signified those believers were in Christ by the baptism of the Holy Spirit (1 Corinthians 12:13).

Therefore, I believe the participants in the Rapture include only believers who lived between the Day of Pentecost and the Rapture to come. These people are called church-age believers.

What is the church age? The church age is the era we live in right now when Jesus is saving Jews and Gentiles and forming them into one body of which He is the Head. The church age will end someday with the Rapture, just as suddenly and dramatically as it began on the Day of Pentecost, when Christ's body of believers is called up to meet Him in the air. While there are several reasons for the Rapture, the primary purpose for the Rapture is to end the church age. The Lord Jesus will come to remove His bride and escort her back to the Father's house.

The Rapture is often more specifically called "the Rapture of the church" because it only applies to believers in this current age.

What Happens to Old Testament Believers?

If only church-age believers are resurrected when the Rapture occurs, people often wonder what will happen to those who were saved before the beginning of the church age—often called Old Testament believers. When will they be resurrected and receive their glorified bodies?

God will resurrect the bodies of Old Testament believers in conjunction with His second coming to earth after the Tribulation.

Two passages in the Old Testament place the resurrection of Old Testament believers at the end of the Tribulation period.

> LORD, in distress we searched for you.
> We prayed beneath the burden of your discipline.
> Just as a pregnant woman
> writhes and cries out in pain as she gives birth,
> so were we in your presence, LORD.
> We, too, writhe in agony,
> but nothing comes of our suffering.
> We have not given salvation to the earth,
> nor brought life into the world.
> But those who die in the LORD will live;
> their bodies will rise again!
> Those who sleep in the earth
> will rise up and sing for joy!
> For your life-giving light will fall like dew
> on your people in the place of the dead!
>
> ISAIAH 26:16-19

> At that time Michael, the archangel who stands guard over your nation, will arise. Then there will be a time of anguish greater than any since nations first came into existence. But at that time every one of your people whose name is written in the

> book will be rescued. Many of those whose bodies lie dead and buried will rise up, some to everlasting life and some to shame and everlasting disgrace. Those who are wise will shine as bright as the sky, and those who lead many to righteousness will shine like the stars forever.
>
> DANIEL 12:1-3

Daniel 12:1 clearly points to a future time of distress that will be the worst in all of human history. I believe this parallels the Great Tribulation that Jesus speaks of in Matthew 24:21. Notice that in Daniel 12:2, the resurrection of Old Testament believers follows this time of trouble, and then 12:3 follows with a reference to the coming messianic kingdom. This sequence locates the resurrection of Old Testament saints *after* the Great Tribulation and *before* the millennial kingdom of Christ. It's placed in between these two future events. That means Old Testament saints will be resurrected in conjunction with the second coming of Christ, which ends the Tribulation and paves the way for the Millennium.

How Long Will the Rapture of the Church Take?

First Corinthians 15:52 says the events of the Rapture will happen "in a moment, in the twinkling of an eye" (NASB). The Greek word for *moment* is *atomos*, from which we get our English word *atom*. *Atomos* refers to something that is indivisible, that cannot be divided. When Paul wrote these words, no one could imagine splitting the *atomos*. Today, we would translate this "in an instant," "in a split second," or "in a flash."

The second phrase that describes the duration of the Rapture is "in the twinkling of an eye." The Greek word for *twinkling* is *rhipe*. This might refer to the time it takes for light to reflect in the human eye. Others believe that it refers to the time it takes to blink your eye—"in the blink of an eye." Blinking is the quickest movement in the human body. People everywhere understand what "in the blink of an eye" means.

The main point is clear. All the events of this Rapture will happen instantaneously. In a flash. It will all happen so quickly that it will be completely unobservable to the human eye. Like replaying in slow motion a split-second catch in a football game, the Lord slows down the Rapture film for us so we can see exactly what will happen. But don't let God's slow-motion version of Rapture in 1 Thessalonians fool you. The Rapture will occur in a split second. Suddenly, corpses all over the world will be raised and reunited with perfected spirits, and living believers everywhere will be caught up to heaven and transformed body, soul, and spirit. The Rapture will shock the world. It will change everything.

The Seven Raptures of the Bible

Many people find the Rapture—an instant disappearance of millions of people—difficult to accept. It just seems too strange and bizarre. After all, they argue, nothing like this has ever happened before. But that's actually not true. It may surprise you to know that several raptures have occurred before in history. The Bible records at least six. While none of these past events involved more than one person, they do illustrate the future Rapture of the church.

Six Historical Raptures

RAPTURE OF ENOCH (GENESIS 5:24; HEBREWS 11:5)

In the days before the Flood, "Enoch walked with God; and he was not, for God took him" (Genesis 5:24, NASB). He didn't die. God took him directly to heaven.

RAPTURE OF ELIJAH (2 KINGS 2:1, 11)

The famous prophet Elijah was caught up to heaven in a chariot of fire without dying.

RAPTURE OF ISAIAH (ISAIAH 6:1-3)

Isaiah was briefly transported to heaven and came back to earth. Unlike Enoch and Elijah, Isaiah returned to earth, fulfilled his ministry, and eventually died. Nevertheless, Isaiah experienced a personal rapture to heaven.

RAPTURE OF JESUS (REVELATION 12:5)

The word *harpazo*, meaning "snatched away," is used to describe the ascension of Jesus to heaven from earth.

RAPTURE OF PHILIP (ACTS 8:39-40)

The word *harpazo* is also used to describe this event. Philip vanished into thin air. He was bodily translated, not to heaven, but from one geographical location to another twenty miles away.

RAPTURE OF PAUL (2 CORINTHIANS 12:2-4)

At some point in his life, Paul was "caught up" to paradise (heaven) and then returned to earth. This was a personal rapture of Paul. When Paul described to believers being "caught up" in 1 Thessalonians 4:17, he knew what he was talking about. He had experienced his own personal rapture. And he couldn't wait for all believers to experience what he had known.

The first six raptures in the Bible have already occurred. The Rapture of the church is the one rapture event that's still to come. It's the one that these others foreshadow.

By reviewing the first six raptures, what do they teach us about the one Rapture that's still to come?

Literal. The Rapture of the church won't be a symbolic event. Given the literal fulfillment for the six raptures that have occurred, we can know the final, future one will be literally fulfilled as well.

Physical Transfer. In each of the historical raptures, people were physically transferred from one location to another. Five of the six involved a transfer from earth to heaven. Philip was moved from one place on earth to another.

Sudden. All of the historical raptures happened suddenly with little warning. Enoch is a perfect example. He was there and then "he was not." This will be the case with the Rapture of the church.

The Mystery of the Rapture[6]

First Corinthians 15:51 says, "Behold, I tell you a mystery; we will not all sleep, but we will all be changed" (NASB). This verse was mounted on the door of the nursery in the church where I grew up. It reflects what happens in many nurseries, but thank God it will be true for millions of His children when Jesus descends from heaven. Raptured believers will never experience the sting of death but will be raptured into the presence of the Lord in the clouds. This transformation is the "mystery" of the Rapture. Raptured believers will do an end run on the grave, cheating death and denying the grim reaper millions of victims. But why is the Rapture called a mystery?

A mystery in the New Testament is not some Sherlock Holmes puzzle to solve. It's not even something that's hard to figure out. Ephesians 3:5 defines a mystery as that "which in other generations was not made known to the sons of men, as it has now been revealed to His holy apostles and prophets in the Spirit" (NASB). Ephesians 3:9 says a mystery is what "God, the Creator of all things, had kept secret from the beginning." Colossians 1:26 further describes the mystery this way: "This message was kept secret for centuries and generations past, but now it has been revealed to God's people." A mystery in the New Testament is a truth that was never revealed prior to its unveiling and that man could never figure out apart from divine revelation.

The concept of believers being caught up to heaven without dying was a brand-new truth. It was a mystery. It was hidden in God until he revealed it through Paul in 1 Corinthians 15.[7] Until 1 Corinthians 15 was written, and the mystery of the Rapture was unveiled, the only way for a believer to get to heaven was through death. Of course, Enoch and Elijah went straight to heaven without dying. They both experienced a rapture. But these two exceptions out of billions prove the rule: believers had to die to get to heaven.

I like the story of a Sunday school teacher whose assignment was to explain to the six-year-olds in his class what someone had to do in order to go to heaven. In an attempt to discover what the kids already believed about the subject, he asked a few questions.

"If I sold my house and my car, had a big garage sale, and gave all my money to the church, would *that* get me into heaven?"

"NO!" the children all answered.

"If I cleaned the church every day, mowed the yard, and kept everything neat and tidy, would *that* get me into heaven?"

"NO!"

"Well then," he said, "if I was kind to animals and gave candy to all the children and loved my wife, would that get me into heaven?"

"NO!"

"Well then, how *can* I get into heaven?"

A boy in the back row stood up and shouted, "You gotta be dead!"[8]

Until the time of Paul this answer was presumably correct. But in 1 Corinthians 15, that all suddenly changed. The Lord unveiled His glorious mystery through Paul: an entire generation of believers will be instantly transformed without tasting physical death. Millions of believers will be clothed in their new, glorified bodies in the time it takes to blink one's eye. This is the thrilling mystery of the Rapture. We may be the terminal generation. We may be the ones who experience this breathtaking event! Think what it would be for all eternity to be part of the generation that never experienced the sting of death. "Amen! Come, Lord Jesus."

Conclusion

My friend Harold Willmington shares a deft illustration to characterize the Rapture. Imagine that you have an old box in the attic that contains some nails, screws, and bolts that you need. But since the box sat in the attic for a long time it's also filled with dust, paper, and splinters of wood. The quickest, easiest way to retrieve the things you want and leave the unwanted stuff behind would be to hold a powerful magnet over the box. With the magnet situated over the box, everything in the box with the same properties as the magnet would immediately fly up out of the box and attach to the magnet. Everything else would be left behind.

The Rapture will occur in a similar way. Jesus will appear in the sky, and everyone who shares His life will fly up to meet Him. All who are "in Christ" will be caught up to meet Him in the air. Those who don't know Him, who don't share His life, will be left behind.[9]

Jesus is not coming for moral, respectable people, for people who faithfully attend church, or for people who observe religious rituals, as good as those things may be. He's coming for those who are "in Christ" through faith in His atoning death and resurrection.

CHAPTER 10

FIVE MAIN VIEWS OF THE TIMING OF THE RAPTURE

THE TIMING OF THE RAPTURE is one of the most debated issues in eschatology. Most Christians agree that the Rapture will occur, but the same is not true when it comes to *when* the Rapture will occur. The key issue is this: will the church go through any or all of the seven-year Tribulation before the Rapture occurs? Or to put it another way—when will the believing be leaving? This question is much more than just a theological, ivory-tower debate. There's a great deal at stake.

If the Rapture occurs in your lifetime, your future will be very different depending on which view is correct. Will you be here to see the Antichrist? Will you be forced to choose whether to take his mark? Will you witness the carnage of God's wrath poured out on the whole world? Or will you be in heaven during this time, experiencing a glorious fellowship and intimacy with the Lamb and His sheep? Will you and I be here for none, half, or all of the Tribulation? It's an important and sobering question. There are five main perspectives today of the timing of the Rapture. Let's briefly examine the five views and some strengths and weaknesses of each of them.

View #1: The Pre-Tribulation Rapture

Pretribulationism—often abbreviated "pre-Trib"—teaches that the church will be raptured before the seven-year Tribulation period begins (i.e., the seventieth week of Daniel). The Tribulation will begin at some point after the Rapture, marked by the Antichrist's seven-year treaty with Israel (Daniel 9:27).

Several arguments are leveled against the pre-Trib position. First, many allege that it teaches two "second comings" of Christ, whereas the Bible presents only one Second Coming. (This objection will be further addressed later on page 149.) However, I argue that the Second Coming is a single event in two phases, which occur at least seven years apart, on either end of the Tribulation.

Another objection stems from the belief that the pre-Trib view did not arise until the 1830s through the teaching of John Nelson Darby. This objection will be answered in more detail on page 177.

A third argument against this view is that pretribulationism is not explicitly taught in the Scriptures. However, while no single verse says Jesus is coming to rapture His saints before the seven-year Tribulation, there are clear statements that He is coming to deliver His people from the coming wrath (1 Thessalonians 1:10; 5:9; Revelation 3:10). Thus, it stands to reason that God will use the Rapture to accomplish this promise. Also, it's important to note that many biblical doctrines, such as the Trinity, the inerrancy of Scripture, and the dual nature of Christ, are not spelled out clearly in one verse.

View #2: The Mid-Tribulation Rapture

The mid-Tribulation view holds that Christ will rapture His church midway through the seven-year Tribulation. Thus, believers will endure the first half of the seven-year Tribulation. Midtribulationists maintain that God's wrath will be restricted to the latter half of the Tribulation, but believers will be raptured to heaven before this.

Midtribulationists point to the frequent mention of 3½ years (42 months or 1,260 days) in Daniel and Revelation as support for their view. They argue that the emphasis on the final 3½ years indicates that it is the time of God's wrath. They usually equate the last trumpet in 1 Corinthians 15:52 with the seventh trumpet in Revelation 11:15 and place the Rapture at that point, although some midtribbers identify the time of the Rapture with Revelation 14:1-4.

However, there are flaws in the mid-Trib view of the Rapture. There are four principal arguments against it. First, the trumpets in 1 Corinthians 15:52 and Revelation 11:15 should not be equated with each other. These two trumpets have notable differences.

	TRUMPET IN 1 CORINTHIANS 15	TRUMPET IN REVELATION 11
SUBJECT	Church	Wicked world
RESULT	Catching up of the church to be with the Lord	Judgment of a godless world
CHARACTER	Trumpet of God's grace	Trumpet of God's judgment
TIMING	Signals the close of the life of the church on earth. It's the last trumpet of the church age.	Marks a climax in the progression of Tribulation judgments

Moreover, simply because the trumpet in 1 Corinthians 15 is called the "last" trumpet does not mean that it is the last trumpet in God's whole prophetic program. As Paul Benware notes, "Those of us in school settings know that during the day there are a number of 'last' bells that ring. The last bell for the eight o'clock class rings but that is not the last bell of the day. 'Last' must be understood in relationship to the context in which it is found."[1] Furthermore, the seventh trumpet in Revelation 11 is not the last trumpet in the Tribulation. At the second coming of Christ a trumpet is blown to gather God's elect (Matthew 24:31). So, the last trumpet argument actually undermines their view.

The last trumpet of the Rapture is the final trumpet of this church age, and it will summon God's people to the great reunion in the sky.

Second, the mid-Trib position denies the doctrine of imminency. This doctrine says that Christ could return at any time and that no prophetic events must transpire ahead of the Rapture. But if the mid-Trib view is correct and Christ can't return until the midpoint of the Tribulation, then there are prophecies that must be fulfilled first. This necessity opposes the doctrine of imminency. Assuming the Tribulation has not even begun, then Christ can't come for at least another 3½ years. (For an explanation of the doctrine of imminency, see page 167.)

Third, midtribbers agree that Christians will be spared from the wrath of God that is poured out on the earth. They hold that the wrath begins at the midpoint of the seven-year Tribulation with the seventh trumpet. The problem here is that Revelation 6:16-17 clearly references God's wrath, and this occurs long before the seventh trumpet of Revelation 11:15.

Fourth, midtribulationists don't even agree among themselves about where the Rapture should be placed in the book of Revelation. Some place it at Revelation 6:12-17, others at Revelation 11:15-17, and still others at Revelation 14:1-4. This inconsistency is a major weakness for this view.

View #3: The Post-Tribulation Rapture

Posttribulationists believe the Rapture and the Second Coming are considered one event separated by a few moments. The Rapture will occur at the end of the Tribulation concurrent with the second coming of Christ. Believers will meet Christ in the air, make a quick U-turn, and accompany Him back to the earth.

Posttribulationists agree that believers are exempt from God's wrath. They believe that the outpouring of God's wrath will be confined to the very end of the Tribulation, when it will be unleashed only on unbelievers.

Advocates support their post-Tribulation view with a number of arguments. Let me mention just a few. First, it is simple and streamlined. There is one Second Coming and only one phase to that coming. It eliminates the need for a two-stage coming of Christ. Second, posttribulationists often assert that the word *meet* (*apantesis*) in 1 Thessalonians 4:17 means to go out and meet someone, like a visiting dignitary, and escort the individual back to the place you came from. This narrow, technical meaning of the word suggests that, after believers are caught up to meet the Lord in the air, they will accompany Him back to earth instead of following Him to heaven. However, there is no indication that this escorting back must happen immediately. Douglas Moo, who is a proponent of posttribulationism, agrees: "this argument can be given little weight—the word does not *have* to bear this technical meaning, nor is it certain that the return to the point of origin must be *immediate*."[2] This leaves room for other views of the timing of the Rapture, not just posttribulationism.

Third, posttribulationists see the trumpets mentioned in Matthew 24:31; 1 Thessalonians 4:16; and 1 Corinthians 15:52 as being one and the same. Since the trumpet in Matthew 24:31 happens at the end of the Tribulation, posttribulationists contend it must be the same as the last trumpet in 1 Corinthians 15:52. Yet the only similarity between these trumpets is that they draw the Lord's people together. By contrast, the differences are greater.

	TRUMPET IN 1 THESSALONIANS 4:16 AND 1 CORINTHIANS 15:52	TRUMPET IN MATTHEW 24:31
SUBJECT	Church	Jewish believers in the Great Tribulation
CIRCUMSTANCES	Connected with raising of believers who have died	No mention of resurrection. Focus is on regathering living believers who have been scattered over the earth
RESULT	Uniting of the raised dead with the living dead in a great meeting with the Lord in the air	The elect are living believers who are regathered from all over the earth to meet the Lord, who has returned to the earth in an open display of glory
SIGNS	Preceded by no signs	Preceded by many signs

Posttribulationism has some holes, however. First, Revelation 19 constitutes a major problem for posttribulationists. Revelation 19:11-21 is the most comprehensive and detailed account of the second coming of Christ found anywhere in the Bible. Yet it contains no mention of a resurrection or rapture. This silence is quite compelling. If the Rapture were posttribulational, why would this key feature be totally missing? As John Walvoord notes, "If details like the casting of the beast and the false prophet into the lake of fire are mentioned and the specific resurrection of the tribulation saints is described, how much more the Rapture and translation of the church as a whole should have been included if, as a matter of fact, it is part of this great event. They have no scriptural proof for a posttribulational Rapture in the very passages that ought to include it."[3]

Second, as has already been pointed out, the wrath of God is not confined to the end of the Tribulation as posttribbers maintain. God's wrath is specifically mentioned as early as the sixth seal judgment in Revelation 6:12-17. God's wrath is global in scope and devastates the entire earth. It is difficult to understand how believers could be protected from this wrath since it is universal and there is no indication that anyone on earth is fully spared from its effects.

Third, posttribulationists maintain that the Rapture happens at the same time as the Second Coming. Believers will be caught up to meet the Lord Jesus in the air as He is coming from heaven to judge the world. Then they will come right back to earth with Him. But this raises a very important question that often gets overlooked in this discussion: If God has miraculously preserved the church throughout the entire Tribulation, why even have a Rapture? Why bother? It's inconsequential. The Lord won't be delivering us from anything. There's really no purpose in it. Pretribulationism gives meaning to the Rapture: if Christ comes before the Tribulation, His coming is filled with purpose. He is rescuing us from the wrath to come.

View #4: The Partial Rapture

The partial-Rapture view, which was first articulated in the mid-nineteenth century, imagines that there will be multiple raptures that occur throughout the Tribulation. The timing of a person's rapture is based on the depth of their obedience. The partial-Rapture position distinguishes devout, spiritual believers from worldly believers. Faithful, devoted believers who are obediently watching and waiting for Christ's coming will be raptured to heaven before the Tribulation (Matthew 25:1-13; 1 Thessalonians 5:6; Hebrews 9:28; 1 John 2:28). Worldly believers, for their part, will endure some degree of the Tribulation and be caught up in subsequent raptures. One writer describes the partial-Rapture with this creative analogy: "All believers will go home on the same train, but not all on the first section."[4]

This view is the least widely held. The partial-Rapture view has a number of flaws. First, the Bible consistently uses all-inclusive words like *we* and *all* when discussing the participants in the Rapture (1 Corinthians 15:51; 1 Thessalonians 4:14). This suggests that all believers will be raptured at the same time whenever it occurs. According to 1 Thessalonians 4:16 the only condition for being part of the Rapture is that a person be "in Christ" (NASB). Simply stated, all you have to do is trust Christ. There is no other requirement.

Second, the partial Rapture fragments the united body of Christ (1 Corinthians 12; Ephesians 2:14–3:6; 4:1-6, 12-16; Colossians 3:11, 15). All believers are equal in their position before God and their connection with the Head of the body—Jesus Christ. The body of Christ can't go to heaven in pieces. When one part of the body goes, the whole body has to follow. Similarly, if the church—the bride of Christ—marries Christ immediately after the Rapture, as it seems to, then the wedding cannot include only part of the bride, as the partial-Rapture view would suggest. The whole bride of Christ must be present.

Third, all believers are promised immunity from God's wrath during the Day of the Lord (1 Thessalonians 1:10; Revelation 3:10). The partial-Rapture view creates a kind of living purgatory on earth during the Tribulation.

Fourth, since faithful believers are spared from the Tribulation according to the partial-Rapture view, and worldly believers aren't, what need is there to reward believers at the judgment seat of Christ (2 Corinthians 5:10)? The Rapture itself would reward the faithful.

Finally, if the timing of our raptures depends on our own spiritual maturity, how faithful and obedient do we have to be? What degree of devotion and maturity is required to be worthy of inclusion in the first group? The Bible never says clearly. This ambiguity concerning what is specifically required is a serious weakness of this view.

View #5: The Pre-Wrath Rapture

The pre-wrath view holds that the Rapture will occur 5½ years into the Tribulation. It's a "three-quarters Tribulation" view. The calamities up to that point, in this view, result from the wrath of man and the wrath of Satan, not the wrath of God. Pre-wrath rapturists view the events of the sixth seal as signs of the impending Day of the Lord, which they limit to the final quarter of the Tribulation. God's wrath is not poured out until the seventh seal in Revelation. Thus, believers will be raptured between the sixth and seventh seals, just before the wrath of God—the Day of the Lord—begins. In other words, the Day of the Lord commences near the end of the Tribulation, not at the beginning. This view has been popularized by Robert Van Kampen in his book *The Sign* and by Marvin Rosenthal, who wrote *The Pre-Wrath Rapture of the Church.*

A key problem with this timing is that according to 1 Thessalonians 5:1-3 the Day of the Lord comes unexpectedly while people everywhere are saying, "Peace and safety" (NASB). Paul Benware explains:

> According to the pre-wrath view, the sixth seal will just have been broken, which will result in earthquakes and great cosmic disturbances that will cause incredible terror to the inhabitants of the earth (Revelation 6:12-17). In fact, more than one-fourth of the world's population will have been recently destroyed by famines, disease, and widespread warfare on the earth. It does not seem likely that the people of the world will be saying "Peace and safety" when more than a billion people have recently perished and incredible cosmic disturbances are taking place.[5]

No one will be saying, "Peace and safety," at that time. Placing the beginning of the Day of the Lord and therefore the Rapture at that point in the Tribulation doesn't make sense.

While much more could be said about this view, its validity rises and falls on the interpretation of when God's wrath begins. If God's wrath doesn't begin until the seventh seal of Revelation, as proponents suggest, then this view could be legitimate. If, however, God's wrath unfurls from the start of the Tribulation, then this view falls to pieces. One must decide which interpretation makes more sense.

In my opinion, the wrath of God does not begin near the end of the Tribulation, but at the very beginning. The seal judgments in Revelation 6 are opened by the Lamb (Jesus Christ) at the very beginning of the Tribulation (Revelation 6:1-2). He is the source of these judgments. To argue that they are the wrath of man and Satan ignores that the One bringing these judgments forth is the Lamb. While the frequency and intensity of these judgments clearly increase, all of the judgments are the result of God's wrath.

VARIOUS VIEWS OF THE TIMING OF THE RAPTURE

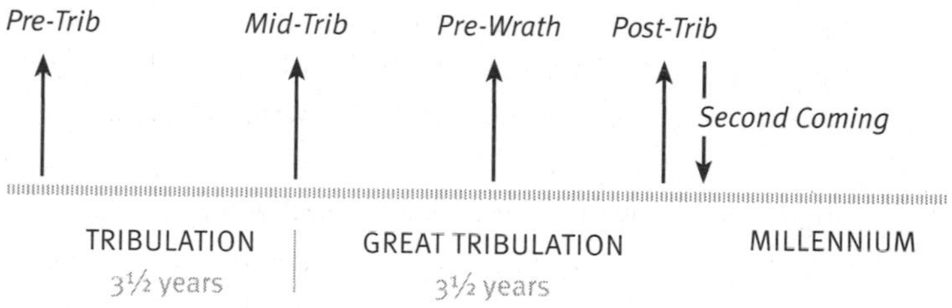

Conclusion

Of these five views, pretribulationism, midtribulationism, and posttribulationism are the most commonly held views and are most popular today. And if you want to simplify it even further, pre-Trib and post-Trib positions are the two dominant views.

When it comes to the timing of the Rapture, the main views all agree that believers are exempt from God's wrath. The ultimate questions then are, When does the wrath begin? and How is the church protected from it?

Pretribbers believe God's wrath begins at the beginning of the Tribulation and that God will keep believers from it by removing them from the entire Tribulation. Midtribbers contend that the second half of the Tribulation is the time of God's wrath and that believers will be taken out before it begins. Pre-wrath proponents maintain that the wrath will begin about three-fourths of the way through the Tribulation and that believers will be raptured at that time and spared from God's wrath. Posttribbers confine the wrath of God to the end of the Tribulation and hold that it will be poured out on unbelievers only, with God protecting believers from it while leaving them on earth until the Second Coming.

The only way to answer these questions and sort through the issues is to study God's Word, examining each relevant passage in its own context, and then to compare Scripture with Scripture in a way that consistently aligns with what each passage teaches.

In the next chapter I will attempt to do that as we examine the support for the pre-Trib view.

CHAPTER 11

SEVEN REASONS FOR THE PRE-TRIB RAPTURE

EVERY VIEW OF THE TIMING of the Rapture has strengths and weaknesses. Whatever view one holds, one must acknowledge its drawbacks. In my opinion, pretribulationism has the best Scriptural support and the fewest drawbacks. So what is the Scriptural evidence for the pre-Trib position? Do people hold to this view simply because it's more appealing than the other views? After all, being caught up to heaven before the terror of the Tribulation doesn't sound too bad, does it?

In this chapter I want to present the seven most compelling biblical arguments for the pre-Trib Rapture position. I have arranged these seven points into a handy acronym that spells out the word *PRE-TRIB*: Place of the Church in Revelation; Rapture versus Return; Exemption from Divine Wrath; Time Gap between the Rapture and the Second Coming; Removal of the Restrainer; Imminency; Blessed Hope. Let's look carefully at the biblical evidence and see if the case can be made for the pre-Trib view.

Place of the Church in Revelation

If the church will experience any or all of the Tribulation, then one would expect that Revelation 4–18—the most detailed description of the Tribulation—would include an account of the church's role during that time period. But remarkably, Revelation 4–18 is silent about the church on earth.

The Greek word for church is *ekklesia*. This word occurs twenty times in the book of Revelation. Revelation 1–3 specifically mentions the church nineteen times. The glorified Lord addresses seven letters to seven specific churches in Asia Minor. In them, the Lord instructs and admonishes each church.

But suddenly, beginning in Revelation 4, the word *ekklesia* disappears. There is an abrupt, deafening silence concerning any presence of the church on earth for fifteen chapters. The word *church,* used nineteen times in Revelation 1–3, is not found once in Revelation 4–18. This absence is arresting and unexplainable if the church continues on earth through any part of the Tribulation.

In Revelation 4:1 the apostle John is lifted up to heaven and transported into the future, where he sees visions of the end of days. He is carried forward in a kind of divine time machine. In the subsequent fifteen chapters, from Revelation 4 through Revelation 18, John watches and describes the events of the Tribulation as they unfold on earth. But the church is absent from any of these events. The church doesn't appear again until chapter 19, where she is pictured as a bride returning to earth with her glorious Bridegroom. This returning from heaven to earth with Christ indicates that the Bride has already been in heaven for some time since she has "prepared herself" (Revelation 19:7). Revelation 22:16 refers to the church again for the final time, specifically using the word *ekklesia.*

The presence and absence of the term *ekklesia* in the book of Revelation is convincing evidence that the church will not be present on earth during the Tribulation and the outpouring of God's wrath.

There are some objections to this argument. Posttribulationists argue that the word *saints* (holy ones) occurs several times in Revelation 4–18, which describes the church as present on earth during the Tribulation (Revelation 13:7, 10; 16:6; 17:6; 18:24).

THE USE OF THE WORD *CHURCH* IN REVELATION		
Revelation 1–3	Revelation 4–18	Revelation 20–22
ekklesia nineteen times	*ekklesia* zero times	*ekklesia* one time (22:16)

Pretribulationists counter that these "saints" are not church-age believers but "Tribulation saints." These are two of three distinct groups of believers: Old Testament saints, church-age saints, and Tribulation saints. The mention of saints in Revelation 4–18 indicates that there will be believers on earth during the Tribulation, but it doesn't prove conclusively that they are church-age believers. We must look at the context to discern which group of saints is in view. I believe the saints in Revelation are Tribulation saints who will be saved after the Rapture.

A second objection from posttribulationists is that if the church is absent during the Tribulation, then she must be in heaven. "What evidence is there in Revelation," they ask, "that the church is in heaven during the Tribulation? Is there any?"

In response to this, I believe the "twenty-four elders" represent the church throughout Revelation 4–19 (Revelation 4:4, 10; 5:5-6, 8, 11, 14; 7:11, 13; 11:16; 14:3; 19:4). The elders appear twelve times in these chapters. And in each instance, they are in heaven worshiping Him who sits on the throne and the Lamb. From their first mention in Revelation 4:4, the twenty-four elders are pictured in heaven, judged, rewarded, and enthroned. This interpretation fits well with the belief that the church will be raptured prior to the Tribulation. Revelation 4–19 consistently pictures the church in heaven, representing it by the twenty-four elders enthroned and crowned, dressed in white, and worshiping the Lamb (Revelation 4:4, 10; 5:5-6, 8, 11, 14).[1]

THERE ARE FOUR MAIN VIEWS concerning the identity of the twenty-four elders: (1) angelic beings; (2) Israel; (3) the church; and (4) all of the redeemed (Israel and the church—twelve tribes + twelve apostles).

Although any of these views is possible, seven key clues convince me that the twenty-four elders represent the church.

The title. They are called elders (*presbuteros*), from which we get our English word *Presbyterian.* In Scripture, elders represent God's people. In the New Testament, the elders of a church are its representatives. In the case of Revelation, these twenty-four elders represent the glorified church in heaven.

I am reminded of the little girl who came home from her Presbyterian Sunday school class. Her mother asked her what the lesson was about. The little girl replied, "We talked about heaven."

"Well," her mother asked, "what did they say about it?"

The little girl said, "The teacher told us that only twenty-four Presbyterians made it to heaven." (Hey, it's a joke.)

The number. The Levitical priesthood in the Old Testament numbered in the thousands (1 Chronicles 24). Since not all of the priests could worship in the Temple at the same time, the priesthood was divided into twenty-four groups, and a representative of each group served in the Temple on a rotating basis. "When these priests met together, even though they were only twenty-four, they represented the whole priesthood and at the same time the whole of the nation of Israel. In a similar way the twenty-four elders mentioned in the book of Revelation may be regarded as a representative body."[2] So whom do Revelation's twenty-four elders represent? In light of the other descriptions of the elders, such as their crowns, clothing, and praise, the best view is that they represent the entire church of Jesus Christ.

The position. They are seated on thrones. Christ promised enthronement specifically to the church (Revelation 3:21).

The crowns. Scripture never pictures angels wearing crowns. And from a pre-Trib perspective, Old Testament believers will not be resurrected and rewarded until after the Tribulation is over. Therefore, the elders cannot represent angels or saved Israel (Daniel 12:1-3). However, church-age believers will receive crowns at the judgment seat of Christ (Revelation 2:10). Since the elders wear crowns, it stands to reason these are the same crowns that the church receives at the judgment seat.

The clothing. The white clothing of the elders is identical to the clothing of church-age believers (Revelation 3:5, 18; 19:8).

The praise. Only church-age believers can sing the song the elders sing in Revelation 5:8-13. The best Greek manuscripts have the word *us* in Revelation 5:10. Neither angels nor Old Testament saints could sing this song of redemption from "every tribe and tongue and people and nation" (5:9, NASB).

The distinction. The elders are clearly distinguished from angels in Revelation 5:11.

Rapture versus Return[3]

The New Testament describes two facets of Christ's second coming: (1) He will come *for* His church to escort her to His Father's house (John 14:3; 1 Thessalonians 4:16), and (2) He will come *with* His saints when He descends from heaven to judge His enemies and establish His glorious one-thousand-year Kingdom on earth (Zechariah 14:4-5; 1 Thessalonians 3:13). How can these facets both be true of Christ's second coming?

I believe pretribulationism best resolves the seeming contradiction. This first facet is what I call the Rapture of the church: the Lord takes believers from earth to His Father's house (John 14:3). The second facet is commonly called the second coming of Christ: believers return with Christ from heaven to the earth (Matthew 24:30). Both describe the Lord's coming, but their differences indicate that they are two unique stages occurring at two separate times. Between these two stages, the Tribulation happens. The first stage—the Rapture—is imminent and signless and could occur at any moment (1 Thessalonians 1:10). The Second Coming, on the other hand, will be preceded by all kinds of signs (Matthew 24:1-29). The same event cannot be both signless and yet preceded by numerous signs. This is patently contradictory. It is difficult for the other views to make sense of the passages that describe these two stages so differently. But, by calling them two stages of the same event, the pre-Trib view successfully harmonizes these two descriptions of Christ's coming.

However, some students of Bible prophecy strongly object to the notion that the Rapture of the church and the second coming of Christ are distinct events. They contend that this perspective is teaching two future comings of Christ, whereas the Bible only presents one event.

On the contrary, I view Jesus Christ's coming as a single event in two stages; these stages are separated by at least seven years, during which the Tribulation happens.

The only definitive way to fully resolve this issue is to set what the Bible says about these events side by side to see if they are describing the same phase. You be the judge! Here are some of the main verses that describe these two stages of Christ's future coming.

RAPTURE
John 14:1-3
Romans 8:19
1 Corinthians 1:7-8; 15:51-53; 16:22
Philippians 3:20-21; 4:5
Colossians 3:4
1 Thessalonians 1:10; 2:19; 4:13-18; 5:9, 23
2 Thessalonians 2:1, 3
1 Timothy 6:14
2 Timothy 4:1, 8
Titus 2:13
Hebrews 9:28
James 5:7-9
1 Peter 1:7, 13; 5:4
1 John 2:28–3:2
Jude 1:21
Revelation 3:10

SECOND COMING
Daniel 2:44-45; 7:9-14; 12:1-3
Zechariah 12:10; 14:1-15
Matthew 13:41; 24:27-31; 26:64
Mark 13:14-27; 14:62
Luke 17:20-37; 21:25-28

Acts 1:9-11; 3:19-21
1 Thessalonians 3:13
2 Thessalonians 1:6-10; 2:8
1 Peter 4:12-13
2 Peter 3:1-14
Jude 1:14-15
Revelation 1:7; 19:11–20:6; 22:7, 12, 20

THE RAPTURE	THE RETURN (SECOND COMING)
Christ comes in the air (1 Thessalonians 4:16-17)	Christ comes to the earth (Zechariah 14:4)
Christ comes for His saints (1 Thessalonians 4:16-17)	Christ comes with His saints (1 Thessalonians 3:13; Jude 1:14)
Believers depart the earth (1 Thessalonians 4:16-17)	Unbelievers are taken away (Matthew 24:37-41)
Christ claims His bride	Christ comes with His bride
Christ gathers His own (1 Thessalonians 4:16-17)	Angels gather the elect (Matthew 24:31)
Christ comes to reward (1 Thessalonians 4:17)	Christ comes to judge (Matthew 25:31-46)
Not in the Old Testament (1 Corinthians 15:51)	Predicted often in the Old Testament
There are no signs. It is imminent.	Portended by many signs (Matthew 24:4-29)
It is a time of blessing and comfort (1 Thessalonians 4:17-18)	It is a time of destruction and judgment (2 Thessalonians 2:8-12)
Involves believers only (John 14:1-3; 1 Corinthians 15:51-55; 1 Thessalonians 4:13-18)	Involves Israel and the Gentile nations (Matthew 24:1–25:46)

Will occur in a moment, in the time it takes to blink. Only His own will see Him (1 Corinthians 15:51-52)	Will be visible to the entire world (Matthew 24:27; Revelation 1:7)
Tribulation begins	Millennium begins
Christ comes as the bright morning star (Revelation 22:16)	Christ comes as the Sun of Righteousness (Malachi 4:2)

Dr. John Walvoord concludes that these "contrasts should make it evident that the translation of the church is an event quite different in character and time from the return of the Lord to establish His kingdom, and confirms the conclusion that the translation takes place before the tribulation."[4]

John MacArthur summarizes this point in favor of the pre-Trib viewpoint.

> Scripture suggests that the Second Coming occurs in two stages—first the Rapture, when He comes *for* His saints and they are caught up to meet Him in the air (1 Thessalonians 4:14-17), and second, His return to earth, when He comes *with* His saints (Jude 1:14) to execute judgment on His enemies. Daniel's seventieth week must fall *between* those two events. That is the only scenario that reconciles the imminency of Christ's coming *for* His saints with the yet unfulfilled signs that signal His final glorious return *with* the saints.[5]

Exemption from Divine Wrath

It's common to hear people say that pretribbers are just escapists. We just want a view that removes us from all the world's troubles. Because of this stereotype, many people strongly object to the notion that the church will be raptured before the Tribulation. They argue that it's arrogant for believers today to think that of all the generations of believers who have lived, we are somehow so special that we will be exempt from the coming Tribulation if the Rapture occurs in our lifetime. Clearly, the pre-Trib position is the most positive view of the future for believers, and some may be tempted to hold it for that reason alone. But we can't adopt a biblical view simply because it's the most appealing.

Let me be very clear. I *do not* believe that Christians are spared from the troubles and trials of this life. Even very serious trouble. Believers in every generation have faced their share of trouble (James 1:2-4). Some have faced terrible persecution and even martyrdom. Even a quick reading of the Bible would prove this point. Jesus Himself told His disciples, "In the world you have tribulation" (John 16:33, NASB). The apostle Paul said, "Through many tribulations we must enter the kingdom of God" (Acts 14:22, NASB). True believers face the common trials of life. They fall ill, have family and marriage problems, deal with emotional stress, experience discouragement and depression, face harassment and intimidation for their faith, lose their jobs, and die. We live in a fallen, sin-cursed world.

But the troubles of this life that we all face are vastly different from the wrath of God poured on a sinful planet during the future Tribulation. It's the difference between tribulation and *the* Tribulation. We all face tribulation in a *general* sense today (John 16:33; 2 Thessalonians 1:4; Revelation 1:9). But the wrath during the seven-year Tribulation is wrath in a *specific* sense. Today, people endure the wrath and persecution from men and the wrath and persecution from Satan. While the wrath of man and Satan will still be around during the Tribulation, the Tribulation will be more defined by the wrath of God than anything else.

It doesn't make sense, though, for God's people to endure God's wrath. Part of what salvation in Christ means is that God saves us from the wrath we deserve (Ephesians 2:3-5; 1 Thessalonians 5:9). This has been God's pattern—not to judge the righteous with the wicked. Lot and his family were rescued from Sodom when God poured out His wrath on the cities of the plain (Genesis 18–19). Also, Enoch's rapture to heaven before the Flood illustrates this biblical principle as well (Genesis 5:23-24). God saves His people from His wrath upon sin.

The Bible promises that church-age believers will be exempt from the coming wrath of God during the Tribulation (1 Thessalonians 1:9-10; 5:9; Revelation 3:10). But why? What is it about the Tribulation that necessitates our absence from this time? The Tribulation is the product of God's wrath upon wickedness. The book of Revelation clearly refers to God's wrath at least seven times (6:17-18; 14:8-10; 14:19; 15:7; 16:1, 19; 19:15). The wrath of God commences with the first seal (Revelation 6:1) and continues all the way until the Second Coming (Revelation 19:11-21).

Three of the other Rapture positions believe God's wrath doesn't begin right at the start. Proponents of the pre-wrath Rapture believe God pours out His wrath only in the final quarter of the Tribulation. They believe that the wrath of God doesn't begin until the opening of the seventh seal (Revelation 8:1-7). For them, all the devastation in the first six seals is due to the wrath of man and the wrath of Satan.

Similarly, midtribulationists maintain that God's wrath is reserved for the second half of the Tribulation. Christians will be raptured just before the wrath of God begins at the midpoint of the Tribulation. Although there is some difference of opinion, most midtribbers equate the Rapture with the blowing of the seventh trumpet in Revelation 11:15-17.

Posttribulationists limit God's wrath to the very end of the Tribulation and believe that God will protect believers through it rather than remove them from it.

Pre-wrath and midtribulationism agree with pretribulationism's belief that God will protect His people from His wrath by snatching them away from earth before His wrath is poured out on the world. The differences between these views stem from disagreement over when God's wrath actually begins. Does it begin with the first seal as pretribulationists argue or with the seventh seal as pre-wrath proponents suggest or with the seventh trumpet as midtribulationists believe or at the very end of the Tribulation as posttribulationists believe? And will God rapture people from earth to protect them from His wrath as pretribulationists, midtribulationists, and pre-wrath rapturists believe, or will He somehow spare them from His wrath without removing them from earth as posttribulationists believe?

In my view, the problem with the pre-wrath, mid-Trib, and post-Trib views is that all nineteen judgments in Revelation 6–18 are God's wrath.[6] The *entire* Tribulation is made up of consistent judgment from God Himself against a rebellious world. The seal judgments, opened at the onset of the Tribulation, are unleashed one by one, not by man or Satan, but by the Lamb Himself (Revelation 6:1). This is God's doing.

Jesus opens the seals, and a living creature calls each of the four horsemen to gallop across the earth in devastating judgment. To argue that the wrath of God is restricted to the latter half, last quarter, or very end of the Tribulation disregards that Jesus sets in motion the judgments contained in the seal judgments that commence the Tribulation. Moreover, the imagery of the first four seal judgments—the famine, sword, pestilence, and wild beasts—is often linked with God's wrath elsewhere in the Bible (Jeremiah 14:12; 15:2; 24:10; 29:17; Ezekiel 5:12, 17; 14:21). The whole Tribulation period is the outpouring of God's wrath; this requires that Christ's bride be exempt from this entire time of trouble, not just some part of it.

Why would God leave His bride on earth to endure His wrath? It makes no sense. J. F. Strombeck explains the conflict, "One is forced to ask, how could the Lamb of God die and rise again to save the Church from wrath and then allow her to pass through the wrath that He shall pour upon those who reject Him? Such inconsistency might be possible in the thinking of men, but not in the acts of the Son of God."[7]

Evidence for Exemption in 1 Thessalonians

Let's take a look at 1 Thessalonians for more evidence that believers are exempt from God's wrath in the coming Tribulation. There are four strong points. First, in 1 Thessalonians 1:9-10 exemption from the coming wrath of the Tribulation is explicitly stated: "You turned to God from idols to serve a living and true God, and to wait for His Son from heaven, whom He raised from the dead, that is Jesus, who *rescues us from the wrath to come*" (italics added, NASB). Some argue that the wrath here is the wrath of hell since Paul has just been discussing the salvation of the Thessalonians. While that interpretation is possible, it seems better to view this as the wrath of the Tribulation that Jesus rescues His people from by His coming. The definite article is present before the word *wrath.* It is *the* wrath, the coming wrath.

Also, it is Jesus, coming from heaven, who delivers us from the wrath to come. His coming is our means of deliverance. This interpretation draws further support from the specific time reference to the wrath in the Day of the Lord in 1 Thessalonians 5:1-6. (I interpret the Tribulation to be an instance of "the Day of the Lord.") The coming of Jesus to rescue His people from *the* wrath offers compelling evidence for the pre-Trib position, assuming the entire Tribulation is God's wrath.

Second, in 1 Thessalonians 4:13–5:9, the sequence of events suggests a chronology we can anticipate. As we have seen, 1Thessalonians 4:13-18 deals with the Rapture of the church. Then, beginning in 1 Thessalonians 5:1 (NASB), Paul shifts to a new topic with the words, "Now as to" (*peri de* in Greek). This Greek phrase is one of Paul's favorite ways to change subjects in his letters. He uses it this way repeatedly in 1 Corinthians 7–16. So, it's clear that he is finished dealing with the Rapture at this point. But what is the next subject in 1 Thessalonians 5:1-9? It's the Day of the Lord (1 Thessalonians 5:2).

Why is this new topic significant? Because it suggests a clear order of events. The Rapture is mentioned first, followed by the Tribulation. The Tribulation is pictured as *separate* from and *subsequent* to the Rapture.

The order is compelling.

The Rapture	1 Thessalonians 4:13-18
The Day of the Lord (Tribulation)	1 Thessalonians 5:1-9

If the discussion of the Rapture precedes the discussion of the Day of the Lord in 1 Thessalonians 4–5, then they can hardly be parts of the same event as posttribulationists maintain.[8] Rather, the chronology of 1 Thessalonians 4–5 supports the pre-Trib position.

Third, in 1 Thessalonians 5:1-5, Paul distinguishes two unique groups. The difference is critical, yet easy to miss. The pronouns in italics are clues to Paul's thinking:

> Now as to the times and the epochs, brethren, *you* have no need of anything to be written to *you*. For *you yourselves* know full

> well that the day of the Lord will come just like a thief in the night. While *they* are saying, "Peace and safety!" then destruction will come upon *them* suddenly like labor pains upon a woman with child, and *they* will not escape. But *you*, brethren, are not in darkness, that the day would overtake *you* like a thief; for *you* are all sons of light and sons of day. *We* are not of night nor of darkness. (NASB, ITALICS ADDED)

There's a conspicuous shift from *you* and *we* (the believers) to *they* and *them* (the unbelievers). The shift is significant. The pronouns indicate that when the Day of the Lord arrives, there will be two distinct groups of people. One group will be raptured and escape the wrath, and the other will remain on earth and face its full force.

The Day of the Lord will come upon *them*, and *they* shall not escape (1 Thessalonians 5:3). Then in 1 Thessalonians 5:4 there's an abrupt contrast: "But *you*, brethren, are not in darkness" (NASB). *They* in verse 3 stands in sharp contrast to *you* and *we* in verses 4-11 who will escape. This sharp distinction signals that God's people will not face the coming wrath of the Day of the Lord.

Fourth, 1 Thessalonians 5:9 says clearly, "For God has not destined us for wrath, but for obtaining salvation through our Lord Jesus Christ (NASB)." Believers have an appointment with salvation, not wrath. Many believe that this verse refers to the wrath of hell that Christians will not experience. However, the Thessalonians had already been assured that they would escape the wrath of hell (1 Thessalonians 1:4). Moreover, in the context of 1 Thessalonians 5:1-8, the wrath Paul has just been discussing is not eternal punishment in hell but the wrath of the Day of the Lord. That's the wrath that believers will be delivered from. As John Walvoord says, "In this passage he [Paul] is expressly saying that our appointment is to be caught up to be with Christ; the appointment of the world is for the Day of the Lord, the day of wrath. One cannot keep both of these appointments."[9] Our appointment for salvation and the Rapture is made the moment we trust Jesus Christ as our personal Savior from sin.

Evidence for Exemption in Revelation 3:10-11

> Because you have kept the word of My perseverance, I also will *keep* you *from* the *hour* of testing, that hour which is about to come upon *the whole world*, to test those who dwell on the earth. I am coming *quickly*.
>
> REVELATION 3:10-11 (NASB, ITALICS ADDED)

We can glean at least four important pieces of evidence from Revelation 3:10-11 pertaining to exemption. This passage illuminates the nature of God's protection, the timing of the Rapture, the scope of the Tribulation, and the brevity of the Rapture.

First, the Lord promises to "*keep* you *from*" the time of testing. The words *keep from* are the English translation of the Greek words *tereo ek*. *Tereo* is the Greek word for "keep, preserve, protect," and the Greek preposition *ek* means "out of, out from within." Posttribulationists argue that the word *ek* here means "through"; thus, they read this passage as "I also will keep you through the hour of testing," not "out of" it. But if the Lord had meant that believers would be kept "through" the Tribulation, He would have used the Greek preposition *dia*, which carries this clear meaning. Furthermore, the only other case of *tereo ek* in the New Testament is in John 17:15, which says, "I do not ask You to take them out of the world, but to *keep* them *from* the evil one" (NASB, italics added). The usage of this identical phrase in John 17:15 supports the meaning of *ek* in Revelation 3:10 as "to keep from" or "out from within."[10] It doesn't make sense for God to keep His people *through* Satan—the evil one; he keeps us *from* him.[11]

Second, the Lord promises to keep his people not just from the testing but from "the *hour* of testing." God's people are exempt not just from the trials during the Tribulation but from the very Tribulation itself. We are removed from the whole period of time, not just the trials of it. This phrasing strongly supports the pre-Trib notion of *removal* before the Tribulation, not the post-Trib claim of *protection* through it.

Third, the time of testing will "come upon *the whole world*." The Tribulation is worldwide in scope. What is this time of worldwide testing that believers will escape? I believe, in the book of Revelation, it can only refer to one time—the Tribulation period described in Revelation 6–18.

Fourth, Jesus tells us how this deliverance will be accomplished—"quickly." This "quickly" seems to suggest something brief, not long and drawn out. This brevity, in my opinion, alludes to the instantaneous removal of the church "in the blink of an eye." It will happen that quickly.

Putting these four points together, I clearly see that the Lord will deliver His people *from* the *time* of *worldwide* testing *by* His sudden coming for them at the Rapture. Charles C. Ryrie shares an excellent illustration of the truth in Revelation 3:10.

> As a teacher I frequently give exams. Let's suppose that I announce an exam will occur on such and such a day at the regular class time. Then suppose I say, "I want to make a promise to students whose grade average for the semester so far is A. The promise is: I will keep you from the exam."
>
> Now I could keep my promise to those A students this way: I would tell them to come to the exam, pass out the exam to everyone, and give the A students a sheet containing the answers. They would take the exam and yet in reality be kept from the exam. They would live through the time but not suffer the trial. This is posttribulationism: protection while enduring.
>
> But if I said to the class, "I am giving an exam next week. I want to make a promise to all the A students. I will keep you from the hour of the exam." They would understand clearly that to be kept from the hour of the test exempts them from being present during that hour. This is pretribulationism, and this is the meaning of the promise of Revelation 3:10. And the promise came from the risen Savior who Himself is the deliverer of the wrath to come (1 Thessalonians 1:10).[12]

The promise of Jesus is that He will come quickly, in the blink of an eye, to keep His bride from the time of the Tribulation.

Time Gap between the Rapture and the Second Coming

There are obvious similarities between the Rapture and the second coming of Jesus. In both cases, Jesus descends from heaven. But there are also some differences: on the one hand, Jesus is described as coming *for* His people, while on the other hand, Jesus is described as coming *with* His people. At the Rapture, Jesus meets His people in the air; at the Second Coming, He returns to earth. How do these two descriptions fit together? Are they the same event or different events—or something else? I think that a pre-Tribulation Rapture best resolves this discrepancy.

In this section I want to identify four biblical prophecies that create further disharmony between the Rapture and the Second Coming. It will show more fully that the Rapture and the Second Coming cannot be simultaneous, that there must be an interval of time between them. I aim to show that the Rapture and the Second Coming are indeed bookends to the Tribulation: the Rapture happens before the Tribulation, and the Second Coming happens after. Nonetheless, I maintain that these are two stages of the same event, separated by the events of the Tribulation.

Finally, I believe that after looking at these prophecies, we will see how pretribulationism best harmonizes the relevant Scripture passages. Other views, especially posttribulationism, are forced to devise scenarios that do not allow for a normal passage of time.[13] A pre-Trib Rapture puts the many end times predictions into a logical timeline. The end times will make sense best with a pre-Trib Rapture followed by the Tribulation and then the Second Coming.

Here are four end times events that raise the need for a time interval between the Rapture and the second coming of Christ.

The Judgment Seat of Christ

The New Testament clearly states that all church-age believers must appear before the judgment seat of Christ in heaven. Interestingly, in the detailed accounts of the second coming of Christ, the judgment seat of Christ is never mentioned (e.g., Revelation 19:11-21). Assuming this judgment would require some passage of time, the pre-Trib gap of seven years between the Rapture and the Second Coming would accommodate such a requirement.

The Preparation of Christ's Bride

Revelation 19:7-10 pictures the church as a bride who has been made ready for marriage to her groom. When Christ returns in his second coming, the bride is dressed and ready to accompany Christ back to the earth (Revelation 19:11-18). With this being the case, the church would have to be complete and in heaven in order to be prepared in the way that Revelation 19 describes. This requires a prior removal as well as an interval of time, both of which pretribulationism handles well.

Life in the Millennial Kingdom

A third event that requires some gap of time between the Rapture and the Second Coming is the presence of believers in mortal, physical bodies during the one-thousand-year reign of Christ on earth. Isaiah 65:20-25 seems to suggest that, during the Millennium, people will carry on ordinary occupations such as farming, planting vineyards, and building houses, and they will bear children, populating the messianic kingdom.[14] Revelation 20:1-6 says that, when Christ returns to earth, He will establish His Kingdom on earth that will last for one thousand years. Old Testament saints, church-age believers, and believers who died during the Tribulation will all enter the millennial kingdom in new glorified bodies, having been resurrected at various points prior to the Millennium. Meanwhile, those believers who come to faith in Christ during the Tribulation and survive until the second advent will enter the millennial kingdom of Christ in their natural, human bodies.

Here's the dilemma for the post-Trib view. If all saints were caught up in a post-Tribulation Rapture prior to the Millennium, there would be no people in natural bodies to enter the one-thousand-year reign of Christ. All believers would already have a glorified body. Unbelievers will be in hell. There wouldn't be any believers remaining in natural bodies to populate the Kingdom.

However, pretribulationism does not run into this problem. The seven-year Tribulation between the Rapture and the return of Christ is the time when millions of people will be saved and thus be present in their natural bodies to populate the earth during the Millennium. This is the third reason there must be a time gap between the Rapture and the Second Coming.

The Sheep and the Goats

Matthew 25:31-46 depicts God's judgment of Gentiles. This judgment will occur after the Second Coming and at the beginning of the Millennium. The people gathered at this judgment will be survivors of the Great Tribulation. Jesus will divide the Gentiles into two groups: believers and unbelievers (the sheep and the goats). This dividing up indicates that both believers and unbelievers will be alive on the earth at Jesus' second coming. Why is this noteworthy?

Posttribulationism fails to account for both believers and unbelievers living on earth after the Rapture. If the Rapture and the Second Coming occur together, as posttribulationists believe, and all living believers are caught up to meet Jesus and escort Him back to earth, then there won't be any sheep left on earth when Jesus arrives. All that would be left are goats. The sheep would have all just been raptured and returned with Christ.

The posttribulation view has no need for Jesus to separate the sheep from the goats when He comes to earth, because the Rapture would have already separated them. But if the Rapture occurs before the Tribulation, as pretribulationists argue, many people would come to know the Lord during the Tribulation and before the Second Coming. These Tribulation believers would account for the "sheep" in Matthew 25:31-46. Once again, a pre-Trib position with its time gap between the Rapture and Second Coming is the best way to account for a literal interpretation of this passage.

Removal of the Restrainer

> Now, dear brothers and sisters, let us clarify some things about the coming of our Lord Jesus Christ and how we will be gathered

> to meet him. . . . Don't be fooled by what they say. For that day will not come until there is a great rebellion against God and the man of lawlessness is revealed—the one who brings destruction. He will exalt himself and defy everything that people call god and every object of worship. He will even sit in the temple of God, claiming that he himself is God.
>
> Don't you remember that I told you about all this when I was with you? And you know *what is holding him back*, for he can be revealed only when his time comes. For this lawlessness is already at work secretly, and it will remain secret until *the one who is holding it back* steps out of the way. Then the man of lawlessness will be revealed, but the Lord Jesus will kill him with the breath of his mouth and destroy him by the splendor of his coming.
>
> 2 THESSALONIANS 2:1, 3-8 (ITALICS ADDED)

Second Thessalonians describes the revelation of "the man of lawlessness." I believe this is the Antichrist. Paul describes some of the things he will do, but he says that for now his identity remains a secret and that the lawlessness continues in secret until he is revealed. So what prevents the man of lawlessness from being revealed? Paul shares another force at work—it is "what is holding him back." This force is also "the one who is holding [this lawlessness] back." I call this withholding force "the restrainer." The Greek word *katecho* in both places means to "hold back or restrain."

So who is this person, or what kind of entity is it that is restraining the appearance of the Antichrist? Down through the centuries many candidates have been suggested:

1. The Roman Empire
2. The Jewish State
3. The Apostle Paul
4. The Preaching of the Gospel
5. Human Government
6. Satan

7. Elijah
8. An Unknown Heavenly Being
9. Michael the Archangel
10. The Holy Spirit
11. The Church

St. Augustine was transparent when he said concerning the restrainer, "I frankly confess I do not know what He means." I can sympathize with Augustine. Nonetheless, I believe there are several clues that can help us identify the restrainer. First, the restrainer holds back the man of lawlessness. Second, the restrainer is referred to with both neuter and masculine verbs (participles). The phrase "what is holding him back" uses a neuter verb, suggesting a principle. The phrase "the one who is holding it back" uses a masculine verb, suggesting a person. Third, whatever the restrainer is, he or it must be removable. Last, the restrainer must be powerful enough to hold back the outbreak of evil under the Antichrist.

These four clues permit only one satisfactory identification for the restrainer—God Himself. In this case it is God the Holy Spirit who is the restrainer. But that still leaves some loose ends—why is the Holy Spirit referred to as both a principle and as a person—as a what and a who? And how can the Holy Spirit, who is omnipresent, be removed from the earth? These are legitimate concerns. The Holy Spirit is omnipresent and cannot be removed from the earth. Moreover, millions of people will be saved during the Tribulation (Revelation 7:9-14). The convicting, drawing, regenerating ministry of the Holy Spirit is essential for anyone to be saved both now and in the Tribulation (John 3:5; 16:7-11; 1 Corinthians 12:3). So how can the Holy Spirit be the restrainer? I believe the answer is that the Holy Spirit is at work during this age in and through the church.

There are four key reasons for identifying the restrainer this way. First, this restraint requires omnipotent power. Second, this view adequately explains the change in gender—from neuter to masculine—in 2 Thessalonians 2:6-7. In Greek the word *pneuma* (Spirit) is neuter. But the Holy Spirit is also consistently referred to by the masculine pronoun *He*, especially in John 14–16. Third, Scripture speaks of the Holy Spirit as restraining sin and evil in the world (Genesis 6:3) and in the heart of the believer (Galatians 5:16-17). Finally, the Holy Spirit uses the church and its proclamation and portrayal of the gospel as the primary instrument in this age to restrain evil. We are the salt of the earth and the light of the world (Matthew 5:13-16). We are the temple of the Holy Spirit both individually and corporately (1 Corinthians 3:17; 6:19; Ephesians 2:21-22).

John Phillips clarifies what the church's role is during the church age:

> The church age is a parenthesis in God's dealings with the world. The church, injected supernaturally into history at Pentecost and supernaturally maintained throughout the age by the baptizing, indwelling, and filling works of the Holy Spirit, will be supernaturally removed when this age is over. What is removed then is the Holy Spirit's mighty working through the church. Until that happens, Satan cannot bring his plans to a head. Thus, I believe the restrainer in 2 Thessalonians 2:6-7 is neither the Holy Spirit alone nor the church alone. Rather, the restraining force is both of them together. In Acts 2, on the day of Pentecost, the Holy Spirit came to earth in a new capacity. He came to earth to indwell each individual believer (1 Corinthians 6:19) and the church as a whole (1 Corinthians 3:16). By his Spirit, God empowers his people in this age to restrain evil. That restraining force will be here as long as the church is here.[15]

The great Bible teacher and expositor Donald Grey Barnhouse summarizes this view.

> Well, what is keeping the Antichrist from putting in his appearance on the world stage? *You* are! You and every other member of the body of Christ on earth. The presence of the church of Jesus Christ is the restraining force that refuses to allow the man of lawlessness to be revealed. True, it is the Holy Spirit who is the real restrainer. But as both

> 1 Corinthians 3:16 and 6:19 teach, the Holy Spirit indwells the believer. The believer's body is the temple of the Spirit of God. Put all believers together then, with the Holy Spirit indwelling each of us, and you have a formidable restraining force.[16]

The restrainer then is the work of the Holy Spirit through His people in this present age. Amazingly, our present age is described as the age of restraint. The presence of believers in the world exerts a powerful influence upon the wicked world.

The Rapture will change everything. When the Rapture occurs, the Spirit-indwelt church and its restraining influence will be removed. That will release the world to sin as it never has before. Christians who stand for civic righteousness and law and order will no longer be present exerting their influence. The church's salt and light will be extracted from the earth. For a time at least, only unsaved people will hold government office. Satan will be able to put his plan into full swing by bringing his man onto center stage to take control of the world. Evil will erupt and expand unchecked beyond anything known in the history of man. It will be like the removal of a huge dam. The world will be inundated with evil of unimaginable scope and severity.

Chuck Swindoll describes the results of the removal of the restrainer:

> When the church is "gathered together" and taken to be with Christ in the air, the salt and light will be withdrawn. Then every vestige of goodness will decay; every remnant of truth, unravel. It is at that time when the man of lawlessness will take center stage. Like cages in a zoo suddenly opened, so will it be when the Restrainer is taken out of the way and lawlessness runs wild and rampant in the streets. Ours is a day of grace in which sin, to a large degree, is restrained. It is a day when God does not deal directly with human sin. However, there will come a time when He will step on the scene to deal definitively with sin. And that will be a time of great destruction.[17]

However, the Holy Spirit's return to heaven will not be a complete withdrawal from earth, but a reverse Pentecost of sorts. His activity will be like it was in the Old Testament. Donald Grey Barnhouse agrees:

> When the church is removed at the rapture, the Holy Spirit goes with the church insofar as His restraining power is concerned. His work in this age of grace will be ended. Henceforth, during the Great Tribulation, the Holy Spirit will still be here on earth, of course—for how can you get rid of God?—but He will not be indwelling believers as He does now. Rather, he will revert to His Old Testament ministry of coming upon special people.[18]

Second Thessalonians 2 and the appearance of the restrainer there raise some complicated issues. A pre-Trib Rapture makes sense of 2 Thessalonians 2 and of the restraining power over the man of lawlessness. When the church is raptured, its restraining influence will be removed, leaving a vacuum of righteousness. The absence of this restraining influence will create an environment fit for the Tribulation.

The "mystery of lawlessness" is already active (2 Thessalonians 2:7, NASB), but the Holy Spirit is now restraining sin until He is removed with the Rapture of the church. When this occurs, "the man of lawlessness will be revealed, but the Lord Jesus will kill him with the breath of his mouth and destroy him by the splendor of his coming" (2 Thessalonians 2:8).

Imminency

Imminency is a doctrine held by pretribulationists that is drawn from a number of New Testament passages. These passages present a Rapture that is certain, though not necessarily soon, that could happen at any moment, and that could happen without warning.

- 1 Corinthians 1:7 (NASB)—"Awaiting eagerly the revelation of our Lord Jesus Christ"
- 1 Corinthians 16:22 (NASB)—"Maranatha" (This word means "our Lord, come.")

- Philippians 3:20 (NASB)—"For our citizenship is in heaven, from which also we eagerly wait for a Savior, the Lord Jesus Christ."
- Philippians 4:5 (NASB)—"The Lord is near."
- 1 Thessalonians 1:10 (NASB)—"to wait for His Son from heaven" (The word for *wait* in Greek is in the present tense, which means they were to wait continuously and literally means to "wait up for" like a parent waiting up for and looking for a child that he or she expects to be home at any moment.)
- Titus 2:13 (NASB)—"looking for the blessed hope and the appearing of the glory of our great God and Savior, Christ Jesus" (Why be constantly looking for Christ if He can't come at any moment?)
- Hebrews 9:28 (NASB)—"So Christ . . . will appear a second time for salvation without reference to sin, to those who eagerly await Him." (Why eagerly await His coming if it's a long way off?)
- James 5:7-9 (NASB)—"Be patient, brethren, until the coming of the Lord. . . . For the coming of the Lord is near. . . . Behold, the Judge is standing right at the door."
- 1 Peter 1:13 (NASB)—"Fix your hope completely on the grace to be brought to you at the revelation of Jesus Christ."
- Jude 1:21 (NASB)—"waiting anxiously for the mercy of our Lord Jesus Christ to eternal life"
- Revelation 3:11; 22:7, 12, 20 (NASB)—"I am coming quickly."
- Revelation 22:17, 20 (NASB)—"The Spirit and the bride say, 'Come.' And let the one who hears say, 'Come.' . . . He who testifies to these things says, 'Yes, I am coming quickly.' Amen. Come, Lord Jesus."

All these Scriptures refer to the Rapture and speak of it as though it could occur at any moment. In some ways, anticipating Christ's return could be compared to living in California and waiting for an earthquake. You can be certain, living there, that an earthquake will happen; it's only a matter of time. It may be soon or it may happen a decade from now, but it will most assuredly happen. It could also happen at any moment. And it could happen without warning. Sure, there could be tremors ahead of time, but not necessarily.

This is similar to the way pretribulationists think about the Rapture. When it comes to imminency, they have three main ideas in mind: it could happen at any moment; it could happen without warning; and it will certainly happen, even if it doesn't happen soon.

Any moment. Imminency means that the Rapture could occur at any moment. Other prophetic events *may* take place before the Rapture, but no prophetic event *must* precede it. An imminent event, according to Charles C. Ryrie, is one that is "impending, hanging over one's head, ready to take place. An imminent event is one that is always ready to take place."[19]

Without warning. Since the Rapture could occur at any moment, then one must be ready for it at any time. If signs were required to precede it, then it couldn't occur at any moment. Thus, imminency means that the Rapture is a signless event. But if this is true, then why do we often hear people refer to signs of Christ's coming? It's important to remember that the signs of Christ's coming in the New Testament, such as Matthew 24, portend the second coming of Christ. They are not signs of the Rapture. In the early church God's people were looking for the Savior, not signs. Pretribulationists call the Rapture a signless event.

Certain, but not necessarily soon. Third, imminency means that the Rapture is certain to happen but not necessarily soon. Imminent does not mean soon; rather, it means inevitable.

Imminency, therefore, combines two key elements: certainty and uncertainty. An imminent event is one that is certain to occur, but the timing of it is uncertain.[20] It's common to hear Christians today say things like, "Jesus is coming soon!" The truth is, the Rapture may happen soon, but it may not. Also, people have different understandings of what "soon" means. We simply don't know for sure when it will happen. To be more accurate, believers ought to say, "The Rapture could happen at any moment; it could happen today." I think this more accurately expresses the biblical teaching of imminency.

ARGUMENTS AGAINST IMMINENCY

Although the Scriptures seem to clearly present the idea of the imminency of Christ's return, some challenge the notion of imminency. These opponents argue that the writers of the New Testament did not believe in the imminency of the Rapture.

First, some argue that the gospel had to be preached throughout the world before Christ could return (Acts 1:8). This requirement would contradict the doctrine of imminency because the Rapture would not have been imminent for those who read the gospel. The gospel would have had to first reach the uttermost parts of the earth; this would have made it a sign preceding the Rapture, thus precluding imminency. However, by AD 50 the gospel had already spread into Europe, which at that time was considered "the ends of the earth." Given the understanding that New Testament writers had of Jesus' commission to the disciples, this requirement was already fulfilled by the time Luke wrote the book of Acts (ca. AD 60–62). Moreover, Paul included himself when he spoke of the Rapture in 1 Thessalonians: "We who are still living when the Lord returns will not meet him ahead of those who have died" (4:15). Evidently, Paul didn't see any obstacles to Christ's coming during his lifetime. He believed the Rapture was imminent.

Second, opponents of imminency maintain that John 21:18-19 precludes an any-moment Rapture because it says that Peter had to live to be an old man. This means that John's readers wouldn't have been concerned until Peter had grown old. His old age would have been a sign of sorts. As a sign, it would have precluded imminency. However, Peter himself encouraged believers to look for the coming of the Lord (1 Peter 1:13; 4:7). Peter knew that he might die suddenly (2 Peter 1:14). Also, other believers expected Peter's early death because when Rhoda told the believers in Acts 12 the news of his release from prison, they said, "You're out of your mind!" (v. 15) and when Peter appeared to them, "they were amazed" (v. 16). Apparently John 21:18-19 did not lead readers to believe Peter had to grow old. They seemed to have no expectation that he would live a long life. Moreover, the passage in John 21 was not even written and circulated to the churches until fifteen to twenty years after Peter was already dead, so John 21:18-19 is not an impediment to imminency.

A third argument against imminency is that the Temple had to be destroyed before Christ returned (Matthew 24:1-3). This would have meant that the Temple's destruction would have been a sign, precluding imminency. But that is not the case. Rather, we must understand what Christ meant in Matthew 24. Jesus was not discussing the Rapture or the church; the church was still a mystery and had not yet been revealed, much less established. Matthew 24 does not relate the Temple's destruction to the Rapture. There is not even a hint that the Temple's destruction must precede the Rapture.

JESUS COULD COME TODAY

With these objections put to rest, I believe that the New Testament presents the Rapture as an event that could occur at any moment. So believers should be looking for it all the time.

One of my friends once said that he believes so strongly in the pre-Trib Rapture that he always eats his dessert first when he sits down to eat. Now that's putting your theology into practice!

But the sentiment behind his statement is true. Why? Because only the pre-Trib position allows for an imminent, any-moment, signless coming of Christ for His own. Only those who believe in a pre-Trib Rapture can honestly say, "Jesus may come today." The other views cannot say this. They expect certain events to precede the Rapture, and those events haven't happened yet.

The imminency of the Rapture should fill us with hope, anticipation, and motivation to godly living. Believers should live with this hope every day—Jesus may come today! Only imminency allows for this blessed hope (Titus 2:13). And only pretribulationism accounts for imminency.

When I talk to people who say that they are mid-Trib or post-Trib, I sometimes ask them if they believe Jesus can come back at any time, even today. They often say yes. I then ask them how Jesus can come at any moment if we are not even in the Tribulation yet, and at least half or all of it must pass until the Rapture can occur. Many fail to see the inconsistency between the doctrine of imminency and the notion that some or all of the Tribulation must elapse before it can occur. Only those who hold the pre-Trib view can logically hold that Jesus could come back today.

Maranatha

The doctrine of imminency is a reality that changes how we live in the present age. This expectation certainly changed how the early church lived. The early church adopted a special password to identify themselves and to greet each other: *Maranatha* (1 Corinthians 16:22). It is an Aramaic word that only appears once in Scripture. It consists of three Aramaic words: *Mar* (Lord), *ana* (our), and *tha* (come). It's a kind of one-word prayer—"our Lord, come."

Maranatha only makes sense in light of the imminent view of the Rapture. As Renald Showers says, "If they knew that Christ could not return at any moment because of other events or a time period had to transpire first, why did they petition Him in a way that implied that He could come at any moment?"[21] It's instructive that the early church coined this special greeting to reflect their hourly hope, eager expectation, and ardent anticipation of the Rapture. No doubt this expectation motivated them to pursue personal purity, devoted service, and evangelism. Think of how the church would change today if we were to adopt this greeting for our brothers and sisters in Christ. Think of how our lives would change if this simple greeting were always on the lips of an expectant people.[22]

Blessed Hope

The Rapture is intended to comfort and bless the Lord's people. The New Testament consistently presents it as a sure hope that God's people are to anxiously anticipate. In John 14:1-3, Jesus says,

> Don't let your hearts be troubled. Trust in God, and trust also in me. There is more than enough room in my Father's home. If this were not so, would I have told you that I am going to prepare a place for you? When everything is ready, I will come and get you, so that you will always be with me where I am.

Titus 2:13 says, "We look forward with hope to that wonderful day when the glory of our great God and Savior, Jesus Christ, will be revealed." After describing the Rapture, Paul concludes with this gentle reminder: "Encourage each other with these words" (1 Thessalonians 4:18). The hope of the Rapture is an uplifting encouragement for troubled hearts. It's a blessing and consolation for the Lord's people.

Think about it. If Paul had taught the Thessalonians the mid-Trib or post-Trib view, we would expect the Thessalonians to be filled with either joy over their loved ones who had died and escaped the Tribulation, or otherwise filled with fear and worry in anticipation of enduring the Tribulation themselves. They would be eagerly seeking detailed information about the Tribulation and the Antichrist.

To add to that, if Paul had believed in anything other than a pre-Trib Rapture, what encouragement could he have given them? Would the truth of the Rapture really be that comforting? If God's people would have to endure 3½ years, 5½ years, or all 7 years of the Tribulation before He comes, how much of a comfort would the Rapture be? As I once heard someone say, "That would be the blasted hope, not the blessed hope." Could you honestly get excited about the Rapture if you knew that you had to endure a time on earth when all the nineteen judgments of Revelation 6–16 were being poured out? But in reality, Paul uses the Rapture to encourage the Thessalonians to have hope.

Instead, in 1 Thessalonians 4:13-18, the Thessalonians are filled with neither rejoicing nor fear and worry. They are actually filled with grief and sorrow for those who have died. The believers are grieving because they fear that their loved ones have missed the Resurrection and the Rapture. The Thessalonians express no fear or nagging questions about the approaching Day of the Lord or the appearance of the Antichrist. Why? They were looking for Christ, not the Antichrist. The overall mood in 1 Thessalonians 4 matches the pre-Trib position to a tee, but it's totally inconsistent with either midtribulationism or posttribulationism.[23]

Was Paul a Pretribber? The Rapture in 2 Thessalonians 2:1-3

AFTER WRITING HIS FIRST LETTER to the Thessalonians, Paul had to write another letter to them within a few months—2 Thessalonians. Apparently, someone claiming to be Paul had written a counterfeit letter to the church at Thessalonica (2 Thessalonians 2:2). In this forged epistle, the author had told the believers, who were facing persecution and trouble, that they were already living during the Tribulation period that Paul had described in 1 Thessalonians 5.

This spurious letter threw the Thessalonians into confusion. Paul responded to their distress. "Dear brothers and sisters, let us clarify some things about the coming of our Lord Jesus Christ and how we will be gathered to meet him. Don't be so easily shaken or alarmed by those who say that the day of the Lord has already begun" (2 Thessalonians 2:1-2).

It's clear, given Paul's statement, that the Thessalonians expected that they would be raptured before the Tribulation. Why? If the Thessalonians believed they would have to endure the Tribulation before Christ's coming, why were they so upset at the prospect that the Day of the Lord had already come? They would have been thrilled at seeing prophecy fulfilled, not upset and shaken. The coming of the Day of the Lord would have meant Paul's prophecy in 1 Thessalonians 5 was coming true. The Thessalonians would have anticipated going through the Tribulation.

But they didn't respond with hope or excitement. Their reaction was the opposite. They were "easily shaken" and "alarmed." The phony letter they had received contradicted what Paul had taught them in 1 Thessalonians 4–5—namely that they would be raptured prior to the Tribulation. Being told they were already in the Tribulation blindsided them. It shook them to the core. They faced three disturbing options: either Paul's prophecy in 1 Thessalonians was a lie or they had totally misinterpreted what he said or that the Rapture had already occurred and they had been left behind.

The only logical implication from 2 Thessalonians 2:1-2 is that the Thessalonians believed that the Rapture would occur before the Tribulation. Such a view would have been based on Paul's previous teaching in 1 Thessalonians. Later in 2 Thessalonians 2:3-11, Paul goes on to show the believers that the teaching that they were already in the Day of the Lord was false doctrine and that they had no reason to be afraid.

Conclusion

In this chapter, my goal has been to show that pretribulationism offers the best interpretation of Scripture's prophecy about the end times. We've looked at numerous passages that describe a lot of the details about the end times. A pre-Tribulation Rapture makes the best sense of these details.

In Revelation 1–3, the church (*ekklesia*) is mentioned often and pictured on earth. But there's a transition in chapter 4. In Revelation 4–18, the church is represented by the twenty-four elders around the throne of God in heaven. When the church appears in these chapters, it is always pictured in heaven, not on earth. This shift is best accounted for by a pre-Tribulation Rapture. In 1 Thessalonians 4:13–5:9, Paul discusses the Rapture first and then the Day of the Lord. From this order, we can conclude that the Rapture precedes the Day of the Lord. Pretribulationism accounts for this order.

First Thessalonians 1:10 promises that believers will be delivered from the coming wrath. Additionally, Paul's language in 1 Thessalonians 5:1-6 specifically excludes believers from the Day of the Lord. He does not include himself or believers. By contrast, just prior to 1 Thessalonians 5, Paul uses inclusive language about the Rapture (1 Thessalonians 4:13-18). Pretribulationism accounts for each of these details; a pre-Tribulation Rapture delivers believers from the coming wrath and makes sense of Paul's linguistic shifts.

Scripture talks about four events that require some passage of time between the Rapture and the Second Coming: the judgment seat of Christ, the preparation of Christ's bride (Revelation 19:7-10), earthly believers living in the millennial kingdom (Isaiah 65:20-25), and the separation of the sheep from the goats (Matthew 25:31-46). To make sense of these four events, some sort of gap is necessary between the Rapture and the Second Coming. A pre-Tribulation Rapture provides this gap.

Before the man of sin can be revealed and before the Tribulation can begin, 2 Thessalonians 2:5-7 says the restrainer must be removed. The restrainer, as we saw, is the restraining influence of the Spirit through the church. A pre-Tribulation Rapture accounts for this removal. The church's influence disappears in a pre-Trib Rapture, and this paves the way for the man of sin to rise up and for the Tribulation to begin.

Numerous passages in Scripture picture the coming of the Lord as an imminent event (Philippians 4:5; James 5:7-9; Revelation 3:11; 22:7, 12, 17, 20). It could occur at any moment (1 Thessalonians 1:10). Scripture does not mention any preceding signs that must occur prior to the Rapture. The pre-Trib Rapture position accounts for imminence, but other views don't.

Second Thessalonians reveals that the believers were distraught, believing the Day of the Lord had begun (2 Thessalonians 2:2). If Paul had taught them that they would be in the Day of the Lord, they would not be upset by this. They would have been expecting it. But their fear and worry show that they believed they were going to be raptured before the Day of the Lord. Clearly, the Thessalonians, taught by Paul, believed in a pre-Tribulation Rapture.

In 1 Thessalonians 4:18, Paul saw the Rapture as a reason for comfort and encouragement. What comfort would there be in the Rapture if it happened sometime after the beginning of the Great Tribulation? This simply doesn't make sense. The Rapture is an encouragement only if believers are spared the trials of the Tribulation. A pre-Tribulation view accounts for this thinking.

We've covered a lot of ground in this chapter. While there are other strong arguments in favor of the pre-Trib view, I believe these seven are the strongest. Scripture includes many details in prophecy, and with them we can get a clearer picture of the future. In my opinion, pretribulationism makes the most coherent picture out of the prophetic details we have.

CHAPTER 12

A BRIEF HISTORY OF THE PRE-TRIB RAPTURE VIEW

One of the most common objections to the pre-Tribulation Rapture view is that it can't be right because it didn't arrive on the scene until the 1830s through the ministry and teaching of an Irish Brethren preacher named John Nelson Darby. The argument goes like this: if the Rapture were biblical, it would have appeared earlier in church history. Until recently this argument was largely unanswered, but in the last few years several pre-1830 pre-Trib Rapture statements have been discovered. Three main ones stand out.

Pseudo-Ephraem

The earliest extra-biblical evidence of the pre-Tribulation Rapture position surfaced in the early medieval period in a sermon titled "On the Last Times, the Antichrist, and the End of the World, or Sermon on the End of the World." The sermon is often attributed to Ephraem the Syrian, but most scholars believe it was the product of someone known as Pseudo-Ephraem. This powerful sermon was written sometime between the fourth and sixth centuries. Concerning the timing of the Rapture, the sermon reads as follows:

> We ought to understand thoroughly therefore, my brothers, what is imminent or overhanging. . . . Why therefore do we not reject every care of earthly actions and prepare ourselves for the meeting of the Lord Jesus Christ, so that he may *draw us from the confusion*, which overwhelms all the world? . . . For all the saints and elect of God are gathered together *before the tribulation*, which is to come, and are taken to the Lord, in order that they might not see at any time the confusion which overwhelms the world because of our sins. (italics added)[1]

According to prophecy scholars Thomas Ice and Timothy Demy, Pseudo-Ephraem clearly presents at least three important features found in modern pretribulationism:

> (1) There are two distinct comings: the return of Christ to rapture the saints, followed later by Christ's Second Advent to the earth, (2) a defined interval between the two comings, in this case three and one-half years, and (3) a clear statement that Christ will remove the church from the world before the tribulation.[2]

According to Thomas Ice, "This statement evidences a clear belief that all Christians will escape the Tribulation through a gathering to the Lord and is stated early in the sermon. How else can this be understood other than as pretribulational? The later second coming of Christ to the earth with the saints is mentioned at the end of the sermon."[3]

Pseudo-Ephraem is a clear pre-Trib Rapture statement over one thousand years before J. N. Darby.

Brother Dolcino

In AD 1260, Gerard Sagarello founded a group known as the Apostolic Brethren in northern Italy. At that time it was against church law to form any new ecclesiastical order, so the Apostolic Brethren were subjected to severe persecution. In 1300, Gerard was burned at the stake, and a man named Brother Dolcino took over leadership of the movement. Under his leadership, the order grew and eventually numbered in the thousands. End times prophecy evidently held an important place in the study and teaching of the Apostolic Brethren.

Brother Dolcino died in 1307, and in 1316 an anonymous notary of the diocese of Vercelli in northern Italy wrote a brief treatise in Latin that set forth the deeds and beliefs of the Apostolic Brethren. This treatise was called *The History of Brother Dolcino*. At one point in the treatise the following paragraph appears:

> Again, [Dolcino believed and preached and taught] that within those three years Dolcino himself and his followers will preach the coming of the Antichrist. And that the Antichrist was coming into this world within the bounds of the said three and a half years; and after he had come, that he [Dolcino] and his followers would be transferred into Paradise, in which are Enoch and Elijah. And in this way they will be preserved unharmed from the persecution of the Antichrist. And that then Enoch and Elijah themselves would descend on the earth for the purpose of preaching [against] Antichrist. Then they would be killed by him or by his servants, and this Antichrist would reign for a long time. But when the Antichrist is dead, Dolcino himself, who then would be the holy pope, and his preserved followers, will descend on the earth, and will preach the right faith of Christ to all, and will convert those who will be living then to the true faith of Jesus Christ.[4]

Several points in this remarkable statement bear close similarity to modern pretribulationism:

The Latin word *transferrentur*, meaning "they would be transferred," is the same word used by medieval Christians to describe the rapture of Enoch to heaven.

The subjects of this rapture were to be Brother Dolcino and his followers. This was not a partial-Rapture theory, because Brother Dolcino considered the Apostolic Brethren to be the true church in contrast to the Roman Catholic Church.

The purpose of the Rapture was to preserve the people from the persecution of the Antichrist.

The text presents the "transference" of believers to heaven and the "descent" of the believers from heaven as two separate events.

The text also shows that quite a long gap of time must intervene between the rapture of the saints to heaven and the return of the saints from heaven.[5]

Francis Gumerlock, an expert on the *Brother Dolcino* text, clearly believes that it is a pre-Tribulation Rapture statement. He concludes:

> This paragraph from *The History of Brother Dolcino* indicates that in northern Italy in the early fourteenth century a teaching very similar to modern pre-Tribulationalism was being preached. Responding to some very distressing political and ecclesiastical conditions, Dolcino was engaged in detailed speculations about Christian eschatology and believed that the coming of the Antichrist was imminent. He also believed that the means by which God would protect His people from the persecution of the Antichrist would be through a translation of the saints to paradise.[6]

These two ancient witnesses are sufficient to demonstrate that the pre-Tribulation view isn't a recent invention, but there is one more that must not be overlooked.

Morgan Edwards

Morgan Edwards (1722–1795) was a Baptist who founded Brown University. Edwards believed in a distinct Rapture 3½ years before the start of the Millennium. Edwards first wrote about his pre-Tribulation beliefs in 1742 and later published them in 1788. He taught the following about the Rapture:

> *The distance between the first and second resurrection will be somewhat more than a thousand years.* I say, somewhat more, because the dead saints will be raised, and the living changed at Christ's "appearing in the air" (I Thes. IV. 17); and this will be about three years and a half before the millennium, as we shall see hereafter: but will he and they abide in the air all that time? No: they will ascent to paradise, or to some one of those many "mansions in the father's house" (John xiv: 2), and to disappear during the foresaid period of time. The design of this retreat and disappearing will be to judge the risen and changed saints; for "now the time is come that judgment must begin," and that will be "at the house of God" (I Pet. IV. 17).[7]

Notice that Edwards makes three essential points consistent with the pretribulationist view: (1) He clearly separates the Rapture from the Second Coming by 3½ years. (2) He uses modern pre-Tribulation Rapture verses to describe the Rapture and support his view (see John 14:2 and 1 Thessalonians 4:17). (3) He believed that the judgment seat of Christ (rewarding) for believers will occur in heaven while the Tribulation rages on earth.

The only notable difference between modern pretribulationism and Edwards's belief is the time interval of 3½ years, instead of seven, between the Rapture and the Second Coming. This, however, does not mean that Edwards was a midtribulationist, since he apparently believed that the Tribulation was only 3½ years.[8]

Other Pre-Trib Promoters

In addition to the three primary pre-1830 witnesses, there are several other important sources that support the pre-Trib Rapture. In 1674 Thomas Collier rejected the pretribulational Rapture view, which demonstrates that the view existed. John Asgill authored a book in 1700 "about the possibility of translation (i.e., rapture) without seeing death."[9]

Paul Benware summarizes some of the other more noteworthy examples beginning in the seventeenth century.

> Peter Jurieu in his book *Approaching Deliverance of the Church* (1687) taught that Christ would come in the air to rapture the saints and return to heaven before the battle of Armageddon. He spoke of a secret Rapture prior to His coming in glory and judgment at Armageddon. Philip Doddridge's commentary on the New Testament (1783) and John Gill's commentary on the New Testament (1748) both use the term *rapture* and speak of it as imminent. It is clear that these men believed that this coming will precede Christ's descent to the earth and the time of judgment. The purpose was to preserve believers from the time of judgment. James Macknight (1763) and Thomas Scott (1792) taught that the righteous will be carried to heaven, where they will be secure until the time of judgment is over.[10]

Conclusion

The idea that the pre-Tribulation Rapture is a recent invention and that no one ever taught it before 1830 is an overused "straw man" argument. As you can see, this argument is simply not historically accurate. A person may choose to reject the pre-Tribulation position, but no rejection of this view should be based on this faulty argument.

CHAPTER 13

FALSE CLAIMS ABOUT THE ORIGIN OF THE PRE-TRIB RAPTURE

OVER THE PAST SEVERAL decades numerous conspiracy theories about the origin of pretribulationism have arisen, claiming that John Nelson Darby got his view from his contemporaries.[1] "Evangelical opponents of pretribulationism often put forth theories that cast Darby in a bad light. For example, some say Darby got the idea from Edward Irving (1792–1834), while others say it originated from the prophetic utterance of a fifteen-year old Scottish lassie Margaret Macdonald (1815–1840). Both sources are understood to be tainted since Irving was considered exocentric and heretical and Macdonald's prophetic utterance is thought to be demonic."[2] Is there any evidence that Darby developed his view from these sources, or did it rise from his own study of Scripture?

Let's examine these two conspiracy theories about the origin of the Rapture.[3]

Margaret Macdonald

The most common of these theories is that pretribulationism was invented by a fifteen-year-old girl named Margaret Macdonald from Port Glasgow, Scotland. The story is that in April 1830 Margaret Macdonald gave a prophetic utterance that has been a source of much speculation. Some allege that it contains a pre-Trib Rapture statement that later influenced Darby's own thinking. There are a number of solid reasons why this cannot be true.

First, it is doubtful that Margaret Macdonald's "prophecy" contains any elements related to the pre-Trib Rapture.[4] A simple reading of her statement makes this clear. The statement is quite convoluted, but if Margaret says anything about the Rapture, she seems to describe something more akin to the partial Rapture or even posttribulationism rather than the pre-Trib idea.[5]

Second, no one has ever demonstrated from actual historical facts that Darby was influenced by Macdonald's "prophecy," even if it did contain pre-Trib elements.[6] There has been much speculation and guessing about this but no actual proof of any link between Macdonald and Darby.

Third, Darby clearly held to an early form of the pre-Trib Rapture by January 1827. This is a full three years before Macdonald's prophecy in 1830. According to R. A. Huebner, John Nelson Darby first began to believe in the pre-Trib Rapture and to develop his dispensational perspective while recovering from a riding accident during December 1826 and January 1827.[7] If Huebner's claim is true, and all the evidence points in that direction, then all the conspiracy theories fall to the ground. Darby's view would predate anyone who could have supposedly influenced his thought, undermining the credibility of all the theories of outside influence. Darby's understanding of the pre-Trib Rapture developed, as he maintained, out of his personal thoughts from the study of Scripture. Jonathan David Burnham concludes:

> There is, for example, no proof that Darby "took" his views from a "prophecy" of Margaret Macdonald after he returned from visiting Scotland. Indeed, her so-called prophecy was more in line with the notion of a partial rapture, or even post tribulationism.[8]

Darby's pre-Trib and dispensational thoughts, says Huebner, developed from the following factors: (1) "He saw from Isaiah 32 that there was a different dispensation coming . . . that *Israel and the Church were distinct*."[9] (2) "During his convalescence JND learned that he ought daily to expect his Lord's return."[10] (3) "In 1827 JND understood the fall of the church . . . 'the ruin of the Church.'"[11] (4) Darby also was beginning to see a gap of time between the Rapture and the Second Coming by 1827.[12] (5) Darby said in 1857 that he first started understanding things relating to the pre-Trib Rapture "thirty years ago." "With that fixed point of reference, Jan. 31, 1827," says Huebner, we can see that Darby "had already understood those truths upon which the pre-tribulation rapture hinges."[13] When reading Darby's earliest published essay on biblical prophecy (1829), it is clear that Darby believed the Rapture was the church's focus and hope.[14]

What Do the Scholars Say?

Scholars who have carefully examined the evidence regarding various "Rapture origin" theories do not accept the theories as historically valid. The only ones who have accepted these theories are those who already are opposed to the pre-Trib Rapture. A look at various scholars and historians reveals that they think, in varying degrees, that these Rapture conspiracy theories are without merit. Historian Timothy P. Weber says this about the pre-Trib Rapture:

> The pretribulation rapture was a neat solution to a thorny problem and historians are still trying to determine how or where Darby got it. . . . A newer though still not totally convincing view contends that the doctrine initially appeared in a prophetic vision of Margaret Macdonald. . . . Possibly, we may have to settle for Darby's own explanation. He claimed that the doctrine virtually jumped out of the pages of Scripture once he accepted and consistently maintained the distinction between Israel and the church.[15]

Posttribulationist William E. Bell asserts,

> It seems only fair, however, in the absence of eyewitnesses to settle the argument conclusively, that the benefit of the doubt should be given to Darby. . . . This conclusion is greatly strengthened by Darby's own claim to have arrived at the doctrine through his study of II Thessalonians 2:1-2.[16]

The renowned New Testament scholar F. F. Bruce, who did not agree with pretribulationism, says the following about Darby and his pre-Trib Rapture view:

> Where did he [Darby] get it? The reviewer's answer would be that it was in the air in the 1820s and 1830s among eager students of unfulfilled prophecy. . . . Direct dependence by Darby on Margaret Macdonald is unlikely.[17]

Edward Irving

Another false claim about the origin of the pre-Trib Rapture is that Darby stole the idea from a man named Edward Irving (1792–1834) and his followers, known as the Irvingites, and then claimed it as his own discovery.[18] A closer examination of Irving's teachings reveals that this was not the case.

Irvingite eschatology viewed the entire church age as the Tribulation. The major point was that Babylon (false Christianity) was about to be destroyed and then the Second Coming would occur. Irving also taught that the Second Coming was synonymous with the Rapture.[19] He believed that raptured saints would stay in heaven until the earth was renovated by fire. Then they would return to the earth. In contrast to Darby's view, Irving did not teach a separate Rapture, followed by the Tribulation, culminating in the Second Coming.

Columba Graham Flegg notes,

> Darby introduced the concept of a *secret* rapture to take place at "any moment," a belief which subsequently became one of the

> chief hallmarks of Brethren eschatology. He also taught that the "true" Church was invisible and spiritual. . . . There were thus very significant differences between the two eschatologies, and attempts to see any direct influence of one upon the other seem unlikely to succeed—they had a number of common *roots*, but are much more notable for their points of disagreement. Several writers have attempted to trace Darby's secret rapture theory to a prophetic statement associated with Irving, but their arguments do not stand up to serious criticism.[20]

Other scholars who have researched Irvingite views of Bible prophecy agree with Flegg's informed conclusion that the Irvingites never held to pretribulationism. Ernest R. Sandeen declares,

> This seems to be a groundless and pernicious charge. Neither Irving nor any member of the Albury group advocated any doctrine resembling the secret rapture. . . . Since the clear intention of this charge is to discredit the doctrine by attributing its origin to fanaticism rather than Scripture, there seems little ground for giving it any credence.[21]

John Walvoord's assessment is likely close to the truth:

> Any careful student of Darby soon discovers that he did not get his eschatological views from men, but rather from his doctrine of the church as the body of Christ, a concept no one claims was revealed supernaturally to Irving or Macdonald. Darby's views undoubtedly were gradually formed, but they were theologically and biblically based rather than derived from Irving's pre-Pentecostal group.[22]

Conclusion

It seems clear that John Nelson Darby developed his view of the pre-Trib Rapture from his own study and not from Edward Irving, Margaret

Macdonald, or any other source. Darby, like all of us, was a product of his times. Premillennial thinking was flowering at Trinity College in Dublin when he attended, as was a more literal method of interpretation, which undoubtedly influenced him. Even so, it is highly doubtful that Edward Irving or Margaret Macdonald even held to a pre-Trib Rapture position, let alone that Darby was directly influenced by them or stole and appropriated their view as his own.

Nevertheless, even if it could be demonstrated that Darby was influenced in some way by others, this does not disprove the pre-Trib view. The pre-Trib position is not dependent on John Nelson Darby. He was not the originator of the position. Ultimately, like every other issue of biblical interpretation, the final question is, what does the Bible teach? Tim LaHaye summarizes the issue well:

> John Darby gained his views primarily from his study of the Word of God, the inspiration of the Holy Spirit, and the influence of emerging premillennial biblical literalists, who were moving from the Historical school of interpreting prophecy to the Futurist position. But even if he didn't, that doesn't change anything. The pre-Trib position is supported by Scripture. Surely that is enough![23]

CHAPTER 14

QUESTIONS ABOUT THE RAPTURE

People have all kinds of questions related to the events surrounding the Rapture. While we don't have space to answer them all, here are three questions I most commonly hear about the Rapture.

If All Believers Are Raptured *before* the Tribulation, Who Are the Believers on Earth *during* the Tribulation?

I have argued that Jesus will return to rapture His people before the Tribulation begins. This is the first phase of Christ's second coming. At the end of the Tribulation, the second phase will occur. Jesus will return from heaven to earth at His glorious second coming. Here's how Matthew 24:31 describes it: "He will send forth His angels with a GREAT TRUMPET and THEY WILL GATHER TOGETHER His elect from the four winds, from one end of the sky to the other" (NASB). This raises a very important question. If Jesus raptures all believers before the Tribulation begins, who are these believers ("His elect") who are still on earth during the Tribulation? Did Jesus forget some believers? Do some believers get left behind for some reason?

Pretribulationists, like myself, hold that these "elect" in Matthew 24 are Jewish believers who will be saved after the Rapture during the Tribulation period. These people are often referred to as "Tribulation believers" or "Tribulation saints." In Revelation 7 two groups of Tribulation believers are distinguished: 144,000 Jewish believers (twelve thousand from each of the twelve tribes of Israel; 7:1-8), and a numberless company of Gentiles who will be martyred for their faith (7:9-14). (Posttribulationists say that these "elect" are the church on earth who have survived the Tribulation.)

But if all these Jews and Gentiles are going to come to faith in Christ during the Tribulation and all believers are removed, how will those who are left behind hear the gospel? The Bible doesn't tell us specifically, but we can imagine what will transpire. I've heard many say over the years that it may be that each of the 144,000 Jews will have a personal "Damascus Road experience" like Paul had. Whatever the case, we know that they will be saved and powerfully used by God to spread the gospel message around the globe.

Surely, millions of people will be frantically searching for answers in the aftershock of the Rapture. The Rapture will be a stunning event. People all over the earth will vanish into thin air. It will shock the world beyond what we imagine. The Rapture itself may be the greatest evangelistic tool in human history. Churches may be overflowing as people everywhere try to make sense out of what's happened. No doubt many will turn to the Bible for answers, listen to recorded sermons, watch Christian DVDs, or read Christian books, especially ones about the end times (maybe even this book). Certainly, many will believe in Christ by calling to mind the truth of the gospel that someone took time to share with them before the Rapture. The prospect of this should motivate us to share the gospel wherever and whenever we can. We never know when God may use the power of His gospel to bring people to life.

We don't know for sure what means God will use to save people during the Tribulation. But it will happen. Jesus said that during the Tribulation, "this gospel of the kingdom shall be preached in the whole world as a testimony to all the nations, and then the end will come"

(Matthew 24:14, NASB). May God help us to faithfully do all we can to spread His message while there's still time.

If Believers Are Raptured to Heaven before the Tribulation, Why Does the Bible Tell Us So Much about the Seven-Year Tribulation?

The Bible contains a great deal of very specific information about the seven-year Tribulation (more on this in parts 6-9). Long passages in the Old Testament vividly depict the coming time of worldwide cataclysm. Revelation devotes fourteen chapters to this seven-year period. But this raises a very important question that I have heard many times: If believers will be raptured before the Tribulation, why does God give us so much information about it? Why would the Lord warn believers in such detail about what's ahead if we will not be here?

There are at least three key reasons why God gave us this information and why we should take time to learn about the key events and players in the Tribulation.

First, Revelation is like a final examination in theology. From Genesis to Jude, the Lord reveals great truths about Himself, man, creation, sin, God's Word, salvation, the church, angels, Satan and demons, and the end times. In Revelation 6–18, and elsewhere, God presents the conditions on earth during the Tribulation.

The Tribulation shines the spotlight on many major theological truths. Above all, the Tribulation culminates all that the first sixty-five books of the Bible teach us about God, Satan, and the nature of man. It teaches us that man is totally depraved, easily deceived, and disobedient. We learn that God sovereignly controls history, keeps His promises, and fulfills prophecy. We also discover that God is holy and that He pours out His wrath against sin, but also that He is infinitely gracious and will save millions of people even in history's darkest hour (Revelation 7:9-14).

The Tribulation also uncovers Satan. Thomas Ice and Timothy Demy note, "Satan is unmasked and we see his ultimate intentions and purposes. Such an understanding of his plan, if properly applied, can aid the believer today in spiritual warfare. For example, we note that during the tribulation, Satan uses religion in a false and deceptive way. This stands as a warning for us today."[1] Studying the Tribulation gives us valuable insight for living today.

Second, the Tribulation is a flashing red light concerning the consequences of sin. John MacArthur drives this point home:

> Some have asked why the Lord would warn people during the New Testament times as He does in this message, when He knew they would never live to experience these terrible signs. Indeed, why include this in the Gospel account, where it has stood as a warning to the church in every generation? But a similar question could be asked about Isaiah's prophecy and his warnings about the Babylonian captivity (Isaiah 39:6-7), which did not occur until after all the people in Isaiah's generation were dead. The message is given to be a warning to all about the consequences of sin—and it will stand as a specific warning to those who will actually experience the terrible judgment.[2]

Third, even though believers will not experience the Tribulation, the Lord loves to take His own people into His confidence and tell us what lies ahead. Remember Genesis 18. God came to Abraham and told him that He was going to destroy the wicked cities of Sodom and Gomorrah. This revelation had no immediate impact on Abraham. He didn't live in these cities. He was not going to be there when God's judgment fell. But God told Abraham about it anyway because Abraham was the friend of God (2 Chronicles 20:7; James 2:23). The Lord said to Abraham, "Shall I hide from Abraham what I am about to do, since Abraham will surely become a great and mighty nation, and in him all the nations of the earth will be blessed? For I have chosen him" (Genesis 18:17-19, NASB). This revelation led Abraham to plead for God's mercy and the salvation of the people in these cities.

Similarly, even though believers will not be here during the Tribulation, God has graciously taken us into His confidence and showed us what He will do on earth during the final dark days of this age. Jesus said that we, too, are His friends (Luke 12:4; John 15:14-15). And like Abraham, having received the revelation of what's ahead, we should be moved to pray for those who are still under the wrath of God. What a privilege it is to know the mind of God and His prophetic program for the final seven years of this present age.

Three Views of What Happens to Babies and Young Children at the Rapture[3]

Parents frequently ask what will happen at the Rapture to babies and young children if they are too young to understand what it means to trust Christ for salvation. First, there is no specific Scripture that addresses this subject. Nevertheless, there are three main views on this issue.

View #1: No Children Will Be Included in the Rapture

Those who hold this view emphasize that the Rapture is only for believers and that if a person has not personally believed in Christ, he or she is not eligible for the Rapture. They would point out that in the Flood and Israel's conquest of Canaan, small children were not excluded from the judgment.

View #2: All Infants and Young Children Will Be Raptured to Heaven before the Tribulation

Adherents of this view point out Scripture's strong implication that children who die have a place in heaven. Several passages in the Bible seem to support this position: 2 Samuel 12:20-23; Matthew19:13-15; Mark 10:13-16. Because these passages suggest that all young children or infants who have never put saving faith in Christ go to heaven if they die, many argue that they will also go to heaven in the Rapture. This is the view presented in the Left Behind series. All children under the age of twelve are raptured, regardless of the spiritual condition of their parents.

I do agree that infants and small children who die go to heaven to be with Christ, but I do not believe that this necessarily means they will participate in the Rapture. These are two different issues.

View #3: Infants and Young Children of Believers Will Be Raptured to Heaven before the Tribulation

The third view mediates between views 1 and 2. While one should avoid dogmatism on this issue, I believe this is the best view for two reasons. First, Paul reminds us in 1 Corinthians 7:14 that in a family with a believing parent the children are set apart for him. It's inconceivable to me that the Lord would rapture believing parents to heaven and leave their defenseless children alone in the world for the Tribulation period.

Second, I believe there is biblical precedent for this view. When the Lord flooded the earth during the days of Noah, the entire world was destroyed, including unbelieving men, women, and children. But God delivered Noah, his wife, and his three sons and their wives. Likewise when God destroyed Sodom and Gomorrah, he destroyed all the inhabitants of the cities, including the children of unbelievers. The only ones to escape were Lot and his two daughters. Also, in Egypt at the first Passover, the blood of the lamb on the doorpost protected the believers' households, including their young children. In each of these cases, the children of believers were delivered from judgment, while unbelievers and their children were not.

Noah's three sons and Lot's daughters were not infants or small children and were probably believers themselves, but I believe that these incidents provide biblical precedent for the fact that, when God sends cataclysmic judgment, he rescues both the believer and the believer's children but allows unbelievers and their children to face judgment.

I believe that during the Tribulation the young children of unbelievers will have the opportunity to believe in Christ as they come of age during the Tribulation period. Those who die during the Tribulation before they are old enough to understand the claims of the gospel will be taken to heaven to be with Christ.

Finally, regardless of which view one holds, the one fact we can all rest in is that God is a God of love, compassion, mercy, and justice. Whatever He does when the Rapture occurs will be wise, righteous, and fair. God loves our children more than we do. Indeed, they are "precious in His sight."

CHAPTER 15

THE MEANING OF THE RAPTURE FOR EVERYDAY LIFE

It has always fascinated me that every key New Testament passage on the Rapture contains a practical application closely associated with it. The message is crystal clear—anticipating the Rapture should change the way we live. According to the Bible, understanding the Rapture should have at least six life-changing influences on our hearts.[1]

1. The Rapture Has a Converting Influence on Seeking Hearts

No person knows how much time he or she has left on this earth, either personally or prophetically. Personally, all of us are painfully aware of our mortality. We have no guarantee we will see tomorrow. Prophetically, Christ could come at any moment to take His bride, the church, to heaven, and all unbelievers will be left behind to endure the Tribulation period.

With life's brevity in mind, the most important question for every reader to face is whether he or she has a personal relationship with Jesus Christ as Savior. Salvation through Jesus Christ is a message that contains both bad news and good news.

The bad news is that the Bible declares that all people, including you and me, are sinful and therefore separated from the holy God of the universe (Isaiah 59:2; Romans 3:23). God is holy and cannot simply overlook sin. A just payment for the debt must be made. But we are spiritually bankrupt and have no resources within ourselves to pay the huge debt we owe.

The Good News, or gospel, is that Jesus Christ has come and satisfied our sin debt. He bore our judgment and paid the price for our sins. He died on the cross for our sins and was raised to life on the third day to complete the work of salvation. Colossians 2:14 says that God "canceled out the certificate of debt consisting of decrees against us, which was hostile to us; and He has taken it out of the way, having nailed it to the cross" (NASB). First Peter 3:18 says, "Christ also died for sins once for all, the just for the unjust, so that He might bring us to God" (NASB).

The salvation that Christ accomplished is offered to all of us through faith in Jesus Christ. Salvation from sin is a free gift that God offers to sinful people who deserve judgment. Won't you receive the gift today? Place your faith and trust in Christ, and in Him alone, for your eternal salvation (Acts 16:31). Now that you know the truth of the Rapture and that those who fail to trust Christ will be left behind to endure the Tribulation, won't you respond to the invitation before it is too late? Accept Christ personally by calling upon Him to save you from your sins. Make sure you are Rapture ready!

2. The Rapture Has a Caring Influence on Soul-Winning Hearts

No believer can study Bible prophecy without being gripped by the awesome power and wrath of God. Just a simple reading of Revelation 6–18 reminds us of what is in store for this earth after the Rapture. Scripture also describes the eternal horrors that await those who die without trusting Christ. The Bible brings us face-to-face with what is at stake for those who don't know Christ as their Savior. Second Corinthians 5:20 reminds us of our calling during this present age: "Therefore, we are ambassadors for Christ, as though God were making an appeal through us; we beg you on behalf of Christ, be reconciled to God" (NASB). Those who have already responded to the message of God's grace and forgiveness through Christ know the world's future, and we are Christ's ambassadors, representing Him and His heart to a perishing world. We should care deeply about those who are still lost, willingly give of our material resources to help spread the gospel message, and regularly ask the Lord for opportunities and boldness to share the Good News of Christ. A clear understanding of the Rapture should exert a strong influence on every believer to care about the lost before time runs out.

3. The Rapture Has a Cleansing Influence on Sinning Hearts

When people used to come up to Donald Grey Barnhouse, the pastor of Tenth Presbyterian Church in Philadelphia, and ask him a prophecy question, he would ask them if they knew 1 John 3:2-3. If they said no, then he told them to go look it up and read it before he would answer their question. Barnhouse wanted to make sure that those interested in the Lord's coming were living in light of it.

> Beloved, now we are children of God, and it has not appeared as yet what we will be. We know that when He appears, we will be like Him, because we will see Him just as He is. And everyone who has this hope fixed on Him purifies himself, just as He is pure.
>
> 1 JOHN 3:2-3 (NASB)

A proper understanding of the Rapture should produce a life of holiness and purity. Focusing the mind and heart on Christ's coming can powerfully motivate our efforts toward living a pure life. Note the certainty: "And everyone who has this hope fixed on Him purifies himself, just as He is pure." Here is a perfect prescription for living a life of holiness—focusing on the Rapture. How can we be riveted by the Rapture and live an impure life at the same time? First John 3:3 says it can't happen. Fixing our hope on Christ and His coming is a purifying hope.

In 2011, Harold Camping set two different dates for the Rapture. Of course, he was wrong both times. I always like to say when someone sets a date for the Rapture that you can be sure that's not the day. All date setting is foolish and futile (Matthew 24:36; Luke 21:8). However, I'm sure that Camping's reckless actions did cause some people to reexamine their lives just in case he might be correct.

We are to live as if Jesus could come at any time, and if this becomes real to us it will transform our lives. The Bible declares that we are to always be looking for Christ's coming, not just when someone sets an arbitrary date. "Live sensibly, righteously and godly in the present age, looking for the blessed hope and the appearing of the glory of our great God and Savior, Jesus Christ" (Titus 2:12-13, NASB).

Prophecy and purity are mentioned together in Romans 13:11-14:

> This is all the more urgent, for you know how late it is; time is running out. Wake up, for our salvation is nearer now than when we first believed. The night is almost gone; the day of salvation will soon be here. So remove your dark deeds like dirty clothes, and put on the shining armor of right living. Because we belong to the day, we must live decent lives for all to see. Don't participate in the darkness of wild parties and drunkenness, or in sexual promiscuity and immoral living, or in quarreling and jealousy. Instead, clothe yourself with the presence of the Lord Jesus Christ. And don't let yourself think about ways to indulge your evil desires.

Second Peter 3:10-14 also presents the practical, cleansing effect of prophecy.

> The day of the Lord will come like a thief, in which the heavens will pass away with a roar and the elements will be destroyed with intense heat, and the earth and its works will be burned up. Since all these things are to be destroyed in this way, what sort of people ought you to be in holy conduct and godliness, looking for and hastening the coming of the day of God, because of which the heavens will be destroyed by burning, and the elements will melt

> with intense heat! But according to His promise we are looking for new heavens and a new earth, in which righteousness dwells. Therefore, beloved, since you look for these things, be diligent to be found by Him in peace, spotless and blameless. (NASB)

When anyone says that studying Bible prophecy is impractical or irrelevant to everyday life, they reveal that they don't understand what the Bible says about the personal impact of prophecy. In an immoral, sinful society like ours what could be more important and down to earth than personal purity? Many people view prophecy as having no real impact on everyday life. Living a godly life is the essence of a walk with Christ. What could be more practical?

4. The Rapture Has a Calming Influence on Stirring Hearts

Another practical effect of the Rapture is that it calms us down when our hearts are troubled and stirred up. In John 14:1-3 Jesus says, "Do not let your heart be troubled; believe in God, believe also in Me. In my Father's house are many dwelling places; if it were not so, I would have told you; for I go to prepare a place for you. If I go and prepare a place for you, I will come again and receive you to Myself, that where I am, there you may be also" (NASB).

The word *troubled* means "to be stirred up, disturbed, unsettled, or thrown into confusion." There are many things in our world today to disturb and unsettle us: moral decay, crime, economic uncertainty, terrorism, fear of pandemics, social unrest, and others. Added to these problems are the personal trials and difficulties we all face in our daily lives. Trouble is the common denominator of all humankind (Job 5:7). Often these troubles and difficulties can leave us distraught, distracted, and disturbed. One of the great comforts in times like these is to remember that our Lord will someday return to take us to be with Himself.

In John 14:1-3, Jesus emphasizes three things that can calm our troubled hearts—a person, a place, and a promise. The person is our Lord, the place is the heavenly city (new Jerusalem), and the promise is that He will come again to take us to be with Him forever.

5. The Rapture Has a Comforting Influence on Sorrowing Hearts

Every person has faced or will face the grief of losing a close friend or loved one in death. When death strikes, pious platitudes do little to bring lasting comfort to friends and family. The only real, lasting comfort is the hope that we will see that person again in heaven. God's Word tells us with certainty that we are not to sorrow as people who have no hope because we will be reunited with our saved loved ones and friends at the Rapture.

> Dear brothers and sisters, we want you to know what will happen to the believers who have died so you will not grieve like people who have no hope. For since we believe that Jesus died and was raised to life again, we also believe that when Jesus returns, God will bring back with him the believers who have died.
>
> We tell you this directly from the Lord: We who are still living when the Lord returns will not meet him ahead of those who have died. For the Lord himself will come down from heaven with a commanding shout, with the voice of the archangel, and with the trumpet call of God. First, the Christians who have died will rise from their graves. Then, together with them, we who are still alive and remain on the earth will be caught up in the clouds to meet the Lord in the air. Then we will be with the Lord forever. So encourage each other with these words.
>
> 1 THESSALONIANS 4:13-18

The Rapture and Resurrection should transform the way we view death. Death has lost its sting. God has promised that death will ultimately be abolished and that life will reign. Grief is still appropriate when our friends or loved ones die. Jesus wept at the tomb of Lazarus (John 11:35). Stephen's friends wept loudly over his battered body (Acts 8:2). We miss our loved ones when they die. As Tennyson put so beautifully, "O for the touch of a vanished hand / And the sound of a voice that is still." However, the Bible declares that our weeping is not the weeping of despair. There is deep solace, hope, and comfort for our sorrowing hearts in the truth of God's Word about the future for His children.

6. The Rapture Has a Controlling Influence on Serving Hearts

So many today are unstable and unsettled in Christian work. They are constantly vacillating. Knowing about Christ's coming and future events should cure the problem of instability and inconsistency in Christian labor. In 1 Corinthians 15:58, after presenting the truth of the Rapture and the Resurrection, Paul concludes with a strong admonition: "Therefore, my beloved brethren, be steadfast, immovable, always abounding in the work of the Lord, knowing that your toil is not in vain in the Lord" (NASB). Paul is saying, since you know that Christ will someday come to receive you to Himself, let nothing move you, and be strong and steady in your Christian service. Realizing that Christ could return at any time is to make us energetic and excited about serving the Lord. The first two questions Saul, who later became Paul, asked when he saw the glorified Christ on the road to Damascus were "Who are You, Lord?" and "What shall I do, Lord?" (Acts 22:8, 10, NASB). Many professing Christians today have never moved past the first question. Many believers in Christ are spiritually unemployed!

If the Rapture is a reality to us, it will motivate us to work faithfully for our Lord. The Lord intends for our knowledge of Bible prophecy to translate into devoted service for those around us as we await His return. The principle in the Bible is clear: waiters are workers. When Christ comes we are to "be dressed for service and keep [our] lamps burning" (Luke 12:35).

Warren Wiersbe tells a story of when he was a young man preaching on the last days with all the events of prophecy clearly laid out and perfectly planned. At the end of the service an older gentleman came up to him and whispered in his ear, "I used to have the Lord's return planned out to the last detail, but years ago I moved from the planning committee to the welcoming committee."

Certainly we want to study Bible prophecy and know about God's plan for the future. That's what this book is all about. But we must be careful not to get too caught up in the planning and forget the welcoming. Are you on the welcoming committee for the Lord's coming? Are you living each day to please the Master? May God help our knowledge of the Rapture to transform our lives as we eagerly await the coming of our Savior.

PART 4

The Judgment Seat of Christ

There is a story about a frustrated basketball coach, Cotton Fitzsimmons, who hit on an idea to motivate his team. Before the game he gave them a speech that centered around the word pretend. *"Gentlemen, when you go out there tonight, instead of remembering that we are in last place, pretend we are in first place; instead of being in a losing streak, pretend we are in a winning streak; instead of this being a regular game, pretend this is a play-off game!" With that, the team went onto the basketball court and were soundly beaten by the Boston Celtics. Coach Fitzsimmons was upset about the loss. But one of the players slapped him on the back and said, "Cheer up, Coach! Pretend we won!"*

Many of us appear to be winning in the race of life, but perhaps it is all "pretend." Standing before Christ we will soon see the difference between an actual victory and wishful thinking. We will see what it took to win and what it took to lose. We'll discover that we were playing for keeps.

ERWIN W. LUTZER, *Your Eternal Reward*[1]

CHAPTER 16

STANDING BEFORE THE *BEMA*

GOD'S PROPHETIC PROGRAM for the church will begin with the Rapture. The next major event for the church will be the judgment seat of Christ in heaven. At the judgment seat all believers from the church age—the time between the Day of Pentecost and the Rapture—will appear individually before God to receive rewards or loss of reward based on their life, service, and ministry for the Lord. This will be the first of seven great future judgments that will occur.

The Future Judgments

1. The Judgment Seat of Christ (2 Corinthians 5:10)

   Church-age believers will appear before the judgment seat of Christ in heaven for reward.
2. Old Testament Believers (Daniel 12:1-3)

   All Old Testament believers will be resurrected and rewarded after the Second Coming.

3. Tribulation Believers (Revelation 20:4-6)

   Those who trust Christ during the Tribulation and are martyred will be resurrected and rewarded at the end of the Tribulation.

4. Jews Living at the Second Coming (Ezekiel 20:34-38)

   All Jews who survive the Tribulation will be judged right after the Second Coming. The saved will enter the millennial kingdom, and the lost will be purged.

5. Gentiles Living at the Second Coming (Matthew 25:31-46)

   All Gentiles who survive the Tribulation will be judged immediately after the Second Coming when Christ sits on His glorious throne. This is often referred to as the judgment of the "sheep and the goats." The righteous will enter the millennial kingdom, and the unrighteous will be cast into hell.

6. Satan and Fallen Angels (Revelation 20:10)

   The final judgment of Satan and fallen angels (demons) will take place after the millennial kingdom (Matthew 25:41; 2 Peter 2:4; Jude 6).

7. The Great White Throne (Revelation 20:11-15)

   The judgment of unrighteous people will occur at the end of the Millennium. They will be judged according to their works and cast into the lake of fire.

The Bible is clear that God is not only a judge but also a rewarder.[1] God will judge and reward church-age believers at the "judgment seat of Christ" (2 Corinthians 5:10, NASB).

Romans 13:12 reminds us that "the night is almost gone; the day of salvation will soon be here. So remove your dark deeds like dirty clothes, and put on the shining armor of right living." No one can deny that time is hastening on. The time of the Lord's coming and our final judgment before Him is drawing near. God's judgment is one of life's most sobering thoughts. The great American statesman Daniel Webster was once asked about the greatest thought to ever enter his mind. He responded, "The most important thought that ever occupied my mind is 'my accountability to God.'" What gripped Webster was the knowledge that one day he would stand before God. Years ago I read a quote from the Scottish theologian James Denney, who said, "Is it not a solemn thing to stand at the end of life?" Since every person will face that day, the day when we will stand before our Lord, and give account of our lives to Him, it is incumbent upon us to get ready for it, and part of getting ready is understanding what the Bible says about that future event known as the judgment seat of Christ.

To help us unpack its meaning, the judgment seat of Christ will be considered under seven main headings: the period (when), the place (where), the participants (who), the purpose (why), the principles (how), the pictures (what), and the preparation (getting ready).

The Period of the Judgment

The judgment seat of Christ will occur in heaven immediately after the church is raptured to heaven. First Corinthians 4:5 places this judgment right after the Lord comes at the Rapture: "Don't make judgments about anyone ahead of time—before the Lord returns. For he will bring our darkest secrets to light and will reveal our private motives. Then God will give to each one whatever praise is due." The judgment seat will be the first order of business after the Rapture.

The Place of the Judgment

Since the judgment seat takes place after the Rapture, it makes sense that it will take place in heaven at the judgment seat of Christ. Second Corinthians 5:10 says, "We must all appear before the judgment seat of Christ, so that each one may be recompensed for his deeds in the body, according to what he has done, whether good or bad" (NASB). In ancient times, a *bema*—the Greek word for *judgment seat*—referred to a raised step or platform, much like a judge's bench in a modern courtroom. A *bema* was set up for three major purposes in New Testament times.

First, the bema was a court of justice where people came to have their grievances redressed. Some Jews hauled Paul before the judgment seat of Gallio in the marketplace of Corinth (Acts 18:12). Second, the judgment seat was also a place in a military camp where the commander administered discipline and addressed the troops. Third, the judgment seat was the stand at the athletic games from which the rules were enforced and rewards were distributed. This third picture seems to be the primary backdrop for the judgment seat of Christ in Scripture. The bema is the place where Christ will reward those who have finished the race and obeyed the rules and where He will withhold reward from those who have been unfaithful. It's called the judgment seat "of Christ" because Jesus will be the judge. John 5:22 says, "The Father judges no one. Instead, he has given the Son absolute authority to judge."

The Participants of the Judgment

The judgment seat of Christ is for believers only, and the judgment seat is not optional. In 2 Corinthians 5:10, Paul says that "*we must all* stand before Christ to be judged" (emphasis added), and the context clearly indicates that he is including himself and other believers. The word *we* refers to believers in Christ, and just so we don't miss it, Paul includes the word *all.* No believer is exempt. Every person reading these words will appear at one of two great judgments; there are other, later judgments, and we'll talk about them, but these two judgments are relevant to readers today. Believers will appear at the judgment seat to be rewarded. Unbelievers will appear later at the Great White Throne Judgment to be condemned (Revelation 20:11-15).

The Purpose of the Judgment

To understand the purpose of this judgment, it is important to know what it *is not*. The purpose of the judgment seat of Christ *is not* to determine whether people will enter heaven or hell or to punish sin. This ultimate issue is decided when a person believes in Jesus Christ as his or her Savior from sin. God's Word is clear that His children will never be judged for their sins (John 5:24; Romans 8:1). Our salvation rests wholly on the person and work of Christ in our place.

If the purpose of the judgment seat is not to determine if we get into heaven, what is its purpose? The issue at the judgment seat is not salvation but rewards. Salvation is based wholly on Christ's work for us (Ephesians 2:8-9).

Rewards are based on our works for Christ after we trust in Him. The purpose of the judgment seat of Christ is twofold: to review and to reward.

Review

First, the Lord will review our lives as believers (Romans 14:10-12). At the judgment seat God will evaluate the actions of believers after they came to faith in Christ. Only after conversion is one truly able to serve God with proper motives. Let's look at two key passages that talk about God's judgment of believers.

> We must all appear before the judgment seat of Christ, so that each one may be recompensed for his deeds in the body, according to what he has done, whether good or bad.
> 2 CORINTHIANS 5:10 (NASB)

> Each man's work will become evident; for the day will show it because it is to be revealed with fire, and the fire itself will test the quality of each man's work.
> 1 CORINTHIANS 3:13 (NASB)

Second Corinthians 5:10 says every believer must face judgment "according to what he has done, whether good or bad." But what does Paul mean by "good or bad"? What are these "bad" works? The word *bad* is the Greek word *phaulos,* which refers to "bad" in the sense of worthless, or inferior in quality, not in the sense of evil. They are what we might call *bad* good works. What makes these things bad or worthless? They are done with the wrong motive (1 Corinthians 4:5; Hebrews 4:13). They are good things in themselves, but done for selfish reasons. Such motives are not worthy of reward, despite the good that results from them. (They are probably parallel to the "wood, hay, or straw" in 1 Corinthians 3:12.)

God knows not only what we do, but why we do it. Examining our motives is the most searching aspect of His evaluation. In 2 Corinthians 5:10 the word *appear* means "to be made manifest, disclosed, made known."

At the judgment seat, every believer's conduct, service, and motives will be turned inside out and will appear for what they were. We can often fool other people about our service and motives, and they may think we are doing some great things for God. But we can't fool God, and His reward will be based on His right evaluation of our actions, words, and attitudes.

> Beware of practicing your righteousness before men to be noticed by them; otherwise you have no reward with your Father who is in heaven. So when you give to the poor, do not sound a trumpet before you, as the hypocrites do in the synagogues and in the streets, so that they may be honored by men. Truly I say to you, they have their *reward in full*. . . . When you pray, you are not to be like the hypocrites; for they love to stand and pray in the synagogues and on the street corners so that they may be seen by men. Truly I say to you, they have their *reward in full*. . . . Whenever you fast, do not put on a gloomy face as the hypocrites do, for they neglect their appearance so that they will be noticed by men when they are fasting. Truly I say to you, they have their *reward in full*.
>
> MATTHEW 6:1-2, 5, 16 (NASB, ITALICS ADDED)

"Reward in full" is the translation of a Greek word that means "to be paid in full, to receive a receipt for full payment." Jesus, three times, is saying that if we serve God to receive praise and notoriety from others, we had better enjoy whatever accolades we receive, because that is all we will ever get. Many who we believe will receive great reward may walk away with very little, and those who we are sure will receive hardly anything may be the most rewarded among us. Remember Jesus' words in Matthew 20:16: "Those who are last now will be first then, and those who are first will be last." Jesus judges our motives. He sees it all.

A group of children was lined up in the cafeteria of a Catholic elementary school for lunch. At the head of the table was a large pile of apples. A nun posted a note on the apple tray: "Take only one. Remember, God is watching." Moving further along the lunch line, at the other end of the table was a large pile of chocolate chip cookies. A child had written a note, "Take all you want. God is watching the apples." The truth is—God is watching the apples and the cookies. God knows everything. His omniscient eye not only sees *to us*; He sees *through us*. The first purpose of the bema judgment is to review the lives of believers.

Reward

You might be thinking, *Since that's the case, I probably won't get anything then. I will surely walk away from the bema empty-handed.* We probably all feel that way. I know that at my best I can't think of anything I do without some of my own pride and ego in it. I don't do anything with 100 percent pure motives unless it's something I do so quickly that I don't have any time to think about it. Any reward I get will be purely due to the grace of God. But the Scriptures give us hope and reassurance that our Lord in His grace will reward us.

This is the second purpose of the judgment seat of Christ—to reward. Jim Elliot, the martyred missionary, once said, "He is no fool who gives what he cannot keep to gain what he cannot lose." Those who have faithfully served the Lord and poured out their lives for Him will gain an eternal reward that they can never lose.

I love the words of 1 Corinthians 4:5: "Each man's praise will come to him from God" (NASB). The Lord will find something in the life of every believer to praise and reward. Stop and think about that for a moment. The Lord of the ages, the creator of the universe, the shepherd of the stars, will praise each one who has trusted in Christ.

While many areas of service, conduct, and ministry will undoubtedly bring reward, the New Testament focuses on five specific rewards, sometimes called crowns, that the faithful will receive at the judgment seat. These crowns represent the kinds of conduct and service that the Lord will reward.

1. THE INCORRUPTIBLE CROWN (1 CORINTHIANS 9:24-27, KJV)

The reward for those who consistently practice self-discipline and self-control is the crown that will not fade away.

2. THE CROWN OF RIGHTEOUSNESS (2 TIMOTHY 4:8)

The crown of righteousness is the reward for those who eagerly look for the Lord's coming and live a righteous life in view of this fact.

3. THE CROWN OF LIFE (JAMES 1:12; REVELATION 2:10)

The sufferer's crown is given to those who faithfully endure and persevere under the trials and tests of life.

4. THE CROWN OF REJOICING (1 THESSALONIANS 2:19, KJV)

The soul winner's crown is given to those who win people for Christ.

5. THE CROWN OF GLORY (1 PETER 5:1-4)

The shepherd's crown will be given to those pastors, elders, and church leaders who lovingly, graciously, faithfully shepherd and oversee God's people.

What will we do with these crowns? Will we wear them around the streets of gold to show off? Will we compare them to the number of crowns others have? The Bible is clear that the redeemed, having been rewarded by the Lord, will immediately give all glory and honor to Him for their rewards. The redeemed will fall down and worship the Lord, "and they [will] lay their crowns before the throne and say, 'You are worthy, O Lord our God, to receive glory and honor and power. For you created all things, and they exist because you created what you pleased'" (Revelation 4:10-11). The crowns of the redeemed will be cast at the feet of the Redeemer in humble gratitude to the only one who is worthy of glory, power, and honor.

In addition to these crowns, there appear to be two other main rewards the faithful will receive. The first one is greater responsibility and authority in the coming Kingdom. This present age is training time for reigning time. Believers will occupy various positions of authority in God's Kingdom based on how well we lived our lives here on earth (Luke 19:13-26). The second reward may be an increased capacity and ability to reflect the Lord's glory. Daniel 12:3 says, "Those who are wise will shine as bright as the sky, and those who lead many to righteousness will shine like the stars forever." I once heard a preacher liken God's people in glory to lightbulbs of different wattages in a chandelier. Some will shine fifteen watts, some forty watts, some seventy-five, and still others one hundred.

Whatever our specific rewards will be, the purpose of the judgment seat is this: the person you are today will determine the rewards you will receive tomorrow. Your life here and my life here will impact our lives forever in eternity.

The Principles of the Judgment

How will believers be judged when they stand before the Lord someday? The Bible identifies five basic principles by which Christ will judge our lives.[2]

1. Believers Will Be Judged Fairly

The Lord's judgment will account for how long we have been following Him as well as the opportunities and abilities He has given us. The parable of the workers in the vineyard teaches that those who enter the Lord's service later in life can receive the same reward as the "all day" workers (Matthew 20:1-16). Length of service does not determine the degree of reward. Jesus the righteous judge will make no mistakes. His rewards will be based on what we did with the opportunities, resources, and time that we had to serve Him, however great or small.

2. Believers Will Be Judged Thoroughly

As has already been noted, the Lord will literally turn us inside out at the judgment seat. Every hidden motive, thought, and deed will be exposed (1 Corinthians 4:5). Nothing will escape the scrutinizing eye of the Savior (Hebrews 4:13).

3. Believers Will Be Judged Impartially

God does not show favoritism (Romans 2:11; Colossians 3:25). If anything, God has a stricter standard for those who teach God's Word and lead the Lord's people. They will be held to a higher degree of accountability (Hebrews 13:17). James 3:1 says, "not many of you should become teachers in the church, for we who teach will be judged more strictly." I once heard someone say, "If you are standing in line at the judgment seat and see a line with a bunch of preachers in it, get in another line. It will go faster." That's true. Those who teach God's Word will be held to a higher standard and will be judged both for the accuracy of what was taught and whether or not they lived it out in their lives (Matthew 5:19).

4. Believers Will Be Judged Individually

Every believer will stand alone before the Lord. Notice how Paul moves from the plural to the singular in these passages: "We will all stand before the judgment seat of God. . . . So then each one of us will give an account of himself to God" (Romans 14:10, 12, NASB). "We must all appear before the judgment seat of Christ, so that each one may be recompensed for his deeds in the body, according to what he has done, whether good or bad" (2 Corinthians 5:10, NASB). Each one of us will have to sing solo before the Lord.

Erwin Lutzer captures something of the drama of our judgment day: "Imagine staring into the face of Christ. Just the two of you, one-on-one! Your entire life is present before you. In a flash you see what He sees. No hiding. No opportunity to put a better spin on what you did. No attorney to represent you. The look in His eyes says it all. Like it or not, that is precisely where you and I shall be someday."[3]

5. Believers Will Be Judged Graciously

The fact that we will receive any rewards or praise at all is a testimony to God's grace. Jesus is a kind and gracious judge who will reward us all much more than we could ever imagine (Matthew 20:13-15).

The Pictures of the Judgment

The New Testament uses three images to help us understand what God will be judging at the bema: a building, a manager, and an athlete.

A Building

The picture of the building shows us that what materials we use matters.

First Corinthians 3:10-15 says,

> Because of God's grace to me, I have laid the foundation like an expert builder. Now others are building on it. But whoever is building on this foundation must be very careful. For no one can lay any foundation other than the one we already have—Jesus Christ.
>
> Anyone who builds on that foundation may use a variety of materials—gold, silver, jewels, wood, hay, or straw. But on the judgment day, fire will reveal what kind of work each builder has done. The fire will show if a person's work has any value. If the work survives, that builder will receive a reward. But if the work is burned up, the builder will suffer great loss. The builder will be saved, but like someone barely escaping through a wall of flames.

In this passage Paul is referring specifically to himself and the leaders at the church in Corinth. Paul had laid the foundation while he was in Corinth teaching God's Word for eighteen months (Acts 18:11). When he departed he left that work to others. The main thrust of this passage is how we build the Lord's church. What kind of materials should we use? We must make sure that we are building churches out of precious, spiritual materials that will stand forever. While this passage is aimed at church leaders, these principles can certainly be applied to the life of an individual person. We, too, are building our lives each day and will be held accountable by God for how we have constructed them.

Notice that the foundation of the building and the superstructure are clearly distinguished from each other. The foundation is the Solid Rock, Jesus Christ. He is the only sure foundation on which a life can be built (Matthew 7:24-27). Our salvation rests solely on the foundation. However, the superstructure we build on top of that foundation determines our reward. There is one foundation but many superstructures. And we each select the materials for building our lives. We can select our materials from two basic categories: (1) worthless/temporary, and (2) valuable/lasting. The worthless materials are referred to as "wood, hay, straw," while the valuable materials are "gold, silver, precious stones."

At the church where I pastor, when we have added on to our church building, the final step has always been an inspection by the city. It is the inspector's job to make sure that all the codes have been followed, the proper materials have been used, and the building has been properly constructed. God's Word says that someday the building inspector is coming to inspect our lives. What kind of building are you constructing? Are you building your life of materials that will keep their value when the time of testing comes?

A Steward

The second picture is of a manager and shows us that God is looking for faithfulness (1 Corinthians 4:1-2). God owns everything we have. We are simply stewards, managers, or caretakers of the Lord's gifts and property while He is away.

At the judgment seat the Lord will evaluate how we used the time, treasure, and talents He entrusted to us (Matthew 25:14-30). Rewards will not be based on how much money or talent we possessed or how long we served, but rather how faithful we were with what we were given. The issue for the manager is faithfulness to his master. God will evaluate our faithfulness, not our "success." For God, success is faithfulness. Those who have been faithful managers will one day receive the master's praise: "Well done, my good and faithful servant" (Matthew 25:21).

An Athlete

The third picture is of an athlete. It shows us that discipline and focus are important. This picture is developed in 1 Corinthians 9:24-27.

> Don't you realize that in a race everyone runs, but only one person gets the prize? So run to win! All athletes are disciplined in their training. They do it to win a prize that will fade away,

> but we do it for an eternal prize. So I run with purpose in every step. I am not just shadowboxing. I discipline my body like an athlete, training it to do what it should. Otherwise, I fear that after preaching to others I myself might be disqualified.

Paul's main point is very simple: The same commitment and dedication that make a winning athlete will make a winning Christian. Athletes are willing to subject themselves to the suffering and demands of rigorous training to get a corruptible crown of leaves (or a trophy of plastic, metal, or wood). How much more should Christians be willing to sacrifice for an incorruptible reward in heaven! Just imagine if God's people put the same time, effort, and resources into our Christian lives that we put into our sports. People are willing to invest hundreds of hours and thousands of dollars to improve their tennis backhand or their golf game. What if we were willing to devote the same amount of time and resources into our spiritual race?

We are to live our lives with purpose, dedication, self-control, and discipline, giving maximum effort as we diligently pursue the prize (Philippians 3:12-14). Even the apostle Paul trained himself knowing that he, too, could be disqualified from reward if he lived an undisciplined life. We will only receive rewards as God's athletes if we obey the rules in God's rule book, the Bible. Second Timothy 2:5 reminds us, "Athletes cannot win the prize unless they follow the rules."

I'll never forget watching Ben Johnson shatter the men's 100-meter record in the 1988 Olympics. I was totally amazed. After the race I heard a sports commentator say that he thought the record would stand for one hundred years. But it didn't even stand for one hundred hours. Within a couple of days Ben Johnson had been stripped of his medal for breaking the rules of the games. He was disqualified, his record was deleted, and he was disgraced in front of the entire world. We must sacrifice our own comfort, discipline ourselves, and follow God's rules found in His Word if we are to receive the eternal prize from our Savior.

The Preparation for the Judgment

In school, it doesn't take very long to realize that the most important day is test day. When there is a test, everything is different. The whole mood and atmosphere change. Did you ever notice in class that kids could be talking and goofing around, but if the teacher began to give you the questions on the upcoming test, everyone suddenly got very quiet and began to listen attentively? Knowing the questions ahead of time was helpful.

The great test day is coming for God's children. But like a gracious teacher, God has given us the "test questions" for the judgment seat of Christ beforehand. Knowing these test questions can prepare us to ace the final exam. Here are some of the main areas that will be examined when we stand before the Lord.

1. How we treat other believers (Matthew 10:41-42; Hebrews 6:10)
2. How we employ our God-given talents and abilities (Matthew 25:14-29; Luke 19:11-26; 1 Corinthians 12:4, 7; 2 Timothy 1:6; 1 Peter 4:10)
3. How we use our money (Matthew 6:1-4; 1 Timothy 6:17-19)
4. How well we endure personal injustice and being mistreated (Matthew 5:11-12; Mark 10:29-30; Luke 6:27-28, 35; Romans 8:18; 2 Corinthians 4:17; 1 Peter 4:12-13)
5. How we endure suffering and trials (James 1:12; Revelation 2:10)
6. How we spend our time (Psalm 90:9-12; Ephesians 5:16; Colossians 4:5; 1 Peter 1:17)
7. How we run the particular race God has given us (1 Corinthians 9:24; Philippians 2:16; 3:12-14; Hebrews 12:1)
8. How effectively we control our fleshly appetites (1 Corinthians 9:25-27)
9. How many souls we witness to and win for Christ (Daniel 12:3; 1 Thessalonians 2:19-20)
10. How much the Rapture means to us and shapes our lives (2 Timothy 4:8)

11. How faithful we are to God's Word and God's people (Acts 20:26-28; 2 Timothy 4:1-2; Hebrews 13:17; James 3:1; 1 Peter 5:1-2; 2 John 1:7-8)
12. How hospitable we are to strangers (Matthew 25:35-36; Luke 14:12-14)
13. How faithful we are in our vocations (Colossians 3:22-24)
14. How we support others in ministry (Matthew 10:40-42)
15. How we use our tongues (Matthew 12:36; James 3:1-12)

We have the test questions. Let's get ready. Start cramming for the test so you can get an A. Let's live this day in light of that day, so we can hear those words: "Well done, my good and faithful servant."

Conclusion

Every person on earth has an appointment to stand before God someday. Everyone will be judged. There's no escaping it. The only question is, which judgment will you face? Will you face your Creator as one who trusted in Him or rejected His free offer of eternal life? Every person reading these words should want to participate in the judgment that will occur in heaven immediately following the Rapture—the judgment of believers in Christ. At this judgment the issue will not be sins but service. How did we serve and why did we serve? Jesus Christ will graciously reward His people, giving each of us far more than we deserve or could ever imagine.

The final review and reward at the judgment seat will prepare God's people for the next event in heaven known as the marriage of the Lamb. This event will culminate God's unique prophetic program for the church.

PART 5

The Marriage of the Lamb

A number of weddings are described in the Bible. The first wedding was performed by a very special guest minister. Whatever religious ceremony he may have chosen, it did not include those familiar words: "If any man can show just cause why these two should not be lawfully joined together, let him speak now, or else forever hold his peace." This phrase was unnecessary, for the minister was God himself, and the couple was Adam and Eve (Genesis 2:18-25). Then there was a very unusual wedding in which the bridegroom found out the next morning, by light of day, that he had married the wrong girl (Genesis 29:21-25). One of the most beautiful wedding stories began in a barley field outside the little town of Bethlehem (Ruth 2). Perhaps the most tragic wedding was that between Ahab, King of Israel, and Jezebel, a godless Baal worshiper. This marriage would result in much sorrow and suffering for God's people (1 Kings 16:29-31). Finally, the Savior of men chose a wedding in the city of Cana to perform his first miracle (John 2:1-11). However, the most fantastic and wonderful wedding of all time is yet to take place.

H. L. WILLMINGTON, *The King Is Coming*[1]

CHAPTER 17

A MARRIAGE MADE IN HEAVEN

On April 29, 2011, billions of people around the world watched the royal wedding of Prince William and Kate Middleton. It was the wedding of the new millennium. The cost of the wedding was estimated at around $34 million, compared to the average wedding at $27,000. Here are a few of the staggering prices:

The royal wedding cake: $80,000 (average US price: $540)
Kate Middleton's wedding gown: $434,000 (average US price: $1,099)
The royal wedding flowers: $800,000 (average US price: $1,988)
The ring: $136,000 (average US price: $5,392) The ring, which was originally Princess Diana's, was actually free for the couple. However, Prince Charles purchased it in 1981 for $45,000, and it was estimated to be worth $136,000 in 2011.
Other costs that figured into the $34 million budget included the church service, music, food, decorations, and additional security.

> Prince William and Kate Middleton's wedding actually cost less than the marriage of Prince Charles and Princess Di, which cost somewhere in the neighborhood of $48 million. (Some estimate in today's dollars that could be over $100 million!)[1]

As dazzling and detailed as William and Kate's wedding was, it pales in comparison to a heavenly wedding that is on God's prophetic calendar—the marriage of the Lamb. There are three key future events that comprise God's distinct prophetic plan for the church: the Rapture, the judgment seat of Christ, and the marriage of the Lamb. The church will be caught up to the Father's house, each believer will be rewarded, and then the bride will be presented to her Bridegroom. All this will happen before the church returns with Christ to earth at His second coming.

God Himself is the author of the marriage relationship. It is the first human institution He created. The Bible consistently mentions weddings and marriages to accentuate their importance in God's plan. The Bible mentions at least twenty weddings.[2]

While some of these weddings pleased God and some didn't, the greatest wedding of all time is still to come. The Bible calls it the marriage of the Lamb when the Lord Jesus Christ is joined to His bride, the church, in heaven. It is the next great event in heaven that takes place after the reviewing and rewarding of the saints at the judgment seat of Christ. The main passage in the Bible that describes this joyous event is Revelation 19:7-10:

> "Let us be glad and rejoice,
>   and let us give honor to him.
> For the time has come for the wedding feast of the Lamb,
>   and his bride has prepared herself.
> She has been given the finest of pure white linen to wear."
>   For the fine linen represents the good deeds of God's holy people.
>
> And the angel said to me, "Write this: Blessed are those who are invited to the wedding feast of the Lamb." And he added, "These are true words that come from God."

> Then I fell down at his feet to worship him, but he said, "No, don't worship me. I am a servant of God, just like you and your brothers and sisters who testify about their faith in Jesus. Worship only God. For the essence of prophecy is to give a clear witness for Jesus."

God's Word is clear that a day is coming when the church, the bride of Christ, will be joined to her Bridegroom in heaven. In order to better understand the marriage of the Lamb, we need to consider two main points: (1) the participants in the marriage and (2) the phases in the marriage.

The Participants in the Marriage

Modern weddings have several key participants: the minister, the bride, the bridegroom, the bridesmaids, the groomsmen, the families, and the guests. In a similar way, the marriage of the Lamb will have four key participants.

1. The Host of the Wedding—The Father in Heaven

The Father is the divine host of the marriage of the Lamb. He is the Father of the bridegroom, He selected the bride, He prepares the wedding, and He sends out the invitations (Matthew 22:2-3).

2. The Bridegroom—Jesus Christ

On one occasion, Jesus asked, "Do wedding guests fast while celebrating with the groom?" (Luke 5:34). John the Baptist answered this question: "No one can receive anything unless God gives it from heaven. You yourselves know how plainly I told you, 'I am not the Messiah. I am only here to prepare the way for him.' It is the bridegroom who marries the bride, and the best man is simply glad to stand with him and hear his vows. Therefore, I am filled with joy at his success" (John 3:27-29).

3. The Bride—The Church

The bride is a clear New Testament picture of the church (Ephesians 5:25-26).

4. The Guests—Old Testament and Tribulation Saints

The marriage of the Lamb will occur in heaven where the church is joined to Christ, but the marriage supper that follows the wedding will take place later on earth during the millennial kingdom. Guests will be invited to the marriage supper: "Blessed are those who are invited to the wedding feast of the Lamb" (Revelation 19:9). Who are these guests? It appears that they are Old Testament and Tribulation saints who will be resurrected at the second coming of Christ and will join the great banquet in the millennial kingdom (Matthew 22:1-14). The marriage ceremony will only involve the church, but the marriage feast will include Old Testament and Tribulation saints.

The Phases of the Marriage

Just as every wedding has certain people who participate in the ceremony, a wedding also has a schedule of events that must occur. Almost every wedding I perform has an order of events that is handed out to the guests.

A wedding in ancient Israel had four main steps or phases. The ancient wedding ceremony is a picture with spiritual parallels to the church of Jesus Christ and even to each individual believer's relationship to Christ.

Phase 1: The Selection of the Bride by the Father

Obviously, the first step to any marriage ceremony is choosing a bride. In ancient Israel the official selection was made by the father with input, consultation, and no doubt encouragement by the son and his mother. God's Word declares that, before the world was created, God the Father selected a bride for His beloved Son (Ephesians 1:4). The Father has already selected the bride for His Son.

Phase 2: The Betrothal of the Bride and Groom

When a selection had been made, the father of the groom contacted the father of the bride. If the proposed marriage was acceptable, the two families entered into a binding contract of betrothal that spelled out the terms of the marriage, the financial arrangements, etc. The betrothal period was similar to our modern engagement, but as you can see it was much more formal and legally binding.

The betrothal agreement was solemnized by three acts: (1) a solemn oral commitment in the presence of witnesses, (2) a pledge of money, and (3) a written pledge or contract. The betrothal document was a binding contractual agreement between the families that could only be broken by death or divorce. The betrothed couple were considered to be husband and wife, and any violation of the relationship was considered adultery and punishable by death. The betrothal period was normally one year for virgins and one month for widows. During this time preparations for the wedding and marriage were carried out. Remember that Joseph and Mary were betrothed when she became pregnant with Jesus (Matthew 1:18). Joseph, not knowing initially that this was of the Lord, planned to "send her away," which meant to give her a bill of divorce. That's how sacred this betrothal was in Jewish culture.

An important part of the betrothal process was the gifts of betrothal. There were three important parts to these gifts. First was the "marriage present" that the bridegroom gave to the bride's father. Second, the bride's father gave the dowry to his daughter (and ultimately to the groom). This gift might include servants, valued possessions, or land. Third, the bridegroom gave a gift to the bride called the "bridegroom's gift." This gift was often jewelry or clothes.

Just as God chose believers to be the bride of Christ, he has also betrothed us to our Bridegroom (2 Corinthians 11:2-3).

The betrothal stage of the ancient marriage parallels our present experience as believers. The church is presently in the betrothal stage of God's schedule for the marriage. Believers have been selected by the Father and betrothed to Christ and are waiting for Him to come and take us to be His bride. The Father of the Bridegroom has paid the price for our purchase as the bride of Christ. He offered up His own Son as a sacrifice on the cross. The Bridegroom is also the sacrificial Lamb (1 Peter 1:18-19). Moreover, as part of our betrothal to Christ, the Father has given every believer in Christ an amazing dowry—the indwelling Holy Spirit (Ephesians 1:13-14). Because we are betrothed to Christ and have the dowry of the Holy Spirit, our salvation is absolutely secure! The divine Bridegroom will never violate His betrothal, and the Father will never take back His dowry.

We don't know how long the betrothal stage will last. However, as we await our Bridegroom, like a virtuous bride, we are to keep ourselves spiritually pure and undefiled (Ephesians 5:25-27).

Phase 3: The Marriage of the Bride and Groom

In the ancient Near East, when the betrothal period was complete, the bride and groom were officially joined as husband and wife at a presentation ceremony. The presentation ceremony would occur when the father of the groom told his son, "Go, son, and get your bride and bring her home!" To add to the drama and excitement, this would often be done in the evening. The anxious son would leave his father's house and in a torch-lit procession go to the home of his bride. Once there he would announce that he had come to receive his bride to himself. The marriage ceremony consisted mainly in the "taking" of the bride. The bridegroom literally "took a wife." When the bridegroom entered the bride's home, her father would place her hand in the bridegroom's hand and "present" her to him.

Someday, at the appointed time, the Father in heaven will tell His Son, "Go, Son, and get Your bride and bring her home!" Christ will come and rapture His bride, and she will be presented to Him as a glorious, unblemished bride. At this point, the Father will have fulfilled His legal contract when He betrothed us to Christ.

We are still awaiting this presentation phase of the marriage. We are waiting for our Bridegroom to come to take us to Himself. We are waiting to hear the midnight cry, "Look, the bridegroom is coming! Come out and meet him!" (Matthew 25:6).

Phase 4: The Marriage Supper or Celebration

After the bride was presented to the bridegroom, he would lead a joyous procession back to his father's house. The party was joined on the journey by young virgins who were waiting to catch sight of the procession as it passed by. These young women were friends of the bride and bridegroom (Matthew 25:1-13).

Upon the wedding party's return to the father's house, a feast was ready for family and friends, much like what we call the wedding reception today, except much more elaborate (John 2:1-11). Unlike our weddings and receptions today, the bridegroom was the center of attention, not the bride. He was king for the time of the feast.

The wedding feast was supervised by a faithful steward or close friend and usually lasted from one to seven days—sometimes even up to fourteen days if the parents were wealthy. To refuse an invitation to the wedding feast was a gross insult to the family (Matthew 22:1-10).

How do these phases apply to us? God's Word says that Jesus is coming for us, His bride, to take us to His Father's house where He has been preparing a place for us for two thousand years (John 14:1-3). After we are presented to our heavenly Bridegroom, the greatest celebration in history will break loose—the marriage supper of the Lamb. While some believe the marriage supper will occur in heaven, it appears that it will take place on earth, spilling over into the millennial kingdom. The length of the wedding feast in ancient times was determined by the wealth of the bridegroom's father. When Christ takes His bride, His heavenly Father, whose wealth is infinite, will throw a party that will last not for seven days but for one thousand years. Jesus frequently compared the millennial kingdom to a wedding feast (Matthew 8:11; 22:1-14; 25:1-13; Luke 14:16-24).

Getting Ready for the Big Day

One of the chief concerns of every bride to be is what she is going to wear at her wedding and wedding reception. The bride spends hours and hours and hours and . . . painstakingly looking at dresses, shoes, veils, jewelry, and all the accessories. Not to mention all the time just before the wedding getting a manicure and pedicure, getting her hair done, and making sure her makeup is just right. No detail of preparation is left to chance.

The marriage of the Lamb should be no different. Revelation 19:8 reminds us that every believer will be present at the wedding feast dressed in the finest white linen, which the Bible says represents the righteous deeds we have done. These good deeds are not so we can enter heaven. God has already invited us and made the way. However, what we will wear to the wedding feast will be the garment we sew ourselves. I once heard a Bible teacher say, "Has it ever occurred to you that at the marriage of the bride to the Lamb, each of us will be wearing the wedding garment of our own making?" How we are dressed on that day will depend on the life we have lived for Christ. Make sure that you will be beautifully dressed on that day by living for Christ today. The marriage of the Lamb is an event that is certain to happen. Someday the Bridegroom will come to take His bride to His Father's house. Make sure you are living a pure life for your loving Bridegroom.

PART 6

The Worst Is Yet to Come

On the evening of May 3, 1999, a tornado in southwest Oklahoma metastasized into a monster cyclone and thundered northeast, effortlessly flattening a sixty-mile swath through town after town, neighborhood after neighborhood. When the steamroller finally ran out of energy, it had totally destroyed 1,500 homes, damaged 8,093 homes, and killed 44 people. Ninety-five percent of Mulhall, Oklahoma, was destroyed.

After the storm, meteorologists determined that the wind speed generated by the tornado peaked at 318 mph, the highest winds ever recorded on planet earth. The storm may have even created a new tornado rating of F6. The day after the tornado the local news stations ran nonstop footage of the damaged areas. The scene was heartbreaking and indescribable. A few days later I had the opportunity to view some of the damaged area in person. I was stunned. It looked like a scene out of some post-Apocalypse movie. Twisted, scarred trees with all the bark stripped off littered the landscape, and all the grass was sucked out of the ground, leaving acres of exposed earth in its wake.

As overwhelming as this F6 tornado was, the Bible says that someday God is going to unleash His own tornado of judgment on this earth—an F6 tornado of God's devastating judgment—a time the Bible calls "the Tribulation."

CHAPTER 18

COMING TO TERMS WITH THE TRIBULATION

Timing the Tribulation

MANY PEOPLE WHO HOLD to the pre-Tribulation Rapture view have assumed that the Rapture of the church is the event that begins the seven-year Tribulation. But that is not necessarily the case. The main purpose of the Rapture is to end the church age. Meanwhile, it is the covenant of peace between the Antichrist and the nation of Israel that inaugurates the Tribulation and starts the end times clock ticking (Daniel 9:27).

This peace agreement could be signed very soon after the Rapture, but there could be several days, weeks, months, or even years between the Rapture and the signing of this treaty. The Bible never tells us how much time passes between the Rapture and the beginning of the Tribulation, but it seems to me that it probably will not be too long, because part of the purpose of the Rapture is to deliver God's people from the coming wrath of the Tribulation, and if the Tribulation is too far in the future, there would be no reason for the Rapture to occur. But between the Rapture and the beginning of the Tribulation, however long, there will be further preparation and stage setting for the events of the end times. Once the stage is set and all the players are in place, the treaty will be enacted.

The seven-year covenant brokered by the Antichrist will apparently usher in a temporary peace for the Middle East, and one that will briefly encompass the entire world (1 Thessalonians 5:1-3). It will appear to fulfill the world's dream. Daniel 9:27 describes this treaty that begins the Tribulation. This verse teaches us at least five key things about this future peace agreement:

1. It will be between Israel and the Antichrist but will almost certainly involve others. Since the Antichrist will rise from a reunited Roman Empire centered in Europe, Europe in its final form will be the key player.
2. It will *begin* the final seven-year period of the Tribulation.
3. It will be a "firm" covenant; this firmness may indicate that it will initially be forced or compelled. It may be a "take it or leave it" deal for Israel and its neighbors. It is also possible that this means the Antichrist will enforce or make strong a covenant that already exists.
4. It will eventually give Jews the right to offer sacrifices in a rebuilt Temple. This fact assumes a Jewish Temple must be rebuilt.
5. It will be broken by the Antichrist himself at the midpoint of the treaty.

Charles Dyer, a respected prophecy teacher and author, summarizes the nature of this covenant.

> What is this "covenant" that the Antichrist will make with Israel? Daniel does not specify its content, but he does indicate that it will extend for seven years. During the first half of this time Israel feels at peace and secure, so the covenant must provide some guarantee for Israel's national security. Very likely the covenant will allow Israel to be at peace with her Arab neighbors. One result of the covenant is that Israel will be allowed to rebuild her temple in

> Jerusalem. This world ruler will succeed where Kissinger, Carter, Reagan, Bush, and other world leaders have failed. He will be known as the man of peace![1]

The coming time of tribulation will begin with a treaty between the Antichrist and Israel and will last seven years. (For more about Daniel 9:27, see chapter 5, where there is a fairly detailed explanation of the "seventy weeks" of Daniel and the final "week" of seven years.)

Tribulation Terms and Titles

J. Dwight Pentecost provides ten descriptive, biblical words that characterize the coming Tribulation: wrath, judgment, indignation, trial, trouble, destruction, darkness, desolation, overturning, and punishment. He concludes his discussion of the Tribulation with this statement: "No passage can be found to alleviate to any degree whatsoever the severity of this time that shall come upon the earth."[2] The Tribulation will be the darkest hour in human history.

THE TERMS OF THE TRIBULATION

One of the best ways to understand what the Tribulation will be like is to note the terms, expressions, and phrases the Bible uses to describe this terrible time. The following is a list of all the significant terms and expressions in the Bible for the coming Tribulation period.

OLD TESTAMENT TRIBULATION: TERMS AND EXPRESSIONS[3]

TRIBULATION TERMS	OLD TESTAMENT REFERENCES
Birth Pangs	Isaiah 21:3; 26:17-18; 66:7; Jeremiah 4:31; Micah 4:10
Day of the Lord	Obadiah 1:15; Joel 1:15; 2:1, 11, 31; 3:14; Amos 5:18, 20; Isaiah 2:12; 13:6, 9; Zephaniah 1:7, 14; Ezekiel 13:5; 30:3; Zechariah 14:1

Great and Terrible Day of the Lord	Malachi 4:5
Day of Wrath	Zephaniah 1:15
Day of Distress	Zephaniah 1:15
Day of the Lord's Wrath	Zephaniah 1:18
Day of Desolation	Zephaniah 1:15
Day of Vengeance	Isaiah 34:8; 35:4; 61:2; 63:4
Day of Jacob's Trouble	Jeremiah 30:7
Day of Darkness and Gloom	Zephaniah 1:15; Amos 5:18, 20; Joel 2:2
Day of Trumpet	Zephaniah 1:16
Day of Alarm	Zephaniah 1:16
Day of the Lord's Anger	Zephaniah 2:2-3
Day of Destruction, Ruin from the Almighty	Joel 1:15
Day of Calamity	Deuteronomy 32:35; Obadiah 1:12-14
Trouble, Tribulation	Deuteronomy 4:30; Zephaniah 1:16
One Week = [Daniel's] Seventieth Week	Daniel 9:27
The [Lord's] Strange Work	Isaiah 28:15, 18, 21
Time/Day of Distress, Anguish	Daniel 12:1; Zephaniah 1:15
The Indignation/The Lord's Anger	Isaiah 26:20; Daniel 11:36
The Time of the End	Daniel 12:9
The Fire of His Jealousy	Zephaniah 1:18

NEW TESTAMENT TRIBULATION: TERMS AND EXPRESSIONS	
TRIBULATION TERMS	NEW TESTAMENT REFERENCES
The Day	1 Thessalonians 5:4 (NASB)
Those Days	Matthew 24:22 (NASB); Mark 13:20 (NASB)
The Day of the Lord	1 Thessalonians 5:2; 2 Thessalonians 2:2; 2 Peter 3:10
The Wrath	1 Thessalonians 5:9; Revelation 11:18
The Wrath to Come	1 Thessalonians 1:10
The Great Day of Their Wrath	Revelation 6:17
The Wrath of God	Revelation 15:1, 7; 14:10, 19; 16:1
The Wrath of the Lamb	Revelation 6:16
The Hour of Trial	Revelation 3:10
The Tribulation	Matthew 24:29 (NASB); Mark 13:24 (NASB)
[Time of] Tribulation	Mark 13:19 (NASB)
The Great Tribulation	Matthew 24:21 (NASB); Revelation 2:22 (NASB); 7:14 (NASB)
The Hour of Judgment	Revelation 14:7
Birth Pangs	Matthew 24:8; 1 Thessalonians 5:3

Why the Tribulation?[4]

Why would God pour out His wrath and judgment on the world He created? Why is such a time of unspeakable trouble necessary? Scripture provides us at least five reasons for the Tribulation. Each reason relates to a specific group or person: Israel, the Gentiles, God, Satan, and believers.

1. TO PREPARE ISRAEL (A PURPOSE FOR ISRAEL)

The Tribulation will bring the Jewish people to their knees in submission to God. God will use this "time of trouble for my people Israel" to prepare the nation for her Messiah (Jeremiah 30:7). God will put Israel in a vise grip from which there is no earthly hope of deliverance. God will refine the rebellious nation in the fire of the Tribulation period (Zechariah 13:8-9). Pentecost states, "God's purpose for Israel in the Tribulation is to bring about the conversion of a multitude of Jews, who will enter into the blessings of the kingdom and experience the fulfillment of all Israel's covenants."[5]

Many of the Jewish people will cry out to God for salvation from their sins during the Tribulation. They will implore God to pierce the heavens and come down to save them (Isaiah 64:1-2, 5-6, 8-9). God will mercifully answer this prayer of confession, will save many in Israel, and will bring them into the millennial kingdom under the reign of their Messiah (Jeremiah 30:8-24).

2. TO PUNISH SINNERS (A PURPOSE FOR GENTILES)

God will use the Tribulation to punish the godless Gentile nations and all unbelievers for their sin, especially for rejecting His Son and receiving the Antichrist (Revelation 16:2).

Pentecost says, "This world will receive this divine visitation because of the world's rejection of Jesus Christ as the Savior. . . . The world will worship the beast, and divine judgment will come upon them because they have despised God, rejected His Son, and acknowledged a demon-possessed man as their only king and deity."[6]

Revelation 6–18 describes this sobering purpose. According to Revelation 3:10, one purpose of the Tribulation is "to test those who dwell on the earth" (NASB). The word *test* refers to painful trials that God sends to bring out what is in people. It pictures putting metal in a crucible to discover its worth. The judgments of the Tribulation are God's way of testing "those who dwell on the earth."

The phrase "those who dwell on the earth" occurs eleven times in the book of Revelation. It is not so much a term of geographical location but moral condition. The entire horizon of their lives is dominated by earthly ambition, not the will of God. Revelation consistently pictures "earth dwellers" as the objects of God's wrath because of their hardened rebellion against Him. God gives up to evil those who continue rejecting Him even in spite of His judgments. His testing proves that they are earthly minded and don't care about God.

According to Isaiah 24–27, often called Isaiah's Apocalypse, no one will be able to hide from God's judgment during the Tribulation. "Look! The Lord is coming from heaven to punish the people of the earth for their sins. The earth will no longer hide those who have been killed. They will be brought out for all to see" (Isaiah 26:21).

3. TO PROVE GOD'S POWER (A PURPOSE FOR GOD)

About 3,500 years ago, the Pharaoh of Egypt mocked the God of heaven: "Who is the Lord? Why should I listen to him and let Israel go?" (Exodus 5:2). God heard his brazen challenge, and in the next eight chapters of Exodus, God shows Pharaoh, his magicians, and all the people who He is. When God is finished with the ten plagues, Pharaoh is begging the children of Israel to leave.

In a similar show of foolish bravado the Antichrist will deny the true God and declare himself to be god. God will once again pour out His plagues to prove His power and to vindicate His reputation. Only this time it will be on a worldwide scale. Many of the Tribulation judgments described in Revelation are the same as or similar to the ten plagues of Egypt. God will prove to a rebellious world that He alone is God (Revelation 15:3-4).

4. TO PORTRAY SATAN'S TRUE CHARACTER (A PURPOSE FOR SATAN)

God will use the Tribulation to fully unmask Satan for what he is—a liar, a thief, and a murderer. When God removes all restraints (2 Thessalonians 2:7), Satan will be fully manifest as the world experiences the final firestorm from the dragon. Realizing that his time is short, the devil will pour out his venom with force and violence (Revelation 12:12).

5. TO PROVIDE SALVATION (A PURPOSE FOR BELIEVERS)

The Lord will graciously use the Tribulation to drive men to Himself in repentance and trust. He will harvest more souls during this time than anyone can count. There will be great revival during the Great Tribulation (Revelation 7:9-10, 13-14).

While the Tribulation will be a time of unparalleled turmoil and may be difficult for us to understand, God will use it to accomplish His sovereign purposes.

Can People Who Hear the Gospel before the Rapture and Reject It Be Saved during the Tribulation?

Almost all students of end times prophecy would agree that people will be saved during the Tribulation period. Revelation 7:9-14 indicates that the Tribulation will be a time of great revival. While the Tribulation will be a time of judgment, it will also be a time that God will use to bring many to salvation. Saving the lost is one of God's chief purposes for the Tribulation period. Speaking of the Tribulation, Joel 2:32 says, "Everyone who calls on the name of the LORD will be saved, for some on Mount Zion in Jerusalem will escape, just as the LORD has said. These will be among the survivors whom the LORD has called."

However, many respected students of Bible prophecy contend that God will preclude anyone who rejects Christ *before* the Rapture from being saved *during* the Tribulation. They hold that God will send strong delusion upon them. Support for this view is usually based on 2 Thessalonians 2:9-12.

> This man will come to do the work of Satan with counterfeit power and signs and miracles. He will use every kind of evil deception to fool those on their way to destruction, because they refuse to love and accept the truth that would save them. So God will cause them to be greatly deceived, and they will believe these lies. Then they will be condemned for enjoying evil rather than believing the truth.

It is critical to remember the context of these verses. Paul is describing what happens *during* the Tribulation period, not *before* the Rapture. It refers to those who witness the deception of the Antichrist, believe his message, and reject the truth. Those who do this will be condemned by God. He will confirm them in their unbelief and send strong delusion on them so that they will believe the lie.

I believe that many who have clearly rejected the gospel before the Rapture will continue to reject it after the Rapture. After all, it won't get easier to be a Christian after the Rapture, but rather more difficult, since the Antichrist will openly persecute those who receive Christ and refuse to take his mark (Revelation 13:7, 16-17). However, to say that it is impossible for anyone to receive God's mercy during the Tribulation is expanding 2 Thessalonians 2:9-12 beyond what the context allows. Commenting on this passage, John Walvoord says,

> But we have to remember the context of this passage. It is focused on people who reject Christ during the tribulation and receive Antichrist not on people who reject Christ before the rapture. The Scriptures definitely teach that God will send strong delusion to those who do not believe after the church is gone. God will judge their hearts, and if they deliberately turn away from the truth He will permit them to believe a lie. They will honor the man of sin as their god and as their king, instead of acknowledging the Lord Jesus Christ. The result will be "that all may be condemned who did not believe the truth but had pleasure in unrighteousness" (v. 12).[7]

God will use the horror of the Tribulation period to bring millions of sinners to faith in His Son (Revelation 7:9-14). Among this numberless crowd, certainly some who rejected the Lord before the Rapture will reconsider and humbly accept Jesus Christ as the Son of God—the One who purchased a pardon from sin for them on the cross.

What a gracious Savior!

PART 7

The Beginning of Birth Pains

The First 3½ Years

The nations are indeed at the crossroads, and impending events cast their shadow on every aspect of human life. The world is moving faster and faster like a colossal machine out of control whose very power and momentum inevitably will plunge it into ultimate disaster.

Apart from the Bible, the world does not have a ray of hope. Our most brilliant leaders have not found an answer. . . . The present world crisis is not a result of any one factor, but a concurrence of causes and effects which combine to set the world stage for a conflict. . . . Whatever the future holds, it is going to be dramatically different than the past. In this dark picture only the Scriptures chart a sure course and give us an intelligent explanation of world-wide confusion as it exists today. The present world crisis in the light of the Scriptures reveals the existence of remarkable components in almost every area which may lead to a dramatic climax of world history. The present crises in every area of human life all point to the same conclusion, that disaster awaits the nations of the world.

JOHN F. WALVOORD, *The Nations in Prophecy*[1]

CHAPTER 19

THE RISE OF THE GROUP OF TEN

AFTER THE THREE UNIQUE events in heaven that involve the church of Jesus Christ—the Rapture, the judgment seat, and the marriage of the Lamb—biblical prophecy turns to earth and the events unfolding there.

Reuniting of the Roman Empire

The Scriptures describe a world situation, not unlike what we have today, as the great events of the end times commence. According to the Bible, the world will be divided into three main power blocs: the Western confederacy led by the Antichrist (Daniel 7:8), the Southern and Northern coalition comprised of Russia and a group of North African and Middle Eastern nations (Daniel 11:40-41; Ezekiel 38), and the Eastern alliance known as the "kings from the East" (Revelation 16:12). The Western confederation of nations will reconstitute the Roman Empire.

According to Scripture, ten leaders will ally together to protect the interests of the West. This "group of ten" could be something like the G-7, G-8, or G-20 forums that have been established among nations. In Daniel 2:42-44, the group of ten is symbolized as ten toes on a great statue, and in Daniel 7:7 and 7:24 by ten horns on a beast that represents the last world empire—the Roman Empire in its final form. Many interpreters of biblical prophecy believe that the European Union could be the embryonic form of what Scripture predicts and could ultimately fulfill this predicted alliance of nations.

How the European Union relates to this ten-leader group is uncertain, but it appears to be a picture similar to what the Bible predicts. Whatever the case, this Western power bloc will embody the revived Roman Empire and will have the economic and political power needed to control the Mediterranean region. Its final leader, the Antichrist, will eventually wrest control from three of the ten leaders and consolidate power very much like the Roman Empire did in the past (Daniel 7:8). To help us understand the biblical basis for this future empire, let's pause for a moment and look back to the ancient prophecies that foretell a future Roman Empire.

The ABCs of Bible Prophecy

Daniel 2 and 7 have often been called the ABCs of Bible prophecy because they lay the foundation for all that follows. These two companion chapters describe four great world empires that would rule over Israel in succession. With the benefit of history, we now know that these four empires were Babylon, Medo-Persia, Greece, and Rome. In Daniel 2 these four empires are pictured as four metals in a great statue that the Babylonian King Nebuchadnezzar saw in a dream from God.

THE METALLIC MAN OF DANIEL 2

WORLD EMPIRE	DESCRIPTION
Babylon	Head of Gold
Medo-Persia	Chest and Arms of Silver
Greece	Belly and Thighs of Brass
Rome	Iron
Rome II (The Antichrist's Kingdom)	Feet and Ten Toes of Iron and Clay
Christ's Kingdom	Stone Kingdom That Fills the Earth

In Daniel 7 these same empires are pictured as four great wild beasts that come up out of the Mediterranean Sea.

THE BEASTS OF DANIEL 7	
WORLD EMPIRE	DESCRIPTION
Babylon	Lion with the Wings of an Eagle
Medo-Persia	Lopsided Bear with Three Ribs in Its Mouth
Greece	Leopard with Four Wings and Four Heads
Rome	Terrible Beast with Teeth of Iron and Claws of Bronze
Rome II (The Antichrist's Kingdom)	Ten Horns and the Little Horn

Daniel identifies the ten toes and ten horns as ten kings (Daniel 2:44; 7:24). Many prophecy students hold that the ten toes and ten horns represent ten nations that will emerge in the end times or ten regional powers that will encompass the entire world, but since the little horn in Daniel 7:8 clearly symbolizes a person, it is most consistent to interpret the other ten horns as individuals as well. Yet, we know from history that the Roman Empire never existed in a ten-king form. It was never ruled by ten leaders. Moreover, both the great image and the final beast are completely, suddenly destroyed. By contrast, the historic Roman Empire gradually deteriorated and declined until the western part of the empire fell in AD 476 and the eastern leg was cut off in AD 1453. A more gradual process could hardly be imagined. This is not the sudden destruction of the feet of the image (Daniel 2:34) and the ten-horn stage of the beast (Daniel 7:7) that Daniel predicted. This prophecy remains unfulfilled.

It is better to interpret Daniel as picturing both the Roman Empire of history but also the Roman Empire of the end times—or what we might call Rome II. Notice the parallels between Daniel 2 and 7, especially in the final phase of the Roman Empire.

PARALLELS BETWEEN DANIEL 2 AND 7		
WORLD EMPIRE	DANIEL 2	DANIEL 7
Babylon	Head of Gold	Lion with the Wings of an Eagle
Medo-Persia	Chest and Arms of Silver	Lopsided Bear with Three Ribs in Its Mouth
Greece	Belly and Thighs of Bronze	Leopard with Four Wings and Four Heads
Rome	Iron	Terrible Beast with Large Iron Teeth
Rome II (Reunited Roman Empire)	Iron and Clay (Ten Toes)	Ten Horns and Little Horn

Interpreting the Future in Light of the Past

The principal reason for believing in the revival of the ancient Roman Empire is the simple fact that Daniel's prophecy hasn't been completely fulfilled. For those who believe the Bible, the prophecies about the future are just as literal as the prophecies already fulfilled in history. Daniel's prophecies about the four world empires were literally fulfilled, but one final phase of the fourth empire is still awaiting fulfillment. The final stage of the Roman Empire as Daniel envisioned it has yet to appear on the stage of world history. It will emerge prior to the second coming of Christ.

Revelation 13 and 17 confirm it: ten kings—symbolized by ten horns—are mentioned in conjunction with the revival of the Roman Empire (Revelation 13:1; 17:3, 12-13). This future manifestation will be a confederation of ten world leaders and will encompass the same basic geography as the ancient Roman Empire. This final Roman Empire will evidently begin as some form of republic and then progress to a dictatorship following the pattern of the historic Roman Empire.

In previewing both the historic Roman Empire and the future one, Daniel skips the intervening centuries, moving from historical Rome to end times prophecy. This "prophetic skip" is consistent with a pattern in other Old Testament prophecy. Prophecy from the Old Testament will frequently detail events that are prophetically fulfilled up to, and including, the first coming of Christ; then it will skip to end times prophecy, describing the Great Tribulation and the events that culminate there (e.g., Isaiah 9:6-7; Zechariah 9:9-11).

Three Stages of the Roman Empire to Come

The future Roman Empire, it appears, will go through three main phases. First, ten kings will appear within the boundaries of the old Roman Empire. They are the group of ten described in Daniel 2 and 7.

Second, a strong man whom we call the Antichrist will emerge and consolidate these ten leaders and the territory they represent into a united empire and probably extend its borders in various directions. As he makes this move, three of the ten leaders will object to his power play and will be killed (Daniel 7:8, 24). They will be replaced, and the ten kings will submit to the authority of the Antichrist and relinquish their power to him (Revelation 17:12-13). The ten kings will turn over "their kingdom to the beast" (Revelation 17:17, NASB). At this point, the Antichrist will rule over the reunited Roman Empire.

Third, the Roman Empire will, by declaration or edict, extend its power over the entire earth. This will make the Antichrist ruler of the world. The power vacuum created by the destruction of the Gog coalition (Ezekiel 38–39; see chapter 24) may be the impetus for this expansion. This final stage will erupt dramatically like a roman candle but will quickly fizzle, lasting only 3½ years. The Antichrist's kingdom will end with the campaign of Armageddon and the second coming of Christ.

It is probable that the revived Roman Empire will include nations from Europe and possibly even from Northern Africa and Western Asia, since the revived Roman Empire includes the three preceding empires, Babylon, Medo-Persia, and Greece, that included territory in Asia. Since Israel is the center of biblical interest, it would only be natural for the empire to include this area, especially given that the Holy Land will evidently be under the influence of the Roman Empire because of the treaty between the Antichrist and Israel, and because of his subsequent double cross and invasion of the land (Daniel 9:27; 11:40-45).

THREE PHASES OF THE REUNITED ROMAN EMPIRE	
Phase 1	The empire is ruled by ten leaders—the group of ten.
Phase 2	The Antichrist subdues three of the leaders and takes over. The ten leaders relinquish their authority to him.
Phase 3	The Antichrist extends the rule to the entire earth.

Although the specific identity of the ten world leaders cannot be determined at this time, there has been much speculation concerning the iron and clay that form the toes of the image described in Daniel 2:41-43.

> The feet and toes you saw were a combination of iron and baked clay, showing that this kingdom will be divided. Like iron mixed with clay, it will have some of the strength of iron. But while some parts of it will be as strong as iron, other parts will be as weak as clay. This mixture of iron and clay also shows that these kingdoms will try to strengthen themselves by forming alliances with each other through intermarriage. But they will not hold together, just as iron and clay do not mix.

Iron does not mix with the clay, so the feet appear to be the weakest portion of the entire structure. This mixture also illustrates that these kingdoms will try to strengthen themselves by forming alliances. But they will not hold together. They will not mix. Since the legs of iron represent the strength of the ancient Roman Empire, the clay must in some sense suggest political weakness or instability.

It is best to interpret the mixture as representing the diverse racial, religious, or political factions that ultimately contribute to the downfall of this revived Roman Empire. Strong nations will intermingle with weak nations. "This means that the empire of the Antichrist will have its internal problems, making for weakness."[1]

The European Union reflects the characteristics of iron and clay today, its inherent strength and weakness. The EU has great economic and political clout, but its diverse culture, language, and politics are also ever present. It represents the joining of strong nations with weak ones just as Daniel predicted. One can easily see how the EU could eventually become the feet and toes of iron and clay. While the current EU is not the fulfillment of the prophecies in Daniel and Revelation, the events in Europe today could be a prelude to the end times Roman Empire that Daniel prophesied about over 2,500 years ago.

CHAPTER 20

SATAN'S CEO—THE ASCENT OF THE ANTICHRIST

SOME ESTIMATE THAT, since the days of Adam, approximately one hundred billion human beings have been born. Over seven billion are alive today. However, the greatest human, apart from Jesus Himself, has yet to make his appearance upon our planet.[1] The Bible predicts this satanic superman will splash onto the world scene and rule the world for the final 3½ years before the return of Christ. He plays a central role in the events of end times prophecy. More than one hundred passages of Scripture describe the origin, nationality, character, career, conquest, and doom of the final world ruler known as the Antichrist. Clearly God wants His people to know something about the coming prince of darkness.

The Aliases of the Antichrist

No one name or title can fully capture the character and cunning of the coming world ruler. A. W. Pink says it well: "Across the varied scenes depicted by prophecy there falls the shadow of a figure at once commanding and ominous. Under many different names, like the aliases of a criminal, his character and movements are set before us."[2]

Here are ten aliases for the coming Antichrist that begin to sketch a composite portrait of the various aspects of his career and character.

Titles of the Antichrist

the little horn (Daniel 7:8)
a king, insolent and skilled in intrigue (Daniel 8:23)
the prince who is to come (Daniel 9:26)
the one who makes desolate (Daniel 9:27)
the king who does as he pleases (Daniel 11:36-45)
a foolish shepherd (Zechariah 11:15-17)
the man of destruction (2 Thessalonians 2:3)
the lawless one (2 Thessalonians 2:8)
the rider on the white horse (Revelation 6:2)
the beast out of the sea (Revelation 13:1-2)

Antichrist is the name most commonly associated with the final world ruler. It refers both to an individual and to the system he represents (1 John 2:18; 4:3). The word *Antichrist* (*antichristos*) occurs five times in the New Testament. It appears in four verses in the epistles of John (1 John 2:18, 22; 4:3; 2 John 1:7). In 1 John 2:18 John refers to an antichrist (*antichristos*, singular) who is coming in the future, and to antichrists (*antichristoi*, plural) who are already present. Using the singular "the Antichrist" starkly contrasts "antichrists" in the plural. John's distinction clearly denotes that the ultimate Antichrist will be a single individual. By using both the singular and the plural, John indicates that the contemporary antichrists in his day, who were false teachers, embodied the denying, deceiving spirit of the future, final Antichrist. They were forerunners of the Antichrist and were powerful evidence that his spirit was already at work in the world. The renowned New Testament scholar F. F. Bruce agrees: "So it was with John. That Antichrist would come he and his readers knew, and in the false teachers he discerned the agents, or at least the forerunners, of Antichrist, sharing his nature so completely that they could be called 'many antichrists.'"[3]

In other words, John looked beyond his own day and the many

lesser antichrists (small *a*) to the one ultimate Antichrist (capital *A*) who will culminate the manifestation of the lawless system that denies Christ and deceives men. The prefix *anti-* can mean "against"/"opposed to" or "instead of"/"in place of." These meanings are undoubtedly included in the term "Anti" Christ. He will be the archenemy and ultimate opponent of Jesus our Lord. The origin, nature, and purpose of Christ and the Antichrist are diametrically opposed. The Antichrist will be against Christ.

The Antichrist will also be "anti" Christ in the sense of "in place of" Christ. He will parody the true Christ. He will be a counterfeit Christ, a mock Christ, a pseudo-Christ, an imitation Christ.

In John 5:43, Jesus says, "I have come in My Father's name, and you do not receive Me; if another comes in his own name, you will receive him" (NASB). The one coming in his own name will be the world's final false messiah, the Antichrist. He will attempt to be the "alter ego" of the true Christ. A. W. Pink says,

> At every point he is the antithesis of Christ. The word "Antichrist" has a double significance. Its primary meaning is one who is opposed to Christ; but its secondary meaning is one who is instead of Christ. . . . Not only does *anti*-christ denote the antagonism of Christ, but tells of one who is instead of Christ. The word signifies another Christ, a pro-Christ, an alter christus, a pretender to the name of Christ. He will seem to be and will set himself up as the true Christ. He will be the Devil's counterfeit.[4]

As people sometimes point out, Satan never originated anything except sin. For six thousand years he has counterfeited the works of God. With the Antichrist, this pattern continues. He is Satan's ultimate masterpiece—the crowning counterfeit—and a false Christ and forgery of Jesus, the true Christ and Son of God.

The Antichrist will mimic the ministry of the true Son of God in many ways.

CHRIST	ANTICHRIST[5]
miracles, signs, and wonders (Matthew 9:32-33; Mark 6:2)	miracles, signs, and wonders (Matthew 24:24; 2 Thessalonians 2:9)
appears in the millennial Temple (Ezekiel 43:6-7)	sits in the Tribulation Temple (2 Thessalonians 2:4)
is God (John 1:1-2; 10:35-38)	claims to be God (2 Thessalonians 2:4)
is the Lion from Judah (Revelation 5:5)	has a mouth like a lion (Revelation 13:2)
makes a peace covenant with Israel (Ezekiel 37:26)	makes a peace covenant with Israel (Daniel 9:27)
causes men to worship God (Revelation 1:6)	causes men to worship Satan (Revelation 13:3-4)
followers sealed on their foreheads (Revelation 7:3-4; 14:1)	followers sealed on their foreheads or right hands (Revelation 13:16-18)
worthy name (Revelation 19:16)	blasphemous names (Revelation 13:1)
married to a virtuous bride (Revelation 19:7-10)	married to a vile prostitute (Revelation 17:3-5)
crowned with many crowns (Revelation 19:12)	crowned with ten crowns (Revelation 13:1)
is *the* King of kings (Revelation 19:16)	is called "the king" (Daniel 11:36)
sits on a throne (Revelation 3:21; 12:5; 20:11)	sits on a throne (Revelation 13:2; 16:10)
sharp sword from his mouth (Revelation 19:15)	bow in his hand (Revelation 6:2)
rides a white horse (Revelation 19:11)	rides a white horse (Revelation 6:2)
has an army (Revelation 19:14)	has an army (Revelation 6:2; 19:19)
violent death (Revelation 5:6; 13:8)	violent death (Revelation 13:3)
resurrection (Matthew 28:6)	resurrection (Revelation 13:3,14)
Second Coming (Revelation 19:11-21)	second coming (Revelation 17:8)

1,000-year worldwide kingdom (Revelation 20:1-6)	3½-year worldwide kingdom (Revelation 13:5-8)
part of a holy Trinity (Father, Son, and Holy Spirit) (2 Corinthians 13:14)	part of an unholy trinity (Satan, the Antichrist, and false prophet) (Revelation 13)

The Appearance of the Antichrist

The Antichrist will debut on the world stage at the beginning of the Tribulation after the Rapture. One can only imagine the chaos and confusion that will grip the world after the Rapture and the desperate cry for someone to bring things under control.

Arthur Bloomfield also connects the Antichrist's coming to a great crisis. "Great men of history, famous and infamous, are products of their times. And though we cannot exclude the sovereignty of God, it is easy to see why success or failure is sometimes born of ripe times and circumstances. The Antichrist himself will be a product of his time. A figure so sensational could come only out of sensational times. A world crisis will produce the Antichrist."[6]

Chuck Swindoll describes the rise of the Antichrist in the wake of the Rapture.

> This man will emerge after the Rapture, probably to calm the chaotic waters troubled by the unexplained departure of so many Christians. He will be primed and ready to speak. He will stand before not only a nation but a world and will win their approval. Like Hitler, he will emerge on a scene of such political and economic chaos that the people will see him as a man with vision, with pragmatic answers and power to unite the world.[7]

According to 2 Thessalonians 2:6-7, the Antichrist can only be revealed when the Holy Spirit is removed at the Rapture. "He who now restrains" (NASB) refers to the Holy Spirit working in and through the church. The fact that the restrainer must be removed before the Antichrist can be revealed tells us that "Satan must wait on God's timing, so he is defeated before he ever begins his final assault on God. He can't make his move until God releases the restraining power of the Holy Spirit indwelling the church."[8] Satan does not know the exact time of Christ's return or when the restraint will be removed, so he must have a potential candidate for the Antichrist ready in every generation. Also, since the identity of the Antichrist cannot be known until after the Rapture, no one today should spend time trying to figure out who he is or come up with possible candidates. All such attempts are speculative and futile. I like to tell people, "If you ever do figure out who the Antichrist is, I've got bad news: you've been left behind."

The Attributes of the Antichrist

Revelation 13, using the image of a beast out of the sea, describes the coming world ruler in great detail. Much of what is revealed about the Antichrist in Revelation 13 and also Revelation 17 builds upon and amplifies what the prophet Daniel wrote. Putting Daniel and Revelation together, we can develop a character profile for this final world ruler. He will be the most incredible leader the world has ever known. A. W. Pink writes,

> For six thousand years Satan has had full opportunity afforded him to study fallen human nature, to discover its weakest points, and to learn how to best make man do his bidding. The devil knows full well how to dazzle people by the attraction of power. . . . He knows how to gratify the craving for knowledge. . . . He can delight the ear with melodious music and the eye with entrancing beauty. . . . He knows how to exalt men to dizzy heights of worldly greatness and fame, and how to control that greatness so that it may be employed against God and His people.[9]

John Phillips etches this chilling description:

> The world will go delirious with delight at his manifestation. He will be the seeming answer to all its needs. He will be filled with all the fullness of Satan. Handsome, with a charming,

> rakish, devil-may-care personality, a genius, superbly at home in all the scientific disciplines, brave as a lion, and with an air of mystery about him to tease the imagination or to chill the blood as occasion may serve, a brilliant conversationalist in a score of tongues, a soul-captivating orator, he will be the idol of all mankind.[10]

While there are many attributes and activities of the Antichrist, here are six of the chief identifying characteristics of the coming Antichrist.

He Will Be a Gentile, Not a Jew[11]

One of the most asked and most debated questions about the Antichrist is his ethnic background. As far back as the second century AD, scholars were writing about this issue. The debate springs from how readers interpret the prefix "anti-" in front of the name Christ. On the one hand, if "anti-" means opposed to Christ as the ruler of Gentile world power, then the Antichrist is probably a Gentile. On the other hand, if "anti-" means in place of Christ as a false messiah, then many would contend this makes it more likely that he would be a Jew. Let's first consider the case made for a Jewish Antichrist.

The consistent view of the church during the closing decades of the second century was that the Antichrist would be a Jewish false messiah from the tribe of Dan. Irenaeus (c. 120–202) held this view. He based his conclusion on Jeremiah 8:16 and the fact that Revelation 7:4-8 omits the tribe of Dan from the list of the tribes of Israel. Some also appeal to Jacob's prophecy concerning Dan in Genesis 49:17: "Dan shall be a serpent in the way, a horned snake in the path, that bites the horse's heels, so that his rider falls backward" (NASB). The serpent there is interpreted as Satan, and is then related to what Revelation 13 says about the Antichrist. Later, Jerome (AD 331–420) also held this view.

The other specific Scripture that is most often used to substantiate the Jewish heritage of the Antichrist is the King James Version of Daniel 11:37, which says, "Neither shall he regard the God of his fathers. . . ." Those who maintain that the Antichrist is a Jew believe that his rejection of "the God of his fathers" proves his Jewishness. The entire argument rests on the phrase "the God of his fathers."

There are some challenges, however, to the argument that the Antichrist is Jewish. First, it is unclear why Dan is omitted from the list of tribes in Revelation 7:4-8. The best explanation I'm aware of is that Dan was the first tribe to go into idolatry after the people moved into the Promised Land (Judges 18).[12]

Second, Daniel 11:37 (KJV) could equally apply to a Gentile whose parents were followers of Christ as to parents of Jewish heritage. Similarly, in 1 John 2:18-19 where the title "Antichrist" appears, the issue is apostasy from Christianity, not from Judaism. At its most basic, Daniel 11:37 simply says that the Antichrist will totally reject whatever religion his ancestors practiced. Moreover, most of the more recent Bible translations (ASV, RSV, NASB, and NIV) translate the KJV word *God* (*elohim*) as "gods." As Arnold Fruchtenbaum observes, "In the whole context, Daniel 11:36-39, the term *god* is used a total of eight times. In the Hebrew text, six of these times it is in the singular and twice in the plural, one of which is the phrase in verse 37. The very fact that the plural form of 'god' is used in a context where the singular is found in the majority of cases makes this a reference to heathen deities and not a reference to the God of Israel."[13] The Septuagint, the Greek translation of the Old Testament, also uses the plural "gods." These translations more faithfully reflect the Hebrew text.[14]

As you can see, no matter your translation, the key verse—Daniel 11:37—used by those who believe the Antichrist is a Jew is far from conclusive. Instead, it makes better sense that the coming Antichrist is a Gentile. I believe the Bible clearly teaches this. There are at least four good reasons for this conclusion.

First, biblical typology points to the Gentile origin of the Antichrist. The only historical person who is specifically identified as a "type" or preview of the person and work of the Antichrist is Antiochus Epiphanes, who was a Syrian monarch in the second century BC. Antiochus has been aptly dubbed the "Old Testament Antichrist." He provides a sneak preview of what the Antichrist will be like. If the precursor to the Antichrist was a Gentile, then it makes sense that the Antichrist would also be a Gentile.

Second, the origin of the Antichrist is symbolized by the beast in Revelation 13:1: "Then I saw a beast rising up out of the sea." The word *sea* when used symbolically in the book of Revelation and the rest of Scripture symbolizes the Gentile nations. This is confirmed in Revelation 17:15 where "the waters . . . represent masses of people of every nation and language." Alternately, the word *sea* could mean "the abyss" or "the deep" (11:7; 17:8). If this is true, then the fact that he comes up out of the sea would be describing his satanic, demonic origin from the underworld.

Third, the Antichrist is presented in Scripture as the final ruler of Gentile world power. His reign is the final phase of the "times of the Gentiles" and their rule over Israel (Luke 21:24, NASB). He will sit on the throne of the final world empire and raise his fist in the face of God. Having a Jew as the last world ruler over Gentile power does not seem likely.

Fourth, one of the primary activities of the Antichrist will be persecuting the Jewish people, invading Israel, and desecrating the rebuilt Jewish Temple (Daniel 7:25; 9:27; 11:41, 45; 2 Thessalonians 2:4; Revelation 11:2; 12:6; 13:7). It doesn't make sense that a Jew would be the final great persecutor of his own people. Gentiles have always led the way in persecuting the Jews. For these reasons, I believe the Antichrist will be a Gentile.

He Will Mesmerize the World with His Words (Daniel 7:8, 11; 11:36; Revelation 13:5)

The Antichrist will inspire the whole world with his charisma and eloquence. Over and over again, biblical passages draw attention to his mouth speaking great words. When he talks, everyone else will listen. As A. W. Pink says,

> He will have a mouth speaking very great things. He will have a perfect command and flow of language. His oratory will not only gain attention but respect. Revelation 13:2 declares that his mouth is "as the mouth of a lion" which is a symbolic expression telling of the majesty and awe-producing effects of his voice. The voice of a lion excels that of any other beast. So the Antichrist will outrival orators ancient and modern.[15]

He Will Rise from Obscurity As a Great Peacemaker (Daniel 9:27; Revelation 17:11-12)

The Antichrist will emerge from relative obscurity to take the international political scene by storm. He won't attract much attention when he first enters the political arena. Daniel 7:8 characterizes him as the "little" horn among the ten horns in a reunited Roman Empire. But he will quickly rise in the ranks and be elected by the group of ten to rule over the whole empire (Revelation 17:13). He will be the consummate unifier and diplomat. He will acquire power using the stealth of diplomacy. His platform will be peace and prosperity. Emerging with an olive branch in his hand, he will weld together opposing forces with ease. The dreams of the United Nations will be realized in his political policies. He will even temporarily solve the Middle Eastern political situation, which may well earn him accolades such as the Nobel Prize or being anointed *TIME* magazine's man of the year. He will bring such peace to the Middle East that the Temple Mount area in Jerusalem will be returned to Jewish sovereignty (Daniel 9:27). He will undoubtedly be hailed as the greatest peacemaker the world has ever seen.

He Will Establish a One-World Economy (Daniel 11:43; Revelation 13:16-17)

The Antichrist will be Satan's CEO of the world's economy. He will set interest rates, prices, stock values, and supply levels. Everything will be nationalized or internationalized and placed under his personal control. With the chaos created by the Rapture and the collapse of the world economy predicted in Revelation 6:5-6, people will be willing to give all power over to one man. Much like the Germans turned to Hitler after the runaway inflation in Weimar Germany, the world will turn to the man who seems to have answers for the crushing problems they're facing. From the midpoint of the Tribulation until the second coming of Christ, no one will be able to buy or sell without the Antichrist's permission (Revelation 13:16-17). People all over the world will be compelled to take his mark. His one-world economy will be run by his sidekick the false prophet (Revelation 13:11-18).

He Will Rule the World (Revelation 6:2; 13:2)

At the midpoint of the Tribulation, the Antichrist's mask will come off, and he will replace his olive branch with a sword. He will subjugate the whole world. All the greatness of Alexander and Napoleon will pale compared to him. No one will be able to stand in the way of his conquest. He will crush everything and everyone before him. He will be the final great Caesar over the Roman Empire. "Who is like the beast, and who is able to wage war with him?" (Revelation 13:4, NASB).

He Will Claim to Be God (2 Thessalonians 2:4; Revelation 13:8)

The Antichrist, Satan's prodigy, will achieve what no other religious leader has ever done. He will do what neither Muhammad nor Buddha nor any pope has ever been able to do: unite the world in worship. All the religions of the world will be brought together in the worship of one man. He will proclaim that he is God and require the world to worship him (2 Thessalonians 2:4; Revelation 13:8).

Just think what genius and power and deception it will take to pull this off! Religion divides so many people. Some people have very strong feelings about it and are easily angered and frustrated by those who disagree with them. Religion separates. But that will all change some day, and preparation is well under way for the acceptance of worshiping a man. The world, like never before, is looking for a great leader, a messiah, a savior to solve the profound predicaments the earth faces today. The planet is well down the road toward worshiping the ultimate idol.

John Phillips describes the Antichrist this way:

> The Antichrist will be an attractive and charismatic figure, a genius, a demon-controlled, devil-taught charmer of men. He will have answers to the horrendous problems of mankind. He will be all things to all men: a political statesman, a social lion, a financial wizard, an intellectual giant, a religious deceiver, a masterful orator, a gifted organizer. He will be Satan's masterpiece of deception, the world's false messiah.

> With boundless enthusiasm the masses will follow him and readily enthrone him in their hearts as the world's savior and god.[16]

To better envision the Antichrist, Harold Willmington provides this helpful analogy. The coming world ruler will possess the following traits:

the leadership of a Washington and Lincoln
the eloquence of a Franklin Roosevelt
the charm of a Teddy Roosevelt
the charisma of a Kennedy
the popularity of an Ike
the political savvy of a Johnson
the intellect of a Jefferson[17]

Antichrist Abridged

There is much more to say about the coming Antichrist. However, in the interest of brevity, here are two lists that outline more fully when he will appear, what he will do, what he will be like, and how he will come to his end.

ANTICHRIST ACTIVITIES[18]
1. He will appear in "the time of the end" of Israel's history (Daniel 8:17).
2. His manifestation will signal the beginning of the Day of the Lord (2 Thessalonians 2:1-3).
3. His manifestation is currently being hindered by the "restrainer" (2 Thessalonians 2:3-7).
4. His rise to power will come through peace programs (Revelation 6:2). He will make a covenant of peace with Israel (Daniel 9:27). This event will signal the beginning of the seven-year Tribulation. He will later break that covenant at its midpoint.
5. Near the middle of the Tribulation, the Antichrist will be assassinated or violently killed (Revelation 13:3, 12, 14).

6. He will descend into the abyss (Revelation 17:8).
7. He will be raised back to life (Revelation 11:7; 13:3, 12, 14; 17:8).
8. The whole world will be amazed and will follow after him (Revelation 13:3).
9. He will be totally controlled and energized by Satan (Revelation 13:2-5).
10. He will assassinate three of the ten kings in the reunited Roman Empire (Daniel 7:24).
11. The kings will give all authority to him (Revelation 17:12-13).
12. He will invade the land of Israel and desecrate the rebuilt Temple (Daniel 9:27; 11:41; 12:11; Matthew 24:15; Revelation 11:2).
13. He will mercilessly pursue and persecute the Jewish people (Daniel 7:21, 25; Revelation 12:6).
14. He will set himself up in the Temple as God (2 Thessalonians 2:4).
15. He will be worshiped as God for 3½ years (Revelation 13:4-8).
16. His claim to deity will be accompanied by great signs and wonders (2 Thessalonians 2:9-12).
17. He will speak great blasphemies against God (Daniel 7:8; Revelation 13:6).
18. He will rule the world politically, religiously, and economically for 3½ years (Revelation 13:4-8, 16-18).
19. He will be promoted by a second beast who will lead the world in worship of him (Revelation 13:11-18).
20. He will require all to receive his mark (666) to buy and sell (Revelation 13:16-18).
21. He will establish his political and economic capital in Babylon (Revelation 17).
22. He and the ten kings will destroy Babylon (Revelation 18:16).
23. He will kill the two witnesses (Revelation 11:7).
24. He will gather all the nations against Jerusalem (Zechariah 12:1-2; 14:1-3; Revelation 16:16; 19:19).

25. He will fight against Christ when He returns to earth and suffer total defeat (Revelation 19:19-20).

26. He will be cast alive into the lake of fire (Daniel 7:11; Revelation 19:20).

TOP TEN KEYS TO THE ANTICHRIST'S IDENTITY
1. He will not be recognized until after the Rapture of believers to heaven.
2. He will begin insignificantly and then rise to world prominence as the Pied Piper of international peace.
3. He will be a Gentile world leader from the geographical area of the Roman Empire.
4. He will rule over the reunited Roman Empire (the "Unholy" Roman Empire).
5. He will make a seven-year peace covenant with Israel.
6. He will be assassinated and come back to life.
7. He will break his treaty with Israel at the midpoint of the Tribulation and invade the land.
8. He will sit in the Temple of God and declare himself to be God.
9. He will desecrate the Temple in Jerusalem by having an image of himself placed in it.
10. He will rule the world politically, economically, and religiously for 3½ years.

Conclusion

As you can see, Scripture teaches that there is a future, final human opponent of Jesus Christ who will rise during the Tribulation. For seven years he will capture world headlines, dominate geopolitics, and implement his plans. He will embody evil as a visible, vigorous enemy of Jesus Christ. Yet, in the final battle when Christ returns, he will be defeated, and Christ will establish His Kingdom on the earth.

Scriptural teaching about the Antichrist is not given to make us anxious but to make us aware. God has revealed this information to us not for us to become preoccupied with the Antichrist or to recklessly speculate about his identity but to show us where this world is headed and to assure us that God is still in control. Our awareness of God's final victory over the Antichrist and evil reassures believers that both the present and the future are firmly in God's grasp.

CHAPTER 21

THE FINAL FALSE PROPHET

REVELATION 13 DESCRIBES the two world leaders who will rise in the end times. These two men are called "beasts" or wild animals to emphasize their vicious, cruel nature. Revelation 13:1-10 describes the attributes and activities of the beast who rises from the sea. He is the Antichrist. Warren Wiersbe summarizes the portrait of him with five key words: wound (13:3a), wonder (13:3b), worship (13:4, 8), words (13:5), and war (13:6-10).[1]

The Antichrist, however, will not rise to power alone. Revelation 13:11-18 introduces a second beast that comes up out of the earth. Also known as the "false prophet," he will serve as the lieutenant for the Antichrist, preparing the way and catapulting him to power and unparalleled success. Using stunning miracles, signs, and wonders, the false prophet will convince the world that the Antichrist is the leader they've been looking for—the man with a plan—the man who can solve the world's problems.

Both the Antichrist and the false prophet will be energized from hell.

Scripture indicates that Satan will be the ultimate power behind the Antichrist. Satan (the dragon) gives his authority to the Beast (Revelation 13:2, 4). Satan himself will indwell, energize, and control the Antichrist. Likewise, the false prophet is described as speaking with the voice of a dragon, which is a picture of Satan (13:11). This indicates that the false prophet is a foul mouthpiece for Satan.

The world has always had false prophets and false teachers. One of Satan's chief methods of operation is to use false messengers to counterfeit and corrupt the message of God. But this strategy of Satan will increase dramatically in the end times.[2]

The Bible says that in the last days of planet earth, many false prophets will perform great signs and wonders and spew out lies (Matthew 24:24). In this mass of deception one false prophet will rise high above all the others in his ability to capture the world's attention. Although a great deal has been written about the Antichrist, comparatively little has been written about the false prophet. Yet he is a central figure in the coming events of the Tribulation. In this chapter we'll take a look at some of the characteristics of the false prophet.

The Unholy Spirit

He is called "the false prophet" three times in Revelation (16:13; 19:20; 20:10) and is also known as the second beast in Revelation 13:11-18. He is the final person in the unholy trinity of the end times (Revelation 16:13; 19:20–20:2; 20:10). Just as the Holy Spirit gives glory to Christ and points men to Him, the false prophet will glorify the Antichrist and lead people to trust and worship him. As Donald Grey Barnhouse says, "The devil is making his last and greatest effort, a furious effort, to gain power and establish his kingdom upon the earth. He knows nothing better than to imitate God. Since God has succeeded by means of an incarnation and then by means of the work of the Holy Spirit, the devil will work by means of an incarnation in Antichrist and by the unholy spirit."[3] In hell's trinity, Satan is a counterfeit Father (anti-Father), the Antichrist is a counterfeit Son (anti-Christ), and the false prophet is a counterfeit of the Holy Spirit (anti-Spirit). This is the infernal trinity.

Here are five key ways the false prophet counterfeits the ministry of the Holy Spirit:

HOLY SPIRIT	FALSE PROPHET
points men to Christ	points men to the Antichrist
instrument of divine revelation	instrument of satanic revelation
seals believers to God	marks unbelievers with the number of the Antichrist
builds the body of Christ	builds the empire of the Antichrist
enlightens men with the truth	deceives men by miracles

The Satanic John the Baptist

Whereas the Antichrist will primarily be a military and political figure, the false prophet will be a religious figure. He will be a kind of "satanic John the Baptist" preparing the way for the coming of the Antichrist. The false prophet will be the chief propagandist and spokesman for the Beast. He will lead the world in the false worship of its emperor. The Antichrist and the false prophet are mentioned together in four places in Revelation.

1. Revelation 13:1-18	They share a common goal.
2. Revelation 16:13-14	They share a common agenda for the world.
3. Revelation 19:20	They share a common sentence.
4. Revelation 20:10	They share a common destiny.

Thomas Ice and Timothy Demy note this close connection: "The Antichrist and the False Prophet are two separate individuals who will work toward a common, deceptive goal. Their roles and relationships will be that which was common in the ancient world between a ruler (Antichrist) and the high priest (False Prophet) of the national religion."[4]

Facts about the False Prophet

Revelation 13:11-18 emphasizes three key facts about the false prophet: his deceptive appearance, his devilish authority, and his deadly activity.

His Deceptive Appearance (Revelation 13:11)

"Then I saw another beast come up out of the earth. He had two horns like those of a lamb, but he spoke with the voice of a dragon." The conflicting descriptions here—a wild beast, a lamb, and dragon—reflect the false prophet's total deceptiveness.

He has the nature of a wild beast.	He is hostile to God's flock. He ravages God's people.
He has the appearance of a lamb.	He looks gentle, tender, mild, and harmless. No one is afraid of a lamb.
He has the voice of a dragon.	He is the voice of hell itself belching forth the fiery lies of Satan. When he speaks, he becomes Satan's mouthpiece.

John Phillips summarizes the deceptive appearance and deadly approach of the false prophet:

> The dynamic appeal of the false prophet will lie in his skill in combining political expediency with religious passion, self-interest with benevolent philanthropy, lofty sentiment with blatant sophistry, moral platitude with unbridled self-indulgence. His arguments will be subtle, convincing, and appealing. His oratory will be hypnotic, for he will be able to move the masses to tears or whip them into a frenzy. . . . His deadly appeal will lie in the fact that what he says will sound so right, so sensible, so exactly what unregenerate men have always wanted to hear.[5]

Just like slick propagandists throughout history, the false prophet will not be what he appears. He will be a dangerous concoction and contradiction. He will sell the vision of the Antichrist, making it palatable.

His Devilish Authority (Revelation 13:12)

The second beast will have great authority delegated to him by the Antichrist. He will exercise "all the authority of the first beast" (Revelation 13:12).

The false prophet's mission will be to use that authority to cause the world to worship the Antichrist. He will carry out the plans and wishes of the Antichrist and lead the worldwide cult of Antichrist worship. Satan will empower the false prophet just as he empowers the Antichrist. Like Joseph Goebbels with Hitler, the false prophet will be inspired by the same authority and will share the same diabolical agenda as the Antichrist.

His Deadly Activity (Revelation 13:13-18)

In ranching there's a special animal known as a Judas goat that is used to herd animals. Named after Judas Iscariot, the traitor of Christ, this goat is trained to mix with the sheep and lead them around, often into pens and onto trucks. One of the functions of this goat is to lead the unsuspecting sheep to the slaughterhouse. Like a Judas goat, the false prophet will gain the world's confidence and enthrall the masses, all the while leading them to their destruction. He will seduce the world with his words and stun the world with his wonders. Six deadly activities of the false prophet are presented in this section. These activities reveal how he will use his influence and experience during the days of the Great Tribulation.

1. HE COMES UP OUT OF THE EARTH (REVELATION 13:11)

Biblical scholars disagree about the ethnicity of the false prophet. Some believe he will be a Jew, while others maintain that he will be a Gentile. Those who believe he will be of Jewish ancestry point to Revelation 13:11. The first beast or Antichrist comes up out of the sea, which may indicate he is a Gentile. The second beast or false prophet, on the other hand, comes up out of the earth or land. Proponents of a Jewish false prophet interpret the word *earth* as a reference to the land of Israel, so that if the beast is "coming up out of the earth," he must be Jewish.

While it's certainly possible that *earth* refers to Israel, it seems better to see the word *earth* in contrast to heaven. Thus, it is better to see the false prophet as a Gentile just like the first beast. Since the second beast works so closely with the Antichrist, whom I believe to be a Gentile, it makes more sense that he, too, will be a Gentile. Together they persecute the Jewish people, so it is doubtful the false prophet is persecuting his own people. His coming up out of the earth is meant to contrast him with the Holy Spirit who comes down from heaven. The false prophet is "earthly" in the fullest sense of the word. The earth is his domain and only focus. Nonetheless, we have to admit that the Bible is inconclusive on this matter.

2. HE WILL BRING DOWN FIRE FROM HEAVEN AND PERFORM OTHER MIRACLES (REVELATION 13:13-14)

The false prophet will mimic the miracles of the two witnesses just like Egyptian magicians counterfeited the miracles of Moses (Exodus 7:11-13, 22; 8:7; Revelation 11:4-6). "Even though this is yet a future event, the lesson to be learned for our own day is that one must exercise discernment, especially in the area of religion—even when miracles appear to vindicate the messenger."[6]

3. HE WILL ERECT AN IMAGE TO THE ANTICHRIST FOR ALL THE WORLD TO WORSHIP (REVELATION 13:14-15)

This image, called the abomination of desolation, will be placed in the Temple in Jerusalem (Matthew 24:15). Like the image of Nebuchadnezzar on the plain of Dura (Daniel 3), all will have to bow to this image or die.

4. HE WILL RAISE THE ANTICHRIST FROM THE DEAD (REVELATION 13:14)

While this is not stated explicitly in the text, it is strongly implied. Revelation 13 mentions the death and resurrection of the Antichrist three times (verses 3, 12, 14), and it is mentioned again in Revelation 17:8. Since the false prophet is a miracle worker who deceives the world, it is probable that Satan will use the false prophet as his human instrument to raise the Antichrist back to life.

5. HE WILL GIVE LIFE TO THE IMAGE OF THE BEAST (REVELATION 13:15)

The image that is erected in the Beast's honor will be unlike any other image ever created. Like something out of a science-fiction movie or the *Twilight Zone*, the statue will be animated. It will speak and breathe. Satan's deception will reach its zenith under the final world ruler and his passionate promoter.

6. HE WILL CONTROL WORLD COMMERCE ON BEHALF OF THE BEAST FORCING EVERYONE TO TAKE THE MARK OF THE BEAST (REVELATION 13:16)

The crowning achievement for the false prophet will be the global registration of all people. He will use a totally controlled economy to secure the rule of the first beast, the Antichrist. No one will be able to buy or sell without pledging allegiance to the Beast, receiving his mark, and submitting to the global registration system.

Revelation 13:16-17 sets forth the false prophet's economic program. "He causes all, the small and the great, and the rich and the poor, and the free men and the slaves, to be given a mark on their right hand or on their forehead, and he provides that no one will be able to buy or to sell, except the one who has the mark, either the name of the beast or the number of his name" (NASB).

Notice the universal scope of his control. It extends to "all." He will exercise ironfisted control over the basic fundamentals of any economy—supply (no one will be able to sell) and demand (no one will be able to buy).

No one will be able to shop at the mall, eat at a restaurant, fill up at gas stations, pay utility bills, buy groceries, get prescriptions filled, pay to get the lawn mowed, or pay the mortgage without the mark of the Beast. It's the Tribulation trademark.

Conclusion

The two beasts of the end times will work in tandem to rule the final world empire. They will be entirely energized by Satan, forming an unholy trinity with him that will deceive the world. Human evil will be focused and embodied in these two men unlike any time in history. Knowing God's plan for history in advance gives believers confidence that God will ultimately triumph over evil—even the greatest concentration of evil under the Antichrist and the false prophet. This should calm our hearts and fill us with hope even when evil is rampant and often appears out of control.

TEN IDENTIFYING FEATURES OF THE FALSE PROPHET FROM REVELATION 13
rises out of the earth (13:11)
controls religious affairs with deceptive speech (13:11)
motivated by Satan, the dragon (13:11)
promotes worship of the first beast (13:12)
performs signs and miracles (13:13)
deceives the whole world (13:14)
empowers the image of the Beast (13:15)
kills all who refuse to worship (13:15)
controls all economic commerce (13:17)
controls the mark of the Beast (13:17, 18)

CHAPTER 22

RIDERS ON THE STORM

The Seven Seal Judgments

THE BOOK OF REVELATION previews how Jesus Christ, by means of judgment, becomes King. The judgment that ultimately leads to the establishment of that Kingdom begins in Revelation 6:1 with the opening of the first seal on the scroll. This is the beginning of the Tribulation.

Before that, Revelation 4–5 presents a scene in heaven where a seven-sealed scroll is introduced. The scroll is a will or testament that contains the inheritance of the Kingdom. In ancient times, a will was secured with seven seals by the seven individuals who witnessed its execution. The seals must be removed and the scroll must be opened for the Lord Jesus Christ to inherit the Kingdom that His Father has given Him (Psalm 2:8).

When we get to Revelation 6:1, the scene changes dramatically. The theme of Revelation 4–5 is *worship,* but the subject of Revelation 6 is *wrath.* John is transported back to earth for the breaking of the seven seals on the scroll. No more throne in heaven. No more angels flying around the throne. No more twenty-four elders casting their crowns before the throne. No more heavenly choirs singing praises to the Creator and Redeemer. This is the beginning of the seven seals, the beginning of Christ's ascent to His throne as King.

The First Seal—Rider on a White Horse

At the breaking of the first seal, John gets his very first glimpse of the future Tribulation, and the main action of the end times begins. He sees a lone rider on a white charger bent on conquest—the first of the four horsemen of the Apocalypse (Revelation 6:1-2). There are four main views on the identity of the first horseman of the Apocalypse.

View #1: Military Conquest

Revelation 6:2 says that the rider goes forth "conquering and to conquer" (NASB). Some believe that this rider pictures military conquest that leads naturally to the bloodshed, poverty, and famine symbolized in the next three horsemen.[1]

However, the next horse, the red one, seems to clearly symbolize war and bloodshed. This interpretation would make the first two seals almost indistinguishable from one another, which seems redundant and unnecessary. Moreover, the second seal takes peace from the earth (Revelation 6:4). For the rider to remove peace from the earth, peace must first exist there. Therefore, the conquest of the first rider must represent bloodless conquest and victory through diplomacy.

View #2: The Proclamation of the Gospel

The first horse is white, the color often associated with Christ or something good in Revelation (1:14; 2:17; 3:4, 5, 18; 6:11; 7:9, 13; 14:14; 19:11, 14; 20:11). Also, the bow that the rider is holding is sometimes used as a symbol of divine victory (Habakkuk 3:9). Based on this imagery, some view the rider on the white horse as the preaching of the gospel of Christ that will win its victories in spite of a hostile, evil environment.[2]

The chief problem with this view is that the four horsemen are all to be interpreted together as a kind of unit. And we must remember that they are all judgments. With this in mind, it would be strange to include the effective preaching of the gospel among the other horsemen that bring nothing but destruction and devastation. The fact that the rider carries a bow, which is an instrument of war, is also inconsistent with the spread of the gospel. Moreover, in the parallel passage in Matthew 24:4-8, the judgments of the four horsemen are described by Jesus as "the first of the birth pains." For the rider on the white horse to represent the preaching of the gospel seems out of place given this context.

View #3: Jesus Christ

One of the most popular views is that this rider represents Christ. Proponents maintain that only Christ can ride a white horse. As I mentioned above, in Revelation, white consistently symbolizes Christ or something associated with Him (1:14; 2:17; 3:4, 5, 18; 4:4; 6:11; 7:9, 13; 14:14; 19:11, 14; 20:11). Moreover, in Revelation 19:11-21, the rider on the white horse is clearly Christ, so why not interpret this rider the same way?

I believe there are three convincing reasons why the rider on the white horse *does not* represent Jesus. First, there are significant contrasts between the riders in Revelation 6:2 and Revelation 19:11-19.

RIDER ON THE WHITE HORSE (REVELATION 6:2)	RIDER ON THE WHITE HORSE (REVELATION 19:11-19)
carries a bow without any arrows	wields a sword
wears a *stephanos* or victor's crown	wears many crowns—the *diadema* or kingly crown
initiates war	destroys His enemies and brings an end to war
commences the Tribulation	climaxes the Tribulation

This rider bears the unmistakable marks of a counterfeit, and we should expect the Antichrist to imitate Christ.

Second, the four horses and their riders have an essential likeness to one another. The other three horsemen are all evil powers of tragedy and destruction. It makes no sense to put Christ in the same ballpark as the other three horsemen.[3]

Third, Christ is the Lamb opening the seals in Revelation 6:1. He is the only one worthy to open the seven seals (Revelation 5:2-8). He controls the contents of the seals. It would be strange for Him to open the seal judgments and also constitute the contents of one of the seals.

View #4: The Antichrist

Two key points strongly favor identifying this rider as the coming world dictator—the Antichrist. First, the most convincing evidence is the way Revelation 6–7 parallels Matthew 24:4-14. These passages are so similar that Matthew 24 is often referred to as the "mini Apocalypse."

PARALLELS BETWEEN MATTHEW 24:4–14 AND REVELATION 6–7

MATTHEW 24	REVELATION 6–7
false Christs (24:4-5)	rider on the white horse (6:1-2)
wars and rumors of wars (24:6-7)	rider on the red horse (6:3-4)
famine (24:7)	rider on the black horse (6:5-6)
famines and plagues (24:7; Luke 21:11)	rider on the pale horse (6:7-8)
persecution and martyrdom (24:9-10)	martyrs (6:9-11)
terrors and great cosmic signs (Luke 21:11)	terror (6:12-17)
worldwide preaching of the gospel (24:14)	ministry of the 144,000 (7:1-8)

Viewing Revelation 6–7 as parallel to Matthew 24:4-14 gives us the key clue from the very lips of Jesus in establishing the horsemen's identification. All four of the horsemen represent major movements that will be at work at the end of days. To be precise, the rider on the white horse is a wave of false messiahs that will appear after the Rapture. The sudden disappearance of all the true believers will open the floodgates for an outbreak of deception and counterfeit Christs who will claim to have the answers for the world's chaos. Eventually, one man will quickly stand out head and shoulders above the rest. He will be the decisive fulfillment of the rider on the white horse—the ultimate anti-Messiah. We know him best as the Antichrist.

Second, Revelation 6:2 says, "a crown was given to him" (NASB). John uses the verb *was given* (*edothe*) repeatedly in Revelation (9:1, 3, 5; 13:5, 7, 14, 15).[4] This verb lets the reader know that God is in control and is directing all the events in Revelation from His throne. Notice Revelation 13 uses it frequently in describing the way that God gives power to the coming world ruler. This notion of divine permission fits perfectly with the view that the rider on the white horse is the Antichrist.

For these reasons, I believe the rider is the coming false messiah who will deceive the world and convince them that he is a man of peace. He will ride forth at the beginning of the Tribulation to bring peace in the midst of global upheaval and turmoil. The image in Revelation 6:2 supports this peace-bringing interpretation. The rider wears a victor's crown and has a bow but no arrows. This imagery seems to symbolize a bloodless victory. The bow indicates the threat of war, but it never materializes because the rider gains the victory through peaceful negotiations. He brings what the world wants more than anything else—worldwide peace and safety (1 Thessalonians 5:1-3). This fits with the rider on the red horse who comes and takes peace from the earth (Revelation 6:3-4). This peace is brought to earth by the first rider on the white horse, the Antichrist.

As Billy Graham says, "Who, therefore, is the rider on the white horse? He is not Christ, but a deceiver who seeks to capture the hearts and souls of men and women. He is one who seeks to have people acknowledge him as Lord instead of the true Christ."[5] David Jeremiah aptly calls this rider "The Dark Prince on a White Horse."[6]

The Second Seal—Rider on the Red Horse

When the Lamb opens the second seal, John hears the summons from the second living being saying, "Come!" Then the second horse thunders forth (Revelation 6:3-4). There is almost universal agreement among scholars that this horse and rider represent war, international strife, and civil upheaval. The promised peace of the white horse is swiftly shattered by the war of the red horse.

The Third Seal—Rider on the Black Horse

Umberto Boccioni's painting *The City Rises* portrays the four horsemen of the Apocalypse in a modern, urban setting. The oil painting is on a massive six-foot-six-inch by nine-foot-ten-inch canvas hanging in the Museum of Modern Art in New York City. It singles out the horror of the third horse and its rider. Boccioni depicts the black horse as a tornado, spinning wildly above the other horsemen.[7] What an apt depiction. The war of the red horse will result in famine and poverty—represented by the black horse (Revelation 6:5-6).

During the Tribulation famine, the purchasing power of a denarius will drop far below what is normal (Revelation 6:6, NASB). A denarius will buy a measure of wheat or three measures of barley. A denarius was equal to an average day's wages. A measure (*koinix*) of grain was slightly less than a modern quart—the basic portion of food for one person for one day. In other words, the world will suffer hyper-inflation. Food prices will skyrocket so high it will take everything a person can earn in one day just to buy enough food for one day for himself. The prices listed here are about 1,000 percent more than the average prices in the Roman Empire at the time John was writing Revelation. As John Walvoord says, "To put it in ordinary language, the situation would be such that one would have to spend a day's wages for a loaf of bread with no money left to buy anything else. The symbolism therefore indicates a time of worldwide famine when life will be reduced to the barest necessities, for famine is almost always the aftermath of war."[8]

With the world economy suffering runaway inflation, the quality of food people can afford will quickly deteriorate. People will resort to lower quality food just to put something on the table for their families. In the ancient world, wheat was the main food and barley was a lesser quality grain with less nutritional value. It was often used to feed animals. During this future famine, people will quit buying the normal foods they have been used to and will turn to cheaper foods. By eating food of grossly inferior quality, a family of three will have enough to eat for one day; whereas only one person could eat the more expensive wheat. In terms of today's market, it will require a full day's wages just to buy a day's worth of meat and potatoes for one person, or a day's worth of macaroni and cheese for a whole family. The world will be swallowed up by the rider on the black horse. The world will writhe in the clutches of stabbing hunger. The global economic collapse and food shortage will set the stage for the Antichrist to move into position to begin seizing control of the world economy as described in Revelation 13.

The Fourth Seal—Rider on the Pale Horse

As the earth reels from the devastation of the first three horsemen, the rider on the fourth horse will appear (Revelation 6:7-8). The word used to describe the fourth horse's color is *ashen* or *pale.* The Greek word *chloros* is the source for our English word *chlorine*. It usually denotes a pale green color. Revelation uses it elsewhere to describe the color of grass and vegetation (8:7; 9:4). However, in Revelation 6:8 the word "designates the yellowish green of decay, the pallor of death. It is the pale ashen color that images a face bleached because of terror. It recalls a corpse in the advanced state of corruption."[9]

Chuck Swindoll describes the carnage of the pale rider: "In this terrifying scene, John saw the grim reaper and the grave digger moving together across the face of the earth. Death slays the body while Hades swallows up the soul. These two symbols represent the massive number of deaths that will follow in the wake of the first three horsemen. One-quarter of the world's population will be lost in their rampage."[10]

The fourth horseman will use four means to wreak his havoc: war, famine, disease, and the wild beasts of the earth. The first three are straightforward, but there are three main interpretations of "wild beasts of the earth" (Revelation 6:8, NASB).

One view suggests that some wild animals will become especially ferocious during the Tribulation because their normal food supplies are disrupted. They will look for prey and take advantage of the defenseless, and God will use them to terrorize and destroy.[11]

Another view sees the wild beasts of the earth as referring to the military and political leaders who overpower, oppress, and persecute their subjects. Revelation uses the Greek word for "wild beast" (*theerion*) thirty-eight times, and the word always refers to the coming Antichrist or the false prophet. It occurs most frequently in Revelation 13, where the two "wild beasts" rise to power and afflict the world.[12] This word evokes the vicious, brutal, bestial character of the Antichrist's kingdom.

A third view believes the wild beasts refer to animals and birds that originate many plagues such as AIDS, Ebola, bird flu, and other deadly diseases.

I believe the best view of these wild beasts is the second view. It seems best to identify the wild beasts with international political and military rulers since the book of Revelation uses the term this way every other time. Whichever of these views is correct, these wild beasts will be a key part of the fourfold devastation of the pale rider.

The Fifth Seal—Martyrs

The fifth seal depicts the martyrdom of believers on earth during the Tribulation (Revelation 6:9-11). After the Rapture, many will come to faith in Christ and will suffer persecution. The fifth seal pictures these martyrs in heaven praying for vindication.

One important question about the fifth seal is, how will the deaths of believers be a judgment for the world? Remember, the seals are divine judgments. The death of God's people brings judgment in two ways. First, the removal of God's people, the salt and light of the world, will allow darkness and corruption to overrun the earth unchecked. It will be a case of the blind leading the blind. Second, as the enemies of God murder His people, they are unknowingly heaping more judgment upon themselves. Also, God will answer these martyrs' prayers for vindication when He pours out His wrath on His enemies.

The Sixth Seal—Devastation

When the sixth seal is opened, the devastating cataclysms of the end times will be unleashed (Revelation 6:12-14). These disasters produce sheer panic on earth as all people—rich and poor, great and small—cry out in dread and hide themselves like frightened animals in the caves and crevices of the earth. Instead of fleeing to the God of mercy for refuge and humbly bowing before Him in worship, they conceal themselves in caves, consumed with frenzied fear (Revelation 6:15-16).

The Seventh Seal—Seven Trumpets

Between the sixth and seventh seals there is an intermission. Then the seventh seal is opened in Revelation 8:1. When it is opened there is "silence throughout heaven for about half an hour." John Walvoord says, "Though thirty minutes is not ordinarily considered a long time, in this case it indicates that something tremendous is about to take place. It may be compared to the silence before the foreman of a jury reports a verdict; for a moment there is perfect silence and everyone awaits that which will follow."[13] The stunned silence in Revelation may result from the anticipation that more judgments are coming. The seventh seal is not the end; when it is opened it contains seven trumpets of judgment.

Although some view the seven seals, trumpets, and bowls as parallel and simultaneous, the fact that the seventh seal contains the seven trumpets indicates that the seven trumpets follow the seven seals and that the seven bowls in turn follow the seven trumpets. Also, since the judgments in each series are different and intensify as the Tribulation progresses, the succession view is best. This chart shows how these three series of judgments relate to one another.

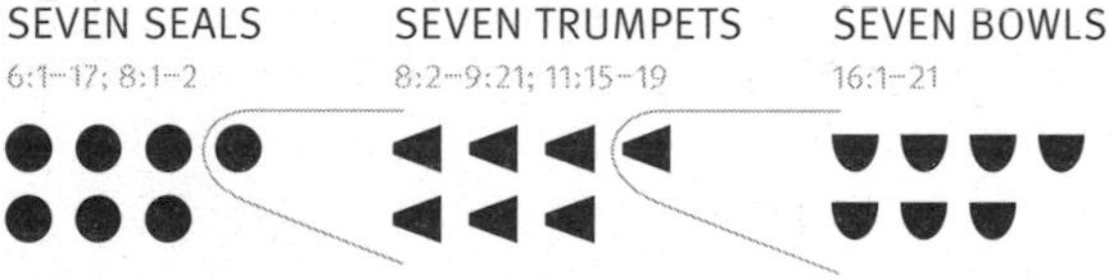

In Revelation 5, Jesus receives the seven-sealed scroll in heaven. The scroll contains His inheritance, which is the kingdom of this world. For that inheritance to be realized, the seven seals must be opened. As Christ opens each seal, judgment is unleashed, but the end of the seals is not the end of the Tribulation. The seventh seal contains another series of judgments—the seven trumpets. However, before the trumpets sound, an interlude introduces two groups who will play a key role in the end times.

Who Is Able to Stand?

Revelation 6 ends with the sobering question, "For the great day of their wrath has come, and who is able to stand?" (NASB). In light of all the devastation let loose in the seal judgments, one might reasonably conclude that no one could possibly stand. Revelation 7, however, reveals that two distinct groups of the redeemed will stand strong during the Tribulation. One group will stand strong on earth under the hand of God's protection, while the other group, after suffering martyrdom for their faith, will stand before God's throne in heaven. We'll meet these two groups in the next chapter.

CHAPTER 23

THE 144,000

At most sporting events you can purchase a program that lists the players for each team and includes their jersey numbers and some other information about them such as height, weight, and what position they play. Without a program, it's often difficult to identify them correctly. The same is true in the study of end times prophecy. There are several key players whose identities are crucial to understanding what's happening. God highlights these players and provides important information about them. One set of key actors in the end times is a mysterious group of 144,000 people who faithfully serve the Lord. They are listed in Revelation 7:1-8 and discussed again in Revelation 14:1-5. The 144,000 have been the subject of considerable speculation. Who is this congregation of God's people?[1]

The Identity of the 144,000

The most common view is that the 144,000 represent the church of Jesus Christ, which is understood as the true, spiritual Israel. Proponents often identify the 144,000 in Revelation 7:1-8 with the great multitude in Revelation 7:9-17. George Eldon Ladd, who held this view, says, "They represent the same people—the church—seen in two stages of her history in the end times: first, standing on the threshold of the great tribulation, and later having passed through this time of tribulation, martyred but victorious."[2] While this view is very popular and is held by many commentators I highly respect, I disagree with this position for three main reasons.

First, Revelation 7:4 says, "one hundred and forty-four thousand sealed from every tribe of the sons of Israel" (NASB). This is important because the word *Israel* is never used for the church in the New Testament, and there is no clear example of this in the early church until AD 160.[3] The noted Lutheran scholar J. A. Seiss states why he believes Revelation 7 refers to Jews:

> As I read the Bible, when God says "children of Israel," I do not understand Him to mean any but people of Jewish blood, be they Christians or not; and when He speaks of the twelve tribes of the sons of Jacob, and gives the names of the tribes, it is impossible for me to believe that He means the Gentiles, in any sense or degree, whether they be believers or not. . . . I know of no instance in which the descendants of the twelve tribes of Israel include the Gentiles.[4]

Why would the Holy Spirit begin to mix the church and Israel in the book of Revelation, the final book in the New Testament, when He has so carefully distinguished the two groups in the previous twenty-six books of the New Testament? Why begin to identify the church as the true, spiritual Israel at this late point in the New Testament? It does not make good sense and is inconsistent.

Second, if one holds to the pre-Tribulation timing for the Rapture, the church is already in heaven as pictured by the twenty-four elders in Revelation 4–5. Thus, it doesn't make sense that the group in Revelation 7, which is on earth, would be the church. The church has already been raptured.

Third, it is interesting that Jews and Gentiles are clearly distinguished from one another in Revelation 7. The 144,000 Jews are listed in 7:1-8 while 7:9-17 presents an innumerable host of "every nation and tribe and people and language." Merging these two groups does not do justice to the distinctions that Revelation 7 makes.

REVELATION 7:1-8	REVELATION 7:9-17
Jews (from twelve tribes of Israel)	Gentiles (from every nation, tribe, people, and language)
numbered—144,000	not numbered—"a great multitude which no one could count" (NASB)
standing on earth	standing before God's throne
sealed for protection	ascended after persecution

Furthermore, Revelation 7 clearly distinguishes between Jews and Gentiles, but this distinction is inconsistent with the New Testament picture of the church—Jews and Gentiles are seen as one in the body of Christ (Galatians 3:27-28; Ephesians 3:6). Since Galatians 3 and Ephesians 3 unite Jews and Gentiles as one and since Revelation 7 does not reflect that unity, the Rapture must reinstitute a division between Jews and Gentiles. Revelation 7 reflects that division.

So then, who are these 144,000 servants of God? If the Scriptures are interpreted literally, then the 144,000 are a literal group of 144,000 Jewish men—12,000 from each of the twelve tribes of Israel raised up by God during the Tribulation to serve Him. They are not *spiritual* Israel (the church), but *actual* Israel. As John F. Walvoord says, "Israel's tribes are still in existence, and God certainly knows who they are."[5]

The Characteristics of the 144,000

Two main texts in Revelation describe the 144,000: 7:1-8 and 14:1-5. Revelation 7 is an intermission before the seventh seal is opened. It's like a flashback to the beginning of the ministry of the 144,000 and gives a panorama of their activity. Revelation 14:1-5 pictures the 144,000 at the end of the Tribulation. These texts highlight six main characteristics that provide insight into the identity and ministry of these 144,000 servants of God.

1. PURCHASED

The 144,000 "had been purchased from the earth" (Revelation 14:3, NASB). The word *purchased* means to "redeem or pay the price for something." The precious blood of Christ purchased these servants of God. They have been bought for a price. They belong to the Lord as His special possession.

2. PREPARED

The 144,000 are prepared for God's service by being given His seal (Revelation 7:3-4). On earth during the Tribulation, the followers of the Beast will bear his mark on their right hand or forehead (Revelation 13:16). During this same time, the Lord will identify His people by placing a seal of ownership on their foreheads (Revelation 14:1).

Revelation 7 and 13 use two different Greek words distinguishing these marks from each other. In Revelation 7, God seals the 144,000 on their foreheads. The word used there, *sphragizo*, symbolizes the spiritual sealing mentioned throughout the New Testament (John 3:33; 6:27; 2 Corinthians 1:22; Ephesians 1:13; 4:30). But in Revelation 13, where followers of the Antichrist are given a mark, the word *charagma* refers to a literal brand, tattoo, or etching.

The seal of the 144,000 sets them apart and prepares them for God's service. As Robert Thomas says, "It was not uncommon for a soldier or a guild member to receive such a mark as a religious devotee. The mark was a sign of consecration to deity. The forehead was chosen because it was the most conspicuous, the most noble, and the part by which a person is usually identified. It will be obvious to whom these slaves belong and whom they serve."[6]

3. PROTECTED

God's seal not only prepares the 144,000 for service, but it also protects them. The seal is God's pledge of security. God seals the 144,000 before allowing the four angels to bring their judgment on the earth (Revelation 7:1-3). The 144,000 will be protected from the wrath of God and Satan during the Tribulation (Revelation 9:4).

In Revelation 14:1-5, John sees the 144,000 at the end of the Tribulation standing triumphantly on Mount Zion—the city of Jerusalem. Notice he doesn't see 143,999. All 144,000 have been divinely preserved by the Lord. Not one has been overlooked. They have come all the way through the Tribulation and are still standing triumphant and victorious on the earth. God will preserve and protect His sealed servants for seven years through the horror of the Tribulation. His pledge of security will be fulfilled.

4. PURE

The 144,000 are pure virgins who have not defiled themselves with women (Revelation 14:4). Many interpret this figuratively—meaning they are spiritually undefiled and pure, separated from the corruption and pollution of false religion. However, Scripture's explicit statement that they are not defiled with women suggests that these servants of God are male, celibate servants of God. In light of the pressures of the Tribulation period, they are called by God to abstain from a normal married life and devote themselves totally to the Lord's service (1 Corinthians 7:29-35).

5. PERSISTENT

The 144,000 persevere in their service for the Lord even under the direst circumstances. During the terrible days of the Tribulation they constantly "follow the Lamb wherever He goes" (Revelation 14:4, NASB). Jesus is the Lamb, but He is also the Shepherd. He knows the way, and the 144,000 follow Him wherever He leads.

6. PREACHERS

These Jewish servants fearlessly proclaim the gospel of Christ during the Tribulation period. There appears to be a cause-and-effect relationship in Revelation 7 between the 144,000 Jewish believers in verses 1-8 and the innumerable crowd of Gentile believers in verses 9-17. The ministry of the

144,000 brings about salvation for millions of people. They will be the greatest evangelists the world has ever seen. These sealed servants of God will fulfill Matthew 24:14: "This gospel of the kingdom shall be preached in the whole world as a testimony to all the nations, and then the end will come" (NASB). Revelation 7 provides a panorama of God's saving work during the Tribulation.

The 144,000 reveal God's passion to save people even in the midst of the unspeakable judgment of the Tribulation. To the very end, the Savior will graciously continue "to seek and save those who are lost" (Luke 19:10).

Conclusion

The 144,000 are important for three reasons. First, they reveal God's faithfulness to His promises. God seals them in Revelation 7 and keeps them to the end of the Tribulation. They make it all the way through under God's protecting hand. God keeps His promises. Second, we learn that even in judgment, God is merciful. God will use the 144,000 as messengers of mercy during the Tribulation. Every judgment of God beginning with Noah all the way to the Tribulation, including the judgment of God's own Son on the cross, reveals God's mercy. Third, these Jewish witnesses will help fulfill the prophecy Jesus gave in Matthew 24:14. The 144,000 will spread the good news of Jesus all over the globe during the Tribulation, and the end won't come until they're finished.

CHAPTER 24

THE BATTLE OF GOG AND MAGOG

Ezekiel 38–39

The greatest threat to modern Israel's continued existence has not yet occurred. In spite of Israel's ingenuity and proven ability to defend itself, according to the Bible, the Jewish people will one day face their greatest military test. One of the most dramatic events of the end times is an invasion of Israel by a vast horde of nations from every direction. The prophet Ezekiel describes this invasion, known as the Battle of Gog and Magog (Ezekiel 38–39). This coalition of invading nations will be motivated by a seething desire to eradicate Israel, enrich themselves, and entangle Israel's allies in the war. The West, led by the group of ten and the Antichrist, will be tied to Israel by the covenant in Daniel 9:27; thus, any attack against Israel will constitute an attack against the Western confederacy. The group of ten's bold move to make the peace treaty with Israel and her neighbors and consolidate absolute power over the Middle East will apparently result in a disastrous countermove by the nations listed in Ezekiel 38–39. The invading coalition attacks Israel in part as a direct challenge—a strategic power play—against the Antichrist and the group of ten. Israel's guard will be down as a result of the treaty with the Antichrist, so the attack will catch the country totally by surprise. Only the supernatural intervention of God will deliver Israel from total annihilation.

To help understand Ezekiel 38–39, we will use five standard questions of journalism: who, when, why, what, and how.

Who? The Participants (Ezekiel 38:1-7)

The prophecy of the Battle of Gog and Magog begins with a list of ten proper names in 38:1-7, or what we might call "God's Most Wanted List."

> The word of the Lord came to me saying, "Son of man, set your face toward *Gog* of the land of *Magog*, the prince of *Rosh*, *Meshech* and *Tubal*, and prophesy against him and say, 'Thus says the Lord God, "Behold, I am against you, O Gog, prince of Rosh, Meshech and Tubal. I will turn you about and put hooks into your jaws, and I will bring you out, and all your army, horses and horsemen, all of them splendidly attired, a great company with buckler and shield, all of them wielding swords; *Persia*, *Ethiopia* and *Put* with them, all of them with shield and helmet; *Gomer* with all its troops; *Beth-togarmah* from the remote parts of the north with all its troops—many peoples with you. Be prepared, and prepare yourself, you and all your companies that are assembled about you, and be a guard for them."'"
>
> EZEKIEL 38:1-7 (NASB, ITALICS ADDED)

Gog

The name Gog, which occurs eleven times in Ezekiel 38–39, is a name or title of the leader of the invasion. Gog is clearly an individual since he is directly addressed several times by God (38:14; 39:1) and is called a prince (38:2; 39:1).

The other nine proper names in Ezekiel 38:1-7 are specific geographical locations: Magog, Rosh, Meshech, Tubal, Persia, Cush (often translated as Ethiopia), Put, Gomer, and Beth-togarmah. Ezekiel used ancient place names familiar to the people of his day. The names have changed many times throughout history, but the geographical territory remains the same. Regardless of what names they may carry at the time of this invasion, a literal interpretation holds that these specific geographical areas will be involved. Let's briefly look at each of these ancient locations and examine them; then we'll identify the modern counterpart.

Magog

According to the Jewish historian Josephus, the ancient Scythians inhabited the land of Magog.[1] The Scythians were northern nomadic tribes who inhabited territory from Central Asia across the southern steppes of modern Russia. Magog today probably represents nations from the former Soviet Union: Kazakhstan, Kirghizia, Uzbekistan, Turkmenistan, and Tajikistan. Afghanistan could also be part of this territory.

Rosh[2]

Bible scholars have often identified Rosh with Russia. But this conclusion has not been unanimous. Two key questions must be answered to properly identify Rosh: (1) Is Rosh a common noun or a proper name? and (2) Does Rosh have any relation to Russia?

COMMON NOUN OR PROPER NAME?

The word *rosh* in Hebrew simply means "head, top, summit, or chief." It is a very common word used in all Semitic languages. Most Bible translations translate *rosh* as a common noun—"chief." The King James Version, Revised Standard Version, English Standard Version, New American Bible, New Living Translation, and New International Version all adopt this translation. However, the Jerusalem Bible, New English Bible, and New American Standard Bible all translate Rosh as a proper name indicating a geographical location.

The weight of evidence favors translating Rosh in Ezekiel 38–39 as a proper name. Five arguments support this view. First, the eminent Hebrew scholars C. F. Keil and Wilhelm Gesenius both hold that a proper noun is the better translation of Rosh in Ezekiel 38:2-3 and 39:1, referring to a specific geographical location.[3]

Second, the Greek translation of the Old Testament, the Septuagint, translates Rosh as the proper name *Ros*. This translation is especially significant since the Septuagint was translated only three centuries after Ezekiel was written—obviously much closer to the original than any modern translation. The modern translations of Rosh as an adjective can be traced to the Latin Vulgate of Jerome.[4]

Third, in their articles on Rosh, many Bible dictionaries and encyclopedias (*New Bible Dictionary*, *Wycliffe Bible Dictionary*, and *International Standard Bible Encyclopedia*) support taking it as a proper name in Ezekiel 38.

Fourth, Rosh is mentioned the first time in Ezekiel 38:2 and then repeated in Ezekiel 38:3 and 39:1. If Rosh were simply a title, it would be dropped in these two places, because when titles are repeated in Hebrew, they are generally abbreviated.

Fifth, the most impressive evidence in favor of taking Rosh as a proper name is simply that this translation in this context is the most natural. G. A. Cooke translates Ezekiel 38:2, "the chief of Rosh, Meshech and Tubal." He calls this "the most natural way of rendering the Hebrew."[5]

The compelling evidence of biblical scholarship indicates that Rosh be understood as a proper name—the name of a specific geographic area.

WHERE IS ROSH?

Having established that Rosh should be translated as a proper name for a geographical area, our next task is to determine what location Rosh is referring to. There are two key reasons for understanding Rosh in Ezekiel 38–39 as a reference to Russia.

First, linguistically and historically, there is substantial evidence that in Ezekiel's day there was a group of people known variously as Rash, Reshu, or Ros who lived in what today is southern Russia.[6] Egyptian inscriptions as early as 2600 BC identify a place called Rosh (*Rash*). A later Egyptian inscription from about 1500 BC refers to a land called Reshu that was located to the north of Egypt.[7] Other ancient documents include a place named Rosh or its equivalent in various languages. The word appears three times in the Septuagint (LXX), ten times in Sargon's inscriptions, once in Ashurbanipal's cylinder, once in Sennacherib's annals, and five times in Ugaritic tablets.[8] While the word has a variety of forms and spellings, it is clear that the same people are in view. Rosh was apparently a well-known place in Ezekiel's day.

After providing extensive evidence of the origin and early history of the Rosh people, and then tracing them through the centuries, Clyde Billington concludes:

> Historical, ethnological, and archaeological evidence all favor the conclusion that the Rosh people of Ezekiel 38–39 were the ancestors of the Rus/Ros people of Europe and Asia. . . . Those Rosh people who lived to the north of the Black Sea in ancient and medieval times were called the Rus/Ros/Rox/Aorsi from very early times. . . . The Rosh people of the area north of the Black Sea formed the people known today as the Russians.[9]

The great Hebrew scholar Wilhelm Gesenius, who died in 1842, noted that Rosh is "undoubtedly the Russians."[10]

Second, geographically, Ezekiel 38–39 emphasizes repeatedly that at least part of this invading force will come from the "remote parts of the north" (38:6, 15; 39:2, NASB). The Bible usually provides directions in reference to Israel, which, on God's compass, is the center of the earth (Ezekiel 38:12). If you draw a line directly north from Israel, the land that is most remote or distant to the north is Russia.

Meshech and Tubal

Scripture normally mentions Meshech and Tubal together. In his notes on Ezekiel 38:2, C. I. Scofield identifies Meshech and Tubal as the Russian cities of Moscow and Tobolsk: "That the primary reference is to the northern (European) powers, headed up by Russia, all agree. . . . The reference to Meshech and Tubal (Moscow and Tobolsk) is a clear mark of identification."[11]

While the names do sound alike, this is not a proper method of identification. Meshech and Tubal are mentioned two other times in Ezekiel (27:13; 32:26). In Ezekiel 27:13, they are mentioned as trading partners with ancient Tyre. It is highly unlikely that ancient Tyre (modern Lebanon) was trading with Moscow and the Siberian city of Tobolsk. The preferred identification is that Meshech and Tubal are the ancient Moschoi and Tibarenoi in Greek writings, or Tabal and Musku in Assyrian inscriptions. These ancient locations are in present-day Turkey. This identification is best understood as referring to modern Turkey.

Persia

The words *Persia*, *Persian*, and *Persians* are found thirty-five times in the Old Testament. In Ezekiel 38:5, Persia is best understood as modern-day Iran. The ancient land of Persia became the modern nation of Iran in March 1935, and then the name was changed to the Islamic Republic of Iran in 1979.

Ethiopia (Cush)

Modern versions often translate the Hebrew word *Cush* in Ezekiel 38:5 as "Ethiopia." Ancient Cush was called Kusu by the Assyrians and Babylonians, Kos or Kas by the Egyptians, and Nubia by the Greeks. Secular history locates Cush directly south of ancient Egypt, extending south past the modern city of Khartoum, which is the capital of modern Sudan. Thus, modern Sudan inhabits the ancient land of Cush.

Libya (Put)

Some ancient sources indicate that Put or Phut was a North African nation. The New Living Translation documents this identification in footnotes for a number of passages, including Isaiah 66:19; Jeremiah 46:9; and Ezekiel 27:10; 30:5; 38:5. From the *Babylonian Chronicles*, tablets that recorded ancient Babylonian history, it appears that Put was the "distant" land to the west of Egypt, which would be modern-day Libya and could possibly include nations farther west such as modern Algeria and Tunisia. The Septuagint renders the word *Put* as *Libues*.

Gomer

Gomer has often been identified by Bible teachers as Germany, or more particularly East Germany before the fall of Communism. This identification is superficial and not the literal meaning of the word in its cultural and historic context. Gomer is probably a reference to the ancient Cimmerians or *Kimmerioi*. Ancient history identifies biblical Gomer with the Akkadian *Gi-mir-ra-a* and the Armenian *Gamir*. Beginning in the eighth century BC, the Cimmerians occupied territory in what is now modern Turkey. Josephus noted that the Gomerites were identified with the Galatians who inhabited what today is central Turkey.[12]

Beth-togarmah

The Hebrew word *beth* means "house," so Beth-togarmah means the "house of Togarmah." Ezekiel 27:14 mentions Togarmah as a nation that traded horses and mules with ancient Tyre. Ezekiel 38:6 states that the armies of Beth-togarmah will join in, too, from the distant north. Ancient Togarmah was also known as Til-garamu (Assyrian) or Tegarma (Hittite), and its territory is in modern Turkey, north of Israel. Again, Turkey is identified as part of this group of nations that attack Israel to challenge the group of ten.

THE GOG COALITION

ANCIENT NAME	MODERN NATION
Rosh (Rashu, Rasapu, Ros, and Rus)	Russia
Magog (Scythians)	Central Asia and possibly Afghanistan
Meshech (Muschki and Musku)	Turkey
Tubal (Tubalu)	Turkey
Persia	Iran
Ethiopia (Cush)	Sudan
Libya (Put or Phut)	Libya
Gomer (Cimmerians)	Turkey
Beth-togarmah (Til-garamu or Tegarma)	Turkey

Based on these identifications, Ezekiel 38–39 predicts an invasion of the land of Israel in the last days by a vast confederation of nations from north of the Black and Caspian Seas, extending to modern Iran in the east, as far as modern Libya to the west, and to Sudan in the south. Therefore, Russia will have at least five key allies: Turkey, Iran, Libya, Sudan, and the Central Asian nations of the former Soviet Union.

Who's Missing

You might have noticed several nations that *are not* listed in this coalition. For instance, there's no specific mention of Israel's neighboring nations such as Egypt, Syria, Jordan, Lebanon, Saudi Arabia, or Iraq (ancient Babylon). Their absence raises a legitimate question—why are they omitted? There are several possible answers to the question.

First, one possibility is that these nations will be destroyed prior to the Battle of Gog and Magog. Prophecy teachers who posit this refer to an earlier "Psalm 83 War" in which the near enemies of Israel are destroyed before the Tribulation period begins. I don't hold this view, partly because it misinterprets Psalm 83. Psalm 83 is a community or corporate lament in which Asaph is calling upon the Lord to deal with the enemies of the nation. I believe that Psalm 83, like Psalm 2, is simply a presentation of the age-old hatred for Israel by its neighbors and the confidence that the Lord will one day intervene to destroy them. If there were a "Psalm 83 War," one would expect the prophets to describe it somewhere in detail, but I don't see it anywhere in the Prophets.

A second explanation is that these nations could be part of the treaty the Antichrist forges between Israel and her neighbors. The nations may be at "peace" with Israel and abstain from this invasion.

A third possibility is that these nations could be part of the invasion even though they are not specifically mentioned. After listing the allies in the Battle of Gog and Magog, Ezekiel adds, "and many others" (Ezekiel 38:6). Some interpret this phrase to include other nations surrounding Israel. When one looks on a map it's clear that the nations mentioned in Ezekiel 38:1-6 are what we might call the "distant enemies" of Israel. They represent the farthest geographic enemies of Israel in every direction—Russia to the north, Iran to the east, Sudan to the south, and Libya to the west. It could be that Ezekiel lists the perimeter nations and then includes the near enemies in the words "and many others."

When? The Period (Ezekiel 38:8)

While there is general agreement about many of the details in Ezekiel 38–39, the timing of the battle is the most debated issue. Scholars have located the battle at almost every major point in the end times from the Rapture all the way to the end of the Millennium. So, when will the Battle of Gog and Magog occur? Are there any significant clues to help narrow down the time? Ezekiel 38:7-11, 14, 16 provides the keys.

> Be prepared, and prepare yourself, you and all your companies that are assembled about you, and be a guard for them. After many days you will be summoned; in the latter years you will come into the land that is restored from the sword, whose inhabitants have been gathered from many nations to the mountains of Israel which had been a continual waste; but its people were brought out from the nations, and they are living securely, all of them. You will go up, you will come like a storm; you will be like a cloud covering the land, you and all your troops, and many peoples with you. Thus says the Lord God, "It will come about on that day, that thoughts will come into your mind and you will devise an evil plan, and you will say, 'I will go up against the land of unwalled villages. I will go against those who are at rest, that live securely, all of them living without walls and having no bars or gates. . . .'" Therefore prophesy, son of man, and say to Gog, "Thus says the Lord God, 'On that day when My people Israel are living securely, will you not know it? . . . And you will come up against My people Israel like a cloud to cover the land. It shall come about in the last days that I will bring you against My land, so that the nations may know Me when I am sanctified through you before their eyes, O Gog.'" (NASB)

In the Past?

Some argue that due to the mention of swords, spears, and horses this battle must have already occurred. It is true that the weapons are ancient weapons and the transportation is ancient transportation. How do we account for these ancient weapons if this invasion is in the end times? There are two plausible answers to this question.

First, by the time this event is fulfilled, it could be that nations will have to resort back to archaic weapons and means of transportation due to depleted resources or a sweeping disarmament agreement. Albert Einstein reportedly said, "I know not with what weapons World War III will be fought, but World War IV will be fought with sticks and stones."[13] He could be right. John Walvoord favors this view. "A second solution is that the battle will be preceded by a disarmament agreement between nations. If this were the case, it would be necessary to resort to primitive weapons easily and secretly made if a surprise attack were to be achieved. This would allow a literal interpretation of this passage. . . . Whatever the explanation, the most sensible interpretation is that the passage refers to actual weapons pressed into use because of the peculiar circumstances of that day."[14]

A second explanation is that Ezekiel described weapons in language that the people of that day could understand. The focus clearly is not the weapons. The point is that the invaders will use weapons of destruction and there will be all-out warfare. Moreover, the main point of Ezekiel's great prophecy is that a specific group of nations will attack Israel, intent on completely destroying her.

Either explanation is possible, but the main point is that no invasion even remotely similar to the one described here has ever occurred in Israel's history, despite the claims by some preterists.[15] John Walvoord says it succinctly: "There has never been a war with Israel which fulfills the prophecies of Ezekiel 38-39."[16]

In the Future?

This battle will occur in the future, in the end times, but when in the future? What indications do we have in Ezekiel 38–39 about the timing of this invasion? Capable Bible scholars have offered several opinions, and there has been considerable disagreement. Every view has problems. Various scholars have placed the invasion at almost every point in the end times. Some believe the battle will take place before the Rapture (this is the view in the Left Behind series); others believe it will occur between the Rapture and the Tribulation; others believe it will take place in connection with the Battle of Armageddon at the end of the Great Tribulation. Some believe it occurs at the end of the Millennium, since Revelation 20:8 refers to Gog and Magog. Others maintain that it will unfold in phases throughout the Tribulation: Phase one (Ezekiel 38) will occur at the middle of the Tribulation, while phase two (Ezekiel 39) will transpire at the end of the Tribulation.

SEVEN VIEWS OF THE TIMING OF EZEKIEL 38–39
1. before the Rapture
2. between the Rapture and the beginning of the Tribulation
3. first half of the Tribulation (some put it close to the midpoint)
4. end of the Tribulation (equates Ezekiel 38–39 with Armageddon)
5. two phases (Ezekiel 38 at the midpoint; Ezekiel 39 at the end)
6. beginning of the Millennium
7. end of the Millennium

Chronological Clues

We are not left to our own speculation in timing the events of Ezekiel 38–39. The text gives us clues that suggest when this battle will take place.[17] One important clue places the battle between the national and spiritual rebirths of Israel. This clue rises from the broader context of Ezekiel's prophecy. The battle in Ezekiel 38–39 is placed between the regathering of Israel in Ezekiel 37 and the restoration of the Jewish people as they worship in the millennial Temple in Ezekiel 40–48. As John Phillips notes, "The prophet put it between a discussion of the physical rebirth of the nation of Israel (chap. 37) and a long description of Israel's spiritual rebirth (chaps. 40-48). In other words, Russia's brief day of triumph lies somewhere between those two crucial events. . . . The prophet deliberately sandwiched Russia's 'date with destiny' between Israel's political and spiritual rebirths."[18] This context narrows the time frame down to the period between 1948—when the modern nation of Israel came into being—and the beginning of the millennial kingdom.

The phrases "latter years" (Ezekiel 38:8, NASB) and "last days" (38:16, NASB) are our next clues. These Old Testament terms refer to the "last days" for Israel, which extends from the beginning of the Tribulation to the Millennium. I believe this clue renders it highly unlikely that the battle would happen any time before the Tribulation. The Tribulation period inaugurates the "latter years" for Israel. The battle will happen after that.

Another clue places the battle at a time when Israel is at rest in its ancient homeland (Ezekiel 38:8, 11, 14). There have not been too many times in God's prophetic program when Israel has been at rest. The Jewish people have been scattered over the face of the earth and persecuted in many places. So when might this period of rest occur? There are a number of views.

WHEN ISRAEL IS AT PEACE

Some argue that Israel is at rest and living securely today, and they believe this prophecy could be fulfilled at any time. They maintain that Israel is living in great prosperity and is enjoying security.

While that is true to some degree, no matter how hard one might try to stretch the meaning of these words, Israel is not really at rest today. Today an armed truce and a no-man's-land separate Israel from their enemies. At the time of this writing, Israel is an armed camp, living under a tenuous truce with only two of their Arab neighbors—Egypt and Jordan—and both of those agreements could be jeopardized at any time by current events in the Middle East. Their other neighbors would love nothing more than to drive every Israelite into the Mediterranean Sea and kill all of them. The reason that they do not is that, humanly speaking, Israel has a good army that is more than a match for its neighbors. Every young Israeli man is required to have three years of military training and every young woman, two years of military training. While the women are trained for jobs that are not necessarily combatant, they also learn to use weapons, so that if they need to fight, they can. After military training, many of them are settled in villages near the border, where they can serve a double purpose—following their civilian job, whatever it is, and serving as guards for the border of Israel. If the nations of Ezekiel 38–39 should invade the Middle East today, it would not fulfill this prophecy because Israel is not at rest. Israel's current state of unrest does not correspond to Ezekiel's prophecy.

Another point when Israel will be at rest is during the millennial kingdom. But Isaiah 2:4 expressly tells us that there will be no war in the millennial kingdom. So the invasion cannot occur during the millennial reign of Christ.

Still others suggest that Israel will be at rest during the Tribulation just before the second coming of Christ. They maintain that the prophecy of Gog and Magog will be fulfilled at that time in conjunction with the final Battle of Armageddon. This view equates Ezekiel 38–39 with Revelation 19. One point in favor of this view is that both of these battles are great end times conflagrations in the land of Israel and both mention the birds feeding on the carnage (Ezekiel 39:17-19; Revelation 19:17-18).

However, while there are certainly similarities between the two passages, a few significant differences demonstrate that they are two separate wars.

GOG AND MAGOG	ARMAGEDDON
Invasion is led by Gog.	Invasion is led by the Antichrist.
Gog is destroyed.	The Antichrist and the false prophet are destroyed. No mention of Gog.
Israel is at peace at the time of the invasion.	There is no mention of Israel's peace.
Armies gather to plunder Israel.	Armies gather to fight against Christ.
Occurs during the first half of the Tribulation.	Occurs at the end of the Tribulation.
Russia and her allies invade Israel.	All nations invade Israel.
Occurs so that all the nations will know that He is God.	Occurs to destroy the nations.

Another reason this war cannot happen during the latter half of the Tribulation is that Israel will not be at rest during the Great Tribulation, for Christ told the Jewish people in Israel to flee to the mountains to escape their persecutors (Matthew 24:15-16). Therefore, the invasion Ezekiel describes cannot be a part of the Battle of Armageddon at the end of the Tribulation.

The Preferred View

In my view, only one future period clearly fits Ezekiel's description. Only one view places the battle between the physical and spiritual rebirth, transpires in the "last days" for Israel, occurs before the Millennium, and happens while Israel is at rest. That time is after the Rapture when Israel has signed a peace treaty with the Antichrist. This is the first half of the Tribulation or what's called Daniel's seventieth week, prophesied in Daniel 9.

The seven-year peace treaty will guarantee protection for the people of Israel. Israel will be able to relax. This peacetime moment in Israel's history fits the prophetic scenario perfectly. With these guarantees of secure borders and international peace, Israel will turn her energies toward increasing wealth rather than defense. But the peace treaty will be shattered less than four years later.

This timing of the invasion also fits well with the inauguration of the global empire of the Antichrist, which begins at the midpoint of the seven-year Tribulation. Something significant must happen to launch the Antichrist to world power. The decimation of the Gog coalition would leave a massive power vacuum and provide a plausible explanation for the Antichrist's sudden rise. Since the Antichrist is allied with Israel and probably committed to her security, he may try to take credit for the destruction of Gog's army. He could possibly even claim to have some powerful weapon that caused the destruction. In any case, he will certainly seize the opening and "spin" it all to his own advantage. The Antichrist's rise to world power midway through the Tribulation is another reason that favors placing Ezekiel 38–39 shortly before the midpoint of the Tribulation.

John Phillips agrees: "Only one period fits all the facts. . . . The invasion, then, takes place *after* the Rapture of the church, *after* the rise of the

Beast in the West, *after* the signing of the pact with Israel, and just *before* the Beast takes over the world. Indeed it is the collapse of Russia that makes his global empire possible."[19]

The main objection to this timetable is Ezekiel 39:9, which says that in the wake of the battle, the inhabitants of Israel will make fires with the weapons for a period of seven years. This would mean that if this invasion occurs during the first half of the Tribulation, the weapons would be burned throughout the second half of the Tribulation and even on into the first years of the Millennium. While this is admittedly a problem for this timeline, it is not unexplainable. Jews could continue to burn the weapons during the last half of the Tribulation and the first 3½ years of the Millennium. This would fulfill the prediction of Ezekiel 39:9.

Accounting for all the factors of Ezekiel 38–39, the best option with the fewest drawbacks is to place the events during the first half of the Tribulation. Whatever view one holds of the timing of Ezekiel 38–39, "we should not be dogmatic and unbending on the issue of the precise timing of the Ezekiel invasion. Many fine scholars have debated this issue through the centuries, and that fact alone is enough to cause one to be humble in the face of this interpretive difficulty. Yes, we should examine the issue and come to our own conclusion. But we should show grace to those who hold to a different position."[20]

Why? The Purpose (Ezekiel 38:9-12)

The fourth key issue that Ezekiel 38–39 addresses is the purpose of this invasion. The passage gives both the human and the divine purposes for the invasion. The invading forces will have four main goals. First, there's land. The invaders will desire to acquire more territory (Ezekiel 38:8). Any military invasion of this magnitude and scope always includes land.

Second, there's money. The invaders will come to plunder Israel and amass wealth (Ezekiel 38:12). One might wonder, *What wealth does Israel have?* No one knows for sure what this will entail, but discoveries of vast gas reserves off the coast of Israel could be part of the equation as oil becomes more scarce in the future, triggering energy wars.[21] Make no mistake—greed will be a key motive behind the Gog invasion.

Third is racism. The invading horde will come to destroy the people of Israel and wipe them off the face of the earth (Ezekiel 38:10, 16). This is in keeping with the hatred we see for the Jewish people in Israel's neighbors today.

Fourth is power. These nations will use this attack to challenge the Antichrist, who will be Israel's ally as a result of the peace treaty (Daniel 9:27). Their attack on Israel will also be an attack against the Western confederacy, attempting to draw it into an open confrontation.

Finally, while the invaders will have their evil intent, God will also have His own motivation. He says that through this attack He will be sanctified in the eyes of the nations: "My holiness will be displayed by what happens to you, Gog. Then all the nations will know that I am the Lord" (Ezekiel 38:16).

What? The Product (Ezekiel 38:13-23)

When the forces invade Israel, there will be no stopping them. They will be bent on war and destruction. The timing will seem perfect, and the invaders will not back down. It will look like the biggest mismatch in history. The Arab invasions of Israel in 1967 and 1973 will pale in comparison. The Jewish people will be unable to overcome their enemies by their own strength and ingenuity. Gog and his army will cover Israel like a cloud. It will look like Israel is finished.

However, God will come to the rescue of His people. God will quickly annihilate the invaders by supernatural means. Here's how Ezekiel describes it:

> This is what the Sovereign Lord says: When Gog invades the land of Israel, my fury will boil over! In my jealousy and blazing anger, I promise a mighty shaking in the land of Israel on that day. All living things—the fish in the sea, the birds of the sky, the animals of the field, the small animals that scurry along the ground, and all the people on earth—will quake in terror at my presence. Mountains will be thrown down; cliffs will crumble; walls will fall to the earth. I will summon the sword against you

> on all the hills of Israel, says the Sovereign Lord. Your men will turn their swords against each other. I will punish you and your armies with disease and bloodshed; I will send torrential rain, hailstones, fire, and burning sulfur!
>
> EZEKIEL 38:18-22

Ezekiel 38–39 describes what we might call the "One-Day War" or even the "One-Hour War" or "When Gog Meets God." God will mount up in His fury to destroy these godless invaders. God will rescue His helpless people using four weapons.

1. A great earthquake (Ezekiel 38:19-20). According to Jesus, the coming Tribulation will be a time of many terrible earthquakes (Matthew 24:7). This specific earthquake will be used by God to conquer and confuse these invaders.
2. Infighting among the troops (Ezekiel 38:21). In the chaos after the powerful earthquake, the armies from each of the nations will turn against each other. Just think about it—the troops from the various invading nations will speak many different languages. They will probably begin to fight anyone that they can't identify.
3. Disease (Ezekiel 38:22). Gog and his troops will experience a horrible, lethal plague that will add to the misery and devastation.
4. Torrential rain, hailstones, fire, and burning sulfur (Ezekiel 38:22). Just as God destroyed Sodom and Gomorrah, He will pour fire from heaven on the invading army.

These nations will brashly swoop down on Israel to take her land, but the only piece of land they will claim in Israel will be their burial plots (Ezekiel 39:12). They will set out to bury Israel, but God will bury them.

How? The Prophetic Significance

Is the world stage being set for the fulfillment of this incredible prophecy? Many major developments point toward the fulfillment of Ezekiel's prophecy, but three key elements stand out.

First, the Jewish people are back in their land, fulfilling the major precondition for this invasion. Second, the nations predicted in Ezekiel 38 all have the will and desire to wipe out the Jewish people, and these nations are forming alliances with one another. Third, according to Ezekiel 39:2, 4, Israel will possess the "mountains of Israel" when this invasion occurs. God tells the future invaders: "I will turn you around and drive you toward the mountains of Israel, bringing you from the distant north. . . . You and your army and your allies will all die on the mountains." The famous Six-Day War in Israel in 1967 helped set the stage to fulfill this prophecy. Before the Six-Day War the mountains of Israel were in the hands of the Jordanian Arabs, with the exception of a small strip of West Jerusalem. Only since that war have the mountains *of* Israel been *in* Israel. Thus many pieces of the prophetic puzzle are already in place for the fulfillment of this prophecy.

Conclusion

Events in the Middle East today strikingly foreshadow this coming invasion. The continued unrest and smoldering hatred for Israel are necessary ingredients for what the Bible predicts. Nations are rising and falling. The world is focused on the Middle East. Israel is in the crosshairs. No one knows when the Lord will come or how much time remains before the Battle of Gog and Magog plunges the Middle East into war. There will undoubtedly be many twists and turns, some expected and others we could never imagine in today's climate. But God's Word is clear—when the world stage is set, this invasion will occur right on time in the unfolding of God's end times script.

PART 8

The Antichrist Takes Over

The Middle of the Tribulation

The times will be intense: everything will be at the maximum—the greatest advances in science, the greatest destructive power in the hands of wicked people, the greatest war of all time threatening to break out, the greatest activity in the forces of the heavens, especially in the evil spirit world. The most sensational and unexpected changes will come about. Everything will be expressed in extremes. Exaggeration will be almost impossible. And with it all will come the most marvelous and miraculous prophetic fulfillments.

ARTHUR E. BLOOMFIELD, *How to Recognize the Antichrist*[1]

CHAPTER 25

SATANIC WARFARE AND WORSHIP

THE MIDPOINT OF THE TRIBULATION marks a major turning point in the end times. Three significant events occur at that juncture that pave the way for the final half of the Tribulation: (1) satanic warfare in heaven and on earth, (2) worship of the Antichrist and creating an idol of him, and (3) the death and resurrection of the Antichrist. Let's look at the first two of these events.

Satanic Warfare

Many people are surprised that Satan currently has access to the presence of God in heaven (Job 1). But someday that access will be forever cut off. This restriction will occur, according to Scripture, at the midpoint of the Tribulation. Satan's exclusion from heaven is prophesied in Revelation 12. This highly symbolic chapter depicts two great conflicts involving Satan (the dragon) and his demonic forces—one in heaven and the other on earth. Though distinct, these battles are very closely related.

Phase 1: War in Heaven—Angels and Demons (Revelation 12:7-12)

In the first satanic conflict, a titanic clash occurs in heaven between Satan accompanied by his demonic minions and Michael the archangel with the angelic host (12:7-8). Michael and the angels will defeat Satan's army, expelling them from heaven and casting them down to the earth.

When Satan is kicked out of heaven at the midpoint of the Tribulation, there will be several significant changes. "First, he will no longer be able to gain an audience with God to accuse the Lord's people. Second, he will no longer have access to the presence of God and be granted permission to test and tempt the saints."[1] Third, knowing that his time is short, Satan will wreak as much havoc as possible. He will institute a scorched earth policy. As John Walvoord says, "From this point on in Revelation, therefore, Satan and his hosts are excluded from the third heaven, the presence of God, although their temporary dominion over the second heaven (outer space) and the first heaven (the sky) continues. Satan's defeat in heaven, however, is the occasion for him to be sent down to earth and explains the particular virulence of the great tribulation time."[2] One of the things that will make the Great Tribulation so terrible is the extreme rage of Satan that he will unfurl.

Phase 2: War on Earth—Satan v. Israel (Revelation 12:13-17)

Following Satan's defeat and expulsion from heaven, he will immediately turn his anger toward Israel. He will try to erase them from the face of the earth. This is the second war in Revelation 12. Revelation 12:1 pictures Israel as a woman "clothed with the sun, and the moon under her feet, and on her head a crown of twelve stars" (NASB). This description is an allusion to Joseph's dream in Genesis 37:9-10 where the people of Israel are clearly in view. Also, the woman gives birth to Jesus in Revelation 12:2, 5, which further links the woman to Israel since Scripture says that the Messiah will come from Israel (Isaiah 9:6).

Satan focuses his fury on the woman and tries to wipe out the Jewish people once and for all to thwart the promises of God. He will embark on an all-out, worldwide campaign of anti-Semitism. This will mark the culmination of Satan's agelong war against the Jewish people. But his attempts always backfire. Have you ever noticed that every time Satan tries to wipe out the Jews, they end up with a holiday? After Pharaoh's brutal enslavement, they got Passover. After Haman's plot in Esther to wipe them out, they got the Festival of Purim. After the atrocities of Antiochus Epiphanes in the intertestamental period, they got Hanukkah, or the Feast of Lights. And after Hitler's holocaust, they got May 14, 1948—the rebirth of the modern state of Israel. Satan's final assault against Israel will also fail. It will result in the repentance of Israel, the second coming of Jesus, and the establishment of the messianic kingdom.

Satan tried to kill Jesus to keep Him from fulfilling His ministry (Revelation 12:5). That was Plan A. When he failed, Satan moved to Plan B—to destroy the people whom Jesus will rule over when He comes again. Arthur Bloomfield describes Satan's plan:

> Satan's attempt to destroy the Jews is of long standing. A number of times in history the Jews have narrowly escaped; in fact, the history of Israel is a history of narrow escapes. . . . The history of the Jews is a history of expulsion from one country after another. When Satan gets the upper hand, the Jews are in trouble. . . . God's whole future program revolves around Israel. . . . When Christ comes again, according to the prophet Zechariah, His feet shall stand upon the Mount of Olives that is before Jerusalem. The Jews will be the nucleus of the new kingdom. If Satan is to win this war and retain control of the earth, he must of necessity destroy all the Jews. That would prevent the establishing of the kingdom of God in the world. This is basic in the program of Satan.[3]

Satan's fury against Israel will last for 1,260 days (3½ years) according to Revelation 12:6, 14. This is the second half of the Tribulation. God will supernaturally protect Israel from Satan's onslaught, symbolized by a ferocious flood flowing from the dragon's mouth (Revelation 12:14-16). Satan will use the Antichrist as his primary tool for carrying out his extermination plan. A description of the Antichrist immediately follows in Revelation 13. As the Antichrist carries out Satan's scheme, he will break his covenant with Israel at the Tribulation's midpoint. This will mark the beginning of his reign of terror for Israel.

THE PRIMARY ACTIVITIES OF SATAN IN THE END TIMES
He will lead the false, unholy trinity (Revelation 13:2; 16:13).
He and his demonic army will be cast out of heaven by Michael the archangel (Revelation 12:7-9).
He will persecute the Jewish people (Revelation 12:13-15).
He will know that his time is short, so he will pour out his wrath on the earth (Revelation 12:12).
He will accuse God's people before the throne (Revelation 12:10).
He will deceive the world (Revelation 12:9; 20:8, 10).
He will foment and lead the final rebellion against God (Revelation 20:7-10).

PROPHETIC NAMES AND TITLES FOR THE DEVIL
Satan (Revelation 2:9)
the devil (Revelation 2:10; 12:9)
a great red dragon (Revelation 12:3)
the great dragon (Revelation 12:9)
the serpent of old (Revelation 12:9)
the accuser (Revelation 12:10)
the one who deceives the whole world (Revelation 12:9; 20:10)

Satanic Worship—The Abomination of Desolation

As the satanic war rages in heaven and spills over to the earth, another event on earth will set in motion a series of dramatic events that will compel the entire world to worship the Antichrist. This event will involve the Antichrist, the false prophet, and the rebuilt Temple in Jerusalem. This future sanctuary will be the third Jewish Temple, or what is often called the "Tribulation Temple."

During at least part of the first half of the Tribulation, the Jewish people, under their peace treaty with the Antichrist, will rebuild their Temple and begin offering sacrifices there (Daniel 9:27). However, midway through the seven-year Tribulation, that will all change. Likening the seven years to one week, Daniel 9:27 (NASB) says, "In the middle of the week he [the Antichrist] will put a stop to sacrifice and grain offering; and on the wing of abominations will come one who makes desolate, even until a complete destruction, one that is decreed, is poured out on the one who makes desolate." At this point, the Antichrist will break his treaty with Israel and commit an act that is most often called "the abomination of desolation." Scripture refers to this sacrilege several times (Daniel 9:27; 12:11; Matthew 24:15; Mark 13:14).

What exactly is the abomination of desolation? First, the word *abomination* refers to an idol or image. Second, the first reference to the abomination of desolation in Daniel 9:27 links it to Antichrist's breaking his covenant with Israel. The phrase "on the wing of abominations" refers to the pinnacle of the Temple, emphasizing the idea of an overspreading influence. In other words, what begins at the Temple will spread to other places.[4] The abomination of desolation then is an idol or image that desolates the Temple and spreads out from there to the entire world. Warren Wiersbe says, "What is the abomination of desolation? It is the image of 'the beast,' set up in the temple in Israel in Jerusalem. An idol is bad enough; but setting it up in the temple is the height of all blasphemy. Since Satan could not command worship in heaven, he will go to the next best place—the Jewish temple in the Holy City."[5]

Antiochus and the Abomination

Bible students already have a good idea of what this abomination will look like because history has already drawn us a picture. The Antichrist's abomination of the Temple will repeat what the Seleucid (Syrian) king, Antiochus IV (Epiphanes), did to the Jewish Temple in 167 BC. Antiochus is often called the "Antichrist of the Old Testament." When he invaded and conquered the city of Jerusalem, his soldiers pillaged the Temple, defiled it by offering a pig—considered unclean—on the Temple altar, stopped the Jewish sacrifices, and instituted pagan worship by erecting a statue of Zeus in the Holy of Holies. (Coincidentally, the face of the statue of Zeus just happened to look like the face of Antiochus.) First Maccabees 1:10-63 and 2 Maccabees 5:1 describe this event.

Amazingly, the prophet Daniel predicted this abomination about four hundred years before it happened.

> It even challenged the Commander of heaven's army by canceling the daily sacrifices offered to him and by destroying his Temple. The army of heaven was restrained from responding to this rebellion. So the daily sacrifice was halted, and truth was overthrown. The horn succeeded in everything it did.
>
> Then I heard two holy ones talking to each other. One of them asked, "How long will the events of this vision last? How long will the rebellion that causes desecration stop the daily sacrifices? How long will the Temple and heaven's army be trampled on?"
>
> The other replied, "It will take 2,300 evenings and mornings; then the Temple will be made right again."
>
> DANIEL 8:11-14

> The next to come to power will be a despicable man who is not in line for royal succession. He will slip in when least expected and take over the kingdom by flattery and intrigue.
>
> DANIEL 11:21

> His army will take over the Temple fortress, pollute the sanctuary, put a stop to the daily sacrifices, and set up the sacrilegious object that causes desecration.
>
> DANIEL 11:31

Antiochus IV committed other atrocities including burning copies of the Torah and forcing people to eat pork and to perform pagan sacrifices in violation of the Mosaic law. Antiochus IV's abomination foreshadows the final abomination by the Antichrist in the end times.

Two Future Phases of the Abomination

Two main phases are involved in the abomination of desolation in the end times.[6] In his initial takeover of Jerusalem, the Antichrist will sit in the very Holy of Holies in the Temple, declaring to the world that he is God, thus establishing the final false religion that he will impose on the entire world (2 Thessalonians 2:3-4). The Antichrist will not be able to sit in the Temple 24/7 to receive worship, so in this second phase of abomination, he will commission an image or idol of his likeness to be constructed to sit in the Temple in his place (Revelation 13:11-15). That an idol will be involved is clear from the meaning of the word *abomination* ("idol") as well as the actions of Antiochus IV in setting up an image.

The Antichrist's right hand man, the false prophet, will be given the authority to do great signs and wonders, deceiving people into worshiping the Beast. His greatest deception will be the construction of an image or likeness of the Antichrist that will come alive. The false prophet will place this image, just as Antiochus IV did, in the Holy of Holies. Jerusalem will be the religious center for the Antichrist, and the Temple will serve as the focus of worship with the living image standing in its inner precinct. All the earth will be required to worship the Beast and his image or face death (Revelation 13:15).

The two phases of the abomination of desolation, therefore, will be the two events that take place inside the Jerusalem Temple's Holy of Holies—the Antichrist's declaration that he is God, and then his setting up an image of himself. The idol will remain there for the final 1,260 days or 3½ years of the Tribulation period. Daniel 12:11 says that the abomination of desolation will stand in the Holy Place for 1,290 days. That is the final 3½ years of the Tribulation (1,260 days) plus thirty extra days. Why an extra thirty days? When Jesus returns at His second coming at the end of the Tribulation, the Antichrist will be destroyed, but evidently the judgments of Christ will take some time to complete, so the image will remain in the Temple for another thirty days beyond that time and then it, too, will be removed and destroyed.

Conclusion

The midpoint of the Tribulation will be marked by an angelic war in heaven that will overflow to the earth when Satan and his fallen angels are expelled from heaven. Realizing that he has a brief time left before Christ's return, Satan will unleash his fury on the earth, with Israel at the vortex of his venom. The Antichrist will be his chosen instrument to erase Israel. As the Antichrist pursues this anti-Semitic agenda, he will break his covenant with Israel, subdue the land, and desecrate the rebuilt Temple, requiring the world to worship his image that will be set up in the Holy of Holies. While these events are unfolding, there is one more event at the midpoint of the Tribulation that will shock the world and change everything. The Antichrist will die and come back to life.

CHAPTER 26

DEAD AND ALIVE

The Assassination and Resurrection of the Antichrist

ANOTHER STUNNING EVENT of the end times that will catapult the Antichrist to global worship as god will be his death and restoration to life. Revelation 13:3-4 describes it.

> I saw that one of the heads of the beast seemed wounded beyond recovery—but the fatal wound was healed! The whole world marveled at this miracle and gave allegiance to the beast. They worshiped the dragon for giving the beast such power, and they also worshiped the beast. "Who is as great as the beast?" they exclaimed. "Who is able to fight against him?"

Revelation 17:8 is a parallel passage.

> The beast you saw was once alive but isn't now. And yet he will soon come up out of the bottomless pit and go to eternal destruction. And the people who belong to this world, whose

> names were not written in the Book of Life before the world was made, will be amazed at the reappearance of this beast who had died.

There are differing opinions about what these texts are describing. First, is it talking about the death and resurrection of a person, or of something else? Second, is it a real resurrection, or is it faked? Let's look at these two questions in turn.

Question #1: Person or Empire?

Some believe that the death and resurrection of the Beast in Revelation 13 refers to the fall of the Roman Empire in AD 476 and its resuscitation in the end times. In other words, these passages are talking about the empire, not an individual person.

It is true that the Beast in Revelation 13 and 17 represents both the empire and its emperor, the kingdom and its king. Often in history a great leader can hardly be distinguished from his kingdom. They are virtually inseparable. For example, Nebuchadnezzar was the embodiment of Babylon. Daniel 2 pictures Babylon as the head of gold on a great statue, but Daniel told King Nebuchadnezzar, "You are the head of gold" (Daniel 2:38). Louis XIV is quoted as saying at one point, "I am France." The question in Revelation 13 is, which one is primarily in view—the empire or the emperor? It seems to me that it is the ruler.

I favor this view for three main reasons. First, the language in Revelation 13 appears for the most part to be referring to an individual. The pronouns *he* and *his* are used repeatedly. The second beast in Revelation 13:11-18 builds an idol to the first beast. Such an idol would be strange if it were an empire instead of a person.

Second, would the entire world really be awestruck by the revival of the Roman Empire? When the Beast is slain and comes back to life, "the whole earth was amazed and followed after the beast" (Revelation 13:3, NASB). John Phillips captures the gravity of such an event: "With this master stroke of miracle, the devil brings the world to the feet of his messiah. . . . It is this miracle of his resurrection that is given as the reason for the popularity of the Beast. No doubt the whole thing will be stage-managed by Satan and the false prophet to make the greatest possible impact upon men. Their propaganda machine will see to it that the miracle is magnified and elaborated to the fullest extent."[1] This resurrection is *the* event that propels the Beast to popularity and compels the world to fall at his feet. This response would be much more likely if it refers to a man. If a great world leader were assassinated with a fatal head wound and then came back to life a few days later, this response would be understandable.

A third reason for applying this to a man is that, as Warren Wiersbe says, "it would be difficult to understand how a kingdom could be slain by a sword. It is best, I think, to apply this prophecy to individual persons."[2] I agree. The leader of the reunited Roman Empire is the primary figure in view in Revelation 13:1-10.

Having concluded that Revelation 13 refers primarily to an individual, we come to the next question: Is the resurrection of the Beast during the Tribulation something that actually occurs, or is it just a cheap trick? Is it real or just a counterfeit?

Question #2: The Resurrection—Real or Faked?

Many scholars argue that since Satan does not have the power to give life, this death and resurrection will be an illusion. The Antichrist will not really die. J. Vernon McGee represents this view.

> Only Christ can raise the dead—both saved and lost. Satan has no power to raise the dead. He is not a life-giver. He is a devil, a destroyer, a death-dealer. . . . I believe the beast is a man who will exhibit a counterfeit and imitation resurrection. This will be the great delusion, the big lie of the Great Tribulation Period. . . . They will not accept the resurrection of Christ, but they sure are going to fake the resurrection of the Antichrist. . . . Nobody can duplicate the resurrection of Christ; they might imitate it, but they cannot duplicate it. Yet Antichrist is going to imitate it in a way that will fool the world—it is the big lie. Believers say, "Christ is risen!" The boast of unbelievers in that

> day will be: "So is Antichrist!" The Roman Empire will spring back into existence under the cruel hand of a man who faked a resurrection, and a gullible world who rejected Christ will finally be taken in by this forgery.[3]

While I wholeheartedly agree that only God has the power to resurrect the dead, I believe Scripture teaches that the Antichrist will parody Christ so completely that the Antichrist will actually die and come back to life. It's a real resuscitation. Let's consider the biblical evidence for this view.

Satan's Increased Power

First, during the Tribulation, the restrainer will be removed, and Satan's power will be unleashed in ways never seen before. The Holy Spirit is now restraining Satan from certain activities (2 Thessalonians 2:6-7). Once the Holy Spirit steps aside, Satan will be more active (2 Thessalonians 2:9). Paul specifically says God will send this activity "so that they will believe what is false, in order that they all may be judged who did not believe the truth, but took pleasure in wickedness" (2 Thessalonians 2:11-12, NASB). With increased power and freedom, Satan will be given the capability of raising the Antichrist back to life.

Revelation 13:3 tells us the Beast will have a "fatal wound [that] was healed." Revelation 13 also says that the false prophet "makes the earth and those who dwell in it to worship the first beast" (13:12, NASB), "performs great signs" (13:13, NASB), "deceives those who dwell on the earth because of the signs which it was given him to perform" (13:14, NASB), and "give[s] breath to the image of the beast, so that the image of the beast would even speak" (13:15, NASB). If Satan has the power to give life to a dead idol, then why is it not also possible for him (with God's permission) to resurrect a man from the dead? [4] Revelation 13 contains the repeated refrain "and it was given to him" (NASB) or "and the beast was allowed" (NLT). This phrase makes clear that God is the One permitting the Antichrist to carry out his plans. His authority is a God-permitted authority. God is sovereign over all that happens. In the same way, God will allow Satan the ability to raise the Antichrist from the dead.

Signs, Wonders, and Miracles

The second reason to believe that the resurrection is authentic is that Jesus, Paul, and John each describe Satan's miraculous works with the very same language used to describe Jesus' miracles (Matthew 24:24; 2 Thessalonians 2:9; Revelation 13:13-15; 16:13-14; 19:20). Scripture consistently presents Satan's "signs, wonders, and miracles" as truly miraculous.

Sign is the most common word used to describe the miraculous works of Christ and His apostles. But these "signs" also describe satanic miracles in the Tribulation (Revelation 13:13-14; 16:14), "and the same combination of words is used: great signs and wonders (Matthew 24:24; Mark 13:22), all power and signs and wonder (2 Thessalonians 2:9)."[5] *Wonder* occurs sixteen times in the New Testament and is always coupled with the word *sign*.[6] The only instance of the word *wonder* that is not describing Christ or the apostles is used to describe the Antichrist's miracles (2 Thessalonians 2:9). The Greek words *dunamis* and *energeia*, translated as "miracle" and "working," always refer to "the workings of God" with one exception, 2 Thessalonians 2:9, which is describing the work of Satan.[7] Philip Edgcumbe Hughes ties it all together:

> It is best to take signs, wonders, and miracles as belonging together rather than as indicating three different forms of manifestation. . . . Thus a sign, which is the word consistently used in the Fourth Gospel for the miraculous works of Christ, indicates that the event is not an empty ostentation of power, but is significant in that, sign-wise, it points beyond itself to the reality of the mighty hand of God in operation. A wonder is an event which because of its superhuman character, excites awe and amazement on the part of the beholder. A miracle (or literally power) emphasizes the dynamic character of the event, with particular regard to its outcome or effect.[8]

As you've no doubt noticed, 2 Thessalonians 2:9 is a key passage here, which says that the man of lawlessness is "the one whose coming is in accord with the activity of Satan, with all power and signs and false wonders" (NASB). It seems like the Bible is telling us that these are miracles similar to the ones done by our Lord. "The word *pseudos* ('false') in 2 Thessalonians 2:9 has to do with the results of the miracles, not with their lack of genuineness or supernatural origin."[9]

Biblical passages that describe miracles performed by the Antichrist and the false prophet use the same language as passages describing Christ's miracles at His first advent. This fact supports the notion that the Tribulation is a unique time in history when God permits Satan to use miracles to deceive those who are rejecting Christ's salvation. Satan will use his power to the full extent, even bringing the Antichrist back from the dead. The language used by the inspired New Testament writers will not allow for a meaning that these satanic works are just sleight of hand magic tricks.

Slain and Has Come to Life

Additional similarities in language point to a true resurrection. Revelation describes the Antichrist's slaying and return to life in much the same way as language about Christ's death and resurrection. Revelation 13:3, 12 describes the fatal wound to the Beast. Revelation 5:6 describes the Lamb as slain (*hos esphagmenon*), which is the same words used of the wound received by the Beast (*hos esphagmenen*) in Revelation 13:3. Because of this close similarity, Charles C. Ryrie concludes, "If Christ died actually, then it appears that this ruler will also actually die. But his wound will be healed, which can only mean restoration to life. . . . He apparently actually dies, descends to the abyss and returns to life. The world understandably wonders after him."[10] Likewise, comparing the statements about Christ's death in Revelation 5:6 and the death of the Beast in Revelation 13, J. B. Smith says, "Since the words in the former instance signify the death of Christ by violence, so truly will the final Roman emperor meet a violent death. In each instance the marks or insignia of a violent death are apparent."[11]

Furthermore, as for the resurrection language, "the word referring to the beast's return to life is similar to the word used of Christ's return to life. Jesus is the One 'who was dead, and has come to life [*ezesen*]' (Revelation 2:8). And the beast will be the one 'who had the wound of the sword and has come to life [*ezesen*]' (13:14)."[12]

Revelation 17:8, 11 supports this when it refers to the Beast, which "was, and is not" (NASB). Gregory Harris notes this phrasing "may well refer to the wounding of the Antichrist in 13:3, 12, and 14. The words 'is not' refer to the physical death of the beast, followed by his ascent from the abyss (17:8), which refers to his return to life (13:14)."[13] John Phillips builds on this notion, saying, "The Beast has two comings. He appears first as the 'beast . . . out of the sea' (13:1), and later, after his assassination, as the 'beast . . . out of the abyss' (17:8)."[14] In other words, the Antichrist will be resurrected from the abyss with hellish powers to deceive the world.

Conclusion

As we said earlier, God is the One who enables Satan and his disciples to do these things in a similar way in which He would use any human instrument to work genuine miracles. Harris says, "The possibility of the beast's return to life (with either God's sovereign permission or His active working) should not be readily ruled out. In other words it is not impossible that the Antichrist should return to life because of the unique status of the Tribulation and the increased capacity of satanic power during that time, as well as God's broadening the parameters of what He will either permit or accomplish directly."[15] God will use Satan for His own purposes (2 Thessalonians 2:11-12).

For these reasons, I believe that the Antichrist will actually die and come back to life in a striking parody of the death and resurrection of Jesus Christ. This stunning event will happen at the midpoint of the seven-year Tribulation and will coincide with Satan's being cast out of heaven (Revelation 12:12). Realizing that time is running out, Satan will duplicate the resurrection of Christ and indwell the Antichrist. These events will be part of the dramatic deception that God will allow during that special season of time at the end of the age. From that point on, the Antichrist, having returned from perdition and being indwelled by Satan, will have the power to perform all kinds of signs, wonders, and miracles and will unleash his final great work of deception.

J. B. Smith describes the impact this astonishing event will have on the world in the end times: "Just as the early spread and the perpetuity of the Christian faith are grounded upon the resurrection of Christ, so the all but universal worship and homage accorded the beast in the last half of the tribulation period can only be accounted for by the resurrection of the fallen emperor of Rome."[16] This event will launch the world into its final dark era—the Great Tribulation—when the Beast will "make his mark."

PART 9

The Great Tribulation

The Final 3½ Years

Then there will be a great tribulation, such as has not occurred since the beginning of the world until now, nor ever will.

JESUS CHRIST, MATTHEW 24:21 (NASB)

CHAPTER 27

THE MARK OF THE BEAST

Will That Be the Right Hand or the Forehead?

When the church I pastor was first establishing our street address at our current site, the postal service told us we could choose any number between 500 and 699 North Coltrane. One man in our church suggested the number 666 N. Coltrane as our church address. It would certainly get people's attention and be easy to remember. Since I love Bible prophecy so much, this suggestion tempted me almost more than I could bear. However, my better judgment finally took over, and we settled for the more mundane 600 N. Coltrane.

The number 666, the so-called mark of the Beast, may be one of the most intriguing issues in all of Bible prophecy. There has probably been more speculation, sensationalism, and silliness about this topic than any other in Bible prophecy. As time has gone on, the true meaning of the mark seems to have almost been lost. The number has been trivialized by repeated association with almost every random occurrence. Here's a list I ran across a few years ago.

Route 666	the way of the Beast
00666	the zip code of the Beast
Phillips 666	the gasoline of the Beast
LXVI	the Roman numeral of the Beast
666k	the retirement plan of the Beast
999	the Australian number of the Beast
IAM666	the license plate of the Beast
666i	the BMW of the Beast

While 666 has been trivialized and sensationalized, it is a serious topic that requires and deserves careful investigation. Questions swirl around the meaning and application of this mark. What is it? When will it be fulfilled? Why 666? What is the purpose of it? Does it have a connection with modern technology?

Is the Mark Past or Future?

The first issue that must be resolved is the time period of this mark. Has the mark of the Beast already been fulfilled, or is it something that still lies in the future?

Many scholars who hold a preterist (past) view of the book of Revelation believe that the Roman Caesar Nero was the Beast. They maintain that the mark of the Beast was completely fulfilled during his reign (AD 54–68).[1] Preterists hold that all or most of the prophecies of Revelation and the rest of the New Testament were fulfilled during the Jewish War (AD 66–70) and destruction of Jerusalem in AD 70. For them, the Beast is not a "future foe; he is a relic of history."[2] The Beast in their view has already appeared on the scene and been defeated by Christ.

Preterists argue that the Greek term "Neron Caesar" written in Hebrew characters is equivalent to 666. They point out that some ancient Greek manuscripts contain the variant number 616 instead of 666 and that the Latin term "Nero Caesar" is equivalent to 616.[3] Proponents also point to the fact that the persecution under Nero lasted about forty-two months or 1,260 days as mentioned in Revelation 13:5.[4]

However, identifying Nero with the beast out of the sea has serious difficulties. First, Revelation was written in AD 95, almost thirty years after the reign of Nero was already over. Therefore, assuming Revelation is prophetic in nature, it cannot be about him.[5] The date of Revelation is the most stubborn problem for the entire preterist viewpoint. The traditional, dominant view of the church from the second century until today is that Revelation was written in AD 95 near the end of Domitian's reign. All of the luminaries in the early church that addressed the issue held to the AD 95 date. This eliminates the preterist view as a viable alternative, including its view that Nero was the beast of Revelation 13.

A second problem is a matter of inconsistent interpretation. Preterists interpret the forty-two months of the Beast's worldwide reign literally, and then turn around and interpret almost every other number in Revelation symbolically. Why take the forty-two months literally and the others symbolically?

Third, and most importantly, Nero never fulfilled the numerous clear statements in Revelation 13. Here are just a few examples:

The Beast will be worshiped by the *entire* world (Revelation 13:8).

All classes of humanity will be forced to take sides (Revelation 13:15). Robert Thomas, a noted New Testament scholar, notes that this language "extends to all people of every civic rank . . . all classes ranked according to wealth . . . covers every cultural category. . . . The three expressions are a formula for universality."[6]

He will force people to take his mark on their right hand or forehead to engage in any commercial transactions.

An image of the Beast will be erected by the false prophet, and all the world must worship it.

The Beast will be slain and come back to life.

The Beast in Revelation 13:1-10 will have an associate, the false prophet, who will call down fire from heaven and give breath to the image (13:11-18).

None of these prophecies were fulfilled during Nero's reign. Neither Nero nor any other Roman emperor ever marked the whole world with 666. Nero had no assistant or propaganda minister like the false prophet as predicted by Revelation 13.[7] But the Antichrist will fulfill all of these prophecies precisely.

Fourth, in order for Nero's name to equal 666 you have to use the precise title Neron Caesar. No other form of his name will work. Moreover, an abbreviated form of the name of the Roman Caesar Domitian (AD 81–96) also equals 666.[8] Revelation 13:17 says specifically that the number equals "the name of the beast or the number representing his name." Neron Caesar was not Nero's name. The word *Caesar* is a title, not part of his name. It would be like adding the word *President* before a person's name today and including that as part of his or her name. This interpretation goes beyond what the text of Revelation 13:17 says.

Fifth, if the relationship of 666 to Nero is so obvious, as preterists claim, why did it take almost 1,800 years for anyone to connect the two?[9] All of the early church fathers who wrote after the time of Nero adopted a futurist view of the beast out of the sea and the number 666.[10] The first ones to clearly suggest a connection between Nero and 666 were four German scholars in the 1830s.[11]

Revelation 13:16-18 clearly says that the number 666 will be the mark proposed for the right hand or forehead. No one in history, including Nero, has even proposed such a number during Tribulation-like conditions, so past guesses as to his identity can be nullified on this basis. Robert Thomas provides wise guidance in this area:

> The better part of wisdom is to be content that the identification is not yet available, but will be when the future false Christ ascends to his throne. The person to whom 666 applies must have been future to John's time, because John clearly meant the number to be recognizable to someone. If it was not discernible to his generation and those immediately following him—and it was not—the generation to whom it will be discernible

> must have lain (and still lies) in the future. Past generations have provided many illustrations of this future personage, but all past candidates have proven inadequate as fulfillments.[12]

Neither Nero nor any other past person fulfilled the detailed prophecies of Revelation 13:1-10. The only conclusion we can reach if we believe the Bible is true is that this must be fulfilled in the future when the final Beast is revealed.

What Is the Mark of the Beast?

Having determined that this mark of the Beast is still to come, the next thing we need to do is define the nature of this future mark. Revelation 13:16-18 is the biblical key that opens the door to the meaning of 666, the mark of the Beast, and the coming one-world economy. This passage is the biblical entry point for any discussion on 666.

> He required everyone—small and great, rich and poor, free and slave—to be given a mark on the right hand or on the forehead. And no one could buy or sell anything without that mark, which was either the name of the beast or the number representing his name. Wisdom is needed here. Let the one with understanding solve the meaning of the number of the beast, for it is the number of a man. His number is 666.

The key issue underlying the mark of the Beast is "worship [of] the image of the beast" (Revelation 13:15, NASB). During the Tribulation, the false prophet, who is the leader of the Antichrist's religious propaganda machine, will head up the campaign of the mark of the Beast (Revelation 13:11-18). The mark of the Beast will force people to declare their allegiance—to the Antichrist or to Jesus Christ. It will be impossible to be neutral or undecided. Those who do not receive the mark will be killed (Revelation 20:4). Scripture is very specific: the false prophet will require a "mark" of loyalty and devotion to the Beast, and it will be "on the right hand," not the left, "or on the forehead" (Revelation 13:16). But what is this "mark"?

The word *mark* appears throughout the Bible. For example, it is used many times in Leviticus as a reference to a mark that renders the subject ceremonially unclean, usually related to leprosy. Clearly, in these cases the "mark" is external and visible.

Interestingly, Ezekiel 9:4 uses *mark* similarly to the way Revelation uses it: "He said to him, 'Walk through the streets of Jerusalem and put a mark on the foreheads of all who weep and sigh because of the detestable sins being committed in their city.'" Here the mark preserved the righteous, similar to the way the blood on the doorposts spared the Hebrews from the death angel in the Exodus. In Ezekiel, the mark is placed visibly on the forehead, which anticipates the practice described in Revelation.

The Greek New Testament uses the word for "mark" or "sign" (*charagma*) eight times, and Revelation contains seven of those. All seven refer to "the mark of the beast" (Revelation 13:16, 17; 14:9, 11; 16:2; 19:20; 20:4). The word *mark* in Greek (*charagma*) means "a mark or stamp engraved, etched, branded, cut, imprinted."[13] Robert Thomas explains how the word was used in ancient times.

> The mark must be some sort of branding similar to that given soldiers, slaves, and temple devotees in John's day. In Asia Minor, devotees of pagan religions delighted in the display of such a tattoo as an emblem of ownership by a certain god. In Egypt, Ptolemy Philopator I branded Jews, who submitted to registration, with an ivy leaf in recognition of their Dionysian worship (cf. 3 Maccabees 2:29). This meaning resembles the long-time practice of carrying signs to advertise religious loyalties (cf. Isaiah 44:5) and follows the habit of branding slaves with the name or special mark of their owners (cf. Galatians 6:17). *Charagma* ("Mark") was a term for the images or names of emperors on Roman coins, so it fittingly could apply to the beast's emblem put on people.[14]

The question for each person alive during the Tribulation will be, will I swear allegiance to the man who claims to be God? Will I give up ownership of my life to him by taking his mark, or will I bow the knee to the true God and lose my right to buy and sell while also risking beheading? (Revelation 20:4). Taking the mark will ultimately be a spiritual decision; the economic benefits will be secondary to this momentous decision every person will face.

What Is the Significance of the Number 666?

Even the most biblically illiterate person has likely heard something about 666 or the mark of the Beast. In the 1976 horror movie *The Omen*, Damien is born on June 6, at six o'clock (666) to symbolize his identification as the coming Antichrist. Around June 6, 2006 (6/6/06), dozens of radio stations interviewed me, and I appeared on Fox News to discuss the superstition surrounding that day. One radio station even offered gifts to the parents of any child born on that day.

There are several explanations of what 666 means. But I believe the best one is the use of a process called "gematria," which refers to the numerical indication of names. In gematria, a numerical value is attributed to each of the letters of the alphabet. If you want to find the numerical total of a word or name, you add together the numerical value of each of its letters. Clearly, in Revelation 13 some kind of numerical value for the Beast's name is intended since the one with wisdom is to "calculate" or "count" the number.[15] To count the number of a name means simply to add up the numbers attached to all the letters in the name.[16]

Hebrew, Latin, Greek, and English all have numerical values for each letter in the alphabet. For the Hebrew language, each of the twenty-two letters is assigned a numerical value as follows: 1, 2, 3, 4, 5, 6, 7, 8, 9, 10, 20, 30, 40, 50, 60, 70, 80, 90, 100, 200, 300, and 400.

Revelation 13:16-18 provides five key clues that aid in interpreting the mark of the Beast and support the use of gematria. Notice the progression of the phrases in the passage:

1. the name of the Beast
2. the number representing his name
3. the number of the Beast
4. the number of a man
5. the number 666[17]

When these five clues are traced through their logical progression, the mark of the Beast equals the number of a man who is the Antichrist. The number of the Antichrist's own name is 666.

As prophecy scholar Arnold Fruchtenbaum notes,

> In this passage whatever the personal name of the Antichrist will be, if his name is spelled out in Hebrew characters, the numerical value of his name will be 666. So this is the number that will be put on the worshipers of the Antichrist. Since a number of different calculations can equal 666, it is impossible to figure the name out in advance.[18]

When the Antichrist begins to appear on the world scene, those who have an understanding of Bible prophecy will be able to identify him by the number of his name. The numerical value of his name will be 666.

Many have grossly misapplied gematria to the names of modern leaders to see if they could be the Antichrist. It has been applied to Henry Kissinger and Lyndon Johnson. It has also been applied to JFK, Mikhail Gorbachev, and Ronald Reagan. I once received a call from a man who told me emphatically that Philip Borbon Carlos, son of Juan Carlos of Spain, is the Antichrist because each of his three names contains six letters, and he is a prominent European leader. The day after Barack Obama was elected president, the Pick 3 number in the Illinois lottery was 666, leading some to irresponsibly view this as a harbinger that he's the Antichrist. Phone books are full of names that might add up to 666 if converted to their numerical value. All such foolish speculation should be avoided.

"Counting the name" is not to be applied in our day, for that would be jumping the gun. Instead, it is to be applied by believers during the

Tribulation. The Antichrist will not be unveiled until the beginning of the Tribulation period or Day of the Lord (2 Thessalonians 2:2-3). At that time people will be able to identify him because the number of his name will be 666 (Revelation 13:18).

Why 666?

One might ask why the Lord planned for the Antichrist's name to equal 666. Many prophecy teachers have pointed out that the triple six refers to man's number, which is the number six or one short of God's perfect number, seven. Remember, man was created on the sixth day. Prophecy scholar John Walvoord writes,

> Though there may be more light cast on it at the time this prophecy is fulfilled, the passage itself declares that this number is man's number. In the Book of Revelation, the number 7 is one of the most significant numbers indicating perfection. Accordingly, there are seven seals, seven trumpets, seven bowls of the wrath of God, seven thunders, etc. This beast claims to be God, and if that were the case, he should be 777. This passage, in effect, says, "No, you are only 666. You are short of deity even though you were originally created in the image and likeness of God." Most of the speculation on the meaning of this number is without profit or theological significance.[19]

M. R. DeHaan, the founder of the Radio Bible Class, also held this position.

> Six is the number of man. Three is the number of divinity. Here is the interpretation. The beast will be a man who claims to be God. Three sixes imply that he is a false god and a deceiver, but he is nevertheless merely a man, regardless of his claims. Seven is the number of divine perfection, and 666 is one numeral short of seven. This man of sin will reach the highest peak of power and wisdom, but he will still be merely a man.[20]

Adam, the first man, was created on the sixth day, while Jesus, the second man, was raised from the dead on Sunday, the "eighth day" of the week (the second first day of the week).[21] It is interesting to me that the number of the name Jesus in Greek is 888, and each of his eight names in the New Testament (Lord, Jesus, Christ, Lord Jesus, Jesus Christ, Christ Jesus, Lord Christ, and Lord Jesus Christ) all have numerical values that are multiples of eight.[22] I don't believe this is a coincidence. Jesus is complete perfection, while man, apart from God, is complete failure.

The number 666 is God's way of demonstrating that the Antichrist, Satan's masterpiece, is a fallen man who is completely under the sovereign control of the great God of the ages.

What Is the Purpose of the Mark?

Why will this mark be required? What's the point? According to Scripture, the mark of the Beast will serve two main purposes during the Tribulation.

First, it will visibly indicate devotion to the Antichrist. The Antichrist's mark, the numerical value of his name, will be etched or imprinted on the right hand or forehead of those who bow their knees to his iron fist. The mark of the Beast will be a satanic counterfeit of the seal of God on the foreheads of the saints (Revelation 7:3).[23] This is just another way Satan will mimic the work of God in the end times. It will serve as a kind of global pledge of allegiance. Taking it will be a visible sign that the marked person has bought into the Antichrist's vision, platform, and purpose. Taking the mark of the Beast will not be an accidental act. Those who take it will make a deliberate choice; they will knowingly align themselves with the Antichrist and his agenda.

Second, the mark will provide economic benefits. It will be one's ticket for business. It will be required for commercial transactions during the latter half of the Tribulation (Revelation 13:17). It will make the global order possible and make sure that no one outside this system can function. The fact that it is an economic passport implies that the mark will be literal and visible. After all, how can it serve as a ticket for all commercial transactions if it is invisible?

Stop and think about it. Every tyrant down through history has dreamed of this degree of control—where he alone decides who can buy or sell. When the Beast or Antichrist seizes power at the middle of the Tribulation, every person on earth will face a momentous decision. Will they take the mark of the Beast on their right hand or forehead, or will they refuse the mark and face death? Will they take the mark that is required for every private and public transaction, or will they stand firm and say no to the Antichrist?

The Antichrist's economic policy will be very simple: take my mark and worship me, or starve. People will be forced to make a spiritual decision to serve the Antichrist and worship the Beast and his image. But it will be far better to refuse the Antichrist and starve or face beheading because by receiving his mark a person will forfeit eternal life. All who take the mark of the Beast will face the eternal judgment of God. Taking the mark will seal their everlasting doom. It will be an unpardonable, irreversible sin. Revelation 14:9-11 says it clearly:

> A third angel followed them, shouting, "Anyone who worships the beast and his statue or who accepts his mark on the forehead or on the hand must drink the wine of God's anger. It has been poured full strength into God's cup of wrath. And they will be tormented with fire and burning sulfur in the presence of the holy angels and the Lamb. The smoke of their torment will rise forever and ever, and they will have no relief day or night, for they have worshiped the beast and his statue and have accepted the mark of his name."

This passage reveals again that taking the mark is not ultimately about economics. God does not condemn people for having economic motives. Taking the mark is a conscious decision to worship the Beast. Worshiping him precedes taking the mark in Revelation 14:9.

Does Modern Technology Relate to the Mark of the Beast?

What exactly will this mark be? What will it look like? What form will it take? The speculation is almost endless. People have speculated about almost every new form of technology. Will it be something as simple as a tattoo? Will it be some kind of ID card? Maybe a national ID card? Will it be a chip placed under the skin? Possibly some kind of bar code of the Beast implanted on the right hand? The mark has been mentioned in relation to Social Security cards, national identification cards, bar code scanners, retina scanners, microchip implant technology, and on and on. As Harold Willmington says, "There's been a lot of sick, sick, sick about six, six, six."

When it comes to the exact nature of the mark of the Beast, we really do not know what it will be, and we should not waste a lot of time thinking about it. We don't know what method the Antichrist will adopt to make his mark. Revelation 13:16 clearly indicates that the mark will be placed "on" or "upon" the hand or forehead, not "in" it. The Greek preposition *epi* in this context means "upon." It will be on the outside, where it can be seen.

The technology is certainly available today to accomplish the purposes of the mark by regulating world commerce and controlling people's transactions. There are also many amazing new means of locating, identifying, and tracking people's lives that foreshadow the global scenario depicted in Revelation 13. It's one more indicator pointing toward the picture Scripture paints of the end times.

TEN KEYS TO UNDERSTANDING THE MARK OF THE BEAST
The mark is future, not past.
The mark is a literal, visible brand, mark, or tattoo.
It will be placed "upon" the right hand or forehead of people during the Tribulation.
The mark will be given as a sign of devotion to the Antichrist and as a passport to engage in commerce.
The mark will be the number 666, which will be the numerical value of the Antichrist's name.
Believers during the Tribulation will be able to calculate the number and identify the Antichrist.

Those who take the mark will be eternally doomed.
Before the Rapture, no one should attempt to identify the Antichrist or his mark—the number 666.
While current technology and methods of identifying and locating people strikingly foreshadow the Antichrist's ability to control the world, no specific, modern technology should be identified as the mark of the Beast. No one can say specifically what technology will be employed to fulfill this prophecy, but what we see today certainly makes such a system not only possible, but probable.
In spite of its association with evil, 666 will be received by those who willfully reject Christ during the Tribulation.

CHAPTER 28

THE TWO WITNESSES

DURING THE GREAT Tribulation Satan will use two men—the Antichrist and the false prophet—to carry out his evil agenda. At the same time, God will raise up two bright lights to shine for Him in the darkness. These lights are two men, called the two witnesses, and Revelation 11:3-14 describes their ministry.

God will anoint these two special witnesses who will minister on His behalf amid the darkness and devastation. Just as John the Baptist was the forerunner for the Messiah, these two witnesses will pave the way for His return. What do we know about the two witnesses? Who are they? What will they do? When will they serve? What will happen to them?[1]

Literal or Symbolic?

The first question concerning the two witnesses is whether or not they are literal individuals who will appear. The two witnesses have been interpreted to symbolize the Old and New Testament, the law and the prophets, or as representatives of all the prophets. However, Scripture clearly identifies the two witnesses as individual people.

They are described as wearing sackcloth, just like John the Baptist. Sackcloth signifies mourning and repentance.

They perform miracles.
They prophesy for God for 1,260 days (3½ years).
They die, and their bodies lie in the street for 3½ days.
They are raised back to life.
They ascend to heaven.

Revelation 11:4 offers further evidence that the two witnesses are real people. There they are called "the two olive trees and the two lampstands that stand before the Lord of all the earth." This imagery alludes to the Old Testament prophet Zechariah, who mentioned two great witnesses in his day—Joshua (the high priest) and Zerubbabel (the civic leader)—two men whom the Lord used to restore the people who returned from the Babylonian captivity. As Bible teacher David Jeremiah says,

> If we look at the prophecy of Zechariah we see, again, two witnesses: Joshua and Zerubbabel (Zechariah 4:1-14). God uses the lampstand and the olive trees as a picture of them. The lampstand burned brightly and the olive tree produced the oil, which was burned by the candelabra. It is a picture of the fact that these two witnesses are going to shine in the darkness of the Tribulation and that they will be fueled by the holy oil of the Spirit of God.[2]

John Walvoord says this about the comparison of the two witnesses to olive trees and lampstands in Revelation 11:4:

> This seems to be a reference to Zechariah 4, where a lampstand and two olive trees are mentioned. . . . The olive oil from the olive trees in Zechariah's image provided fuel for the two lampstands. The two witnesses of this period of Israel's history, namely Joshua the high priest and Zerubbabel, were the leaders of Israel in

> Zechariah's time. Just as the two witnesses were raised up to be lampstands or witnesses for God and were empowered by olive oil representing the power of the Holy Spirit, so the two witnesses of Revelation 11 will likewise execute their prophetic office. Their ministry does not rise in human ability but in the power of God.[3]

Just as Joshua and Zerubbabel ministered to restore Israel to her land and her Lord, so will the two witnesses.[4]

Have They Lived Before?

Having concluded that the two witnesses are real people, the further question is, are they people who have lived before? Many scholars believe that the two witnesses will be two men whom God will raise up in the end times as His special witnesses, not two men who have lived before. Since the two witnesses are never specifically named, this view is certainly possible.

Early Christians such as Tertullian, Irenaeus, and Hippolytus believed Enoch and Elijah will reappear during the Tribulation and will be the two witnesses. Others have held that Moses will be one of the two witnesses along with either Enoch or Elijah. There are several reasons why these men have been identified as the two witnesses.

Enoch

There are two main reasons for identifying Enoch as one of the two witnesses. First, Enoch never died, and the Bible says that "each person is destined to die once and after that comes judgment" (Hebrews 9:27). Of course, this verse is simply establishing the general truth that all must die. There will be millions of exceptions to this general rule at the Rapture. Second, Enoch was a prophet of judgment who announced the coming of the Lord in the days before the Flood (Jude 1:14-15).

Moses

Three main points favor Moses as one of the two witnesses. First, like Moses, the witnesses will turn the rivers to blood and bring other plagues on the earth (Revelation 11:6). Second, Moses and Elijah appeared with Christ on the Mount of Transfiguration, which foreshadowed the glory of Christ at His second coming (Matthew 17:1-11). Third, Moses was a prophet.

One common argument against Moses being one of the two witnesses is that this would mean he would die twice. While this is obviously not common in history, all of the people in the Bible who were resuscitated, like Lazarus, died a second time, so it isn't unprecedented in Scripture.

Elijah

Five main reasons are given for identifying Elijah as one of the two witnesses. First, like Enoch, Elijah never tasted physical death. Second, like Moses, he was present at the Transfiguration. Third, the Scriptures predict that Elijah will come before "the great and dreadful day of the LORD" (Malachi 4:5). Fourth, God used him to prevent rain from falling for 3½ years just like the two witnesses. And fifth, like the two witnesses, Elijah was a prophet.

Conclusion about Their Identity

While certainty about the specific identity of the two witnesses is not possible, I believe these two witnesses are Moses and Elijah for two main reasons. First, both are mentioned in tandem in the final chapter of the Old Testament (Malachi 4:4-5). Second, they appear together with Jesus on the Mount of Transfiguration, which previewed the second coming of Christ (Matthew 16:27–17:5; 2 Peter 1:16-18). Because the two witnesses appear in close connection with the coming of Christ, I believe it is very likely that the two witnesses are Elijah and Moses. These two giants from the past, the great lawgiver and the great prophet, will visit earth again in one of the great encores of all time. They will be end times prophets who will "prophesy for twelve hundred and sixty days" (Revelation 11:3, NASB). They will burst upon the dark scene of the world dressed in sackcloth, the garments of mourning and repentance, and will proclaim God's message of salvation and judgment on the sin-wracked world of the Tribulation. They will warn the world that the end is near.

Powerful Prophets

The two witnesses will be given incredible power by God (Revelation 11:3, 6). Apparently, the two witnesses are the human instruments God uses to call forth the first six trumpet judgments in Revelation 8–9, just like Moses called forth the terrible plagues on Egypt.

Persecuted Prophets

The two witnesses will not only be powerful prophets; they will be persecuted prophets. As you can imagine, the whole world will hate the two witnesses. When they bring plague after plague upon the earth, the Beast (the Antichrist) and his followers throughout the world will view these two witnesses as public enemies number one and number two. But God will supernaturally protect them for 3½ years. They will be invincible (Revelation 11:5). The two witnesses will be a constant irritant and a nagging thorn in the Antichrist's side.

However, when the two witnesses have finished their unprecedented 3½-year ministry, God will allow the Antichrist to kill them (Revelation 11:7). Remember that just like them our times are in God's hand as well. We, too, are invincible until the Lord is finished with us and we have completed our work here for Him. What a comforting, strengthening truth.

The entire world, led by the Antichrist, will celebrate the deaths of these witnesses (Revelation 11:9-10). As Ray Stedman notes, "They keep telling the truth to people who want only to embrace their delusions. They keep blunting the Antichrist's carefully concocted propaganda. . . . The vile and godless society of the world under the Antichrist takes the death of the two witnesses as a cause for global celebration. One is reminded of a saying that was common among ancient Roman generals, 'The corpse of an enemy always smells sweet!'"[5] People all over the world will be so ecstatic these witnesses for God are dead that they will hold a Christmas-like celebration and send gifts to one another—Satan's Anti-Christmas. This is the only mention of any kind of rejoicing or celebrating on earth during the entire Tribulation period. People will be so thrilled to see these men dead that no burial will be allowed. They will want to watch their bodies rot in the street.

Revelation 11:9 makes a brief statement almost in passing: "For three and a half days, all peoples, tribes, languages, and nations will stare at their bodies." There are two ways to understand this prophecy. How broad is the scope of this statement? It could mean that there will be individuals from "all peoples, tribes, languages, and nations" actually in Jerusalem at the time of the death of the two witnesses who will see their bodies lying in the street.

Or this statement could be looking into the future when people from all over the world can see events via television and satellite. It means their bodies will be seen simultaneously by people all over the world. If this is correct, it means that John saw something that has only become possible in the last sixty years, almost two thousand years since he predicted it.

At the time this prophecy was given, and for centuries after, the scope of such a prediction would have seemed impossible. Yet today it's commonplace. It happens 24/7 every day on cable news all around the world, even in many poor Third World countries. As Tim LaHaye says, "Ours is the first generation that can literally see the fulfillment of 11:9 in allowing people of the entire world to see such an awesome spectacle. This is one more indication that we are coming closer to the end of the age, because it would have been humanly impossible just a few years ago for the entire world to see these two witnesses in the streets at a given moment of time."[6]

The worldwide party over the deaths of the two witnesses won't last long, though. After the dead bodies of the two witnesses have lain swelling in the sun for 3½ days, the Lord will raise their bodies back to life from the street in Jerusalem before a horror-stricken world (Revelation 11:11-12). Commentator John Phillips aptly describes the stunning event:

> Picture the scene—the sun-drenched streets of Jerusalem, the holiday crowd flown in from the ends of the earth for a firsthand look at the corpses of these detested men, the troops in the Beast's uniform, the temple police. There they are, devilish men from every kingdom under heaven, come to dance and feast at the triumph of the Beast. And then it happens! As the crowds strain at the police cordon to peer curiously at the two dead bodies, there comes a sudden change. Their color changes from cadaverous hue to the blooming, rosy glow of

> youth. Those stiff, stark limbs—they bend, they move! Oh, what a sight! They rise! The crowds fall back, break, and form again.[7]

What a scene. People all over the earth will see the two witnesses caught up to heaven on their favorite TV newscast as the analysts will sit around discussing its significance.

Which Half of the Tribulation?

The time of the ministry of the two witnesses is clearly stated as 1,260 days or 3½ years, which clearly refers to one of the halves of the seven-year Tribulation. But which half? This question is not a crucial issue, but it does have bearing on one's view of the chronology of many events in the book of Revelation.

There are excellent arguments in favor of each position, and problems with both, but I believe there are four reasons that favor the second half of the Tribulation.

First, the context of Revelation 11:2-3 strongly favors the latter half. Revelation 11:2 says, "Do not measure the outer courtyard, for it has been turned over to the nations. They will trample the holy city for 42 months." The two witnesses are introduced in the very next verse. The context in Revelation 11:2-3 indicates that the two witnesses will minister during the same forty-two month period—1,260 days, or 3½ years—that the Temple is being trampled by the nations and is dominated by the worship of the Antichrist. This corresponds to the latter half of the Tribulation, when the Antichrist will control Jerusalem. Leon Wood agrees:

> These two people, whatever their identity, will begin their work at the time when the Antichrist breaks his treaty with Israel and will continue throughout the difficult months of his oppression and persecution.[8]

Second, the two witnesses face great opposition by the Antichrist. This dynamic fits the second half of the Tribulation better. During the Great Tribulation, the Beast will unleash his full fury.

Third, the blowing of the seventh trumpet—which announces the second coming of Christ at the end of the Tribulation—immediately follows the description of the two witnesses (Revelation 11:15-19). This sequence also points to a ministry during the final half of the Tribulation.

Fourth, when Revelation refers to forty-two months or 1,260 days, it seems to always refer to the latter half of the Tribulation.[9] The same appears to be true of the 1,260-day ministry of the two witnesses (Revelation 11:3).

Whatever timing one has for the ministry of the two witnesses, their presence there encourages us that no matter how dark things may be, the Lord never leaves Himself without a witness. Paul Benware offers this comforting word about the life and ministry of the two witnesses: "These two miracle-working servants of God are lights for the Lord in the morally and spiritually dark city of Jerusalem. The two witnesses are a reminder that even in the worst of times God does not leave Himself without witnesses."[10] This is a stirring challenge for us to be witnesses in the darkness around us.

CHAPTER 29

SEVEN SOUNDING TRUMPETS AND SEVEN SUPER BOWLS

THE BOOK OF REVELATION highlights three series of devastating, intensifying judgments: seven seals, seven trumpets, and seven bowls. As we have already seen, the six seals of judgment will be opened during the first half of the seven-year Tribulation (Revelation 6). The seventh seal contains a second series of seven more judgments—the seven trumpets—which will sound during the second half of the Tribulation (Revelation 8:1-2). The seven trumpets are then followed by seven bowls of wrath that are poured out in rapid succession near the culmination of the Great Tribulation. The seals, trumpets, and bowls are not parallel with one another as some maintain. They are unleashed in sequence spanning the entire seven-year Tribulation.

FIVE REASONS IN FAVOR OF THE SUCCESSION VIEW
The content in the judgments is not identical or similar, as one would expect if they are contemporaneous or parallel.
The seventh seal introduces the seven trumpets, which indicates that the seven trumpets follow the first six seals.

There is an interlude between the sixth and seventh seal and then again between the sixth and seventh trumpet. This speaks of successive action.

The bowls are called the seven last plagues (Revelation 15:1). This fits the idea of successive unfolding of the judgments.

The seventh bowl is introduced with the words "It is finished," which indicate it is the last in a series (Revelation 16:17).

Seven Trumpets of Doom

In his vision, the apostle John watched as the seventh seal was opened and seven angels were given seven trumpets (Revelation 8:1-2). These trumpets represent specific catastrophes, many of which will destroy large portions of the earth (Revelation 8–11). Great disturbances will affect nature and change climates. These judgments are literal, not symbolic. They point to real events. These judgments are not due to man's activity, global warming, or nuclear war; they are the supernatural judgment of God. The first four trumpets will bring natural catastrophes. One-third of the earth will be consumed by fire—by a direct act of God. One-third of the sea will become as blood, and one-third of sea life will be destroyed. As the trumpets continue to sound, one catastrophe after another will afflict the earth. At the sounding of the fifth trumpet, demonic forces from the abyss will swarm the earth like locusts. The forces of hell will be unleashed across the face of the earth to torment people with pain like the sting of a scorpion (Revelation 9:1-12). These demonic creatures are "supernatural soldiers in the kingdom of darkness."[1] But God will limit the demonic invasion to five months and will only allow the demons to torment, not to kill.

The sixth trumpet signals the advance of a great army numbering 200 million that will kill one-third of mankind (Revelation 9:15-16). Some speculate that this passage describes a Chinese invasion of Israel. This conclusion is based on three main points.

1. The army of 200 million is viewed as parallel with the kings from the east in Revelation 16:12 who come from the east into Israel, crossing the dried-up Euphrates River.

2. The modern nation of China could amass an army of this magnitude.
3. The weapons used by this army seem similar to tanks, helicopters, artillery, rocket launchers, and missiles (Revelation 9:17-19).

Ray Stedman believes that Revelation 9:17-19 describes all the armies of the world invading Israel at Armageddon. He likens modern weaponry to the descriptions of that passage:

> What does this description mean? It hardly seems possible that John himself understood what he was looking at. All he could do was record his impressions of future warriors, armor, and weaponry far beyond his ability to imagine. . . . Yet it seems clear that what John envisions for us is the machinery of modern (or future) military destruction translated into the military terminology of his own day. Breastplates of various colors seems to suggest armored chariots—that is, tanks, troop carriers, missile launchers, rocket batteries, artillery pieces, and aircraft. . . . The lions' mouths which spouted fire and smoke suggests cannons, mortars, rocket launchers, and even missiles killing great masses of people with fire, radiation, and even poison gases. The fact that one-third of the human race is destroyed in this conflict strongly suggests that weapons of mass destruction, including nuclear weapons, will be used.
>
> Another intriguing image is that of the horses' tails, described as being like snakes, having heads that inflict injury. These words could apply to various kinds of modern armament—helicopter gunships with rotors mounted on their long tail assemblies, or perhaps missiles which leave a snake-like trail of smoke in their wake and inflict injury with their warheads. Perhaps it is a description of weapons that are yet to be invented.[2]

It is much better to identify this massive army as a second wave of demonic invaders who assault the earth during the Tribulation. There are five reasons I prefer this view.[3]

First, the unleashing of this army is the sixth trumpet judgment. The fifth trumpet judgment is clearly a demonic invasion of earth, and the fifth and sixth trumpet judgments go together since they are the first two of three "terrors" (Revelation 8:13). Second, fallen angels lead this armada just like they do in the fifth trumpet judgment. Thus, since the leaders are four demons, it makes sense that the troops they are leading are also demons (Revelation 9:15). Third, the fearsome description in Revelation 9:17-19 fits supernatural beings much better than modern warfare. Fourth, there are other examples in Scripture of supernatural armies of cavalry. Horses of fire swept Elijah up to heaven (2 Kings 2:11). Horses and chariots of fire protected Elisha at Dothan (2 Kings 6:13-17). Heavenly horses and horsemen from the celestial realm introduce the reign of Christ (Revelation 19:14). The Lord Himself will return riding on a white horse (Revelation 19:11). It seems logical that Satan would parody the coming of the Kingdom with his own infernal cavalry. Fifth, the weapons—fire, brimstone, and smoke—are always supernatural weapons in the Bible, and Revelation associates them with hell four times (14:10-11; 19:20; 20:10; 21:8).

For these reasons, I believe the army of 200 million in Revelation 9:16 is not a human army employing modern or futuristic weapons but a demonic cavalry invading earth—hellish horsemen riding satanic steeds. During the Tribulation period, demons will overrun the earth, afflicting men with great pain and ultimately slaying one-third of the people on earth (Revelation 9:15, 18). In other words, the afflictions of the fifth trumpet will escalate during the sixth trumpet when this demonic armada will be granted the ability to kill one-third of the earth.

Whichever view one holds of the army of 200 million, it will wreak colossal chaos on the earth. This will be a human slaughter in addition to the one in Revelation 6:8. The book of Revelation clearly shows that the combined catastrophes will kill more than half of the world's population.

SEVEN TRUMPET JUDGMENTS
First Trumpet (Revelation 8:7) Bloody Hail and Fire: One-Third of Vegetation Destroyed
Second Trumpet (Revelation 8:8-9) Fireball from Heaven: One-Third of Oceans Polluted
Third Trumpet (Revelation 8:10-11) Falling Star: One-Third of Fresh Water Polluted
Fourth Trumpet (Revelation 8:12) Darkness: One-Third of Sun, Moon, and Stars Darkened
Fifth Trumpet (Revelation 9:1-12) Demonic Invasion: Possession and Torment
Sixth Trumpet (Revelation 9:13-21) Demonic Army of 200 Million: One-Third of Mankind Killed
Seventh Trumpet (Revelation 11:15-19) The Kingdom: The Announcement of Christ's Reign

Timing the Trumpets

Most prophecy teachers agree that the seven seals are opened during the first half of the Tribulation and the seven bowls are poured out near the very end of the Tribulation. The central chronological question revolves around the timing of the trumpets. Are they blown in the first or second half of the Tribulation?

While good arguments can be made for either view, the issue to me centers on the severity of the trumpet judgments. One-third of the earth's population perishes in the sixth trumpet judgment alone. Adding in the one-fourth of the population that dies earlier in the fourth seal judgment (Revelation 6:7-8), that's one-half of the world's population dying during the first half of the Tribulation if the trumpets are located there. Putting the trumpets in the first half of the Tribulation makes the first half of the Tribulation worse than the second half, which contradicts the statement of Jesus that the Great Tribulation (the final 3½ years) will be the worst time in human history (Matthew 24:21). If the devastation of the trumpets is in the first half of the Tribulation, the final half would not fulfill

Christ's prophecy. Thus, it makes better sense to place the trumpets in the second half of the Tribulation.

Seven Super Bowls of Wrath

When the seventh trumpet sounds, the second coming of Christ is announced (Revelation 11:15-17). This makes it clear, then, that the seventh trumpet stretches all the way to Christ's return and thus includes the seven bowls in Revelation 16. "Chronologically, the seventh trumpet both introduces and includes the final period of God's wrath symbolized by the seven bowls in Revelation."[4]

The bowls of wrath clearly represent God's direct judgment. As these successive bowls are poured out, great catastrophes will afflict the earth: the bodies of people will be covered with sores and afflicted with terrible pain; all life in the sea will die; the rivers and fountains of water will become as blood; unnatural heat will scorch the earth as the heavens are disturbed in their normal course. The sun will eventually be darkened, resulting in increasing darkness, changes in climate, and destruction of plant life.

The trumpets and bowls of judgment have striking parallels to the plagues of Egypt. Water will turn to blood, men and women will be afflicted with sores, darkness will envelop the globe, and great hail will pound the earth. Once again God will send forth His plagues, but this time they will fall upon the entire world. God will demonstrate that He alone is the true God who controls all things. There will be no question about it. Yet, instead of being horrified, people will be hardened, despite their knowing that this devastation comes from God. Instead of repenting, they will rebel. Revelation 16:11 says, "They blasphemed the God of heaven because of their pains and their sores; and they did not repent of their deeds" (NASB). What a sobering testimony to the depravity and darkness of the human heart apart from Christ.

In the course of the seven seals and the seven trumpets, an interlude occurs after the sixth judgment, but the seven bowls are not interrupted. They are relentless and rapid in their outpouring. The sixth bowl will dry up the Euphrates River and further prepare the way for the great army invading from the east. The seventh and final bowl will occur during the final War of Armageddon, as the armies of the earth converge on the Middle East for the last, desperate campaign. The entire earth will be literally shaken, its great cities will be destroyed, and the contour of the earth will be changed. Islands will disappear; mountains will be leveled.

SEVEN BOWL JUDGMENTS
1. First Bowl (Revelation 16:2) upon the Earth: Sores on the Worshipers of the Antichrist
2. Second Bowl (Revelation 16:3) upon the Seas: Turned to Blood
3. Third Bowl (Revelation 16:4-7) upon the Fresh Water: Turned to Blood
4. Fourth Bowl (Revelation 16:8-9) upon the Sun: Intense, Scorching Heat
5. Fifth Bowl (Revelation 16:10-11) upon the Antichrist's Kingdom: Darkness and Pain
6. Sixth Bowl (Revelation 16:12-16) upon the River Euphrates: Armageddon
7. Seventh Bowl (Revelation 16:17-21) upon the Air: Earthquakes and Hail

This will be the final hour of divine judgment on a world that refuses to let Christ reign over it. This war and this series of bowl plagues will leave a wake of almost unbelievable destruction of human life and property. It will be exactly what Christ predicted—a time of trouble so great that if it did not end with His own coming to the earth, no human life would survive. This time of trouble will only be the backdrop for God's final dealings with humanity. It will set the stage for the judgments that will come when Jesus Christ returns. But one last piece of business must be finished before the end comes. God must deal once and for all with Babylon.

CHAPTER 30

THE FALL OF BABYLON THE GREAT

REVELATION 16 COMPLETES the pouring out of the seven bowls of wrath and reaches to the campaign of Armageddon. The end is in sight. But before Armageddon is fully described and the second coming of Christ is unveiled in Revelation 19, there is a sudden pause or interlude in the main action. Before Christ returns, one final event must be addressed—the demise of Babylon the Great.[1]

In Revelation one out of every ten verses concerns Babylon. Two entire chapters—Revelation 17–18—are devoted to this city and its destruction. Obviously, Babylon holds a key place in the mind of God and in His final plan for the ages. Babylon, the earthly city, is presented in Revelation 17–18 as a vile prostitute. In sharp contrast the new Jerusalem, the heavenly city, is pictured as the virtuous bride of Christ in Revelation 21–22. The practical implication of these chapters is clear: God's people are to live for heaven, not for earth. However, while the message is clear, the identification of Babylon is more difficult.

There has been a great deal of speculation about the identity of Babylon. This "great prostitute" of the last days has been identified with the

Roman Catholic church and the Vatican, apostate Christendom, the United States, New York City, Rome, or some unknown great metropolis that will emerge in the end times. Preterists, who view the events in Revelation as past, equate Babylon with Jerusalem, which was destroyed by the Romans in AD 70. Some believe that Babylon is used the same way "we might refer to 'Wall Street,' to describe the entire American financial system."[2] What great city is John describing? Seven clues in Revelation 17–18 can help identify this great end times city.

Babylon is a literal city (Revelation 17:18).
Babylon is a city of worldwide importance and influence, probably the capital city of the Antichrist (Revelation 17:15, 18).
Babylon and the Beast (the Antichrist) are very closely connected with one another. The woman (Babylon) is pictured riding on the Beast (the Antichrist) (Revelation 17:3-5, 7).
Babylon is a center of false religion (Revelation 17:4-5; 18:1-2).
Babylon is the center of world commerce (Revelation 18:9-19).
Babylon persecutes the Lord's people (Revelation 17:6; 18:20, 24).
Babylon will be destroyed suddenly and completely at the end of the Tribulation, never to rise again (Revelation 18:8-10, 21-24).

These clues reveal that Babylon will be a great religious and economic capital of the Antichrist's kingdom in the last days. These two systems, religion and commerce, will share the same geographical location under the Antichrist's domain. Babylon will be both a city and a system. But what city does Babylon represent?

Taking all the facts into account, the best view is that Babylon is the literal city of Babylon on the Euphrates in modern Iraq that will be rebuilt in the last days. There are seven main points that favor this identification.

Babylon Means Babylon

First, Revelation specifically refers to the last-days capital of the Antichrist as "Babylon" six times (14:8; 16:19; 17:5; 18:2, 10, 21). It is possible that the name Babylon is a code name for Rome, New York, Jerusalem, or some other world city, but since the text does not indicate that it is to be interpreted figuratively or symbolically, it is best to interpret it as referring to a literal city called Babylon. When John wants to indicate that a geographical location is symbolic, he does so clearly (Revelation 11:8). Otherwise, the geographical places in Revelation are literal: Patmos, Ephesus, Smyrna, Pergamum, Thyatira, Philadelphia, Sardis, Laodicea, and Armageddon. With this established pattern of literal interpretation for places, I believe Babylon should also be taken literally.

Second, Babylon is the most mentioned city in the Bible other than Jerusalem. Scripture refers to Babylon about three hundred times. Throughout Scripture, Babylon symbolizes the epitome of evil and rebellion against God. Consider these examples:

Babylon is the city where man first began to worship himself in organized rebellion against God (Genesis 11:1-11). Babylon was both a literal city and the entire anti-God system that went with it.

Babylon was the capital city of the first world ruler, Nimrod (Genesis 10:8-10; 11:9).

Nebuchadnezzar, king of Babylon, destroyed the city of Jerusalem and the temple in 586 BC.

Babylon was the capital city of the first of four Gentile world empires to rule over Jerusalem.

Since Babylon was the capital city of the first world ruler and Scripture pictures it as Satan's capital city on earth, it makes sense that in the end times, he will once again raise up this city as the capital city of the final world ruler. In Charles Dyer's excellent book *The Rise of Babylon*, he writes, "Throughout history, Babylon has represented the height of rebellion and opposition to God's plans and purposes, so God allows Babylon to continue during the final days. It is almost as though he 'calls her out' for a final duel. But this time, the conflict between God and Babylon ends decisively. The city of Babylon will be destroyed."[3]

Third, Babylon fits the criteria for the city described in Revelation 17–18. As Robert Thomas notes, "Babylon on the Euphrates has a location that fits this description politically, geographically, and in all the qualities of accessibility, commercial facilities, remoteness of interferences of church and state, and yet centrality in regard to the trade of the whole world."[4] Henry Morris highlights the advantages of Babylon as a world capital:

> Babylon is indeed a prime prospect for rebuilding, entirely apart from any prophetic intimations. Its location is the most ideal in the world for any kind of international center. Not only is it in the beautiful and fertile Tigris-Euphrates plain, but it is near some of the world's richest oil reserves. Computer studies for the Institute of Creation Research have shown, for example, that Babylon is very near the geographical center of all the earth's land masses. It is within navigable distances to the Persian Gulf and is at the crossroads of the three great continents of Europe, Asia, and Africa. Thus there is no more ideal location anywhere for a world trade center, a world communications center, a world banking center, a world educational center, or especially, a world capital! The greatest historian of modern times, Arnold Toynbee, used to stress to all his readers and hearers that Babylon would be the best place in the world to build a future world cultural metropolis. [5]

Fourth, the Euphrates River is mentioned by name twice in Revelation (9:14; 16:12). The ancient city of Babylon straddled the Euphrates River. In Revelation 9:14, four fallen angels are being held at the Euphrates River awaiting the appointed time for them to lead forth a host of demons to destroy one-third of mankind. In Revelation 16:12, the Euphrates River dries up to prepare the way for the kings of the east. These references to the Euphrates point to the fact that something important and evil is occurring there. The rebuilt city of Babylon on the Euphrates functioning as a religious and political center for the Antichrist is a good explanation for Revelation's emphasis on the Euphrates River.

Fifth, the prophet Zechariah, writing about twenty years after Babylon's fall to the Medo-Persians, saw a future time when evil would return to its original place in Babylon (Zechariah 5:5-11). In his vision Zechariah sees a woman who is named Wickedness. Then he sees this woman carried away in a basket to the land of Babylon where a temple will be built for her. The parallels between Zechariah 5:5-11 and Revelation 17–18 are striking.

ZECHARIAH 5:5-11	REVELATION 17–18
woman sitting in a basket (5:7)	woman sitting on the beast, seven mountains, and many waters (17:3, 9, 15)
emphasis on commerce (a basket for measuring grain, 5:6)	emphasis on commerce (merchant of grain, 18:13)
woman's name is Wickedness (5:8)	woman's name is "Babylon the Great, Mother of All Prostitutes and Obscenities in the World" (17:5)
focus on false worship (a temple is built for the woman, 5:11)	focus on false worship (18:1-3)
woman is taken to Babylon (5:10-11)	woman is called Babylon (17:5)

God's Word teaches that wickedness will again rear its ugly head in the same place where it began—Babylon. The prostitute in John's vision will fulfill Zechariah 5 when Babylon is established as the city that embodies evil.

Sixth, Isaiah 13 and Jeremiah 50–51 predicted that the city of Babylon would be destroyed suddenly and completely. Babylon was never destroyed in this way but died a long, slow death over many centuries. Since Babylon has yet to be destroyed in the way the prophets predicted, these passages must refer to a future city of Babylon that will be totally destroyed in the Day of the Lord.

Seventh, Jeremiah 50–51 clearly describes the city of Babylon on the Euphrates. The many parallels between Jeremiah 50–51 and the future Babylon in Revelation 17–18 indicate that both are describing the same city.

PARALLELS BETWEEN JEREMIAH 50–51 AND REVELATION 17–18[6]	
JEREMIAH 50–51	REVELATION 17–18
compared to a golden cup (51:7)	17:3-4 and 18:6
dwelling on many waters (51:13)	17:1
involved with nations (51:7)	17:2
named the same (50:1)	18:10
destroyed suddenly (51:8)	18:8
destroyed by fire (51:30)	17:16
never to be inhabited (50:39)	18:21
punished according to her works (50:29)	18:6
fall illustrated (51:63-64)	18:21
God's people flee (51:6, 45)	18:4
heaven to rejoice (51:48)	18:20

Putting all these pieces together, it appears that Babylon will be rebuilt in the last days to serve as the religious and commercial capital for the Antichrist's empire. Wickedness will return to this place for its final stand.

J. Vernon McGee suggests the important role that Babylon is yet to play:

> In that day Babylon will dominate and rule the world. The capital of Antichrist will be Babylon, and he will have the first total dictatorship. The world will be an awful place. In that day everything will center in Babylon. The stock market will be read from Babylon—not New York. Babylon instead of Paris will set the styles for the world. A play, to be successful, will have to be a success in Babylon, not London. Everything in the city will be in rebellion against almighty God, and it centers in Antichrist.[7]

Two Babylons

From the time of Genesis 10–11, Babylon has represented both a city and the religious system that arose in that city. Babylon is a literal geographical location on the Euphrates River, but it also represents the false religious system that began at the tower of Babel when, for the first time, man organized a religion in rebellion against God. Babylon is the birthplace of worldwide religion. The false religion spread out from there to all the other major nations of the earth.

Babylon in its final form in Revelation 17–18 is again a system and a city. The location is clearly the same in both Revelation 17 and 18. However, Revelation 17 and 18 describe two different aspects of the same Babylon—religion and commerce.

Revelation 17: Religious Babylon

Revelation 17 focuses on Babylon's religious character, climaxing in a world religion during the first 3½ years of the Tribulation. The prostitute in Revelation 17 symbolizes a false religious system centered in Babylon. The major indictment against Babylon in Revelation 17 is the city's spiritual idolatry (17:4-5). The prostitute is identified as "Babylon the Great, Mother of All Prostitutes and Obscenities in the World."

Babylon is the "Mother," which means the source, or the polluted fountain from which all spiritual prostitution flows. This identification of Babylon as the source of spiritual unfaithfulness takes us back to the tower of Babel, where it started. Man will again organize in rebellion against the Creator just like at the tower of Babel.

The disappearance of millions of Christians at the Rapture will deepen the religious confusion already evident. The great religious system that began in Babylon after the Flood will return to the forefront. The church institution left on earth after the Rapture—void of true believers—will quickly fall into the hands of opportunists. Arnold Fruchtenbaum identifies Babylon the Prostitute in Revelation 17:

> Babylon the Harlot represents the one-world religious system that rules over the religious affairs during the first half of the

> tribulation. She rules over the nations of the world (the many waters) fully controlling the religious affairs and has the reluctant support of the government. The headquarters of this one world religion will be the rebuilt city of Babylon, the 'mother' of idolatry, for it was here that idolatry and false religion began (Genesis 11:1-9).[8]

Prophecy often uses prostitution, fornication, or adultery to describe idolatry (Isaiah 23:15-17; Jeremiah 2:20-31; 13:27; Ezekiel 16:17-19; Hosea 2:5; Nahum 3:4). New Babylon epitomizes this kind of spiritual prostitution, fornication, and idolatry.

As Robert Thomas says, "She leads the world in the pursuit of false religion whether it be paganism or perverted revealed religion. She is the symbol for a system that reaches back to the tower of Babel (Genesis 10:9-10; 11:1-9) and extends into the future when it will peak under the regime of the beast."[9]

Revelation 18: Commercial Babylon

Revelation 18:1 begins with the words, "After all this." In Revelation, these words generally signal that something new is being introduced or something new is beginning (Revelation 4:1). In Revelation 18, I believe that this phrase signals a shift or change in focus from Babylon's religious aspect in the first half of the seven-year Tribulation to its economic, commercial, and political aspect that dominates the world in the last half of the Tribulation. Babylon is clearly the center of economic power (Revelation 18). The city is connected with the merchants of the earth (Revelation 18:3, 11, 15, 23) and those engaged in maritime commerce (18:17). The long list of goods and cargo associated with Babylon marks the city as an economic juggernaut (18:11-13). The guilt of Babylon in chapter 18 primarily stems from her sensuality associated with materialism and wanton luxury. When Babylon falls, the kings of the earth, the merchants, and the traders of the sea will lament the fall of the nerve center of the world economy. All their dreams will come crashing down. Chuck Swindoll describes the fall of commercial Babylon:

As they watch the empire of the Beast burn amidst its countless treasures, they will also know that their own time is short. Thinking they had gotten in on an opportunity of a lifetime, those who rest in the lap of Babylon's luxury will suddenly realize that the tables have been turned. Like the Nazis in Berlin on the eve of the Allied victory, the reality of the Antichrist's defeat will be obvious as their satanic Reich disintegrates before their eyes.[10]

THE TWO BABYLONS	
RELIGIOUS	ECONOMIC
Revelation 17	Revelation 18
destroyed by the Antichrist and the ten kings	destroyed by God
falls at the midpoint of the Tribulation	falls at the end of the Tribulation

The Doom of Babylon

For the first half of the Tribulation, the woman will ride the Beast (Revelation 17:3), which seems to indicate that false religion will exercise some degree of control over the Antichrist. Since the Antichrist rules the world for the final 3½ years of the Tribulation, the woman cannot be in control of him during that time. Therefore, at the midpoint of the Tribulation, the Antichrist and the ten kings will destroy the religious system of Babylon (Revelation 17:16). The Antichrist will replace the false religious system of Babylon with his own blasphemous system that deifies him.

Babylon itself, with its political and commercial influence, will continue under the rule of the Antichrist for another 3½ years until it is destroyed in the seventh bowl judgment near the end of the Tribulation (Revelation 16:19; 18:16-24). Babylon will fall, never to rise again, just as the Scripture says.

CHAPTER 31

THE CAMPAIGN OF ARMAGEDDON

A YOUNG MAN WAS LEARNING to fly a single-engine airplane, and it was time to do the landing phase of his instruction. The instructor said, "Are you ready to go down?" He said, "Let's do it." So the plane began to descend. The instructor looked over at the young man, and he was cool and calm. There wasn't a sign of nervousness about him—no sweaty palms or biting his lip. The instructor thought this boy would make a great pilot.

The plane descended, and suddenly hit the ground with a thud, bounced fifty feet in the air, hit the ground again and bounced off the runway where it finally stopped. The instructor said, "Son, I have been teaching for a long time, and I believe that is the worst landing ever done by a student pilot." He replied, "Me? I thought *you* were landing the airplane!"[1]

I think a lot of times people feel that way about the world today. They wonder who is in control of this chaotic planet. But we must remember that God is in control, no matter what is happening or what we think. God is landing the plane of history. He is bringing events to their appointed end, and one of the key events that culminates the Tribulation is identified by one ominous word—Armageddon!

In 1945, when the Japanese surrendered, General Douglas MacArthur uttered these sobering words: "We have had our last chance. If we will not devise some greater and more equitable system, Armageddon will be at the door." In 1971, Ronald Reagan, who was then governor of California, told a fellow politician, "For the first time ever, everything is in place for the battle of Armageddon and the second coming of Christ."[2] Again in 1983, President Reagan said, "You know, I turn back to your ancient prophets in the Old Testament and the signs foretelling Armageddon, and I find myself wondering if—if we're the generation that is going to see that come about. I don't know if you've noted any of those prophecies lately, but, believe me, they certainly describe the times."[3] In his book *Till Armageddon*, Billy Graham says, "There is no doubt that global events are preparing the way for the final great war of history—the great Armageddon!"[4]

The Meaning of the Word *Armageddon*[5]

Armageddon. Just the mention of the word brings forth images of cataclysm, carnage, and catastrophe. The word *Armageddon* is found only one time in the Bible (Revelation 16:16), yet this one word is probably the most familiar biblical term from end times prophecy. People everywhere have heard about Armageddon, but like many other terms, the real meaning of the word often gets lost by overuse and misuse. To understand end times prophecy, it is essential to understand the meaning of this word.

The word *Armageddon* is made up of two words in Hebrew: *Har* (mountain) and *Megiddo* (a city in the northern part of ancient Israel). The ancient city of Megiddo was built on a hill, and it is therefore called the mountain of Megiddo—Armageddon. The city of Megiddo overlooks a beautiful, large valley known as the Plain of Esdraelon. The armies of the earth will gather here in the last days and face total defeat by the returning King from heaven (Revelation 16:12-16; 19:19-21).

What Armageddon Is Not

People have a lot of misconceptions about Armageddon. It is not a single battle. People refer to the "battle" of Armageddon as if it were one single conflict, but it is actually a war or campaign involving a series of battles in the land of Israel.

Armageddon is also often equated with the last battle or war on earth, but this is not the case. The last war in history will be the final revolt of Satan in Revelation 20:7-11 called Gog and Magog. This war occurs one thousand years after Armageddon.

What Armageddon Is

Armageddon is the climactic war of the Great Tribulation when all the armies of the earth gather to attack Israel and attempt to finally eradicate the Jewish people. They will capture Jerusalem, but then Jesus Christ will return to destroy the invading armies and deliver the faithful Jewish remnant.

Ten Main Passages That Describe Armageddon

The War of Armageddon is the subject of many biblical passages. Here are ten key Scriptures:

1. Psalm 2
2. Isaiah 34:1-16
3. Isaiah 63:1-6
4. Joel 3:1-17
5. Zechariah 12:1-9
6. Zechariah 14:1-15
7. Malachi 4:1-5
8. Revelation 14:14-20
9. Revelation 16:12-16
10. Revelation 19:19-21

Seven Key Titles of Armageddon

As with many main end times events and characters, the campaign of Armageddon has several different names and titles in Scripture.

1. the day of the Lord's vengeance (Isaiah 34:8)
2. the winepress of God (Isaiah 63:2; Joel 3:13; Revelation 14:19-20)
3. the great and awesome day of the Lord (Joel 2:31, NASB)
4. the harvest (Joel 3:13; Revelation 14:15-16)
5. the day . . . burning like a furnace (Malachi 4:1)
6. the great and terrible day of the Lord (Malachi 4:5, NASB)
7. the war of the great day of God, the Almighty (Revelation 16:14)

The Scope of the Campaign

The campaign of Armageddon will be spread out over twenty thousand square miles. It will encompass the entire land of Israel from Megiddo in the north to Edom and Bozrah in the south, spanning two hundred miles from north to south and one hundred miles from east to west. The battle will be the most intense in three specific areas.

1. *The Valley of Jehoshaphat* (Joel 3:2, 12). This name is probably another title for the Kidron Valley. Jewish, Christian, and Muslim traditions locate the place of final judgment for the nations in the Kidron Valley. This valley runs east of Jerusalem and between the city and the Mount of Olives.

   The Valley of Jehoshaphat is only mentioned by name two times in the Bible (Joel 3:2, 12). The word *Jehoshaphat* means "Yahweh judges," so it is a fitting place for God's judgment to be poured out. Zechariah locates the final judgment of the nations near the city of Jerusalem (Zechariah 14:1-5).
2. *The Plain of Esdraelon* (also known as the Valley of Jezreel, the Valley of Taanach, and the Plains of Megiddo). This plain is twenty miles long and fourteen miles wide. The armies of the earth will gather here, allied with the Antichrist, and meet their doom.

3. *Bozrah/Edom* (Isaiah 34:1-5; 63:1). Bozrah is a city east of the Jordan River in the ancient nation of Edom (modern nation of Jordan). It is near the rock city of Petra. After descending to the Mount of Olives, Christ will lead His army down to Edom to rescue the hiding Jewish remnant there. When He returns from Edom, His clothes will be stained with blood, and His sword will be drenched in blood (Isaiah 34:6; 63:1-3). The wicked people of Bozrah will be slaughtered to such an extent that the mountains will flow with blood and the land will be soaked in blood (Isaiah 34:2-7).

The most vivid description of the severity and brutality of Armageddon is found in Revelation 14:17-20.

> Another angel came from the Temple in heaven, and he also had a sharp sickle. Then another angel, who had power to destroy with fire, came from the altar. He shouted to the angel with the sharp sickle, "Swing your sickle now to gather the clusters of grapes from the vines of the earth, for they are ripe for judgment." So the angel swung his sickle over the earth and loaded the grapes into the great winepress of God's wrath. The grapes were trampled in the winepress outside the city, and blood flowed from the winepress in a stream about 180 miles long and as high as a horse's bridle.

This passage raises an important interpretive question: Will blood really flow as deep as a horse's bridle, about four feet deep, for a distance of two hundred miles—from Megiddo in the north to Bozrah in the south? Some believe that it will. Others maintain that this cannot be interpreted literally and that the language is exaggerated to impress the reader with the massive extent of the slaughter and bloodletting.

While either of these views is possible, I do not believe that this passage necessarily means that there will be a river of blood flowing four feet deep. I believe that the picture here is drawn from the imagery of the winepress.

When the grapes were put into the winepress, there would be people in the winepress who would stomp around on the grapes so that the juice would be released down into a collection vat. Using this image, in Revelation 14:19 the winepress is "the great winepress of God's wrath." The Lord is the One who is doing the stomping, but He is stomping on people, not grapes. And what pours out is blood, not grape juice (Isaiah 63:2-3; Joel 3:13; Revelation 19:15). The imagery suggests that the stomping of His judgment is so intense that the blood from His winepress will splash out as high as a horse's bridle.

This is a picture of the ferocity of God's judgment. The Lord is saying that at Armageddon He is going to throw all the nations into His great winepress and that His intense, blood-splattering judgment will extend throughout Israel from Megiddo to Bozrah.

Why Do the Nations Gather at Armageddon?

Scripture never clearly states why a massive army assembles in Israel. Some believe they will gather from all over the world to challenge the Antichrist. After all, by the end of the Tribulation, with all God's judgments pouring forth, the world will be in terrible shape. The nations may view the Antichrist as the source of the trouble and want to destroy him.

Others believe that the armies are gathered to finally eradicate the Jewish people. This campaign, energized by Satan, will be his last effort to get rid of the Jews and thwart the promises of God. Of these two options, the second one makes more sense to me because Revelation 16:13-16 indicates that the unclean spirits (demons) that gather the armies together will emanate from Satan, the Antichrist, and the false prophet.

It doesn't make sense that the Antichrist would gather the armies together to destroy himself. So I believe the armies gather in Israel in a final anti-Semitic, satanic surge to rid the world of the Jewish people. Whatever the initial reason is, though, Scripture reveals that as the armies gather in Israel, they will see the Lord Jesus coming from heaven and galvanize their efforts and animosity toward Him (Revelation 19:19).

Seven Key Phases of Armageddon

Since Armageddon is a military campaign and not just one single battle, it will play out in several distinct phases that are outlined in Scripture. As we have seen, Armageddon will transpire over the entire land of Israel in several different locations. Therefore, putting all the major pieces of Armageddon together in chronological order is a difficult task, so I would certainly not insist on every detail. However, the following is a proposed chronology of the key phases of Armageddon as presented in Scripture:

Phase 1

The Euphrates River dries up, preparing the way for the kings of the east (Revelation 16:12).

Phase 2

The Antichrist's allies assemble (Revelation 16:12-16). The armies assemble to annihilate the Jews once and for all.

Phase 3

The armies attack Jerusalem, and it falls (Zechariah 14:1-3).

Phase 4

Jesus Christ returns personally to the Mount of Olives (Zechariah 14:4).

Phase 5

Christ and the armies of the Lord destroy the armies gathered against Jerusalem in the Valley of Jehoshaphat (Joel 3:9-17; Zechariah 12:1-9; Zechariah 14:3).

Phase 6

Christ descends upon Bozrah/Edom—in modern Jordan—to destroy its inhabitants and to deliver the Jewish remnant (Isaiah 34:1-7; 63:1-5; Joel 3:19). Earlier, when the Antichrist breaks his covenant with Israel and sets up the abomination of desolation, one-third of the Jewish people will flee into the hills and the wilderness, where they will be supernaturally protected by God for 3½ years from the ravages of the Antichrist and Satan (Revelation 12:6, 14). The Scriptures seem to indicate that they will hide in the rock city of Petra in the southern part of modern Jordan (Micah 2:12-13; Daniel 11:41).[6]

Phase 7

The armies at Armageddon are destroyed (Revelation 16:16; 19:19-21). At Armageddon, the Antichrist will rally the remaining troops to fight against the Lord Jesus and His army (Revelation 19:19). The Antichrist and his armies will suffer total, cataclysmic defeat at the mighty hand of the King (Psalm 2:9; 2 Thessalonians 2:8). Jesus won't have to lift a finger. The sword of His word will smite the nations (Revelation 19:15). John Phillips describes the end of the Armageddon campaign:

> With what panoply and pomp the armies march across the plains of Galilee, file through the passes and deploy on the fertile fields of Megiddo! . . .
>
> Then suddenly it will be over. In fact, there will be no war at all, in the sense that we think of war. There will be just a word spoken from Him who sits astride the great white horse. Once He spoke a word to a fig tree, and it withered away. Once He spoke a word to howling winds and heaving waves, and the storm clouds vanished and the waves fell still. Once He spoke a word to a legion of demons bursting at the seams of a poor man's soul, and instantly they fled. Now He speaks a word, and the war is over. The blasphemous, loud-mouthed Beast is stricken where he stands. The false prophet, the miracle-working windbag from the pit is punctured and still. The pair of them are bundled up and hurled headlong into the everlasting flames. Another word, and the panic-stricken armies reel and stagger and fall down dead. Field marshals and generals, admirals and air commanders, soldiers and sailors, rank and file, one and all—they fall. And the vultures descend and cover the scene.
>
> Thus ends the battle of Armageddon![7]

The Aftermath of Armageddon

In the wake of this war, two key events will happen. First is the great bird supper (Matthew 24:28; Luke 17:37; Revelation 19:17-21): carcasses will fill the entire region; the birds of the air will gather to feed on the carnage. Second, the Antichrist and the false prophet will be cast alive into the lake of fire forever (Revelation 19:20). These two pawns of Satan will be the first two occupants of the lake of fire.

Thus ends the campaign of Armageddon. There will be no more war on earth for one thousand years.

PART 10

The Second Coming

Then I saw heaven opened, and a white horse was standing there. Its rider was named Faithful and True, for he judges fairly and wages a righteous war. His eyes were like flames of fire, and on his head were many crowns. A name was written on him that no one understood except himself. He wore a robe dipped in blood, and his title was the Word of God.

REVELATION 19:11-13

As it did in 4:1, heaven opened before John's wondering eyes. But unlike 4:1, heaven opens this time not to let John in, but to let Jesus out. The time has come at last for the full, glorious revelation of the sovereign Lord. This is the time to which all of Revelation (as well as all of redemptive history) has been pointing.

JOHN MACARTHUR JR., *Revelation 12-22*

CHAPTER 32

HERE COMES THE KING

NEWSPAPERS HAVE A SPECIAL kind of font they reserve only for mega-events when ordinary headlines and bold print just won't cut it. They call it "Second Coming type." It's the kind and size of font that jumps off the page, grabs the reader by the throat and screams, "READ ME!" It's the kind of font they used when Pearl Harbor was attacked, when the allies defeated Hitler, when President Kennedy was assassinated, and even in one of the greatest blunders in American journalism history—Thomas Dewey's "defeat" of Harry Truman in the 1948 presidential election.

Why do they call it "Second Coming type"? Why give this title to the font used for such sensational events? The reason, of course, is that there simply is no bigger event in history than the second coming of Jesus Christ. "Ironically, when He comes, Second Coming type will sit unused on the presses. Why? Because there will be no time left to put out a flash street edition to announce His return!"[1]

The Cornerstone of Bible Prophecy

The climactic event of the Great Tribulation and human history is the second coming of Jesus Christ when Jesus returns to this earth as King of kings and Lord of lords to judge His enemies, end Satan's deception, and set up His Kingdom on earth that will last for one thousand years. There is nothing more dear to God's people and more clearly stated in the Bible than the fact that Jesus Christ is coming again.

The Old Testament contains many references to the Second Coming. Twenty-three of twenty-seven New Testament books explicitly refer to the second coming of Christ to this earth—His visible, literal, physical, glorious return. Three of the remaining four books are one-chapter books (Philemon, 2 John, 3 John), and the book of Galatians implies the Second Coming in 1:4. There are 260 chapters in the New Testament and over three hundred references to the second coming of Christ. Jesus referred to His coming about twenty times, and His followers are commanded nearly fifty times to be ready for His coming. Christ Himself stated the truth of His second advent emphatically.

> As the lightning flashes in the east and shines to the west, so it will be when the Son of Man comes. Just as the gathering of vultures shows there is a carcass nearby, so these signs indicate that the end is near.
>
> Immediately after the anguish of those days,
>
> the sun will be darkened,
> the moon will give no light,
> the stars will fall from the sky,
> and the powers in the heavens will be shaken.
>
> And then at last, the sign that the Son of Man is coming will appear in the heavens, and there will be deep mourning among all the peoples of the earth. And they will see *the Son of Man coming on the clouds of heaven* with power and great glory.
>
> MATTHEW 24:27-30 (ITALICS ADDED)

> Jesus replied, "You have said it. And in the future you will see *the Son of Man seated in the place of power at God's right hand and coming on the clouds of heaven.*"
>
> MATTHEW 26:64 (ITALICS ADDED)

Human history culminates with the second coming of Jesus Christ. Although entire books have been written on this breathtaking event, we will focus on four important points about the Second Coming—the place, the people, the purpose, and the pattern of Christ's coming.

The Place of the Second Coming

Jesus will return to the earth from the same place He left—the Mount of Olives. Three key passages help identify this as the place of His return. First, Zechariah 14:4 addresses the second coming of Christ: "In that day His feet will stand on the Mount of Olives, which is in front of Jerusalem on the east; and the Mount of Olives will be split in its middle from east to west by a very large valley, so that half of the mountain will move toward the north and the other half toward the south" (NASB).

Second, the Mount of Olives is where Jesus gave His great prophetic discourse, which included the signs of His coming (Matthew 24–25).

Third, when Jesus ascended to heaven from the Mount of Olives (Acts 1:9-11), the angels said that he would return just as He had left. Jesus will return to the Mount of Olives, where He will make a perfect two-point landing.

The People Who Will Accompany the Second Coming[2]

A Christian woman was once talking to a servant of Christ about the assurance of her salvation in Christ and said, "I have taken a one-way ticket to glory and do not intend to come back." To this the man of God replied, "You are sure going to miss a lot. I have taken a round-trip ticket. I am not only going to meet Christ in glory, but I am coming back with Him in power and great glory to the earth."

When Jesus Christ returns from heaven to destroy the Antichrist, judge the nations, and establish His glorious Kingdom on earth, He will not be alone. He will be accompanied by a great crowd. This crowd will follow in His entourage as He splits the clouds riding on a white stallion. This crowd will be made up of both angels and redeemed human beings. All believers in Christ have a round-trip ticket. All who have been raptured will return to the earth with Jesus at His second coming, the climax of the Tribulation.

Here are a few of the most familiar verses that describe the crowds of heaven that return with the conquering Christ.

> Then the LORD my God will come, and all his holy ones with him.
> ZECHARIAH 14:5

> When the Son of Man comes in his glory, and all the angels with him, then he will sit upon his glorious throne.
> MATTHEW 25:31

> When our Lord Jesus comes again with all his holy people. Amen.
> 1 THESSALONIANS 3:13

> When the Lord Jesus appears from heaven. He will come with his mighty angels . . .
> 2 THESSALONIANS 1:7

> Listen! The Lord is coming with countless thousands of his holy ones.
> JUDE 1:14

> I saw heaven opened, and a white horse was standing there. Its rider was named Faithful and True, for he judges fairly and wages a righteous war. . . . The armies of heaven, dressed in the finest of pure white linen, followed him on white horses.
> REVELATION 19:11, 14

Just imagine what it will be like to follow the King of kings and Lord of lords and to lead the mighty angels who come in flaming fire as the Lord God Omnipotent returns to reign.

The Purposes of the Second Coming[3]

At least seven key reasons for the second coming of Christ can be discerned from Scripture.

Christ Is Coming to Fulfill His Promise

The coming of Christ to earth will fulfill the numerous promises that He will come again (Zechariah 14:4; Matthew 25:31; Acts 1:9-11).

Christ Is Coming to Defeat the Antichrist and His Armies (Revelation 19:19-21)

Jesus will crush the gathered horde at Armageddon who is under the authority of the Antichrist. In a futile, foolish show of bravado, the assembled armies will turn against Christ as He descends from heaven. In the briefest battle in history, the King of kings and Lord of lords will prevail effortlessly.

Christ Is Coming to Regather and Restore Faithful Israel

The most frequently mentioned promise in the Old Testament is God's promise that He will one day regather and restore the nation of Israel (Isaiah 43:5-6; Jeremiah 30:10; 33:6-9; Ezekiel 36:24-38; 37:1-28). The promise will be fulfilled in two distinct ways—a physical regathering and a spiritual regathering.

The physical regathering of Israel began in 1948 when the modern state of Israel was born, and it continues today. This regathering will continue until the midpoint of the Tribulation. It is a *physical* regathering of the Jewish people to their *land* in unbelief in preparation for the Tribulation. When the Tribulation begins, Israel will be persecuted and scattered for the final time.

The spiritual regathering will happen when, at the Second Coming, Christ will gather the believing Jews together and restore them as His people

(Isaiah 11:11). This will be their *spiritual* regathering to the *Lord* in belief in preparation for the Millennium. In Matthew 24:30-31, Jesus says, "And then the sign of the Son of Man will appear in the sky, and then all the tribes of the earth will mourn, and they will see the SON OF MAN COMING ON THE CLOUDS OF THE SKY with power and great glory. And He will send forth His angels with A GREAT TRUMPET and THEY WILL GATHER TOGETHER His elect from the four winds, from one end of the sky to the other" (NASB). The believing Jewish remnant will be regathered, and the Lord will fulfill His covenant promises to them.

TWO REGATHERINGS OF ISRAEL	
THE PRESENT (FIRST) REGATHERING	THE PERMANENT (FUTURE) REGATHERING
worldwide	worldwide
return to part of the land	return to all the land
return in unbelief	return in faith
restored to the land only	restored to the land and to the Lord
sets the stage for the Tribulation	sets the stage for the Millennium
discipline	blessing

Christ Is Coming to Judge the Living

When Christ returns, all the Gentiles who survived the Tribulation will appear before Him. He will determine if they can enter His Kingdom (Matthew 25:31-46). This judgment is called the judgment of the "sheep and the goats." Christ will also gather all living Jews in the wilderness to determine who can enter the Kingdom (Ezekiel 20:33-38).

Christ Is Coming to Resurrect the Dead

After the Second Coming (Revelation 19:11-21), one of the next events is the resurrection of Old Testament and Tribulation believers to reign with Christ (Revelation 20:4-6; Daniel 12:1-4).

Christ Is Coming to Bind the Devil (Revelation 20:1-3)

After Christ returns and defeats the Antichrist, the first thing He'll do is bind Satan in the bottomless pit for one thousand years.

Christ Is Coming to Establish Himself as King (Revelation 19:16)

Christ will return as King of kings and Lord of lords! He will sit on His glorious throne and reign over the earth (Isaiah 9:6-7; Daniel 2:44; Matthew 19:28; Luke 1:32-33).

The Pattern of His Coming

The nature of the Lord's coming is directly set forth in Scripture. There are eight key words that effectively describe how Jesus will return to the earth at His second coming.

Personally

Jesus will not send someone else to represent Him like great leaders often do. He Himself will return. Acts 1:11 says, "This Jesus, who has been taken up from you into heaven, will come in just the same way as you have watched Him go into heaven" (NASB). In His final words, in Revelation 22:20, Jesus says, "Yes, I am coming quickly" (NASB).

Literally

The coming of Jesus is not a mystical or figurative coming. It is literal. It is real. He came literally the first time to Bethlehem, and He will come literally again. Acts 1:9-11 recounts the ascension of Christ, saying, "After saying this, he was taken up into a cloud while they were watching, and they could no longer see him. As they strained to see him rising into heaven, two white-robed men suddenly stood among them. 'Men of Galilee,' they said, 'why are you standing here staring into heaven? Jesus has been taken from you into heaven, but someday he will return from heaven in the same way you saw him go!'"

Scripture promises that Jesus will come back to earth literally just as He literally ascended to heaven.

Visibly

Jesus will not come back secretly, disguised, or undercover. Those who claim that He has already come, or that He is presently on earth hiding out somewhere, are mistaken. His coming will not be hidden but will be visible to all the world. Matthew 24:23-27 describes His coming:

> If anyone tells you, "Look, here is the Messiah," or "There he is," don't believe it. For false messiahs and false prophets will rise up and perform great signs and wonders so as to deceive, if possible, even God's chosen ones. See, I have warned you about this ahead of time.
>
> So if someone tells you, "Look, the Messiah is out in the desert," don't bother to go and look. Or, "Look, he is hiding here," don't believe it! For as the lightning flashes in the east and shines to the west, so it will be when the Son of Man comes.

Revelation 1:7 says it plainly:

> Look! He comes with the clouds of heaven.
> And everyone will see him—
> even those who pierced him.
> And all the nations of the world
> will mourn for him.
> Yes! Amen!

Suddenly

The second coming of Jesus will be swift and sudden. It will not occur over a long, drawn-out period or in stages. It will come suddenly like a thief in the night and will crash unexpectedly like lightning in the sky.

> As the lightning flashes in the east and shines to the west, so it will be when the Son of Man comes.
>
> MATTHEW 24:27

> I will come to you suddenly, as unexpected as a thief.
>
> REVELATION 3:3

Dramatically

Jesus' coming, just like His birth, will be accompanied by dramatic signs and wonders in the heavens. It will be the most dramatic event in human history.

> Immediately after the anguish of those days,
>
> the sun will be darkened,
> the moon will give no light,
> the stars will fall from the sky,
> and the powers in the heavens will be shaken.
>
> MATTHEW 24:29

> There will be strange signs in the sun, moon, and stars. And here on earth the nations will be in turmoil, perplexed by the roaring seas and strange tides. People will be terrified at what they see coming upon the earth, for the powers in the heavens will be shaken.
>
> LUKE 21:25-26

Gloriously

Jesus will return with splendor, grandeur, and overpowering brilliance.

> At last, the sign that the Son of Man is coming will appear in the heavens, and there will be deep mourning among all the peoples of the earth. And they will see the Son of Man coming on the clouds of heaven with power and great glory.
>
> MATTHEW 24:30

> The Lord Jesus will be revealed from heaven with His mighty angels in flaming fire.
>
> 2 THESSALONIANS 1:7 (NASB)

Triumphantly

Jesus will return as King of kings and Lord of lords. He is coming back to take over!

All the armies of the earth will assemble at Armageddon to face Him, yet amazingly no struggle or battle of any kind is recorded. There will not be any struggle. Jesus will defeat the amassed armies without any effort (Psalm 2:9). All Jesus will have to do to completely vanquish His enemies is speak the words "Drop Dead!" He will slay His enemies with "the breath of His mouth" (2 Thessalonians 2:8, NASB). Revelation 19:19-21 describes His conquest:

> Then I saw the beast and the kings of the world and their armies gathered together to fight against the one sitting on the horse and his army. And the beast was captured, and with him the false prophet who did mighty miracles on behalf of the beast—miracles that deceived all who had accepted the mark of the Beast and who worshiped his statue. Both the beast and his false prophet were thrown alive into the fiery lake of burning sulfur. Their entire army was killed by the sharp sword that came from the mouth of the one riding the white horse. And the vultures all gorged themselves on the dead bodies.

Certainly

There is no doubt that He will come again. In Matthew 24:35 Jesus says, "Heaven and earth will disappear, but my words will never disappear." Everything Jesus says about His coming is sure. It's a done deal.

Conclusion

The first time Jesus came, he allowed Himself to be mocked, persecuted, abused, and finally crucified between two thieves on a Roman cross. God in human flesh humbled Himself so that He could purchase a pardon for our sins and taste death for every person (Hebrews 2:9). But when He comes again, the story will be much different. He will come in power and great glory. Every creature will bow before Him and be subject to His authority (Philippians 2:11). Only those who have accepted by faith what He accomplished at His first coming are ready for His second coming.

CHAPTER 33

SEVENTY-FIVE DAYS TO GLORY

BOOKS ABOUT THE END TIMES frequently overlook the interval of time between the second coming of Christ and the official inauguration of the millennial kingdom. The Millennium will not commence the day after the end of the Great Tribulation. There will be a seventy-five-day interval.

This interval could be likened to the time between the election of a US president in November and the official inauguration in January. During this time, the president-elect appoints cabinet members, prepares his agenda, and doles out the spoils of victory to his faithful supporters.

Daniel 12:11-12 presents this interlude. Daniel 12:1-3 describes the time of coming Tribulation for Israel and then the resurrection of Old Testament saints. The Tribulation for Israel will last 1,260 days, which is 3½ years (Daniel 12:7). This is the latter half of the seven-year Tribulation. Then, after these great events we read the enigmatic words in Daniel 12:11-12: "From the time the daily sacrifice is stopped and the sacrilegious object that causes desecration is set up to be worshiped, there will be 1,290 days. And blessed are those who wait and remain until the end of the 1,335 days!"

As you can see, three future time periods are clearly delineated: 1,260 days, 1,290 days, and 1,335 days. Many commentators interpret these numbers symbolically, but as Leon Wood objects, "the numbers are so near in size that no symbolism would fit them. Moreover, numbers mentioned earlier in Daniel (e.g., 2,300 days, 8:14) have been found to be literal."[1]

So, what are we to make of these three time periods? The 1,260 days is not too difficult since this time period is frequently set forth in Daniel and Revelation as the final 3½ years of the Tribulation. The 1,290 days is thirty days beyond the end of the Tribulation, and the 1,335 days is another forty-five days beyond that. These time periods describe an interval of time between the end of the Tribulation and Christ's second coming and the beginning of the Millennium.

While we cannot be certain about everything that will transpire during this time, it is safe to say that during this time period Christ will remove the abomination of desolation, cast the Antichrist and the false prophet into the lake of fire (Revelation 19:20), throw Satan into the abyss (Revelation 20:1-3), judge those living on the earth (Matthew 25:31-46), resurrect and reward Old Testament and Tribulation saints (Daniel 12:1-3), and assign responsibilities for the administration of His Kingdom. During this interval, the celebration of the marriage supper will begin on the earth (Revelation 19:7-10), and possibly the construction of the millennial Temple will commence as well (Ezekiel 40–48). The fact that those who make it to the 1,335 days are blessed means that they have made it to the beginning of the millennial kingdom (Daniel 12:12). They have come through the judgments and are allowed to enter the kingdom. Leon Wood describes this time period:

> Whatever occasion falls at the conclusion of these days is something good and desirable. There will be blessing for all those who attain it. The thought is thus suggested that it will be the actual starting point of the Millennium. Those who will have passed the judgment of Christ, during the preceding thirty days, would be those who will attain to it, after these

forty-five additional days. What will be the need of these forty-five days? It may be the time necessary for setting up the governmental machinery for carrying on the rule of Christ. The true border of Israel (from the River of Egypt to the Euphrates, Genesis 15:18) will have to be established and appointments made of those aiding in the government. A period of forty-five days would again seem reasonable in which to accomplish these matters.[2]

John Phillips agrees, but adds a few more details:

No light is shed on the extra two and one-half months that follow. It might be that thirty days will be necessary for completing the mopping-up operations against the vast armies that have been deployed by both the East and the West at Megiddo and for bringing to an end all further hostilities worldwide. Also, the land of Israel will need to be cleansed of the dead. The temple, defiled by the Antichrist, will probably be demolished, too, before true worship can be established. Maybe all of these activities will take up the first month. Then, too, we learn from other Scriptures that the Lord intends to set up His throne in the Valley of Jehoshaphat, near Gethsemane, and to judge the nations in accordance with the criteria of Matthew 25. Possibly it will take the extra month and a half to gather the surviving people of the world from earth's remotest bounds to this great assize. The sheep will be separated from the goats. Swift doom will overtake those who sided with the Antichrist, who wore his mark, and who cooperated with his anti-Semitic laws. The remnant of the Jews and the redeemed from among the Gentiles will go on into the millennial kingdom, the nucleus of the new kingdom.

In any case, God pronounces them "blessed." The word, as usual, is plural. It can be rendered, as in Psalm 1:1 and elsewhere, "O the blisses of the person who . . ." or "Happy, happy is the one who . . ." The millennial kingdom will be worth waiting for.[3]

Three Time Periods in Daniel 12

1,260 days: the last half of the seven-year Tribulation

1,290 days: an addition of thirty days during which time the abomination of desolation continues in the Temple before its removal

1,335 days: forty-five more days after the 1,290 day period. The abomination of desolation will be removed, the Antichrist and false prophet will be cast into the lake of fire, Satan will be bound, the nations will be judged, Old Testament and Tribulation saints will be resurrected and rewarded, the marriage supper will begin, positions of authority will be meted out to God's people, and possibly the millennial Temple will be built or at least begun.

The Millennium will begin following the seventy-five-day interval. The King will take His throne, and the Kingdom of God will come to earth.

> May all the godly flourish during his reign.
>   May there be abundant prosperity until the moon is no more.
> May he reign from sea to sea,
>   and from the Euphrates River to the ends of the earth. . . .
> All kings will bow before him,
>   and all nations will serve him.
>
> PSALM 72:7-8, 11

PART II

Satan's Chain and the Saints' Reign

A larger body of prophetic Scripture is devoted to the subject of the millennium, developing its character and conditions, than any other one subject.

J. DWIGHT PENTECOST, *Things to Come*[1]

The Bible is replete with prophecies of a coming age of peace and prosperity. It will be a time when war will be utterly unknown. Not a single armament plant will be operating, not a soldier or sailor will be in uniform, no military camps will exist, and not one cent will be spent for armaments of war, not a single penny will be used for defense, much less for offensive warfare. Can you imagine such an age, when all nations shall be at perfect peace, all the resources available for enjoyment, all industry engaged in the articles of a peaceful luxury.

DR. M. R. DEHAAN, *The Great Society*[2]

CHAPTER 34

THE MILLENNIUM

JESUS WINS. All Christians can agree on a few things, and this is one of them. It's one of those nonnegotiables. In the end, Jesus will reign over the whole world as King. That's part of what the Millennium means—that Jesus will rule over everything. But how will the Millennium come about, and when will it occur? Is it present now, or is it future? Will it be a literal thousand years, or does it simply symbolize a really long time? This is where opinions differ. Although Christians all agree that Jesus will rule the world, there's still debate about how and when that will happen. Let's take a look at the issues on the table.[1]

The One-Thousand-Year Reign

People have always dreamed of a utopia, a great society, a paradise on earth, a return to the Garden of Eden. The Bible is clear that sinful men and women can never produce such a society on earth in their own strength and ingenuity. However, when the Lord Jesus returns to this earth, God's Word tells us that the next great event, the culmination of history, is the one-thousand-year reign of Jesus on earth as King of kings and Lord of lords—or simply, the millennial kingdom. During this era the world will flourish under the rule of the Prince of Peace, basking in unrestricted peace and prosperity. Immediately after Christ returns and destroys the Antichrist and his armies (Revelation 19:11-21), Satan is bound and Christ reigns for one thousand years (Revelation 20:1-6). The words *a thousand years* appear six times in Revelation 20:1-7.

Ten Key Texts on the Millennium

While Revelation 20:1-6 is the only Bible passage that records the length of Christ's reign on the earth, it is certainly not the only passage to refer to His messianic kingdom. The Old Testament has large passages on the messianic kingdom. More prophetic material is devoted to the subject of the Millennium than to any other topic. Therefore, it is critical that we gain at least a basic understanding of the millennial kingdom. For starters, here is a list of ten of the most important Old Testament passages on the coming kingdom.

1. Isaiah 2:1-5
2. Isaiah 11:1-16
3. Isaiah 32:1-20
4. Isaiah 35:1-10
5. Isaiah 60:1-22
6. Jeremiah 31:1-40
7. Jeremiah 33:1-26
8. Ezekiel 37:14-28
9. Amos 9:11-15
10. Zechariah 14:6-21

Seven Key Titles of the Millennium

The title for an event helps shed light on its nature. A title summarizes in a word or brief phrase the essence of the event. God has given us several key biblical titles that capture the essence of the coming messianic kingdom.

1. the Kingdom of Heaven (Matthew 3:2; 8:11)
2. the Kingdom of God (Mark 1:15)
3. the Kingdom (Matthew 16:28)
4. the world to come (Hebrews 2:5)
5. times of refreshing (Acts 3:19, NASB)
6. the period of restoration of all things (Acts 3:21)
7. a Kingdom that cannot be shaken (Hebrews 12:28)

With this brief introduction in mind, let's examine the three main views of the timing and nature of the Millennium.

Are We in the Millennium Now?

Three Main Views of the One-Thousand-Year Reign

In the Bible, the millennial kingdom is that phase when Jesus Christ rules and reigns in God's Kingdom. To help us understand the millennial reign of Christ, we need to begin by examining the three main views: amillennial, premillennial, and postmillennial. As you can see, the word *millennial* is at the core of these terms. *Millennium* means "a thousand years." This term is derived from the Latin words *mille* ("a thousand") and *annus* ("year"). Although the word itself never appears in the Bible, the duration of this kingdom is specifically stated six times in Revelation 20:1-7: one thousand years.

Two Main Points of Agreement

As with most divergent perspectives, there are points of agreement.

1. Jesus Christ is King of kings and Lord of lords, and He rules or will rule over a glorious Kingdom.
2. Jesus Christ will one day return to this world literally, physically, visibly, and gloriously as the Judge of all the earth.

These points are nonnegotiables that bind us together as believers in Jesus Christ, our coming Lord. That said, there are significant disagreements in exactly how these truths play out, and they affect almost every key event of the last days. This is not just some study in irrelevant theory. Which view you hold will determine how you understand the characters, chronology, and consummation of the end times.

Two Main Points of Disagreement

There are many differences between these three views of the last days, but two main points of disagreement distinguish these three views: (1) *When* will Jesus reign? Is it present or yet to come? (2) *How* will Jesus reign? Spiritually in heaven or literally on earth? Let's look at each of these views and see how they answer these two critical questions.

The Amillennial View

WHEN WILL JESUS REIGN?

Amillennialists believe that the Kingdom of Christ is unfolding during the present age, between the first and second advents of Christ. The prefix *a-* before the word *millennium* denotes the opposite of the word *millennium* and so literally means "no millennium." However, this is not exactly reflective of amillennialism—amillennialists *do* believe in a millennial kingdom of Christ, but it is not a future, literal, earthly kingdom. Instead, the one thousand years symbolize a "long period of time." Amillennialists teach that Satan was bound at the first coming of Christ as a result of Christ's death and resurrection (Revelation 20:1-3).

HOW WILL JESUS REIGN?

For the amillennialist, Christ is reigning in a present spiritual Kingdom. Amillennialists deny that the reign of Jesus will be a literal, physical kingdom on earth. Instead, Christ reigns spiritually over the church in the hearts of believers and in heaven over the souls of the redeemed.

The amillennial position is very simple and streamlined. Amillennialists believe that Christ will return someday to judge all humanity and usher in eternity. They deny both a literal seven-year Tribulation before the second coming of Christ and a literal one-thousand-year reign after His second coming.

HISTORY OF AMILLENNIALISM

The amillennial position is the prevailing view of the Roman Catholic church, the Greek church, and a large portion of Protestantism. This view is usually traced back to Tyconius, who had a powerful influence on St. Augustine (AD 354–430). Augustine wrote extensively on the one thousand years in Revelation and viewed it as having reference to the whole church age. This was also the view of the Reformers such as John Calvin and Martin Luther.

FUTURE EVENTS ACCORDING TO THE AMILLENNIAL SYSTEM
1. a parallel development of both good (God's Kingdom) and evil (Satan's kingdom) during this present age
2. the second coming of Christ
3. the general resurrection of all people
4. a general judgment of all people
5. eternity

THE TIMELINE OF AMILLENNIALISM

The Premillennial View

WHEN WILL JESUS REIGN?

Premillennialism teaches that Jesus Christ will return before ("pre-") the millennial kingdom. Christ inaugurates the millennial kingdom in His return to the earth after the seven-year Tribulation.

HOW WILL JESUS REIGN?

Premillennialists hold that the millennial kingdom will be a physical, earthly kingdom of one thousand literal years. Jesus Christ will rule and reign over the earth from His earthly throne in Jerusalem. Unlike amillennialism and postmillennialism, the millennial kingdom will not be gradually cultivated by the conversion of souls over an extended period of time. Instead, Christ will establish the kingdom suddenly and powerfully in His glorious coming to earth. Satan will be bound during those one thousand years (Revelation 20:1-3), the Curse will be reversed, the Jewish people will be restored to their ancient land in fulfillment of the Abrahamic Covenant, and Christ will reign over the earth in righteousness, peace, and joy.

Many premillennialists agree with amillennialists and postmillennialists that Jesus is ruling over the church during this present age and that He reigns in the hearts of His people. He was, is, and always will be the Sovereign of the universe. There is disagreement among premillennialists about the nature of any present form of the Kingdom. However, all premillennialists would agree that this present rule is not the same as the millennial kingdom described in Revelation 20:1-6. Christ's rule from David's throne on earth will be literally fulfilled in the future.

Charles C. Ryrie defines the premillennial view this way: "The millennium is the period of a thousand years of the visible, earthly reign of the Lord Jesus Christ who, after His return from heaven, will fulfill during that period the promises contained in the Abrahamic, Davidic and new covenants to Israel, will bring the whole world to a knowledge of God, and will lift the curse from the whole creation."[2]

Among premillennialists there are two subgroups. Historic premillennialists normally do not distinguish between Israel and the church. They generally believe that the church will remain on earth throughout the Tribulation. Dispensational premillennialists, on the other hand, consistently distinguish Israel from the church and for this reason believe that the church will be raptured to heaven before the beginning of the seventieth week of Daniel (the Tribulation).

HISTORY OF PREMILLENNIALISM

Premillennialism was the view of the early church. At that time, it was referred to as "chiliasm," which comes from the Greek word for one thousand. The essence of this view was the view held by such early church fathers as Papias, Clement of Rome, Barnabas, Ignatius, Polycarp, and Justin Martyr. Tertullian (AD 160–230), a lawyer and Christian apologist, vigorously defended the notion of an earthly kingdom that would last one thousand years.

After the third century, with the rise of Augustine's view of a spiritual Kingdom, premillennialism began to wane and amillennialism prevailed. Premillennialism made a dramatic comeback in the seventeenth century and really took hold in the mid-nineteenth century. It is currently a popular way of understanding the end times. Modern premillennialists include Donald Grey Barnhouse, Charles C. Ryrie, John Walvoord, J. Dwight Pentecost, James Montgomery Boice, J. Vernon McGee, Hal Lindsey, Tim LaHaye, John MacArthur, Adrian Rogers, David Jeremiah, Thomas Ice, Chuck Smith, and Chuck Swindoll.

FUTURE EVENTS ACCORDING TO THE PREMILLENNIAL SYSTEM
increase of apostasy as the church age draws to a close
the Rapture of the church (Premillennialists disagree over the timing of the Rapture. They hold to any of the five views presented earlier in our examination of the Rapture.)
seven-year Tribulation period on earth
the campaign of Armageddon
the second coming of Christ to earth
the one-thousand-year reign of Christ on earth (Satan is bound)
the release of Satan
the Great White Throne Judgment
the creation of a new heaven and new earth
eternity

THE TIMELINE OF PREMILLENNIALISM

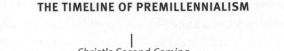

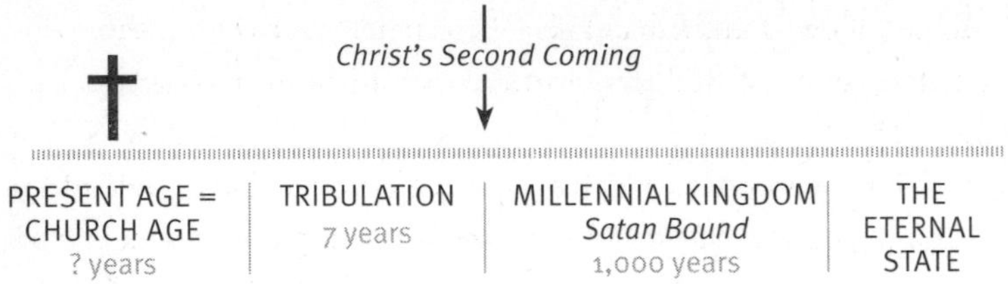

The Postmillennial View

WHEN WILL JESUS REIGN?

Postmillennialists maintain that Jesus Christ will return to earth after ("post-") the Millennium. Consequently, the Millennium is the entire period of time between the first and second comings of Christ. Christ returns after the Millennium is completely over.

HOW WILL JESUS REIGN?

Jesus' reign is spiritual and political for postmillennialists. The millennial kingdom is not a literal thousand years but a golden age that the church will usher in during this present age by preaching the gospel. This golden age will arrive gradually as the gospel spreads throughout the earth until the whole world is eventually Christianized. The Millennium will grow as believers in Christ exercise more and more influence over the affairs of this earth. Ultimately, the gospel will prevail, and the earth will become a better and better world, after which time Christ will appear to usher in eternity. The best-known advocate of this view in recent years is Loraine Boettner. He summarizes the postmillennial view very well:

> Postmillennialism is that view of the last things which holds that the kingdom of God is now being extended in the world through the preaching of the gospel and the saving work of the Holy Spirit in the hearts of individuals, that the world eventually is to be Christianized and that the return of Christ is to occur at the close of a long period of righteousness and

peace commonly called the millennium. It should be added that on the postmillennial principles the Second Coming of Christ will be followed immediately by the general resurrection, the general judgment, and the introduction of heaven and hell in their fullness.

The millennium to which the postmillennialist looks forward is thus a golden age of spiritual prosperity during this present dispensation, that is, the Church Age. This is to be brought about through forces now active in the world. It is to last an indefinitely long period of time, perhaps much longer than a literal one thousand years. The changed character of individuals will be reflected in an uplifted social, economic, political and cultural life of mankind. The world at large will then enjoy a state of righteousness which up until now has been seen only in relatively small and isolated groups: for example, some family circles, and some local church groups and kindred organizations.

This does not mean that there will be a time on this earth when every person will be a Christian or that all sin will be abolished. But it does mean that evil in all its many forms eventually will be reduced to negligible proportions, that Christian principles will be the rule, not the exception, and that Christ will return to a truly Christianized world.[3]

HISTORY OF POSTMILLENNIALISM

Postmillennialism arrived on the scene much later than amillennialism or premillennialism, but it enjoyed great popularity, becoming the major millennial view of the eighteenth and nineteenth centuries. Daniel Whitby (1638–1726), a Unitarian minister from England, is usually credited with the development of this view. With all the advances in technology, science, and the burgeoning industrial revolution, the idea that man could bring in the Kingdom of God made perfect sense. However, the outbreak of World War I followed closely by World War II dealt postmillennialism a blow from which it has never fully recovered. Modern reconstructionists, theonomists, and adherents of dominion theology are postmillennialists.

FUTURE EVENTS ACCORDING TO THE POSTMILLENNIAL SYSTEM
progressive improvement of conditions on earth as the end draws near, culminating in a golden age as the world is Christianized
the second coming of Christ
the general resurrection of all people
a general judgment of all people
eternity

THE TIMELINE OF POSTMILLENNIALISM

SUMMARY OF THE THREE MILLENNIAL VIEWS

	AMILLENNIAL	PREMILLENNIAL	POSTMILLENNIAL
When Will Christ Reign?	Between the first and second comings (present reign)	immediately after the Second Coming (future reign)	between the first and second comings, but arriving by degrees (present reign)
How Will Christ Reign?	Christ rules over a spiritual Kingdom in the hearts of believers on earth and over the souls of the redeemed in heaven (spiritual reign).	Christ will rule personally over a literal, physical, earthly kingdom with Satan bound and the Curse reversed (earthly reign).	Christ rules in the hearts of believers as the church brings in the Kingdom by the triumph of the gospel in this world (spiritual reign).

Who's Right?

The big question I know you are asking right now is, Who's right? Which of these three views most accurately reflects the teachings found in the Bible?

The view that I hold is the premillennial view. I believe this view is far superior to either of the other views. It is an integral part of this whole book. The premillennial view is the best view for six main reasons. To make these points easier to remember I've developed the acronym PREMIL. This acronym serves as a reminder that the premillennial view of the end times is the best view.

PREMIL—Six Reasons for the Premillennial View

Like one of my friends said at a prophecy conference, "I'm so sold on premillennialism that when the doctor tells me to open my mouth and say, 'Ah,' I say, 'Pre.' I'm so premillennial I won't eat 'Post' Toasties." I'm not that bad, but I do believe the premillennial view best represents what the Scriptures teach. Let me share six reasons why. First, premillennialism best fulfills God's promises to Abraham and David. Second, it offers the clearest interpretation of the Resurrection in Revelation 20:4-6. Third, premillennialism is the earliest view. Fourth, it also gives us the most natural reading of Revelation 20:1-6. Fifth, premillennialism best explains Satan's current role and his future incarceration during the Millennium. Finally, it maintains the consistent literal interpretation of Scripture.

Together these reasons can be remembered using the acronym PREMIL.

Promises of God
Resurrection in Revelation 20:4-6
Earliest View
Most Natural Reading of Revelation 20:1-6
Imprisonment of Satan
Literal Use of Numbers in Revelation

Let's look at each of the six reasons to see how they support the premillennial view.

Promises of God

Of the millennial views, only premillennialism believes in the literal fulfillment of God's covenants with Abraham and David.[4] As we saw in chapter 6, God unconditionally, unilaterally promised Abraham three things in Genesis 12:1-3 and 15:18:

1. God would bless Abraham personally and the whole world would be blessed through him.
2. God would give Abraham many descendants.
3. God would give Abraham and his descendants a specific piece of land forever.

Clearly, God has literally fulfilled the first two aspects of His promise. God gave Abraham many descendants, and God has blessed the world through Abraham via the Jewish Scripture and the Jewish Savior. If the first two aspects of this covenant have been fulfilled literally, then it seems logical to conclude that the land promise will also be literally fulfilled. And since this promise has never been fulfilled in history and is unconditional, the promise must still be future. The land promised to Abraham fits perfectly with the idea of a one-thousand-year reign of Christ on earth, during which Israel will occupy all the land promised to them in Genesis 15:18 and Christ will rule from the city of Jerusalem.

God made another promise that still awaits fulfillment. In 2 Samuel 7:12-16, God promised King David that one of his descendants would sit on his throne and reign over his kingdom forever. While God did not promise that this rule would continue uninterrupted, He did promise that David's dynasty would maintain the right to rule and that one of David's descendants would rule forever. This promise was applied specifically to Jesus when He was born (Luke 1:32-33).

Amillennialists and postmillennialists argue that God fulfilled His promise because Christ sits on His throne in heaven ruling over the church. Premillennialists, on the other hand, contend that Christ must literally sit on David's throne on earth and rule over David's kingdom, the nation of Israel. The New Testament reinforces this literal interpretation.

In Acts 1:6-7, Jesus reaffirmed that the kingdom would be restored to Israel in the future:

> When the apostles were with Jesus, they kept asking him, "Lord, has the time come for you to free Israel and restore our kingdom?" He replied, "The Father alone has the authority to set those dates and times, and they are not for you to know."

Jesus had promised the disciples that in His kingdom they would sit on twelve thrones judging the twelve tribes of Israel (Matthew 19:28). Understandably, they were anxious to find out when this great event would happen. Notice that Jesus did not correct the disciples' statement that the kingdom would be restored to Israel. If they entertained an erroneous view of the kingdom, surely Jesus would have corrected them, especially since He had just spent forty days teaching them about the Kingdom of God (Acts 1:3). However, Jesus didn't correct their view of Israel and the kingdom; He simply pointed out that they were not to be concerned about the timing of that event. Just before His ascension back to heaven, Jesus confirmed to His disciples that the kingdom would be restored to Israel (Acts 1:6-7). And the future millennial kingdom of Christ is the only time mentioned in Scripture when the Davidic Covenant could be literally fulfilled.

Resurrection in Revelation 20:1-6

Revelation 20:4-6 gives us details about the Resurrection that point toward premillennialism. First, Revelation 20:4 mentions believers coming to life: "They all came to life again, and they reigned with Christ for a thousand years."

Amillennialists have interpreted Revelation 20:4-6 in two different ways. They argue that this passage either refers to the new spiritual life following conversion or a believer's life in heaven after death during the current age.[5] In either interpretation, the resurrection is spiritual. Kim Riddlebarger states the amillennial view of Revelation 20:5 succinctly:

"The first resurrection is spiritual and not bodily and occurs before, not after the second advent."[6]

Premillennialists maintain that the resurrection in Revelation 20:5 refers to physical, bodily resurrection at the end of history. Nothing in the text indicates the regeneration of the soul, but everything points to a resurrection of the body. The phrase "they came to life again" in Greek is the verb *ezesan*, which appears twelve times in the book of Revelation and normally refers to physical life. Only one time in Revelation does it refer to the believer's spiritual life (3:1).

Second, Revelation 20:5-6 uses the word *resurrection* (*anastasis* in Greek). Of the forty-two times this word appears in the New Testament, forty-one of those times it refers to bodily resurrection. Clearly that is what it means here as well. The dead who come to life reign with Christ for one thousand years.

Finally, in Revelation, this passage on the resurrection of the dead follows on the heels of John's account of the second coming of Christ (19:11-21). Therefore, the Millennium must occur after the return of Christ and the resurrection of the dead, both of which have yet to occur.

Earliest View

The early church believed in a premillennial return of Christ for the first two to three centuries of church history. The view was known as *chiliasm*, and those who held this view were known as *chiliasts*, from the Greek word for one thousand: *chilioi*. Almost all the luminaries in the early church held this view. Papias, the bishop of Hierapolis, was a companion of Polycarp and a disciple of the apostle John, who wrote the book of Revelation. This ties Papias directly to the original source, and Papias believed in a literal one-thousand-year reign of Christ on the earth. Irenaeus (c. 120–202), Apollinaris, Tertullian (160–230), Victorinus, and Lactantius all promulgated the tradition of the literal Millennium. *The Epistle of Barnabas* (c. 130) takes the one thousand years literally. Justin Martyr (100–165) in his *Dialogue with Trypho* states, "But I and every other completely orthodox Christian feel certain that there will be a resurrection of the flesh, followed by 1,000 years in the rebuilt, embellished, and enlarged city of Jerusalem, as was announced by the prophets Ezekiel, Isaiah, and others." Premillennialism was the church's earliest view of the end times.

Most Natural Reading

The premillennial position is the clearest, most natural way to understand the flow and sequence of events in Revelation 19–22. Revelation 20:1-6 is the only passage in the Bible that specifically mentions the one-thousand-year reign of Christ, and it follows immediately after the second coming of Christ in Revelation 19:11-21.

Those who reject the idea of a future, literal, earthly kingdom following Christ's second coming argue that Revelation 20 reverts back to the present age before Christ's return. But there is nothing in the text to signal this shift. To the contrary, John's repeated use of the words "then I saw" (thirty-two times in the book of Revelation) moves the action along in a chronological sequence as John is seeing new visions (e.g., Revelation 19:11, 19; 20:1, 4, 11; 21:1). The Millennium follows the return of Christ in this sequence of events that John is seeing unfold. This is the most natural reading of Revelation.

Imprisonment of Satan

The binding of Satan in Revelation 20:1-3 lies at the heart of the millennial issue. Both amillennialists and postmillennialists contend that the binding of Satan occurred at the first coming of Christ and that Satan is bound right now during this present age. They often view the casting of Satan from heaven in Revelation 12:7-9 as parallel with Luke 10:18-19. They point to Mark 3:27 and Matthew 12:25-29 as the fulfillment of the binding of Satan during the earthly ministry of Christ. For them, Satan's activity and power are restricted during this present age. However, this contradicts the way Satan is pictured in the New Testament. Satan is called "the ruler of this world" (John 12:31; 14:30), "the god of this world" (2 Corinthians 4:4), "an angel of light" (2 Corinthians 11:14), "the commander of the powers in the unseen world" (Ephesians 2:2), and he is "like a roaring lion, looking for someone to devour" (1 Peter 5:8). The devil schemes against believers (2 Corinthians 2:11; Ephesians 6:11), hinders us (1 Thessalonians 2:18), accuses us (Revelation 12:10), and blinds the minds of the lost (2 Corinthians 4:4). Satan is anything but bound today. He is aggressively opposing the work of God. As someone once said, "If Satan is bound today he must have an awfully long chain." Satan is characterized as the arch-deceiver in the New Testament. Yet, Revelation 20:3 says that when he is bound Satan will "not deceive the nations anymore." This does not fit the current situation. It demands a later time after the Lord's coming.[7]

Revelation 20:1-3 is very precise and specific in its description of Satan's binding. It describes four distinct actions by the angel who binds him. Satan is "laid hold of," "bound," "[thrown] into the abyss," and the abyss is "shut and sealed over him" (NASB). The language is very compelling and clear. Nothing even similar to this happened at the first coming of Christ. But it will happen when Christ returns, after which Christ will reign for a thousand years (Revelation 20:4-6). As New Testament scholar Harold Hoehner says, "There is no indication that Satan has freedom to exercise any power during that period of time. This binding of Satan for 1,000 years cannot have reference to the present time but must speak of a future period of time, namely, the Millennium."[8]

The release of Satan after the Millennium also favors a literal interpretation of the one thousand years (Revelation 20:7). If taken literally, this means that after it ends, Satan will be released for a short time, will deceive the nations, suffer total defeat, and finally be cast into the lake of fire. But if one believes the one-thousand-year reign of Christ refers to the present church age and that Satan is bound until Christ's second advent, when will Satan be released for a short time? It's difficult to fit his release into the chronology of events. Amillennialists and postmillennialists believe that when Christ returns there will be final judgment and the new heaven and new earth will begin. They have a serious problem explaining Satan's release at the end of the one thousand years, which they take to be the present age. The release of Satan is further support that this time period should be interpreted literally.

Literal Use of Numbers

Revelation 20:1-7 specifically mentions "a thousand years" six times. This repetition emphasizes its importance and points toward its literalness. Why repeat a time period six times if it's not literal? Moreover, most, if not all, the other time-specific time periods and numbers mentioned in Revelation can be interpreted literally: "ten days" (Revelation 2:10), "144,000" (7:4; 14:1), "five months" (9:5, 10), "200 million" (9:16), "forty-two months" (11:2; 13:5), and "1,260 days" (11:3; 12:6). In Revelation whenever the number "thousand" is used, it refers to something definite. For example, the 144,000 (Revelation 7:4-8; 14:1, 3); 1,260 days (11:3); 7,000 killed in an earthquake (11:13); and 1,600 stadia (14:20) and 12,000 stadia, which is the measurement of the new Jerusalem (21:16). There is no indication in Revelation 20 that anything other than a literal time period of one thousand years is intended here.

Additionally, when John mentions a time period that is general or nonspecific, he identifies it as such by phrases like "a little longer" (Revelation 6:11) or "little time" (12:12). Revelation 20:3 says that at the end of the one thousand years Satan will be released for "a little while." If the one thousand years symbolizes a "long while," why didn't John say so? He uses the specific language and nonspecific language in the same context. He does it again in Revelation 20:8, writing, "as numberless as sand along the seashore." Rather than giving a specific number, John uses an image that refers to a very large number. The specific and nonspecific numbers used in the same context point toward a literal understanding of the one thousand years.

Conclusion

In Revelation 5:9-10 the four living creatures and the twenty-four elders in heaven fall down before the Lord and sing a new song.

> They sang a new song with these words: "You are worthy to take the scroll and break its seals and open it. For you were slaughtered, and your blood has ransomed people for God

> from every tribe and language and people and nation. And you have caused them to become a Kingdom of priests for our God. *And they will reign on the earth.*" (ITALICS ADDED)

The final words of this heavenly hymn are instructive. They speak of a reign that is future ("will reign") and earthly ("on the earth"). Only the premillennial view does justice to these words of revelation from God.

Taking all the relevant evidence into account, it is best to interpret the one thousand years in Revelation 20 as a literal Millennium when Jesus Christ will reign with His saints on the earth after His second coming. But this raises another important question: What is the purpose of the reign of Christ on earth? Why does there need to be a Millennium in the program of God? Why not just move straight from the Second Coming to the final judgment and eternity?

CHAPTER 35

WHY THE MILLENNIUM?

According to the amillennial and postmillennial systems, we are currently in the Millennium. Someday when Christ returns, there will be a general resurrection, one great judgment, and then eternity will begin. The premillennial position, on the other hand, believes that Christ will come to establish His messianic kingdom on earth. But why will there be a literal, earthly Millennium? What purposes will it fulfill? Why is it necessary? The Millennium will serve at least three important functions in the plan of God.[1]

To Reward the Faithful

The first reason we need the Millennium is so God can reward the faithful. He will do this by giving them authority to reign over the earth. When Jesus Christ returns to this earth, He will bring His saints with Him (Jude 1:14; Revelation 19:14). After He defeats the armies of the Antichrist at Armageddon and judges the nations, He will establish His Kingdom on the earth.

While the Millennium will include things like worshiping and serving our Lord, Scripture emphasizes our ruling and reigning with Christ. The Bible says that all believers from every age will reign with Christ for a thousand years. Consider what these verses say about what God's people will be doing in the Kingdom.

> In the end, the holy people of the Most High will be given the kingdom, and they will rule forever and ever. . . . Until the Ancient One—the Most High—came and judged in favor of his holy people. Then the time arrived for the holy people to take over the kingdom. . . . Then the sovereignty, power, and greatness of all the kingdoms under heaven will be given to the holy people of the Most High. His kingdom will last forever, and all rulers will serve and obey him.
>
> DANIEL 7:18, 22, 27

> Don't you realize that someday we believers will judge the world? And since you are going to judge the world, can't you decide even these little things among yourselves? Don't you realize that we will judge angels? So you should surely be able to resolve ordinary disputes in this life.
>
> 1 CORINTHIANS 6:2-3

> To all who are victorious, who obey me to the very end,
>
> To them I will give authority over all the nations. They will rule the nations with an iron rod and smash them like clay pots.
>
> They will have the same authority I received from my Father, and I will also give them the morning star!
>
> REVELATION 2:26-28

> Then I saw thrones, and the people sitting on them had been given the authority to judge. And I saw the souls of those who had been beheaded for their testimony about Jesus and for proclaiming the word of God. They had not worshiped the beast

> or his statue, nor accepted his mark on their foreheads or their hands. They all came to life again, and they reigned with Christ for a thousand years. . . . Blessed and holy are those who share in the first resurrection. For them the second death holds no power, but they will be priests of God and of Christ and will reign with him a thousand years.
>
> REVELATION 20:4, 6

What an exciting prospect! We will rule the nations with Christ for a thousand years on earth. We will even judge the angels.

During this present age, God is testing believers to determine their future position of authority and responsibility in the millennial kingdom. Believers will be given rulership in the kingdom over men and angels based on what we did with the treasures and talents God entrusted us with here on earth (Luke 19:11-26). Some will be governors over ten cities; some will rule over five cities. All believers will reign, but the extent and responsibility of that reign is being determined right now in your life and mine. As it has been said, "this is training time for reigning time."

To Redeem Creation

The second reason we need the Millennium is so God can finally reverse His curse on creation and fulfill His original purpose for the earth. When Adam and Eve sinned in the Garden of Eden, God pronounced a series of five curses. These five curses were given against the serpent, Satan, the woman, the man, and nature (Genesis 3:14-19). From that time until today, the earth has been cursed, as evidenced by "thorns and thistles" and the hard work that man must endure to harvest food from the ground. The new crabgrass in the lawn each spring is a small yet vivid reminder of the Curse.

During the millennial kingdom, all animals will revert back to being plant eaters as they were originally in Creation (Genesis 1:30). The wolf and lamb will lie down together in harmony, and a child will be able to play next to a poisonous snake (Isaiah 11:6-9). Someone once pointed out, "If you think we are in the Millennium today, put a wolf in a pen with a lamb and see what happens." P. T. Barnum, the famous circus showman, loved to show visiting preachers his exhibit called "The Happy Family," in which lions, tigers, and panthers squatted around a lamb without any aggression. When visiting preachers asked Barnum if the group ever had any trouble, he would say, "Apart from replenishing the lamb now and then, they get along very well together." We are not in the Millennium now. This world is not what it is supposed to be. It is not what God created it to be, but the Bible declares that someday it will be.

In addition, the entire earth will become amazingly productive and beautiful as even the deserts will blossom like a rose (Isaiah 35:1-7). The whole earth will be like a huge Garden of Eden. God's original purpose was to bring all things under the dominion of humankind and to submit all things to Himself through human beings (Genesis 1:26-27). In the Millennium, God will fulfill His original purpose for humanity and His glorious creation.

Without a literal Millennium under the reign of Christ, God's purpose for this world can never be fully realized. As J. Dwight Pentecost says, "God's purpose for the earth would be unrealized and the problem generated by Satan's rebellion would never be resolved. Thus the physical, literal reign of Christ on the earth is a theological and biblical necessity—unless Satan is victorious over God."[2] The Millennium will bring creation full circle as God brings to pass with the second Adam, Jesus Christ, what the first Adam failed to do (1 Corinthians 15:21-22). James Boice says, "To my mind, however, the best and ultimate reason why there must be a literal millennium is that only in a literal millennium do we have a meaningful culmination of world history."[3]

Johann Sebastian Bach sometimes slept more than he should have. His children had a unique way of waking him up. They would go to the piano and begin to play a composition. When they would get to the last note, they would stop. They wouldn't play the last note. It worked like a charm, and it would always wake him up. He would get up from his sleep, go to the piano, and play the final chord. He couldn't stand to leave it hanging there incomplete—unfinished. In the same way today, we are all waiting for the last note on the final page of God's song of victory. God will not leave His grand composition without striking the final note. That final note is the messianic kingdom of Jesus Christ.[4]

To Realize the Biblical Covenants

The third reason we need the Millennium is to fulfill the biblical covenants. In these covenants, God made very specific promises to Israel. As discussed in chapter 6, God made four great unconditional, one-way, eternal covenants with Abraham and his descendants. These four covenants are the Abrahamic Covenant, the Land Covenant, the Davidic Covenant, and the New Covenant.

None of these four covenants has been literally fulfilled. But Jesus, the Son of David, will fulfill them when He comes to sit on the throne of David and rules over the house of David from the city of David, which is Jerusalem. He will fulfill the Abrahamic Covenant and its promises of the land and descendants; the Land Covenant with its promise of the land; the Davidic Covenant with its promises concerning David's house, throne, and kingdom; and the New Covenant with its promises of a new heart, the forgiveness of sins, and the indwelling of the Spirit for a converted nation. In short, without a literal millennial reign of Christ, these covenants remain incomplete and unfulfilled.

The Millennium is no optional part of God's plan for the end times. It must occur for God to keep His promises to reward the faithful with authority, redeem creation from the Curse, and realize the biblical covenants by fulfilling God's promises.

CHAPTER 36

WHEN THE WORLD IS TURNED RIGHT SIDE UP

One of my friends, who attended Dallas Theological Seminary many years ago, told me that one of his professors walked into class one day and abruptly announced that he had become an amillennialist. Now, at Dallas Seminary, which is strongly premillennial, this was a very bold statement to make. However, the professor went on to explain. He informed the class that he had been having some troubles and had read Isaiah 11 in his Bible the night before. Isaiah describes the pristine conditions on the earth during the coming Millennium. After finishing the chapter, the professor said he sat back in his chair and said, "Ah, Millennium."

When we look at our present world with all its difficulty, depression, and despair and then imagine the millennial kingdom, it is a refreshing thought. Every believer in Christ should be an "Ah-millennialist." We should look forward to that day when the earth will glorify the Lord and paradise will be regained.

Steve Brown told a story on his radio program about the ugliest car he had ever seen. It had a large gash on its side; the door was held together with baling wire; many places on the car were rusted out. The muffler was loose and, with every bump, was hitting the street, sending sparks in every direction. It was hard to tell the original color of the car. The rust had eaten away much of the original paint, and so much of the car had been painted over with so many different colors that any one of them, or none of them, could have been the first coat. The most interesting thing about the car was the bumper sticker. It read, "This is not an abandoned car."

We live in a fallen world. It is often ugly and depressing. Everywhere we turn we find tragedy and heartache. Our world seems to be sitting on the verge of disaster. We might be tempted to wonder if God really cares about this world. But the promise of the Millennium is God's sign that reads, "This is not an abandoned world." Jesus is coming someday to restore paradise on earth.[1]

What Will the Millennium Be Like?

During the millennial reign of Christ, the earth will experience a return to conditions like the Garden of Eden. It will literally be heaven on earth as the Lord of heaven comes to live on the earth among His people. Chuck Swindoll describes the Millennium:

> The book of Revelation promises a golden age in which all weapons of warfare will be fashioned into implements of peace. Prosperity will be shared. Peace will become the banner of all people. The light of justice will illumine every corner of the world.[2]

The Bible has a lot more to say about the coming Millennium than most people realize. Here are ten prominent conditions that will prevail on the earth during the reign of Christ.[3]

1. Peace

All wars will cease as the world unites under the reign of the true King (Isaiah 2:4; 9:4-7; 11:6-9; Zechariah 9:10). We might call this one thousand years the *Pax* Messiah—the messianic peace.

2. Joy

Isaac Watts wrote the song "Joy to the World" to anticipate the glorious second coming of Christ to rule and reign on this earth. Think of some of the words of this song: "Joy to the world! The Lord is come; let earth receive her king. . . . No more let sins and sorrows grow. . . . He rules the world with truth and grace. . . ." This is a song of the Millennium—when full joy will come to the world (Isaiah 9:3-4; 12:3-6; 14:7-8; 25:8-9; 30:29; 42:1; Jeremiah 30:18-19; Zephaniah 3:14-17; Zechariah 8:19; 10:6-7).

3. Holiness

The word *holy* means to be "set apart" to God for sacred purposes. The Kingdom of Christ will be a holy kingdom. Everything in it will be set apart to God for His use. The holiness of the Lord will be manifest in His own person as well as in the citizens of His kingdom. The land, the city, the Temple and the subjects will all be holy unto the Lord (Isaiah 4:3-4; 29:19; 35:8; 52:1; Ezekiel 43:7-12; 45:1; Zechariah 8:3; 14:20-21).

4. Glory

The radiant glory of God will be fully manifest in Messiah's kingdom (Isaiah 35:2; 40:5; 60:1-9; Ezekiel 43:1-5). His glory will fill the earth.

5. Justice or Righteousness

When the millennial kingdom begins, it will be inhabited only by believers. However, these believers will still have human bodies with fallen natures capable of sinning. They will have children who are also still in their mortal flesh. The reigning Messiah will judge man's sin with perfect justice (Isaiah 9:7; 11:5; 32:16; 42:1-4; 65:21-23). He will rule with "a rod of iron" restraining and judging sin so that the prevailing atmosphere in the kingdom will be righteousness (Isaiah 11:1-5; 60:21; Jeremiah 31:23; Ezekiel 37:23-24; Zephaniah 3:1, 13).

6. Full Knowledge

The teaching ministry of the Lord and the indwelling Spirit will bring the inhabitants of the kingdom into a full knowledge of the Lord's ways (Isaiah 11:1-2, 9; 41:19-20; 54:13; Jeremiah 31:33-34; Habakkuk 2:14).

7. Absence of Sickness or Deformity

Politicians are constantly working on plans to provide better health care for their citizens. In the Lord's government, the health plan will be out of this world. The King will heal all the diseases and deformities of His people (Isaiah 29:18; 33:24; 35:5-6; 61:1-2; Ezekiel 34:16). As a result of this universal health care, people will live extended life spans like before the Flood. A person who dies at the age of one hundred will have died very prematurely (Isaiah 65:20).

8. Universal Worship of God

All the inhabitants of the earth will join their hearts and voices in praise and worship to God and His Christ (Isaiah 45:23; 52:1, 7-10; 66:17-23; Zephaniah 3:9; Zechariah 13:2; 14:16; Malachi 1:11; Revelation 5:9-14). This worship during the Millennium will be centered in the rebuilt Temple in Jerusalem (Isaiah 2:3; 60:13; Ezekiel 40–48; Joel 3:18; Haggai 2:7, 9).

Ezekiel 40–48 describes the literal, millennial Temple in detail, including its dimensions, priesthood, worship, sacrifices, and ritual. Some argue that Ezekiel's Temple is symbolic of the church or of God's covenant relationship with His people. On the contrary, there is ample evidence for interpreting it as a literal, end times Temple. The center of Israel's new life will be the Lord Himself, who will return in glory to rule in her midst (Ezekiel 43:1-9). The millennial Temple will meet the need for a royal residence for God's glory. God will reign with this Temple as His throne (Ezekiel 43:7) just as he had done previously in the Tabernacle and the Temple.[4] This interpretation is in harmony with other Old Testament prophetic passages that prophesy the existence of a millennial Temple and sacrifices in that future Temple (Isaiah 2:3; 56:6-7; 60:13; Jeremiah 33:18; Joel 3:18; Haggai 2:7, 9; Zechariah 14:16-21).

A very controversial aspect of the worship in the Millennium is that animal sacrifices will be reinstituted in the massive millennial Temple (Isaiah 56:6-7; 60:7; Ezekiel 43:18-27; 45:17-23; Zechariah 14:16-21). This controversy centers on why these sacrifices would be needed since Christ's death was the final sacrifice for sin. First, this is not a reinstitution of the law of Moses in the messianic kingdom, but a new system of kingdom law. The numerous differences between the laws of Moses and the laws of the Millennium reveal that the systems are not the same.[5] The law of Moses was terminated permanently with the death of the Messiah. Many Jewish rabbis refused to accept the book of Ezekiel into the Hebrew canon for some time because of the way it describes the law in chapters 40–48.[6]

All agree that these sacrifices will not be offered to take away sin. No animal sacrifice can ever take away sin (Hebrews 10:1-2). Only the blood of Christ can wash away sin. So, how do we explain Ezekiel's description of animal sacrifices in the millennial Temple (Ezekiel 43:18-27)? What purpose will they serve?

Some maintain that these sacrifices will, like the Lord's Supper, serve as a powerful memorial to the one sacrifice for sin forever—the sacrifice of Jesus Christ. They will remind people of the holiness of God, the awfulness of sin, and the horrible death the Savior died in our place. The problem is that Ezekiel states that these sacrifices are for atonement. Every mention of "atonement" in Ezekiel 40–48, except 45:15-17, relates to the concept of ceremonial purification or consecration of the Temple or altar.[7] In the one exception in Ezekiel 45:15-17, the purpose would be the same as in the Mosaic system—that is, to provide a graphic picture of the ultimate atoning work of Christ, which alone can pay the ransom price for sin and provide forgiveness.[8]

A better explanation is that these sacrifices serve as ritual purification. During the Millennium, a holy God will be dwelling on earth in the midst of people in their glorified bodies but also in the midst of sinful people living in natural, unglorified bodies. These sacrifices prevent these worshipers from defiling God's holy Temple when they come to worship Him. It is a matter of ritual purification. Jerry Hullinger states, "Ezekiel 40–48 indicates that during the millennium God's glory will return to the temple where sacrificial ritual will take place and in which offerings will make atonement. For Ezekiel the concept of atonement is the same as it was in the Book of Leviticus, namely, an act that wipes away and purges uncleanness. This purgation will be required because the divine presence will once again be dwelling in the land. . . . Impurity is contagious to both persons and sancta. Further, impurity is inimical to Yahweh, who refuses to dwell among a people if uncleanness remains untreated. Because of God's promise to dwell on earth during the millennium (as stated in the New Covenant), it is necessary that He protect His presence through sacrifice."[9]

Sacrifices during the Millennium will not be a substitute for Christ's atoning work. Instead, they will provide ritual purification for unglorified people on earth who approach the holy God in worship.

9. Economic Prosperity

The millennial kingdom will have no need for rescue missions, welfare programs, food stamps, or relief agencies. The world will flourish under the hand of the King of heaven (Isaiah 35:1-2, 7; 30:23-25; 62:8-9; 65:21-23; Jeremiah 31:5,12; Ezekiel 34:26; 36:29-30; Joel 2:21-27; Amos 9:13-14; Micah 4:1, 4; Zechariah 8:11-12; 9:16-17).

10. The Presence of God

The greatest thing about the kingdom is that Christ Himself will be there. God's presence will be fully recognized, and the Lord's people will experience fellowship with the Lord unlike anything they have ever known (Ezekiel 37:27-28; Zechariah 2:10-13). The city of Jerusalem will be called *Yahweh Shammah*, which means "the Lord is there" (Ezekiel 48:35).

A Surprising Twist

This sounds like the perfect ending to the story of Creation and redemption—God dwelling among His people in perpetual peace and prosperity. But it is not the end of the story. There is one more surprising twist to the drama of the ages that none of us could ever imagine if it were not in the pages of Scripture. After Jesus has ruled for one thousand years, Satan will be released to make his final stand.

PART 12

The Second Coming of Satan

As the evening shadows of the Millennial Day fall, the Angel who imprisoned Satan will unlock the "prison house" of the "Bottomless Pit," and Satan will come forth embittered by his forced confinement to vent his anger upon the people of God, a refutation of the claim that the miseries of perdition will lead to repentance. Satan will still be the same malignant being after his 1,000 years of confinement that he was before. His hatred against God and his people will be unquenched.

CLARENCE LARKIN, *The Book of Revelation*[1]

He who lets him loose is, of course, the same who bound him, and sealed him in the prison of the Abyss. God uses even the wickedest of beings, and overrules the worst depravity, to his own good and gracious ends. He allows Satan liberty, and denies him liberty, and gives him liberty again, not because the Devil or the Devil's malice is necessary to him, but to show his power to bring good out of evil, to make even the worst of creatures praise him, and to turn their very wickedness to the furtherance of the purposes they would fain defeat.

J. A. SEISS, *The Apocalypse*[2]

CHAPTER 37

SATAN'S LAST STAND

THERE IS AN OLD SAYING: "The next time Satan comes along and begins to remind you of your past, remind him of his future." The Bible reveals that Satan's future is very bleak. He is doomed to eternal destruction. However, the Bible tells us that he will not go down without a fight. Revelation 20:1-3, 7-10 depicts the final demise of Satan. These verses reveal three important stages in the final revolt or second coming of Satan and his final doom: (1) Satan Bound, (2) Satan Released, and (3) Satan Defeated.

Satan Bound

When Christ returns as King to establish His kingdom, the first order of business is to defeat the gathered armies at Armageddon and imprison the false king, the Antichrist, the usurper to His throne. The second order of business is to seize the power behind the Antichrist, the devil himself. Christ immediately dispatches a powerful angel to bind Satan in the bottomless pit. Satan is sentenced to the longest prison term in history—one thousand years. During Satan's one-thousand-year incarceration, Christ will rule the earth with His resurrected and raptured saints in the millennial kingdom (Revelation 20:4-6).

Satan Released

At the end of the one thousand years, Satan is released for a brief period of time for his last stand (Revelation 20:3). God allows Satan one last shot at world dominion. But why would God release Satan from the abyss? J. Vernon McGee provides valuable insight:

> Apparently Satan is released at the end of the Millennium to reveal that the ideal conditions of the kingdom under the personal reign of Christ do not change the human heart. This reveals the enormity of the enmity of man against God. Scripture is accurate when it describes the heart as "desperately wicked" and incurably so. Man is totally depraved. The loosing of Satan at the end of the 1,000 years proves it.[1]

God's Word clearly teaches that man is sinful both by nature and by practice. Man has been tested in every way and will always fail apart from God and His grace. The millennial kingdom and the second coming of Satan will conclusively prove this.

During the messianic kingdom, people who haven't yet been glorified will still have sinful natures, but the perfect world around them will offer no enticement to sin, nor will Satan and his demons be around to tempt them either. Satan will be bound for one thousand years, and the Lord Jesus Himself will be personally present, ruling and reigning on the restored earth.

In spite of these perfect conditions, a host of people born and raised during the Millennium will still reject the Lord. Only believers will survive the Tribulation to enter the kingdom, and they will all know the Lord and trust in Him, but they will have children during the Millennium, and many of those children will not repent and believe in Christ as their

Savior. They may outwardly conform to avoid judgment, but inwardly they will harbor a rebellious heart against the King of kings. This situation seems unbelievable, but it is true.

When Satan is released at the end of the Millennium, his one-thousand-year prison sentence will not have reformed his character. He will not have changed. And humankind will not have changed either. Satan will gather so many people after his release that "the number of them is like the sand of the seashore" (Revelation 20:8, NASB). This last human confederacy will try to destroy Christ, His city, and His people. Their actions will prove once for all, beyond any doubt, that regardless of a person's heredity, circumstances, or environment, people are incorrigibly sinful apart from God's saving grace. As J. Dwight Pentecost notes, "The millennial age is designed by God to be the final test of fallen humanity under the most ideal circumstances, surrounded by every enablement to obey the rule of the king, from whom the outward sources of temptation have been removed, so that man may be found and proved to be a failure in even this last testing of fallen humanity."[2]

The Millennium and the second coming of Satan will demonstrate once and for all that our hearts are totally depraved and black with sin, that Christ had to pay the ultimate price for us to be forgiven and saved, and that eternal punishment is necessary. The one-thousand-year reign of Christ will prove conclusively that we need a righteousness outside ourselves to live in relationship with a holy God—the very righteousness of Jesus Christ that God credits to all who will simply trust in His Son (2 Corinthians 5:21).

Satan Defeated

The gathering of rebels and the war that defeats them are called "Gog and Magog" in Revelation 20:8. This title has confused many people and led them to equate this battle of Gog and Magog with the one in Ezekiel 38–39. There are two key differences between these two battles that indicate they are not the same.

GOG AND MAGOG IN EZEKIEL 38–39	GOG AND MAGOG IN REVELATION 20:8
Occurs during the Tribulation, before the Millennium described in Ezekiel 40–48	Occurs after the Millennium of Revelation 20:1-6
Enumerates specific nations	Involves all the nations

The two invasions differ in period and participants. The name is the main thing that is the same.

But if these two battles are not the same, then how do we account for them both having the same name? The best way to understand this is to view the term "Gog and Magog" in the same way we use the term "Waterloo" today. When we say today that someone met their "Waterloo," we mean that they experienced a disastrous defeat. It is a shorthand way of describing a crushing military defeat. The same appears to be true here of Gog and Magog.

Instead of giving all the details, John simply alludes to Gog and Magog. In other words, a vast horde of nations will gather against the Lord and His people but will be decimated. It will repeat Ezekiel 38–39.

Another plausible explanation is to view the two uses of Gog and Magog like World War I and World War II. Ezekiel 38–39 will be Gog and Magog I and Revelation 20:7-10 will be Gog and Magog II.

Whatever explanation one adopts, the main point is that this will be one of the shortest battles in history. As this massive mob of rebels gathers on the broad plain of the earth and surrounds Jerusalem, God sends fire down from heaven to destroy them. Immediately, Satan is cast into the lake of fire forever to join the other two members of the false trinity, the Antichrist and the false prophet (Revelation 20:10). The archenemy of God and humanity who first entered in Genesis 3 in the Garden of Eden will exit in Revelation 20, cast into the lake of fire forever.

PART 13

The Great White Throne

We picture the scene: host beyond host, rank behind rank. The millions among the nations of the world, all crowded together in the presence of the One who sits upon the throne, the One who looks intently at each individual. We are accustomed to human judges; we know their partial and impartial verdicts. In the presence of the Almighty, all previous judgments are rendered useless. Many men and women acquitted on earth before a human judge will now be found guilty before God. Men who have been accustomed to perks, special privileges, and legal representation now stand as naked in the presence of God. To their horror they are judged by a standard that is light-years beyond them: The standard is God Himself. . . . For the first time in their lives they stand in the presence of unclouded righteousness. They will be asked questions for which they know the answer. Their lives are present before them; unfortunately, they will be doomed to a painful, eternal existence.

ERWIN W. LUTZER, *Your Eternal Reward*[1]

CHAPTER 38

JUDGMENT DAY

AMERICANS ARE ENAMORED with the drama of a courtroom. There has been a steady stream of TV shows that focus on the courtroom: *Perry Mason*, *L.A. Law*, *Law & Order*, *The People's Court*, *Boston Legal*, and *The Firm*. John Grisham has sold millions of books and movie tickets by focusing on the high stakes of courtroom tension. People in our nation were spellbound for months by the trials of O. J. Simpson and Casey Anthony.

The Bible tells us that the ultimate courtroom drama, the trial of the ages, will occur someday in heaven in the courtroom of God when all those who have rejected Him will have their day in court. This final day of judgment is called the Great White Throne Judgment. The court date for the great white throne is set on God's docket to occur after the millennial kingdom has ended and Satan has been cast into the lake of fire. The scene at this final great judgment is the most fearsome picture in all the pages of the Bible.

> And I saw a great white throne and the one sitting on it. The earth and sky fled from his presence, but they found no place to hide. I saw the dead, both great and small, standing before God's throne. And the books were opened, including the Book of Life. And the dead were judged according to what they had done, as recorded in the books. The sea gave up its dead, and death and the grave gave up their dead. And all were judged according to their deeds. Then death and the grave were thrown into the lake of fire. This lake of fire is the second death. And anyone whose name was not found recorded in the Book of Life was thrown into the lake of fire.
>
> REVELATION 20:11-15

To better understand the final judgment at the end of time, the courtroom scene will be broken down under eight headings: the courtroom, the judge, the defendants, the summons, the evidence, the verdict, the sentence, and the prison.

The Courtroom

Most adults have seen a courthouse, and some have probably been in a courtroom as a juror, witness, or part of a lawsuit. The scene is very imposing. Courtrooms often have high, vaulted ceilings with beautiful paintings and massive chandeliers. In the gallery the people sit on dark wooden benches with high, straight backs. The atmosphere is always serious and silent, except for a few muted whispers. Suddenly the door from the judge's chambers opens and the bailiff enters, commanding all present to rise as the black-robed judge enters the courtroom. When the judge takes a seat behind the bar, court is in session. The parties are called, and the case begins. This scene will someday occur before the bar of God in heaven—only multiplied times infinity.

Every person must wonder sometime during his or her life what it will be like to see the supreme court of the universe—to see the Ancient of Days sitting on His great white throne. God's throne is called great (*mega* in Greek) because it is the highest throne in the universe. It is called white because it is absolutely pure, holy, and righteous. All of the verdicts handed down from this throne are perfectly right, just, and true. This is God's courtroom—God's throne of justice. It is the supreme court of heaven and earth.

The Judge

Notice next who is seated on this majestic throne. It is the Lord Jesus Christ Himself. Jesus Christ is the final judge before whom the unbelieving world will stand. As John 5:22 reminds us, "Not even the Father judges anyone, but He has given all judgment to the Son" (NASB, see also Acts 17:31). In 2 Timothy 4:1 Jesus Christ is called the one who will "judge the living and the dead." David Jeremiah says, "Somewhere between heaven and earth this judgment will take place. Jesus Christ Himself will conduct the trial, and no one is better qualified. He did all He could to save man. Since man has rejected Him, he must be judged by Him."[1]

The Defendants

Revelation refers to the defendants in this courtroom as "the dead, both great and small" (Revelation 20:12). The context makes it clear that this includes everyone who ever died without saving faith in Christ and was never saved by God's grace. This means all unbelievers. There is no one too great to escape judgment here, and there is no one too insignificant to go unnoticed. Alexander the Great, Julius Caesar, Stalin, and Hitler will be there. So will people whose lives were barely a blip in history. The self-righteous will be there. The atheists and terrible sinners will be there. The procrastinators will be there. The religious, unconverted church members will be there. No unsaved person will escape his or her day in God's court. "This multitude is diverse in its religions. We see Buddhists, Muslims, Hindus, Protestants, and Catholics. We see those who believed in one God and those who believed in many gods. We see those who refused to believe in any God at all. We see those who believed in meditation as a means of salvation and those who believed that doing good deeds was the path to eternal life. We see the moral and the immoral, the priest as well as the minister, the nun as well as the missionary."[2]

The Summons

When the Day of Judgment comes, there will be no place to hide. No high-priced lawyers will get the case postponed or dismissed on a technicality. No one will be able to jump bail. Everyone who is summoned must appear.

The dead will be summoned from all kinds of places. "The sea gave up its dead, and death and the grave gave up their dead" (Revelation 20:13). In the ancient world the sea was thought to be the most inaccessible place. No human could venture to the depths of the ocean. People believed that no one buried in the ocean could ever be disturbed. But God makes clear that even the most mysterious, difficult, out-of-the-way, forbidden places are fully accessible to God. The Day of Judgment is sure (Hebrews 9:27).

The Evidence

At this trial the prosecutor's case will be airtight. No relevant evidence will be suppressed. Only two exhibits will be submitted by the prosecution. Exhibit A is called "the books" that are opened (Revelation 20:12). These books are God's infallible records containing a detailed, meticulous account of all the works of every unsaved person.

In the United States, justice is symbolized by a blindfolded woman with scales in her hand. The idea is that she judges impartially, without reference to the parties involved. Yet God judges with eyes wide open. He judges with eyes like fire that can penetrate the most hardened sinner. Nothing will be overlooked.[3] God is keeping a precise account of every person's life in His books (Daniel 7:10). The lost will be doomed because of their sinful deeds recorded in these books. "And all were judged according to their deeds" (Revelation 20:13).

Exhibit B contains even more damning evidence. This exhibit is called the Book of Life. It contains the names of everyone who has ever been saved by God's grace. This huge volume lists all the names of the hopelessly lost sinners who trusted Jesus Christ to save them and pardon them from having to appear at this Great White Throne Judgment. Exhibit B will be consulted to see if the defendant's name appears in the Book of Life. "Anyone whose name was not found recorded in the Book of Life was thrown into the lake of fire" (Revelation 20:15). "The purpose of the Great White Throne Judgment is not to determine if a person is saved. All who will be saved have been saved by this time. This is a judgment of the evil works of the unsaved."[4]

The Verdict

After consulting the books and the Book of Life, Jesus will pronounce the guilty verdict. The gavel of God will fall, and the lost will have no appeal. The guilty verdict will stand for eternity. After the verdict is read, the sentence will be handed down.

The Sentence

The sentence at this judgment will be the harshest sentence imaginable—imprisonment in hell forever, without possibility of parole. The condemned will die a second time; that is, they will be separated eternally from God in the lake of fire (2 Thessalonians 1:9; Revelation 20:14). When the sentence is read, the lost will be transported immediately to the place of eternal confinement.

This sentence may seem harsh to us. It may even seem unfair. But we must remember that God is infinitely just. The price for sin must be paid. Christ Himself personally bore the wrath and punishment of God for human sin (2 Corinthians 5:21). Each person must either accept the infinite pardon Christ has freely offered or pay the infinite price himself or herself. The price must be paid—will we pay it ourselves or accept Christ's payment in our place? That is the supreme choice. Either way, God is perfectly just. Ultimately, we must bow the knee before an infinite God and His wisdom. "To our way of thinking, hell might be considered unjust. But we are not asked to make up the rules by which the game of life is played. Since this is God's universe, He runs it according to His eternal purposes. We must bow to His authority, believing that He does all things well."[5]

The Prison

There are many notorious prisons: Sing Sing, San Quentin, Alcatraz. But they pale in comparison to the eternal dungeon described in God's Word. Hell is a horrifying place too heinous to contemplate. For this reason, many today are trying to do away with hell or at least construct a "kinder, gentler" view of the lake of fire. Yet, despite our denials or redefinitions, the Bible is clear: hell is real. We do not have the liberty to change the truth because we do not like it or fully understand it. As John Walvoord notes, "There either is or is not a future of eternal punishment. Whether we agree with it or not has very little bearing on the issue. The vote against it could be unanimous, and still hell might be a reality. God did not consult us when planning his righteous judgment of the sinful human race. The ultimate question is whether the Bible, which is our only source of information about what happens after death, teaches a doctrine of eternal conscious punishment."[6]

Here are six sobering facts about hell from the pages of the Bible.[7] These are facts that should convince everyone that they never want to end up there.

Fact #1: Hell Is a Place of Awareness and Memory

In hell, people will have continued consciousness and immediate awareness of where they are. In Luke 16:19-31, the rich man knew immediately *where he was*. There will also be identity—the rich man knew *who he was*. There will also be memory. When the rich man asked Abraham for some water to cool the burning of his tongue, Abraham answered, "Child, remember that during your life you received your good things" (Luke 16:25, NASB). We also know from Jesus that the rich man remembered Lazarus (Luke 16:24) and his five brothers who were still alive (Luke 16:27-28). People in hell will have perfect memories and will suffer the mental and emotional anguish of regret.

Fact #2: Hell Is a Place of Conscious Physical, Mental, and Spiritual Torment

The worst part of hell is that there will be torment and agony (Luke 16:28). Jesus said, "The Son of Man will send his angels, and they will remove from his Kingdom everything that causes sin and all who do evil.

And the angels will throw them into the fiery furnace, where there will be weeping and gnashing of teeth" (Matthew 13:41-42). Jesus also said, "If your eye causes you to sin, gouge it out. It's better to enter the Kingdom of God with only one eye than to have two eyes and be thrown into hell, 'where the maggots never die and the fire never goes out.' For everyone will be tested with fire" (Mark 9:47-49). Jesus reported the words of the rich man: "I am in anguish in these flames" (Luke 16:24). Whether this fire is literal, as many believe, or metaphorical, as others maintain, there is no way to put a positive spin on what it means. Hell will be hell.

Fact #3: Hell Is the Only Other Place besides Heaven to Spend Eternity

There are only two places people go after death—paradise or perdition. Jesus said so (Matthew 7:13-14). There is no in-between place. There is no third choice. The rich man went to hades; Lazarus went to paradise. These are still the only two destinations today.

Fact #4: Hell Is a Place Where the Inhabitants Do Not Want Others to Come

The rich man in Luke 16 never complains that it is unfair for him to be there. He bemoans his torment but never says he is there unjustly. However, he longs to warn his brothers who are still alive how to avoid his fate. He has compassion for his five brothers who are still alive. And he knows that his brothers would need to repent (Luke 16:30). The rich man in hades suddenly becomes interested in the gospel! As Erwin Lutzer poignantly says, "We might think this man would have preferred to have his brothers join him in hades for the sake of the companionship. But he was more than willing to never see them again if he only knew that they would be on the other side of the gulf where Lazarus and Abraham were meeting for the first time. Apparently, even in hades there is compassion, a natural human concern about the fate of those who are loved."[8]

Fact #5: Hell Is Just

Just as there will be degrees of reward in heaven for the righteous, the Bible teaches that there will be degrees of punishment in hell for the unrighteous. Punishment will be based on the evidence contained in the books

(Revelation 20:12). The length of the sentence is the same for all the lost, but the severity of the punishment will be based both on the amount and the nature of the sin that one committed and the amount of truth that one refused (Matthew 11:21-23; Luke 12:47-48; Romans 2:5-6).

Fact #6 Hell Is Earned

Hell is what we earn. "The wages of sin is death" (Romans 6:23a). Heaven is what God gives us as a free gift by His grace. "But the free gift of God is eternal life through Christ Jesus our Lord" (Romans 6:23b).

Conclusion

Warren Wiersbe captures something of the drama of the final judgment at the great white throne. "The White Throne Judgment will be nothing like our modern court cases. At the White Throne, there will be a Judge but no jury, a prosecution but no defense, a sentence but no appeal. No one will be able to defend himself or accuse God of unrighteousness."[9] The old song by A. B. Simpson vividly captures the magnitude of that moment as well as the importance of accepting Christ now:

What will you do with Jesus?
Neutral you cannot be.
Someday your heart will be asking,
What will He do with me?

The good news is that you need not appear at this judgment or receive that awful sentence. Jesus suffered the wrath of God on the cross for you and for me. All you have to do to be excused from the Day of Judgment and to spend eternity with God in heaven is receive God's free pardon through faith in Jesus Christ.

PART 14

The Best Is Yet to Come

I pity the man who never thinks about heaven. I use the word in the broadest and most popular sense. I mean by "heaven" the future dwelling place of all true Christians, when the dead are raised, and the world has passed away. Cold and unfeeling must that heart be which never gives a thought to that dwelling place! Dull and earthly must be that mind which never considers "heaven!". . . This world shall not go on forever as it does now. Its affairs shall be at last wound up. The King of kings will come, and take His great power, and reign. The judgment shall be set, the books opened, and dead raised, the living changed. And where do we all hope to go then? Why, if we know anything of true faith in the Lord Jesus Christ, we hope to go to "heaven." . . . Before we go to our eternal home we should try to become acquainted with it. . . . Suffice it to say, that heaven is the eternal presence of everything that can make a saint happy, and the eternal absence of everything that can cause sorrow.

J. C. RYLE, *Heaven*[1]

CHAPTER 39

NEW HEAVEN, NEW EARTH, NEW JERUSALEM

The new millennium began with a bang in Sydney, Australia. At the stroke of midnight on December 31, 1999, elaborate fireworks erupted over Sydney Harbor to the delight of more than one million people who watched from the shores and a vast flotilla of watercraft on the harbor. This was the display to end all displays. It was designed to outdo every other New Year's celebration on planet earth. Nothing compared with the dazzling brilliance of Sydney Harbor on January 1, 2000. The natural beauty of the harbor was brilliantly illuminated on that mild summer night down under. But one feature above all others set apart Sydney's new-millennium success.

Suspended from the giant arch of the Sydney Harbor Bridge, amidst the exploding rockets and the deluge of light pouring like a waterfall from the roadway, hung one word—*Eternity*. Like a message from heaven flashed across the world stage to billions of souls, it shone like a beacon from beyond, warning all who saw it that time is swiftly passing and we are creatures of eternity. This was a sobering sermon in a word.[1] One could write the same word over Revelation 21–22.

Dr. John Walvoord told me a story from many years ago. He was at the Dallas-Fort Worth airport with a man who was the managing editor of a Christian magazine titled *Eternity*. While they were at the airport, they ran into a friend of Dr. Walvoord, and he introduced his friend to the editor. After the introduction and a handshake, the friend asked the man, "What do you do?" to which he responded, "I manage *Eternity*." Dr. Walvoord's friend replied, "That must be an awfully big job."

Think of what a big job it must be to *really* manage eternity. The all-powerful, transcendent Creator manages the cosmos effortlessly. There is not a maverick molecule in the universe. He is the ruler of all eternity!

Eternity is a word that none of us can fully grasp, yet God is eternal and every person will live somewhere forever. What does the Bible tell us about eternity? The two closing chapters of the Bible, Revelation 21–22, tell us a lot.

After the millennial kingdom and the Great White Throne Judgment, the same God who created this present heaven and earth will destroy it and create a new heaven and new earth, ushering in the eternal state.

> Then I saw a new heaven and a new earth, for the old heaven and the old earth had disappeared. And the sea was also gone. And I saw the holy city, the new Jerusalem, coming down from God out of heaven like a bride beautifully dressed for her husband.
>
> I heard a loud shout from the throne, saying, "Look, God's home is now among his people! He will live with them, and they will be his people. God himself will be with them. He will wipe every tear from their eyes, and there will be no more death or sorrow or crying or pain. All these things are gone forever."
>
> And the one sitting on the throne said, "Look, I am making everything new!" And then he said to me, "Write this down, for what I tell you is trustworthy and true." And he also said, "It is finished! I am the Alpha and the Omega—the Beginning and the End. To all who are thirsty I will give freely from the springs

> of the water of life. All who are victorious will inherit all these blessings, and I will be their God, and they will be my children.
>
> "But cowards, unbelievers, the corrupt, murderers, the immoral, those who practice witchcraft, idol worshipers, and all liars—their fate is in the fiery lake of burning sulfur. This is the second death."
>
> REVELATION 21:1-8

Revelation 21–22 presents at least five key points about the eternal state, or what we often call heaven.[2]

The Cremation of the Present Heaven and Earth

Before the new heaven and new earth can be created, the present heaven and earth must be destroyed. The old heaven and the old earth will disappear. The Bible mentions this event several times (Psalm 102:25-26; Isaiah 34:4; 51:6; Matthew 24:35; 2 Peter 3:10, 12; Revelation 21:1).

> Look up to the skies above,
> and gaze down on the earth below.
> For the skies will disappear like smoke,
> and the earth will wear out like a piece of clothing.
> The people of the earth will die like flies,
> but my salvation lasts forever.
> My righteous rule will never end!
>
> ISAIAH 51:6

> Heaven and earth will disappear, but my words will never disappear.
>
> MATTHEW 24:35

> The day of the Lord will come as unexpectedly as a thief. Then the heavens will pass away with a terrible noise, and the very elements themselves will disappear in fire, and the earth and everything on it will be found to deserve judgment.
>
> 2 PETER 3:10

This destruction will occur right before the Great White Throne Judgment (Revelation 20:11). Just think what it will be like for all the people gathered at the great white throne. As they await God's judgment and their inevitable punishment, they will behold the entire universe going up in smoke—the sudden, fiery demolition of the universe. It will all "flee away" or "disappear." God will display His power and show them the futility of all that they craved and cherished on this earth. By the spoken word, God will simultaneously break up every atom in the cosmos, and the entire universe will disintegrate (2 Peter 3:7, 10-13).

However, many respected commentators and theologians believe that the present heaven and earth will not be destroyed and re-created but that they will be renewed and transformed.[3] Here's the issue: Will this present creation undergo renovation or re-creation? Will there be a major cosmic renovation or a universal destruction and rebuild?

While there are good arguments for both positions, I believe the Scripture teaches that creation will be totally dismantled and put back together again. I agree that the earth will be renewed and restored during the millennial reign of Christ. It will be paradise restored for one thousand years. However, at the end of the messianic age, it appears to me that the restored earth is burned up and created anew.

The Bible describes what we might call "uncreation." Revelation 21:1 says that the present heaven and earth will have "passed away" (NASB), "had disappeared" (NLT), or "ceased to exist" (NET). Whatever the wording, it means creation will go out of existence. Revelation 21:4 uses the same Greek word when it says, "He will wipe every tear from their eyes, and there will be no more death or sorrow or crying or pain. All these things are *gone forever*" (italics added). It is clear that these things—the tears, death, sorrow, crying, and pain—have disappeared. They are not simply renovated or made new. To be consistent we should give the same meaning to this word where it appears in Revelation 21:1. Therefore, the notion of destruction and re-creation seems to be the simplest, most straightforward reading of the relevant texts of Scripture. John Walvoord says,

> The most natural interpretation of the fact that earth and sky flee away is that the present earth and sky are destroyed and will be replaced by the new heaven and new earth. This is also confirmed by the additional statement in 21:1, where John sees a new heaven and a new earth replacing the first heaven and first earth. Frequent references in the Bible seem to anticipate this future time when the present world will be destroyed (Matthew 24:35; Mark 13:31; Luke 16:17; 21:33; 2 Peter 3:10). . . . Passages such as Revelation 20:11 and 2 Peter 3:10 state explicitly that this destruction is literal and physical. It would be most natural that the present heaven and earth, the scene of the struggle with Satan and sin, should be displaced by an entirely new order suited for eternity. The whole structure of the universe is operating on the principle of a clock that is running down. What could be simpler than for God to create a new heaven and a new earth by divine decree in keeping with His purposes for eternity?[4]

Swindoll describes it well: "This isn't a sequel. It isn't simply a reedited version, enhanced with clearer sound, brighter colors, and a smattering of digitally enhanced special effects. This is no reedit; it's a remake!"[5]

The destruction of the present created order will make way for the new creation. The creation of the new heaven and new earth is mentioned in only four places in the Bible: Isaiah 65:17; 66:22; 2 Peter 3:13; and Revelation 21:1.

The Creation of the New Heaven and New Earth

After the present order is destroyed, God will put it all back together again. What all the king's men could not do for Humpty Dumpty, God will do for the universe. He will gather all the building blocks of the original creation and make a brand-new universe. The Greek word for "new" in Revelation 21:1 is *kainos,* which denotes something not just new in time but new qualitatively. Something that is different and superior to the old. It will be a perfect place existing in a perfect environment. One of today's Christian music artists says it well: "I can only imagine."[6]

The Conditions of the New Heaven and New Earth

The Bible does not tell us a great deal about the eternal state, but what it does record is exciting. It is a place of perfection characterized both by what *is* there and what *is not* there.

Three Things That Will Be There

1. the Holy City, new Jerusalem
2. God Himself dwelling among His people
3. righteousness (2 Peter 3:13)

Twelve Things That Will Not Be There

1. no more sea—because all chaos and disorder (symbolized by the sea in ancient times) will be gone (Revelation 21:1)
2. no more tears—because all hurt will be removed (Revelation 21:4)
3. no more death—because mortality is swallowed up by life (Revelation 21:4)
4. no more mourning—because all sorrow will be perfectly comforted (Revelation 21:4)
5. no more crying—because joy will reign supreme (Revelation 21:4)
6. no more pain—because all diseases will be expelled (Revelation 21:4)
7. no more thirst—because every desire will be satisfied (Revelation 21:6)
8. no more wickedness—because all evil will be banished (Revelation 21:8, 27)
9. no more Temple—because God will be everywhere (Revelation 21:22)
10. no more night—because the glory of God will shine (Revelation 21:23-25; 22:5)

11. no more closed gates—because God's door will always be open (Revelation 21:25)
12. no more curse—because the death of Christ has lifted it (Revelation 22:3) [7]

Based on this comforting list, some have described heaven as the blessed place of "no more." Steven Lawson has compiled an expanded list of "no mores."

> There will be no funeral homes, no hospitals, no abortion clinics, no divorce courts, no brothels, no bankruptcy courts, no psychiatric wards, and no treatment centers.
>
> There will be no pornography, dial-a-porn, no teen suicide, no AIDS, no cancer, no talks shows, no rape, no missing children . . . no drug problems, no drive-by shootings, no racial tension, and no prejudice.
>
> There will be no misunderstandings, no injustice, no depression, no hurtful words, no gossip, no hurt feelings, no worry, no emptiness, and no child abuse.
>
> There will be no wars, no financial worries, no emotional heartaches, no physical pain, no spiritual flatness, no relational divisions, no murders, and no casseroles.
>
> There will be no tears, no suffering, no separations, no starvation, no arguments, no accidents, no emergency departments, no doctors, no nurses, no heart monitors, no rust, no perplexing questions, no false teachers, no financial shortages, no hurricanes, no bad habits, no decay, and no locks.
>
> We will never need to confess sin. Never need to apologize again. Never need to straighten out a strained relationship. Never have to resist Satan again. Never have to resist temptation.
>
> Never![8]

The perfection of the city is also seen when contrasted to the original Creation in Genesis. What started in Genesis is brought to completion in Revelation. Everything will come full circle in eternity.

GENESIS	REVELATION
heavens and earth created	new heaven and earth
sun created	no sun
night established	no night
seas created	no seas
rivers in the Garden of Eden	river in the new Jerusalem
Curse announced	no Curse
death enters	death exits
man denied access to the tree of life	access to the tree of life restored
sorrow and pain begin	sorrow and pain end

The Capital of the New Heaven and New Earth (Revelation 21:9–22:5)

As John looks at the new heaven and new earth in his vision, the spotlight shifts suddenly to a descending metropolis, the new Jerusalem, the Holy City coming down out of heaven from God. The city is a colossal cube—1,500 miles long, wide, and deep. It contains 3.375 billion cubic feet of space. How big is that? To help us envision it, we can think of a map of the United States. The footprint of the city would be about the same as drawing a square from Miami up to Maine then westward to Minneapolis then south to Houston and then back to Miami. And that's just the ground level. The towering city rises 1,500 miles.

John sees this cubed city the size of a continent floating through space, approaching the new earth. This city is the current dwelling place of God, the angels, and the souls of departed saints, yet one day it will descend to the new earth (Revelation 21:2-3).

I believe this heavenly city will come down and rest on the new earth and serve as the capital city of the new heaven and new earth. The new Jerusalem will be the capital of the eternal state. It will be the metropolis of eternity. The fact that this city is mentioned in conjunction with the new earth and that the city has huge foundation stones seem to suggest that it will rest on the new earth (Hebrews 11:10). What will this capital city of eternity be like? What will be there? Revelation 21–22 describes the indescribable.

The Glory of God

The glory of God will be the main feature of this city (Revelation 21:11, 23). It is described in terms of light, precious stones, and gold polished to mirror brilliance. The celestial skyline dazzles as the light of God shines on the beauty of the city. The glory of God will be overpowering and overwhelming. The flashing city is a 1,500-mile cube. The Holy of Holies in the Tabernacle, the dwelling place of God on earth, was a perfect cube measuring fifteen feet on every side. Likewise, the Holy of Holies in Solomon's Temple was a thirty-foot cube. The new Jerusalem, also a perfect cube, will be like a huge Holy of Holies, a cosmic Temple, where God dwells eternally. The parallels between the new Jerusalem and the Garden of Eden (a river, the tree of life, and God's presence) and the Holy of Holies have led some to call the new Jerusalem the "Edenic Temple-City."[9] This is an apt description. Here are a few of the other key features of this city.

The Wall of Jasper

The wall surrounding the city is 216 feet thick and 1,500 miles high and is made of jasper, which could refer to a diamond or a gem that looks like ice. The gigantic wall looks like a shimmering sheet of ice.

The Twelve Gates

The gates of the city, which are never closed, provide open access and entrance for the Lord's people (Revelation 21:25). Each gate is made from a single pearl. The names of the tribes of Israel are written on the gates. Stop and think for a moment about the lives of the twelve sons of Jacob that the tribes were named after. They were devious, sinful men who even sold their brother Joseph into slavery and lied to their aged father. Genesis 38, which recounts the sins of Judah, is one of the most sordid chapters in the Bible. The fact that God etches the names of these men on the gates of His Holy City is an eternal witness to God's amazing grace.

These names on the gates of heaven should reassure us all that "even the worst of sinners can enter heaven by God's redeeming grace."[10]

The Twelve Foundation Stones

The foundation stones reveal the permanence of the city (Hebrews 11:10). They are inlaid with twelve precious gems: jasper (diamond), sapphire (deep blue), agate (green), emerald (green), onyx (layered stone of red), carnelian (blood red), chrysolite (golden yellow), beryl (sea green), topaz (greenish gold or yellow), chrysoprase (gold green), jacinth (violet), and amethyst (purple quartz). The twelve foundation stones bear the names of the twelve apostles. The mention of the twelve tribes of Israel on the twelve gates and the twelve apostles on the twelve foundation stones indicates that the new Jerusalem will be for all of God's people—Israel and the church.

The Street

People often talk about the streets of gold in heaven, but actually there is only one street of gold. Everyone will live on Main Street. And that street will be paved with gold polished to mirror brilliance. Gold is so plentiful to the Creator that He uses it to pave His street.

A River

A river of crystal-clear water will run down Main Street from the throne of God. This is reminiscent of the rivers that watered the Garden of Eden.

The Tree of Life

The tree that man was excluded from when he was expelled from the Garden of Eden will be available to all of God's people for all of eternity.

There will be nothing but the best in this city. There will not be any cinder blocks, shag carpet, or cheap imitations. Only the best will be used. The heavenly city described in Revelation 21–22 is the third heaven that Paul visited in 2 Corinthians 12. It is the place that Jesus is preparing for us (John 14:1-3). It is the Father's house in which there are many dwelling places. He has now been working on it for two thousand years. What a place it will be!

Above all, it is the dwelling place of God. As D. L. Moody once said, "It is not the jeweled walls or pearly gates that are going to make heaven attractive. It is being with God."

For this reason every believer should feel the heavenward pull, the tug of heaven. Our feet are on earth, but our hearts are to be in heaven where Christ dwells (Colossians 3:1-4). Heaven should rest at the center of our worldview and should motivate us to live for the Lamb of glory who dwells in unapproachable light yet made a way for us to dwell with Him forever by shedding His blood on the cross and rising from the dead.

The Citizens of the New Heaven and New Earth

Hebrews 12:22-24 describes the residents of God's new world.

> You have come to Mount Zion, to the city of the living God, the heavenly Jerusalem, and to countless thousands of angels in a joyful gathering. You have come to the assembly of God's firstborn children, whose names are written in heaven. You have come to God himself, who is the judge over all things. You have come to the spirits of the righteous ones in heaven who have now been made perfect. You have come to Jesus, the one who mediates the new covenant between God and people, and to the sprinkled blood, which speaks of forgiveness instead of crying out for vengeance like the blood of Abel.

There are three identifiable groups in the new Jerusalem besides God Himself and Jesus: angels, church-age believers ("the assembly of God's firstborn children"), and the rest of the people of God from the other ages ("the spirits of the righteous ones in heaven who have now been made perfect"). All who by God's grace have trusted in the person and promises of God will be in heaven.

The Bible is clear about who will be in heaven, but it also leaves no doubt about who won't be there. Revelation 21:8 describes eight kinds of people who will not be there. The list does not refer to isolated acts of sin in these areas but describes the direction and pattern of one's life.

1. cowards—those who are ashamed of Christ (Matthew 10:33)
2. unbelievers—those who neglect or reject Christ
3. the corrupt—those who live impure, polluted lives
4. murderers—those who practice murder. A person who commits murder can be saved by God's grace. King David is a perfect example.
5. the immoral—those who live a lifestyle of sexual sin outside the bonds of monogamous, heterosexual marriage
6. those who practice witchcraft—those who delve into occult practices
7. idol worshipers—those who submit to some created thing in order to receive from it what only God can give. An idol is not just a graven image but anything that absorbs the heart and imagination more than God. Colossians 3:5 says, "A greedy person is an idolater, worshiping the things of this world."
8. liars—those who habitually deceive and mislead others

While these will be excluded, all of God's people of all the ages will have eternal access to the new heaven, the new earth, and the new Jerusalem. Of course, the key issue is, will you be there? Will you be a citizen of the new heaven and new earth and new Jerusalem? Heaven is a prepared place for a prepared people. Have you received God's offer of salvation? That is the key issue in all of life. It's fascinating to know what will happen to this world in the future, but it's much more important for you to know your future. It's thrilling to understand *The End*, but how much more important to know about *Your End*. If you have never done so, why not turn to the Lord now and recognize these four great truths about yourself and the Savior?

I am a sinner (Romans 3:23).
I need a Savior. I cannot save myself (Ephesians 2:8-9).
Jesus Christ, who died in my place and rose again, is my Savior (1 Corinthians 15:1-3).
I trust Him alone to be my Savior from sin (Acts 16:31).

Why not trust in Jesus now as your Savior from sin? Trusting Christ will bring a new beginning that will secure your perfect ending.

THE END

Appendix 1: A Proposed Chronology of the End Times

IT'S NOT EASY TRYING to fit together all the pieces of the end times into a chronological sequence. This outline is my best attempt to put the pieces together. I don't insist on the correctness of every detail in this outline, but my prayer is that it will help you get a better grasp of the overall flow of events in the end times.

I. EVENTS IN HEAVEN

A. The Rapture of the Church (1 Corinthians 15:51-58; 1 Thessalonians 4:13-18; Revelation 3:10)

B. The Judgment Seat of Christ (Romans 14:10; 1 Corinthians 3:9-15; 4:1-5; 9:24-27; 2 Corinthians 5:10)

C. The Marriage of the Lamb (2 Corinthians 11:2; Revelation 19:6-8)

D. The Singing of Two Special Songs (Revelation 4–5)

E. The Lamb Receiving the Seven-Sealed Scroll (Revelation 5)

II. Events on Earth

A. Seven-Year Tribulation

1. The Beginning of the Tribulation

   a. The seven-year Tribulation begins when the Antichrist signs a covenant with Israel, bringing peace to Israel and Jerusalem (Daniel 9:27; Ezekiel 38:8, 11).

   b. The Jewish Temple in Jerusalem is rebuilt (Daniel 9:27; Revelation 11:1).

   c. The reunited Roman Empire emerges in a ten-nation confederation—the "group of ten" (Daniel 2:40–44; 7:7; Revelation 17:12).

2. First Half (3½ Years) of the Tribulation

   a. The seven seal judgments are opened (Revelation 6; 8:1).

   b. The 144,000 Jewish believers begin their great evangelistic ministry (Revelation 7).

   c. Gog and its allies invade Israel while Israel is at peace under the covenant with the Antichrist. The Gog coalition is supernaturally decimated by God (Daniel 11:40-45; Ezekiel 38–39). This will probably occur somewhere near the end of the 3½-year period. The destruction of these forces will shift the balance of power, enabling the Antichrist to begin his rise to world ascendancy.

3. The Midpoint of the Tribulation

   a. The Antichrist breaks his covenant with Israel and invades the land (Daniel 9:27; 11:40–41).

   b. The Antichrist begins to consolidate his empire by plundering Egypt, Sudan, and Libya, whose armies have just been destroyed by God in Israel (Daniel 11:42-43; Ezekiel 38–39).

c. While in North Africa, the Antichrist hears disturbing news of insurrection in Israel and immediately returns there to destroy and annihilate many (Daniel 11:44).

d. The Antichrist sets up the abomination of desolation in the rebuilt Temple in Jerusalem (Daniel 9:27; 11:45a; Matthew 24:15; 2 Thessalonians 2:4; Revelation 13:5, 15-18).

e. Sometime during these events, the Antichrist is violently killed, possibly as a result of a war or assassination (Daniel 11:45; Revelation 13:3, 12, 14; 17:8).

f. Satan is cast down from heaven and begins to make war with the woman, Israel (Revelation 12:7–13). The chief means he uses to persecute Israel is the two beasts in Revelation 13.

g. The faithful Jewish remnant flee, possibly to Petra in modern Jordan, where God protects them for the remainder of the Tribulation (Matthew 24:16-20; Revelation 12:15-17).

h. The Antichrist is miraculously raised from the dead to the amazement of the entire world (Revelation 13:3).

i. After rising from the dead, the Antichrist gains political control over the ten kings of the reunited Roman Empire. Three of these kings will be killed by the Antichrist and the other seven will submit (Daniel 7:24; Revelation 17:12-13).

j. The two witnesses begin their 3½-year ministry (Revelation 11:2-3).

k. The Antichrist and the ten kings destroy the religious system of Babylon and set up their religious, economic capital in the city (Revelation 17:16-17).

4. Second Half (3½ Years) of the Tribulation
    a. The Antichrist blasphemes God, and the false prophet performs great signs and wonders and promotes false worship of the Antichrist (Revelation 13:5, 11-15).
    b. The mark of the Beast (666) is introduced and enforced by the false prophet (Revelation 13:16-18).
    c. Totally energized by Satan, the Antichrist dominates the world politically, religiously, and economically (Revelation 13:4-5, 15-18).
    d. The trumpet judgments are unleashed throughout the final half of the Tribulation (Revelation 8–9).
    e. Knowing he has only a short time left, Satan intensifies his relentless, merciless persecution of the Jewish people and Gentile believers on earth (Daniel 7:25; Revelation 12:12; 13:15; 20:4).
5. The End of the Tribulation
    a. The bowl judgments are poured out in rapid succession (Revelation 16).
    b. The campaign of Armageddon begins (Revelation 16:16).
    c. Commercial Babylon is destroyed (Revelation 18).
    d. The two witnesses are killed by the Antichrist and are resurrected by God 3½ days later (Revelation 11:7-12).
    e. Christ returns to the Mount of Olives and slays the armies gathered against Him throughout the land, from Megiddo to Petra (Revelation 19:11-16; Isaiah 34:1-6; 63:1-5).
    f. The birds gather to feed on the carnage (Revelation 19:17-18).

B. After the Tribulation

1. Interval of Seventy-Five Days (Daniel 12:12)
    a. The Antichrist and the false prophet are cast into the lake of fire (Revelation 19:20-21).
    b. The abomination of desolation is removed from the Temple (Daniel 12:11).
    c. Israel is regathered (Matthew 24:31).
    d. Jews who survive the Tribulation are judged (Ezekiel 20:30-39; Matthew 25:1-30).
    e. Gentiles who survive the Tribulation are judged (Matthew 25:31-46).
    f. Satan is bound in the abyss (Revelation 20:1-3).
    g. Old Testament and Tribulation saints are resurrected and rewarded (Daniel 12:1-3; Isaiah 26:19; Revelation 20:4).
    h. The millennial Temple is constructed or at least begun (Ezekiel 40–48).
2. One-Thousand-Year Reign of Christ on Earth (Revelation 20:4-6)
3. Satan's Final Revolt and Defeat (Revelation 20:7-10)
4. The Great White Throne Judgment of the Lost (Revelation 20:11-15)
5. The Destruction of the Present Heavens and Earth (Matthew 24:35; 2 Peter 3:3-12; Revelation 21:1)
6. The Creation of the New Heavens and New Earth (Isaiah 65:17; 66:22; 2 Peter 3:13; Revelation 21:1)
7. Eternity (Revelation 21:9–22:5)

Appendix 2: Recommended Books for Further Study

GENERAL/OVERVIEW BOOKS

Benware, Paul N. *Understanding End Times Prophecy: A Comprehensive Approach*. Chicago: Moody, 2006. First published 1995.

Fruchtenbaum, Arnold G. *The Footsteps of the Messiah: A Study of the Sequence of Prophetic Events*. Tustin, CA: Ariel Ministries, 1983.

Hoyt, Herman A. *The End Times*. Winona Lake, IN: BMH Books, 2000. Originally published 1969 by Moody.

Ice, Thomas, and Timothy Demy. *Fast Facts on Bible Prophecy: A Complete Guide to the Last Days*. Eugene, OR: Harvest House, 1997.

LaHaye, Tim. *Understanding the Last Days: The Keys to Unlocking Bible Prophecy*. Eugene, OR: Harvest House, 1998.

LaHaye, Tim, and Thomas Ice. *Charting the End Times: A Visual Guide to Understanding Bible Prophecy*. Eugene, OR: Harvest House, 2001.

Lightner, Robert P. *The Last Days Handbook: A Comprehensive Guide to Understanding the Different Views of Prophecy*. Nashville: Thomas Nelson, 1990.

Pentecost, J. Dwight. *Prophecy for Today: God's Purpose and Plan for Our Future*. Revised edition. Grand Rapids: Discovery House, 1989.

———. *Things to Come: A Study in Biblical Eschatology*. Grand Rapids: Zondervan, 1964. First published 1958 by Dunham Publishing Company.

Phillips, John. *Exploring the Future: A Comprehensive Guide to Bible Prophecy*. 3rd ed. Grand Rapids: Kregel, 2003.

Ryle, J. C. *Are You Ready for the End of Time? Understanding Future Events from Prophetic Passages of the Bible*. 1867. Reprint, Tain, UK: Christian Focus Publications, 2001.

Walvoord, John F. *End Times: Understanding Today's World Events in Biblical Prophecy*. Edited by Charles R. Swindoll. Nashville: Thomas Nelson, 1998.

———. *Prophecy: 14 Essential Keys to Understanding the Final Drama*. Nashville: Thomas Nelson, 1993.

———. *The Prophecy Knowledge Handbook: All the Prophecies of Scripture Explained in One Volume*. Wheaton, IL: Victor Books, 1990.

Willmington, H. L. *The King Is Coming: A Compelling Study of the Last Days*. Revised edition. Carol Stream, IL: Tyndale, 1991. Originally published 1973.

Wood, Leon J. *The Bible and Future Events: An Introductory Survey of Last-Day Events*. Grand Rapids: Zondervan, 2006. Originally published 1973.

THE BOOK OF DANIEL

Boice, James Montgomery. *Daniel: An Expositional Commentary*. Grand Rapids: Baker, 2006. First published 1989 by Zondervan.

Campbell, Donald K. *Daniel: God's Man in a Secular Society*. Grand Rapids: Discovery House, 1988.

Jeremiah, David. *The Handwriting on the Wall: Secrets from the Prophecies of Daniel*. Nashville: Thomas Nelson, 2008. First published 1992 by Word Publishing.

Walvoord, John F. *Daniel: The Key to Prophetic Revelation*. Chicago: Moody, 1971.

Whitcomb, John C. *Daniel: The Coming of Christ's Kingdom*. Winona Lake, IN: BMH Books, 1985.

Wood, Leon. *A Commentary on Daniel*. Grand Rapids: Zondervan, 1998.

THE BOOK OF REVELATION

Hindson, Ed. *Approaching Armageddon: The World Prepares for War with God*. Eugene, OR: Harvest House, 1997.

Jeremiah, David, and C. C. Carlson. *Escape the Coming Night: An Electrifying Tour of the World as It Races toward Its Final Days*. Dallas: Word Publishing, 1990.

MacArthur, John Jr. *Revelation 1-11*. The MacArthur New Testament Commentary. Chicago: Moody, 1999.

———. *Revelation 12-22*. The MacArthur New Testament Commentary. Chicago: Moody, 2000.

Morris, Henry M. *The Revelation Record: A Scientific and Devotional Commentary on the Prophetic Book of the End Times*. Carol Stream, IL: Tyndale, 1983.

Osborne, Grant R. *Revelation*. Baker Exegetical Commentary on the New Testament, edited by Moises Silva. Grand Rapids: Baker Academic, 2002.

Phillips, John. *Exploring Revelation: An Expository Commentary*. Grand Rapids: Kregel, 2001. First published 1987 by Loizeaux Brothers, 1987.

Rogers, Adrian. *Unveiling the End Times in Our Time: The Triumph of the Lamb in Revelation*. Nashville: B&H, 2004.

Stedman, Ray C. *God's Final Word: Understanding Revelation*. Grand Rapids: Discovery House, 1991.

Swindoll, Charles R. *Insights on Revelation*. Grand Rapids: Zondervan, 2011.

Thomas, Robert L. *Revelation 1-7: An Exegetical Commentary*. Chicago: Moody, 1992.

———. *Revelation 8-22: An Exegetical Commentary*. Chicago: Moody, 1995.

Walvoord, John F. *Revelation*. Revised edition. Chicago: Moody, 2011.

THE RAPTURE

LaHaye, Timothy. *No Fear of the Storm: Why Christians Will Escape All the Tribulation*. Portland, OR: Multnomah, 1992.

Ryrie, Charles C. *Come Quickly, Lord Jesus: What You Need to Know about the Rapture*. Eugene, OR: Harvest House, 1996.

Showers, Renald. *Maranatha: Our Lord, Come!* Bellmawr, NJ: The Friends of Israel Gospel Ministry, 1995.

Stanton, Gerald B. *Kept from the Hour: Biblical Evidence for the Pretribulational Return of Christ.* Miami Springs, FL: Schoettle Publishing Company, 1991.

Walvoord, John F. *The Blessed Hope and the Tribulation: A Historical and Biblical Study of Posttribulationalism.* Grand Rapids: Zondervan, 1976.

———. *The Rapture Question.* Revised edition. Grand Rapids: Zondervan, 1979.

DISPENSATIONALISM

Ryrie, Charles C. *Dispensationalism.* Revised edition. Chicago: Moody, 2007.

ISRAEL AND REPLACEMENT THEOLOGY

Diprose, Ronald E. *Israel and the Church: The Origin and Effects of Replacement Theology.* Waynesboro, GA: Authentic Media, 2004.

Horner, Barry E. *Future Israel: Why Christian Anti-Judaism Must Be Challenged.* NAC Studies in Bible and Theology, edited by E. Ray Clendenen. Nashville: B&H, 2007.

Wilkinson, Paul Richard. *For Zion's Sake: Christian Zionism and the Role of John Nelson Darby.* Studies in Evangelical History and Thought. Great Britain: Paternoster, 2007.

SIGNS OF THE TIMES

Jeremiah, David. *What in the World Is Going On? 10 Prophetic Clues You Cannot Afford to Ignore.* Nashville: Thomas Nelson, 2008.

LaHaye, Tim, and Jerry B. Jenkins. *Are We Living in the End Times?* Carol Stream, IL: Tyndale, 1999.

Rhodes, Ron. *Northern Storm Rising: Russia, Iran, and the Emerging End-Times Military Coalition Against Israel.* Eugene, OR: Harvest House, 2008.

Rosenberg, Joel C. *Epicenter: Why the Current Rumblings in the Middle East Will Change Your Future.* Carol Stream, IL: Tyndale, 2006.

THE KINGDOM

McClain, Alva J. *The Greatness of the Kingdom.* Winona Lake, IN: BMH Books, 1968.

Pentecost, J. Dwight. *Thy Kingdom Come: Tracing God's Kingdom Program and Covenant Promises throughout History.* Grand Rapids: Kregel, 1995.

JERUSALEM AND THE JEWISH TEMPLE

Ice, Thomas, and Randall Price. *Ready to Rebuild: The Imminent Plan to Rebuild the Last Days Temple.* Eugene, OR: Harvest House, 1992.

Price, Randall. *The Coming Last Days Temple.* Eugene, OR: Harvest House, 1999.

———. *In Search of Temple Treasures: The Lost Ark and the Last Days.* Eugene, OR: Harvest House, 1994.

———. *Jerusalem in Prophecy: God's Stage for the Final Drama.* Eugene, OR: Harvest House Publishers, 1998.

THE JUDGMENT SEAT OF CHRIST

Benware, Paul N. *The Believer's Payday: Why Standing Before Christ Should Be Our Greatest Moment.* Chattanooga, TN: AMG Publishers, 2002.

Kroll, Woodrow. *Facing Your Final Job Review: The Judgment Seat of Christ, Salvation, and Eternal Rewards.* Wheaton, IL: Crossway, 2008.

Lutzer, Erwin W. *Your Eternal Reward: Triumph and Tears at the Judgment Seat of Christ.* Chicago: Moody, 1998.

Wall, Joe L. *Going for the Gold: Reward and Loss at the Judgment of Believers.* Chicago: Moody, 1991.

THE ANTICHRIST

Hindson, Ed. *Is the Antichrist Alive and Well? 10 Keys to His Identity.* Eugene, OR: Harvest House, 1998.

Pink, Arthur W. *The Antichrist,* Grand Rapids: Kregel, 1988. First published 1923 by Bible Truth Depot.

THE MILLENNIUM

Ryrie, Charles C. *The Basis of the Premillennial Faith.* Neptune, NJ: Loizeaux Brothers, 1953.

Walvoord, John F. *The Millennial Kingdom: A Basic Text in Premillennial Theology.* Grand Rapids: Zondervan, 1959.

HEAVEN AND HELL

Alcorn, Randy. *Heaven.* Carol Stream, IL: Tyndale, 2004.

Criswell, W. A., and Paige Patterson. *Heaven.* Carol Stream, IL: Tyndale, 1991.

Dixon, Larry. *The Other Side of the Good News.* Tain, UK: Christian Focus Publications, 2003.

Ice, Thomas, and Timothy Demy. *The Truth about Heaven and Eternity.* Eugene, OR: Harvest House, 1997.

Kreeft, Peter. *Everything You Ever Wanted to Know About Heaven but Never Dreamed of Asking!* San Francisco: Ignatius, 1990.

Lawson, Steven J. *Heaven Help Us!: Truths about Eternity That Will Help You Live Today.* Colorado Springs: NavPress, 1995.

MacArthur, John F. *The Glory of Heaven: The Truth about Heaven, Angels, and Eternal Life.* Wheaton, IL: Crossway, 1996.

Morey, Robert A. *Death and the Afterlife.* Minneapolis: Bethany House, 1984.

Rhodes, Ron. *The Undiscovered Country.* Eugene, OR: Harvest House, 1996.

Rumford, Douglas J. *What about Heaven and Hell?* Carol Stream, IL: Tyndale, 2000.

Tada, Joni Eareckson. *Heaven.* Grand Rapids: Zondervan, 1996.

Notes

INTRODUCTION

1. "The Top Ten Ways to Know If You Are Obsessed with Prophecy," *The Lamplighter* (September/October 2000).

PART 1: FOUNDATIONS FOR THE FUTURE

1. John F. Walvoord and Mark Hitchcock, *Armageddon, Oil, and Terror* (Carol Stream, IL: Tyndale, 2007), 1–2.

CHAPTER 1: DON'T STOP THINKING ABOUT TOMORROW

1. J. Barton Payne, *Encyclopedia of Biblical Prophecy* (Grand Rapids: Baker, 1980), 674–75.
2. John MacArthur Jr., *The Second Coming of the Lord Jesus Christ* (Valencia, CA: Word of Grace Communications, 1981), 1.
3. Randall Price, *Jerusalem in Prophecy: God's Stage for the Final Drama* (Eugene, OR: Harvest House, 1998), 55.
4. Ibid., 50.
5. Charles Dyer, *World News and Bible Prophecy* (Carol Stream, IL: Tyndale, 1995), 270.
6. Daniel Luckenbill, Ancient Records of Assyria and Babylonia, vol. 2 (Chicago: University of Chicago Press, 1927), 420.
7. This section was adapted from Elliott E. Johnson, "Nahum," in *The Bible Knowledge Commentary*, ed. John F. Walvoord and Roy B. Zuck, vol. 2 (Wheaton, IL: Victor Books, 1985), 1495.
8. Peter Stoner, *Science Speaks* (Chicago: Moody, 1958), 76.

CHAPTER 2: WHAT IS A PROPHET?

1. This chart is from Dr. Charles Dyer's class notes at Dallas Theological Seminary on the prophets.
2. Leon J. Wood, *The Prophets of Israel* (Grand Rapids: Baker, 1979), 16.
3. Hobart E. Freeman, *An Introduction to the Old Testament Prophets* (Chicago: Moody, 2000), 14.

4. John Phillips, *Exploring the Future: A Comprehensive Guide to Bible Prophecy*, 3rd ed. (Grand Rapids: Kregel, 2003), 7.
5. These marks were adapted from Wood, *The Prophets of Israel*, 109–13, and Freeman, *An Introduction to the Old Testament Prophets* (Chicago: Moody, 1968), 102–17.

CHAPTER 3: BRINGING THE FUTURE INTO FOCUS

1. There is a fifth approach that some have adopted recently that is called the eclectic (mixture) view. This is a newer approach to Revelation that attempts to combine the four other views to maximize their strengths and minimize their weaknesses. Some of the more prominent eclectics are Greg Beale, G. R. Beasley-Murray, and Craig Keener. Proponents of this view seek to understand the message to the original audience and take special note of the historical-cultural context of Revelation. They also acknowledge that some of the events will be fulfilled in the final consummation. Although they claim to be eclectic, it seems to me that most who adopt this approach still primarily lean heavily toward idealism. The strength of the eclectic view is its desire to avoid the weaknesses of some of the other positions and present a balanced approach, yet I believe its idealistic leanings leave it open to the same subjective, inconsistent interpretation that plagues the idealistic view. See Grant R. Osborne, *Revelation*, Baker Exegetical Commentary on the New Testament, ed. Moises Silva (Grand Rapids: Baker Academic, 2002), 21.
2. R. C. Sproul, *The Last Days according to Jesus* (Grand Rapids: Baker, 1998), 228.
3. Ibid., 24.
4. Ibid., *The Last Days according to Jesus* (Grand Rapids: Baker, 1998), 158.
5. For a detailed presentation defending the AD 95 date of Revelation, go to pre-trib.org, where a copy of my doctoral dissertation from Dallas Theological Seminary is available. The title of the dissertation is "A Defense of the Domitianic Date of the Book of Revelation." On the website you can also view a debate on the date of Revelation between myself and Hank Hanegraaff that was held in December 2007 in Dallas, Texas.
6. J. Daniel Hays, J. Scott Duvall, and C. Marvin Pate, *Dictionary of Biblical Prophecy and End Times* (Grand Rapids: Zondervan, 2007), 172.
7. *Sermon Central*, accessed December 12, 2011, www.sermoncentral.com/illustrations/illustrations-about-revelation.asp.

CHAPTER 4: IT'S ALL A MATTER OF INTERPRETATION

1. Roy B. Zuck, *Basic Bible Interpretation* (Colorado Springs: David C. Cook, 1991), 242.
2. Charles C. Ryrie, *Dispensationalism* (Chicago: Moody, 1995), 80–81.
3. David L. Cooper, *The World's Greatest Library: Graphically Illustrated* (Los Angeles: Biblical Research Society, 1970), 11.
4. *Webster's New Twentieth Century Dictionary*, 2nd ed., s.v. "literal."
5. Ibid., s.v. "literal interpretation."
6. Paul Lee Tan, *The Interpretation of Prophecy* (Winona Lake, IN: Assurance Publishers, 1974), 29.
7. Tan, *The Interpretation of Prophecy*, 63.
8. Ryrie, *Dispensationalism*, 81.
9. J. C. Ryle, *Are You Ready for the End of Time?* (1867; repr., Tain, UK: Christian Focus Publications, 2001), 49.
10. For a more complete list, see J. B. Smith, *A Revelation of Jesus Christ: A Commentary on the Book of Revelation* (Scottsdale, PA: Herald Press, 1961), 18.

11. Paul Benware, *Understanding End Times Prophecy: A Comprehensive Approach* (Chicago: Moody, 1995), 25.
12. *Dialogue with Trypho*, Justin Martyr.

CHAPTER 5: KEY PROPHETIC PASSAGES

1. J. Dwight Pentecost, *Things to Come* (Grand Rapids: Zondervan, 1958), 316–17.
2. Harold W. Hoehner, *Chronological Aspects of the Life of Christ* (Grand Rapids: Zondervan, 1977), 131.
3. For an excellent, detailed presentation of the entire seventy weeks prophecy, see Ibid., 115–40. Those who deny a future seven-year time of tribulation insist that there is no gap between the end of the sixty-ninth week in AD 33 and the beginning of the seventieth week. They see them as running consecutively. (Gary DeMar, *End Times Fiction* [Nashville: Thomas Nelson, 2001], 42–52.) However, there are at least two insurmountable problems with this view. First, the text of Daniel 9:26-27 clearly denotes a gap of at least thirty-seven years between the end of the sixty-ninth and the beginning of the seventieth week (the time between the triumphal entry of Christ in AD 33 and the destruction of Jerusalem in AD 70). Second, if you do not put a gap of years between the sixty-ninth and seventieth weeks you have the seventy weeks ending in about AD 40. And what great event happened that year? Nothing! DeMar tries to fit the destruction of Jerusalem in AD 70 into the seventieth week, but to do that the final seven years has to be extended to at least thirty-seven years (*End Times Fiction*, 50–51). This kind of twisting to make the numbers fit is contrary to sound biblical interpretation. James Montgomery Boice, a well-known Bible expositor, faces this issue head-on and recognizes the necessity of a gap of time before the final seven years unfold: "But what about the last week? What of the final seven years of the 490-year series? This is a puzzle for almost everyone due to the fact that if we simply add seven years to what we have already calculated, we come to the year A.D. 38 (or 46), and nothing of any particular importance happened in that year. . . . But I tend to think those people are right who see a break in the fulfillment of prophecy at this point. According to them, the fulfillment of this uniquely Jewish prophecy is suspended while the gospel is preached to the Gentiles and the full number of the church is brought in, a church encompassing people from all walks of life, all races and all nations. Then after the members of the church are fully gathered the prophecy will begin to unfold once more with a final week of acute suffering and persecution for the Jewish nation. In this view the last week of Daniel would coincide with a seven-year period of great tribulation mentioned elsewhere. I think there is support for this in Jesus' reference to 'the abomination that causes desolation' mentioned in this passage (v. 27) as well as in Daniel 11:31 and 12:11 as something not to happen immediately, but to be experienced at the very end of the age (Matthew 24:15)." James Montgomery Boice, *Daniel: An Expositional Commentary* (Grand Rapids: Zondervan, 1989), 109–110.
4. For a thorough discussion of the seventy weeks prophecy of Daniel, see Thomas Ice, "The Seventy Weeks of Daniel," in *The End Times Controversy: The Second Coming Under Attack* (Eugene, OR: Harvest House, 2003), 307–53.
5. Those who disagree with the futurist understanding of Daniel 9:27 believe that the one who makes the covenant in Daniel 9:27 is not the Antichrist, but Christ. They believe that the breaking of the covenant and making an end to sacrifices and offerings refers to Christ's death on the cross in AD 33. However, there are two stubborn problems

with this view. First, the nearest antecedent to the pronoun "he" in Daniel 9:27 (NASB) is the "prince who is to come," who is of the same people who destroyed the Temple in AD 70. Clearly, this is a reference to the Romans. This cannot refer to Jesus since He was not Roman. This is a clear reference to the coming Antichrist who will arise from the reunited Roman Empire of the end times (Daniel 7:8). Second, the Bible never indicates that Christ made a seven-year salvation covenant. He lived for about thirty-five years and ministered publicly for over three years. Nowhere do we find a particular seven-year period. Leon Wood sets forth seven convincing reasons for taking "he" in Daniel 9:27 as a reference to the coming prince or Antichrist. Leon Wood, *A Commentary on Daniel* (Grand Rapids: Zondervan, 1973), 258.

6. Daniel 12:4 (NASB) says, "But as for you, Daniel, conceal these words and seal up the book until the end of time; many will go back and forth, and knowledge will increase." These words have often been cited to prove that in the last days people will travel at great speeds ("go back and forth") and that there will be a great increase of knowledge. On the basis of this verse Isaac Newton predicted that the day would come when the volume of knowledge would be so increased that man would be able to travel at speeds up to 50 mph. In response to this suggestion the atheist Voltaire cast great ridicule on Newton and the Bible. Undoubtedly, knowledge has exploded in the last forty years and continues to accelerate at a dizzying pace. All the new technology related to the computer industry alone is unbelievable. However, Daniel 12:4 does not describe an explosion of knowledge in general but a particular kind of knowledge that will increase in the last days. The phrase "many will rush here and there" or "many will go back and forth" is used in the Bible of movement in search of something, often information (Amos 8:12; Zechariah 4:10). Daniel 12:4 is talking about people, primarily Jewish people in this context, running to and fro or back and forth during the end times studying the book of Daniel to find answers about what in the world is going on. This passage goes on to say that knowledge (literally "the" knowledge) will increase. In the context of this passage, "the" knowledge that will increase is the knowledge of God's prophetic program for this world. It is not talking about knowledge in general but knowledge of Bible prophecy. We see this happening today. We understand Daniel's book even better today than he did. We have the Olivet discourse of Jesus in Matthew 24, the book of Revelation, and 2,500 years of history to help us better understand the prophecies of Daniel. As we get closer to the end, knowledge of the end times will continue to increase. But Daniel's prophecy deals primarily with the Jewish people in the end times. For the final generation of Jewish people during the Tribulation, the end times prophecies of Scripture will read like the daily newspaper.
7. John F. Walvoord, *Matthew: Thy Kingdom Come* (Chicago: Moody, 1970), 193.
8. John MacArthur, *The Second Coming* (Wheaton, IL: Crossway, 1999), 81.
9. David J. MacLeod, "The Lion Who Is a Lamb: An Exposition of Revelation 5:1-7," *Bibliotheca Sacra* (July–September 2007): 325–30.
10. William Hendriksen, *More Than Conquerors* (Grand Rapids: Baker, 1967), 109.
11. Charles R. Swindoll, *Insights on Revelation* (Grand Rapids: Zondervan, 2011), 109.
12. MacLeod, "The Lion Who Is a Lamb," 328–29.
13. George Eldon Ladd, *A Commentary on the Revelation of John* (Grand Rapids: Eerdmans, 1972), 82.
14. Charles C. Ryrie, *Revelation* (Chicago: Moody, 1968), 43.
15. Ibid., 44.
16. Ibid.

CHAPTER 6: BACK TO THE FUTURE

1. John F. Walvoord, *The Millennial Kingdom* (Grand Rapids: Zondervan, 1959), 139.
2. J. Dwight Pentecost, *Things to Come* (Grand Rapids: Zondervan, 1958), 71.
3. Walvoord lists ten reasons as evidence that the covenant is unconditional. Walvoord, *The Millennial Kingdom*, 150–52.
4. Paul Benware, *Understanding the End Times: A Comprehensive Approach* (Chicago: Moody, 1995), 44.
5. Charles C. Ryrie, *The Basis of the Premillennial Faith* (Neptune, NJ: Loizeaux Brothers, 1953), 53.
6. Ronald E. Diprose, *Israel and the Church: The Origin and Effects of Replacement Theology* (Waynesboro, GA: Authentic Media, 2004), 12.
7. Ryrie, *The Basis of the Premillennial Faith*, 60.
8. Pentecost, *Things to Come*, 97.
9. Some argue that the land promises were fulfilled in Joshua 11:23 or 1 Kings 4. However, in Joshua 11 it is clear that Israel had not come close to possessing all the land promised to Abraham. The land described in 1 Kings 4 during the reign of Solomon was never actually possessed and occupied by Israel. Solomon collected tribute money from the pagan kings who reigned in those areas. The Land Covenant requires permanent possession of the land promised to Abraham. This was not fulfilled in Joshua or 1 Kings.
10. Pentecost, *Thy Kingdom Come* (Wheaton, IL: Victor Books, 1990), 147.
11. Ibid., 148.
12. Benware, *Understanding the End Times*, 67.
13. Pentecost, *Things to Come*, 128.
14. Lewis Sperry Chafer, *Systematic Theology*, vol. 4 (Dallas: Dallas Seminary Press, 1948), 315–28. For an excellent presentation and defense of a future for national Israel, see Barry E. Horner, *Future Israel: Why Christian Anti-Judaism Must Be Challenged*, NAC Studies in Bible & Theology, ed. E. Ray Clendenen (Nashville: B&H Academic, 2007).

CHAPTER 7: ARE WE LIVING IN THE "END TIMES"?

1. Thomas Ice and Timothy Demy, *The Truth About the Signs of the Times* (Eugene, OR: Harvest House, 1997), 8–9.
2. Ed Hindson, *Final Signs: Amazing Prophecies of the End Times* (Eugene, OR: Harvest House, 1996), 191. Much of the material in this section has been adapted from this book.
3. See Isaiah 2:12; 13:6, 9; Ezekiel 13:5; 30:3; Joel 1:15; 2:1, 11, 31; 3:14; Amos 5:18 (2 times); 5:20; Obadiah 1:15; Zephaniah 1:7, 14 (2 times); Zechariah 14:1; Malachi 4:5.
4. J. Dwight Pentecost, *Things to Come* (Grand Rapids: Zondervan, 1958), 230–32.

CHAPTER 8: WHAT TO LOOK FOR

1. Ed Hindson, *Final Signs: Amazing Prophecies of the End Times* (Eugene, OR: Harvest House, 1996), 196.
2. Thomas Ice and Timothy Demy, *The Truth About the Signs of the Times* (Eugene, OR: Harvest House, 1997), 10–11.
3. Adrian Rogers, *Unveiling the End Times in Our Time* (Nashville: B&H, 2004), 142.
4. Randall Price, "The Divine Preservation of the Jewish People," *Bible Prophecy Blog*, October 1, 2009, http://www.bibleprophecyblog.com/2010/07/divine-preservation-of-jewish-people.html.
5. Amiram Barkat, "Statistics Bureau: Israeli Jews Outnumber Jews in the U.S.,"

Haaretz.com, November 20, 2009, http://www.haaretz.com/print-edition/news/statistics-bureau-israeli-jews-outnumber-jews-in-the-u-s-1.91466.

6. Ibid.
7. John F. Walvoord, *The Church in Prophecy* (Grand Rapids: Zondervan, 1964), 50.
8. J. Dwight Pentecost, *Will Man Survive? The Bible Looks at Man's Future* (Grand Rapids: Zondervan, 1971), 58.
9. John Phillips, *Exploring the Future: A Comprehensive Guide to Bible Prophecy*, 3rd ed. (Grand Rapids: Kregel, 2003), 225, 269.

PART 3: WHEN WILL THE BELIEVING BE LEAVING?

1. Arthur Bloomfield, *How to Recognize the Antichrist* (Minneapolis: Bethany House, 1975), p. 28.

CHAPTER 9: THE MYSTERY OF THE RAPTURE

1. David Gates, David J. Jefferson, and Anne Underwood, "The Pop Prophets," *Newsweek*, May 24, 2004, 48.
2. J. B. Smith, *A Revelation of Jesus Christ: A Commentary on the Book of Revelation* (Scottdale, PA: Herald Press, 1961), 312.
3. This section was adapted from Mark Hitchcock, *The Complete Book of Bible Prophecy*, (Carol Stream, IL: Tyndale, 1999), 184–85.
4. Some point to verses such as Matthew 17:3; Luke 16:22-24; and Revelation 6:9-11 to support the view that deceased believers have a temporary body during the time between physical death and the Rapture. While this view is certainly possible, 2 Corinthians 5:1-4 deals directly with this issue and seems to say that during the intermediate state believers are "naked" or without corporeal existence. Either way, it's clear that the permanent, glorified body is received at the Lord's coming.
5. John MacArthur, *1 Corinthians* (Chicago: Moody, 1984), 444.
6. Material in this section was adapted from *The Complete Book of Bible Prophecy* (p. 184).
7. Actually, 1 Thessalonians was written by Paul before 1 Corinthians, but if you were reading the Bible straight through you would come to 1 Corinthians first.
8. Andy Stanley, *How Good Is Good Enough?* (Sisters, OR: Multnomah Publishers, 2003), 7–8.
9. Harold Willmington, *Willmington's Guide to the Bible*, 30th Anniv. Ed. (Carol Stream, IL: Tyndale, 2011), 746.

CHAPTER 10: FIVE MAIN VIEWS OF THE TIMING OF THE RAPTURE

1. Paul N. Benware, *Understanding End Times Prophecy* (Chicago: Moody, 1995), 219.
2. Gleason L. Archer Jr., Paul D. Feinberg, Douglas J. Moo, *Three Views on the Rapture* (Grand Rapids: Zondervan, 1984), 181.
3. John F. Walvoord, *The Rapture Question*, rev. ed. (Grand Rapids: Zondervan, 1979), 268.
4. Gerald B. Stanton, *Kept from the Hour: Biblical Evidence for the Pretribulational Return of Christ* (Miami Springs, FL: Schoettle Publishing, 1991), 166.
5. *Understanding End Times Prophecy*, 235.

CHAPTER 11: SEVEN REASONS FOR THE PRE-TRIB RAPTURE

1. This excursus was adapted from *The Complete Book of Bible Prophecy* (pp. 119–20).
2. John F. Walvoord, *The Revelation of Jesus Christ* (Chicago: Moody, 1989), 102.
3. Material in this section was adapted from *The Complete Book of Bible Prophecy* (pp. 185–86).
4. Walvoord, *The Return of the Lord* (Grand Rapids: Zondervan, 1955), 88. The quotation

and the first six contrasts in the comparison on page 151 are taken from pp. 87–88 of Walvoord's *The Return of the Lord.*

5. John F. MacArthur, *The Second Coming* (Wheaton, IL: Crossway, 1999), 87.
6. In Revelation, there are three series of seven judgments—the seals, trumpets, and bowls. This, of course, equals twenty-one. But since the seventh seal contains the seven trumpets and the seventh trumpet contains the seven bowls, the total number of specific judgments is actually nineteen rather than twenty-one.
7. J. F. Strombeck, *First the Rapture: The Church's Blessed Hope* (Grand Rapids: Kregel, 1992), 133.
8. Gleason L. Archer Jr., Paul D. Feinberg, Douglas J. Moo, *The Rapture: Pre-, Mid-, or Post-Tribulational?* (Grand Rapids: Zondervan, 1984), 117–18.
9. Walvoord, *The Thessalonian Epistles* (Grand Rapids: Zondervan, 1974), 54.
10. For a thorough, scholarly discussion of this issue and many other issues related to the timing of the rapture see Archer, et al., *The Rapture*, 63–71.
11. Also, if Revelation 3:10 promises to protect believers during the Tribulation, as other views argue, then Revelation 7:9-14 seems to break that promise, if indeed that passage describes the Tribulation. In that passage millions of believers are martyred during the Tribulation. It's much more consistent to understand Revelation 3:10 as a "keeping from" the Tribulation, not "keeping through."
12. Charles C. Ryrie, *Come Quickly, Lord Jesus: What You Need to Know about the Rapture* (Eugene, OR: Harvest House, 1996), 137–38.
13. Of course, the mid-Tribulation view and the pre-wrath view also allow for a time gap between the Rapture and the Second Coming. For the mid-Trib view, the interval is 3½ years, and for the pre-wrath view, it's about 1½ years. But the time gap of at least seven years for the pre-Trib view is the best alternative.
14. Isaiah 65:17 uses the term "new heavens and a new earth" in reference to the millennial reign of Christ. The note in *The MacArthur Study Bible* at Isaiah 65:17 is helpful: "Israel's future kingdom will include a temporal kingdom of a thousand years and an eternal kingdom in God's new creation. The prophet uses the eternal kingdom here as a reference point for both. Isaiah's prophecy does not make clear the relationship between the kingdom's two aspects as does later prophecy (Revelation 20:1–21:8). This is similar to the compression of Christ's first and second advents, so that in places they are indistinguishable (cf. 61:1, 2)."
15. John Phillips, *Exploring 1 and 2 Thessalonians: An Expository Commentary* (Grand Rapids: Kregel, 2005), 120.
16. Donald Grey Barnhouse, *Thessalonians: An Expositional Commentary* (Grand Rapids: Zondervan, 1977), 99–100.
17. Charles R. Swindoll, *Steadfast Christianity: A Study of Second Thessalonians* (Nashville: Thomas Nelson, 1986).
18. Barnhouse, *Thessalonians*, 99–100.
19. Ryrie, *Come Quickly, Lord Jesus*, 22.
20. Renald Showers, *Maranatha: Our Lord Come! A Definitive Study of the Rapture of the Church* (Bellmawr, NJ: Friends of Israel Gospel Ministry, 1995), 127.
21. Ibid., 131.
22. Thomas Ice, "Imminency and the Any-Moment Rapture," *Pre-Trib Perspectives* (October 1999): 4.
23. Richard Mayhue, *1 and 2 Thessalonians: Triumphs and Trials of a Consecrated Church* (Fearn, UK: Christian Focus Publications, 1999), 218–19.

CHAPTER 12: A BRIEF HISTORY OF THE PRE-TRIB RAPTURE VIEW

1. Pseudo-Ephraem, "On the Last Times, the Antichrist, and the End of the World, or Sermon on the End of the World" (sermon), www.pre-trib.org/article-view.php?id=169.
2. Timothy J. Demy and Thomas D. Ice, "The Rapture and Pseudo-Ephraem: An Early Medieval Citation," *Bibliotheca Sacra* 152 (July–September 1995): 12.
3. Thomas Ice, "A Brief History of the Rapture," www.pre-trib.org/articles/view/brief-history-of-rapture.
4. Quoted in Francis Gumerlock, "A Rapture Citation in the Fourteenth Century," *Bibliotheca Sacra* 159 (July–September 2002): 345–46.
5. Ibid., 365–69.
6. Ibid., 361
7. Morgan Edwards, *Two Academical Exercises on Subjects Bearing the Following Titles: Millennium, Last-Novelties* (Philadelphia: Dobson and Lang, 1788), 5–6. The English has been modernized. This entire book is available on the Internet at the following address: www.pre-trib.org/article-view.php?id=178.
8. Ibid., 7.
9. Ice, "A Brief History of the Rapture."
10. Paul N. Benware, *Understanding End Times Prophecy: A Comprehensive Approach* (Chicago: Moody, 1995), 197–98.

CHAPTER 13: FALSE CLAIMS ABOUT THE ORIGIN OF THE PRE-TRIB RAPTURE

1. One of the most ardent supporters of these ideas is Dave MacPherson. See Dave MacPherson, *The Unbelievable Pre-Trib Origin* (Kansas City, MO: Heart of America Bible Society, 1973); *The Late Great Pre-Trib Rapture* (Kansas City, MO: Heart of America Bible Society, 1974); *The Great Rapture Hoax* (Fletcher, NC: New Puritan Library, 1983); *Rapture?* (Fletcher, NC: New Puritan Library, 1987); *The Rapture Plot* (Monticello, Utah: P.O.S.T. Inc., 1994); *The Rapture Plot* (Simpsonville, SC: Millennium III Publishers, 2000).
2. Thomas D. Ice, "John Nelson Darby and the Rapture." Paper presented at the pre-Trib study group in Dallas, Texas, December 7, 2011. This can be viewed online at http://www.pre-trib.org/articles/view/john-nelson-darby-and-the-rapture.
3. I am indebted to my friend Tommy Ice for the material in this chapter. It was adapted from a chapter he wrote in a project we collaborated on together.
4. The following books are some of those that have the full text of Macdonald's utterance: Dave MacPherson, *The Incredible Cover-Up* (Plainfield, NJ: Logos International, 1975), 150-54. Dave MacPherson, *The Great Rapture Hoax* (Fletcher, NC: New Puritan Library, 1983), 125-28. R. A. Huebner, *The Truth of the Pre-Tribulation Rapture Recovered* (Millington, NJ: Present Truth Publishers, 1973), 67–69. Hal Lindsey, *The Rapture: Truth or Consequences* (New York: Bantam Books, 1983), 169–72. William R. Kimball, *The Rapture: A Question of Timing* (Grand Rapids: Baker, 1985), 44–47.
5. The following are some excerpts from Macdonald's utterance: "I saw it was just the Lord himself descending from Heaven with a shout, just the glorified man, even Jesus; but that all must, as Stephen was, be filled with the Holy Ghost, that they might look up, and see the brightness of the Father's glory. . . . Only those who have the light of God within them will see the sign of his appearance. . . . 'Tis Christ in us that will lift us up—he is the light—'tis only those that are alive in him that will be caught up to meet him in the air. I saw that we must be in the Spirit, that we might see spiritual things. John was in the Spirit, when he saw a throne set in Heaven. But I saw that the glory of the ministration of

the Spirit had not been known. I repeated frequently, but the spiritual temple must and shall be reared, and the fullness of Christ be poured into his body, . . . and then shall we be caught up to meet him. Oh none will be counted worthy of this calling but his body, which is the church, and which must be a candlestick all of gold. . . . I felt that those who were filled with the Spirit could see spiritual things, and feel walking in the midst of them, while those who had not the Spirit could see nothing—so that—two shall be in one bed, the one taken and the other left, because the one has the light of God within while the other cannot see the Kingdom of Heaven. . . . Oh there must and will be such an indwelling of the living God as has not been—the servants of God sealed in their foreheads—great conformity to Jesus—his holy holy image seen in his people—just the bride made comely by his comeliness put upon her. This is what we are at present made to pray much for, that speedily we may all be made ready to meet our Lord in the air—and it will be. Jesus wants his bride. His desire is toward us. He that shall come, will come, and will not tarry. Amen and Amen Even so come Lord Jesus." ("Margaret's Revelation," www .bibleprophesy.org/vision.htm.)

6. Ice, "Why the Doctrine of the Pretribulational Rapture Did Not Begin with Margaret Macdonald," *Bibliotheca Sacra* 147 (April–June 1990): 158, 161.
7. Huebner, *Precious Truths Revived and Defended through J. N. Darby*, vol. 1 (Morganville, NJ: Present Truth Publishers, 1991).
8. Jonathan David Burnham, "The Controversial Relationship between Benjamin Wills Newton and John Nelson Darby" (PhD Thesis, St. Anne's College, Oxford University, 1999), 129, f.n. 128.
9. Huebner, *Precious Truths Revived and Defended*, 17.
10. Ibid., 19.
11. Ibid., 18.
12. Ibid., 23.
13. Ibid., 24.
14. J. N. Darby, "Reflections upon the Prophetic Inquiry and the Views Advanced in It" *The Collected Writings of J. N. Darby*, vol. 2 (Winschoten, Netherlands: H. L. Heijkoop, reprint 1971), 1–31.
15. Timothy P. Weber, *Living in the Shadow of the Second Coming: American Premillennialism 1875–1982* (Grand Rapids: Zondervan, 1983), 21–22.
16. William E. Bell, "A Critical Evaluation of the Pretribulation Rapture Doctrine in Christian Eschatology" (PhD dissertation, New York University, 1967), 60–61, 64–65.
17. F. F. Bruce, review of *The Unbelievable Pre-Trib Origin*, by Dave MacPherson, *The Evangelical Quarterly*, 67, no. 1 (January–March 1975): 58.
18. See MacPherson, *The Rapture Plot.* See also Mark Patterson and Andrew Walker, "'Our Unspeakable Comfort' Irving, Albury, and the Origins of the Pretribulation Rapture," *Fides et Historia*, 31, no. 1 (Winter/Spring 1999): 77.
19. Edward Irving, "Signs of the Times in the Church," *The Morning Watch*, vol. 2 (1830): 156.
20. Columba Graham Flegg, *"Gathered under Apostles": A Study of the Catholic Apostolic Church* (Oxford, UK: Clarendon Press, 1992), 436.
21. Ernest R. Sandeen, *The Roots of Fundamentalism: British and American Millenarianism 1800–1930* (Grand Rapids: Baker, 1970), 64.
22. John F. Walvoord, *Blessed Hope and the Tribulation: A Historical and Biblical Study of Posttribulationism* (Grand Rapids: Zondervan, 1976), 47.
23. Tim LaHaye, *The Rapture: Who Will Face the Tribulation?* (Eugene, OR: Harvest House, 2002), 187.

CHAPTER 14: QUESTIONS ABOUT THE RAPTURE

1. Thomas Ice and Timothy Demy, *The Truth about the Tribulation* (Eugene, OR: Harvest House, 1996), 46.
2. John MacArthur, *The Second Coming: Signs of Christ's Return and the End of the Age* (Wheaton, IL: Crossway, 1999), 88.
3. Material in this section was adapted from *The Complete Book of Bible Prophecy* (pp. 187–88).

CHAPTER 15: THE MEANING OF THE RAPTURE FOR EVERYDAY LIFE

1. Material in this chapter was adapted from *The Complete Book of Bible Prophecy* (pp. 137–44).

PART 4: THE JUDGMENT SEAT OF CHRIST

1. Erwin W. Lutzer, *Your Eternal Reward* (Chicago: Moody, 1998), 115.

CHAPTER 16: STANDING BEFORE THE *BEMA*

1. Psalm 58:11; 62:12; Proverbs 11:18; Isaiah 40:10; 62:11; Matthew 5:12; 6:1-2; 10:41-42; Luke 6:35; 1 Corinthians 3:8, 14; Ephesians 6:8; Hebrews 10:35-36; 11:6, 24-26; 2 John 1:8; Revelation 2:23; 11:18; 22:12.
2. These five points were taken from Erwin W. Lutzer, *Your Eternal Reward* (Chicago: Moody, 1998), 25–36.
3. Ibid., 23.

PART 5: THE MARRIAGE OF THE LAMB

1. H. L. Willmington, *The King Is Coming* (Carol Stream, IL: Tyndale, 1991), 41.

CHAPTER 17: A MARRIAGE MADE IN HEAVEN

1. Adapted from Kim Grundy, "William and Kate Wedding Budget," *She Knows Entertainment* (blog), April 25, 2011, www.sheknows.com/entertainment/articles/829395/royal-wedding-will-cost-around-32-million.
2. H. L. Willmington, *The Complete Book of Bible Lists* (Carol Stream, IL: Tyndale, 1987), 193–94.

CHAPTER 18: COMING TO TERMS WITH THE TRIBULATION

1. Charles H. Dyer, *World News and Bible Prophecy* (Carol Stream, IL: Tyndale, 1993), 214.
2. J. Dwight Pentecost, *Things to Come: A Study in Biblical Eschatology* (Grand Rapids: Zondervan, 1964), 235.
3. This list was adapted from *The Complete Book of Bible Prophecy* (p. 69).
4. Material in this section was adapted from *The Complete Book of Bible Prophecy* (pp. 67–68).
5. Pentecost, *Things to Come*, 237.
6. Pentecost, *Will Man Survive?* (Grand Rapids: Zondervan, 1980), 71.
7. John F. Walvoord, *The Thessalonian Epistles* (Grand Rapids: Zondervan, n.d.), 79.

PART 7: THE BEGINNING OF BIRTH PAINS

1. John F. Walvoord, *The Nations in Prophecy* (Grand Rapids: Zondervan, 1967), 13.

CHAPTER 19: THE RISE OF THE GROUP OF TEN

1. Leon Wood, *A Commentary on Daniel* (Grand Rapids: Zondervan, 1973), 71.

CHAPTER 20: SATAN'S CEO—THE ASCENT OF THE ANTICHRIST

1. H. L. Willmington, *The King Is Coming: A Compelling Biblical Story of the Last Days* (Carol Stream, IL: Tyndale, 1981), 81.
2. Arthur W. Pink, *The Antichrist* (1923; repr., Grand Rapids: Kregel, 1988), 9.
3. F. F. Bruce, *The Epistles of John* (Grand Rapids: Eerdmans, 1970), 65.
4. Pink, *The Antichrist*, 62.
5. This chart was adapted from *The Complete Book of Bible Prophecy* (p. 132).
6. Arthur E. Bloomfield, *How to Recognize the Antichrist: What Bible Prophecy Says about the Great Deceiver* (Minneapolis: Bethany House, 1975), 89.
7. Charles R. Swindoll, *Steadfast Christianity: A Study Guide of 2 Thessalonians* (Fullerton, CA: Insight for Living, 1986), 24.
8. Ed Hindson, *Is the Antichrist Alive and Well?: 10 Keys to His Identity* (Eugene, OR: Harvest House, 1998), 22.
9. Pink, *The Antichrist*, 79.
10. John Phillips, *Exploring Revelation: An Expository Commentary* (Grand Rapids: Kregel, 2001), 166.
11. Material in this section was adapted from *The Complete Book of Bible Prophecy* (pp. 195–96).
12. Robert L. Thomas, *Revelation 1-7* (Chicago: Moody, 1992), 481.
13. Arnold G. Fruchtenbaum, *The Footsteps of the Messiah*, rev. ed. (Tustin, CA: Ariel Ministries, 2003), 211.
14. Ibid., 211.
15. Pink, *The Antichrist*, 81.
16. Phillips, *Exploring the Future: A Comprehensive Guide to Bible Prophecy*, 3rd ed. (Grand Rapids: Kregel, 2003), 272.
17. Willmington, *The King is Coming*, 95.
18. This list was adapted from *The Complete Book of Bible Prophecy* (pp. 131–32).

CHAPTER 21: THE FINAL FALSE PROPHET

1. Warren W. Wiersbe, *The Bible Exposition Commentary: New Testament*, vol. 2 (Wheaton, IL: Victor Books, 1989), 605.
2. Material in this chapter was adapted from *The Complete Book of Bible Prophecy* (pp. 134–36).
3. Donald Grey Barnhouse, *Revelation: An Expository Commentary* (Grand Rapids: Zondervan, 1971), 240.
4. Thomas Ice and Timothy J. Demy, *Fast Facts on Bible Prophecy from A to Z* (Eugene, OR: Harvest House, 1997), 78–79.
5. John Phillips, *Exploring Revelation* (Neptune, NJ: Loizeaux Brothers, 1991), 171.
6. Ice and Demy, *Fast Facts on Bible Prophecy*, 78–79.

CHAPTER 22: RIDERS ON THE STORM

1. This view is held by several excellent commentators, including James Montgomery Boice, "The Four Horsemen of the Apocalypse," *God's Word Today* (May 2002): 32–33; Leon Morris, *Revelation*, Tyndale New Testament Commentaries, rev. ed. (Grand Rapids: Eerdmans, 1989), 100–101.
2. George Eldon Ladd, *A Commentary on the Revelation of John* (Grand Rapids: Eerdmans, 1972), 97–99.
3. Robert L. Thomas, *Revelation 1-7* (Chicago: Moody, 1992), 421; W. A. Criswell, *Expository Sermons on Revelation*, vol. 3 (Grand Rapids: Zondervan, 1969), 92.

4. Daniel K. K. Wong, "The First Horseman of Revelation 6," *Bibliotheca Sacra* 153 (April–June 1996): 224.
5. Billy Graham, *Approaching Hoofbeats: The Four Horsemen of the Apocalypse* (Waco, TX: Word Books, 1983), 78.
6. David Jeremiah, *Escape the Coming Night* (Dallas, TX: Word Publishing, 1997), 112.
7. Graham, *Approaching Hoofbeats*, 161.
8. John F. Walvoord, *Revelation*, rev. ed. (Chicago: Moody, 2011), 126.
9. Thomas, *Revelation 1-7*, 436.
10. Charles R. Swindoll, *Insights on Revelation* (Grand Rapids: Zondervan, 2011), 111.
11. Thomas, *Revelation 1-7*, 439.
12. Henry Morris, *The Revelation Record* (Carol Stream, IL: Tyndale, 1983), 117–18.
13. Walvoord, *Revelation*, 149.

CHAPTER 23: THE 144,000

1. Material in this chapter was adapted from *The Complete Book of Bible Prophecy* (pp. 125–27).
2. George Eldon Ladd, *A Commentary on the Revelation of John* (Grand Rapids: Eerdmans, 1972), 116.
3. The one text that is used to support the use of *Israel* for the church is Galatians 6:16, but this view has been soundly refuted. S. Lewis Johnson Jr., "Paul and the 'Israel of God': An Exegetical and Eschatological Case-Study," in *Essays in Honor of J. Dwight Pentecost*, ed. Stanley D. Toussaint and Charles H. Dyer (Chicago: Moody, 1986), 181–96.
4. Joseph A. Seiss, *The Apocalypse: Lectures on the Book of Revelation* (1900; repr., Grand Rapids: Zondervan, 1964), 161.
5. John F. Walvoord, *Revelation*, rev. ed. (Chicago: Moody, 2011), 139.
6. Robert L. Thomas, *Revelation 1-7* (Chicago: Moody, 1992), 473.

CHAPTER 24: THE BATTLE OF GOG AND MAGOG

1. Josephus, *Antiquities* 1.6.1. For more information about the Scythians, see Edwin M. Yamauchi, *Foes from the Northern Frontier* (Grand Rapids: Baker, 1982), 64–109.
2. Material in this section was adapted from *After the Empire* (p. 27ff).
3. C. F. Keil and F. Delitzsch, *Commentary on the Old Testament*, trans. James Martin (1866; repr., Grand Rapids: Eerdmans, 1982), 159. Wilhelm Gesenius and Samuel Prideaux Tregelles, *Gesenius' Hebrew-Chaldee Lexicon to the Old Testament* (1846; repr., Grand Rapids: Eerdmans, 1949), 752.
4. Clyde E. Billington Jr., "The Rosh People in History and Prophecy (Part Two)" *Michigan Theological Journal* 3 (1992): 54–61.
5. G. A. Cooke, *A Critical and Exegetical Commentary on the Book of Ezekiel*, International Critical Commentary, ed. Samuel Rolles Driver, Alfred Plummer, and Charles Augustus Briggs (Edinburgh: T. & T. Clark, 1936), 408–9. Daniel Block supports taking "Rosh" as the name of an ethnic group. See Daniel I. Block, *The Book of Ezekiel, Chapters 25-48*, NICOT (Grand Rapids: Eerdmans, 1998), 434. John Taylor agrees. He says, "If a place-name *Rosh* could be vouched for, RV's *prince of Rosh, Meshech, and Tubal* would be the best translation." See John B. Taylor, *Ezekiel: An Introduction & Commentary*, Tyndale Old Testament Commentaries, gen. ed. D. J. Wiseman (Downers Grove, IL: InterVarsity Press, 1969), 244. Since it appears that there was a place in Ezekiel's day known as Rosh, this is the superior translation. For an extensive, thorough presentation of the grammatical and philological support for taking Rosh as a place name, see James D. Price, "Rosh: An Ancient Land Known to Ezekiel," *Grace Theological Journal* 6 (1985): 67–89.

6. Billington, "The Rosh People (Part Two)," 145–46; Billington, "The Rosh People (Part Three)," 59, 61; James D. Price, "Rosh: An Ancient Land Known to Ezekiel," *Grace Theological Journal* 6 (1985): 71–73; Jon Mark Ruthven and Ihab Griess, *The Prophecy That Is Shaping History: New Research on Ezekiel's Vision of the End* (Longwood, FL: Xulon Press, 2003), 61–62.
7. Billington, "Rosh People (Part Two)," 145–46.
8. Price, "Rosh: An Ancient Land," 71–73.
9. Billington, "The Rosh People (Part Three)," 59, 61.
10. Gesenius, *Gesenius' Hebrew-Chaldee Lexicon,* 752.
11. C. I. Scofield, *Scofield Reference Notes* (1917), http://www.biblestudytools.com/commentaries/scofield-reference-notes/.
12. Josephus, *Antiquities* 1.6.1.
13. John F. Walvoord, *The Nations in Prophecy* (Grand Rapids: Zondervan, 1967), 116.
14. Walvoord, *The Nations in Prophecy,* 115–16.

Some preterists contend that the events in Ezekiel 38–39 have already occurred. Gary DeMar contends that Ezekiel 38–39 was fulfilled by the events described in Esther 9 occurring in about 473 BC in the days of Queen Esther of Persia. DeMar states that the parallels between the battles in Ezekiel 38–39 and Esther are "unmistakable." Gary Demar, *End Times Fiction* (Nashville, TN: Thomas Nelson, 2001), 12–14. DeMar, however, fails to account for several clear differences between Ezekiel 38–39 and Esther 9. A simple reading of the two passages reveals that they cannot possibly be describing the same event. Here are five of the more apparent and problematic inconsistencies.

EZEKIEL 38–39	ESTHER 9
The land of Israel is invaded (38:16).	Jews are attacked in cities throughout the Persian Empire and defend themselves (9:2).
The enemies fall on the mountains of Israel (39:4).	The enemies die throughout the Persian Empire.
Gog, the leader of the invasion, is buried in Israel (39:11). The Jews bury the dead bodies over a period of seven months to cleanse the land of Israel (39:12).	No need to cleanse the land because the bodies are not in the land of Israel.
The invaders are destroyed by a massive earthquake in the land of Israel, infighting, plagues, and fire from heaven (38:19-22). God destroys the enemies supernaturally.	Attackers are killed by the Jewish people themselves assisted by local government leaders (9:3-5).
Invaders are from as far west as ancient Put (modern Libya) (38:5) and as far north as Magog, the land of the Scythians.	The Persian Empire never included these areas. It only extended as far west as Cush (modern Sudan) (8:9) and as far north as the southern part of the Black and Caspian Seas.
God sends fire upon Magog and those who inhabit the coastlands (39:6).	There is nothing even close to this in Esther 9.

15. One important question we might ask at this point is, if Ezekiel 38–39 was fulfilled in the events of Esther 9, why did this escape the notice of everyone in Esther's day? Why is there no mention in Esther of this great fulfillment of Ezekiel's prophecy? And why are there no Jewish scholars in that day or subsequently who recognized this fulfillment? The answer seems quite clear. Esther 9 did not fulfill Ezekiel 38–39. An important Jewish holiday known as Purim developed out of the Esther event (9:20-32). This is a joyous annual holiday to celebrate God's deliverance of Israel from the hand of her enemies. Purim's celebration includes the public reading of the book of Esther, but no tradition has developed or even been heard of in which the Jews read Ezekiel 38–39 in connection with this observance. If Ezekiel 38–39 had been a fulfillment of Esther, then no doubt a tradition of reading that passage would have arisen in conjunction with the celebration.
16. Walvoord, *The Nations in Prophecy*, 105.
17. Ron Rhodes presents an excellent, evenhanded presentation and evaluation of each of these views. Ron Rhodes, *Northern Storm Rising: Russia, Iran, and the Emerging End-Times Military Coalition against Israel* (Eugene, OR: Harvest House, 2008), 179–95.
18. John Phillips, *Exploring the Future: A Comprehensive Guide to Bible Prophecy*, 3rd ed. (Grand Rapids: Kregel, 2003), 343.
19. Ibid., 347–48.
20. Rhodes, *Northern Storm Rising*, 193.
21. Luke Baker, "Israel Asks Itself the $150 Billion Question," *Reuters*, May 25, 2011, http://www.reuters.com/article/2011/05/25/us-economy-israel-steinitz-idUSTRE74O38R20110525.

PART 8: ANTICHRIST TAKES OVER

1. Arthur E. Bloomfield, *How to Recognize the Antichrist: What Bible Prophecy Says about the Great Deceiver* (Minneapolis: Bethany House, 2000), 93.

CHAPTER 25: SATANIC WARFARE AND WORSHIP

1. Charles R. Swindoll, *Insights on Revelation* (Grand Rapids: Zondervan, 2011), 174–75.
2. John F. Walvoord, *Revelation*, rev. ed. (Chicago: Moody, 2011), 197.
3. Arthur E. Bloomfield, *How to Recognize the Antichrist* (Minneapolis: Bethany House, 1975), 129–32.
4. Arnold G. Fruchtenbaum, *The Footsteps of the Messiah*, rev. ed. (Tustin, CA: Ariel Ministries, 2003), 257.
5. Warren W. Wiersbe, *The Bible Exposition Commentary: New Testament*, vol. 2 (Wheaton, IL: Victor Books, 1989), 606.
6. Fruchtenbaum, *The Footsteps of the Messiah*, 256–60.

CHAPTER 26: DEAD AND ALIVE: THE ASSASSINATION AND RESURRECTION OF THE ANTICHRIST

1. John Phillips, *Exploring Revelation: An Expository Commentary* (Grand Rapids: Kregel, 2001), 166–67.
2. Warren W. Wiersbe, *The Bible Exposition Commentary: New Testament*, vol. 2 (Wheaton, IL: Victor Books, 1989), 605.
3. J. Vernon McGee, *Thru the Bible*, vol. 5 (Nashville: Thomas Nelson, 1983), 1000. Some argue strenuously and stridently against this view. Hank Hanegraaff deems an actual

death and resurrection of the Antichrist as preposterous. He says, "If Antichrist could rise from the dead and control the earth and sky . . . Christianity would lose the basis for believing that Christ's resurrection vindicated His claim to deity. In a Christian worldview, Satan can parody the work of Christ through 'all kinds of counterfeit miracles, signs and wonders' (2 Thessalonians 2:9), but he cannot perform the truly miraculous as Christ did. If Satan possesses the creative power of God, he could have masqueraded as the resurrected Christ. Moreover, the notion that Satan can perform acts that are indistinguishable from genuine miracles suggests a dualistic worldview in which God and Satan are equal powers competing for dominance." See Hank Hanegraaff, *The Apocalypse Code: Find Out What the Bible Really Says about The End Times and Why It Matters Today* (Nashville: Thomas Nelson, 2007), xix–xx. Hanegraaff further states, "What is at stake here is nothing less than the deity and resurrection of Christ. In a Christian worldview, only God has the power to raise the dead." See Hank Hanegraaff and Sigmund Brouwer, *The Last Disciple* (Carol Stream, IL: Tyndale, 2004), 394. I agree, but it appears from the clear language used in Revelation that God gives Satan the power to raise the Antichrist from the dead as part of the great delusion.

4. Wiersbe, *The Bible Exposition Commentary*, 605.
5. Gregory H. Harris, "Satan's Deceptive Miracles," 311.
6. Matthew 24:24; Mark 13:22; John 4:48; Acts 2:19, 22, 43; 4:30; 5:12; 6:8; 7:36; 14:3; 15:12; Romans 15:19; 2 Corinthians 12:12; 2 Thessalonians 2:9; Hebrews 2:4.
7. Harris, "Satan's Deceptive Miracles in the Tribulation," *Bibliotheca Sacra* 156 (July–September 1999): 310.
8. Philip Edgcumbe Hughes, *A Commentary on the Epistle to the Hebrews* (Grand Rapids: Eerdmans, 1977), 80–81.
9. Harris, "Satan's Deceptive Miracles," 311.
10. Charles C. Ryrie, *Revelation*, Everyman's Bible Commentary (Chicago: Moody, 1968), 83.
11. J. B. Smith, *A Revelation of Jesus Christ: A Commentary on the Book of Revelation* (Scottdale, PA: Herald Press, 1961), 194.
12. Harris, "The Wound of the Beast in the Tribulation," *Bibliotheca Sacra* 156 (October–December 1999): 467.
13. Ibid., 466.
14. John Phillips, *Exploring Revelation* (Neptune, NJ: Loizeaux Brothers, 1991), 119.
15. Harris, "The Wound of the Beast," 469.
16. Smith, *A Revelation of Jesus Christ*, 195–96.

CHAPTER 27: THE MARK OF THE BEAST: WILL THAT BE THE RIGHT HAND OR THE FOREHEAD?

1. Gary DeMar, *End Times Fiction: A Biblical Consideration of the Left Behind Theology* (Nashville, TN: Thomas Nelson, 2001), 142–45; Kenneth Gentry, *The Beast of Revelation* (Tyler, TX: Institute for Christian Economics, 1989).
2. Kim Riddlebarger, *The Man of Sin: Uncovering the Truth about the Antichrist* (Grand Rapids: Baker, 2006), 11.
3. Gentry, *The Beast of Revelation*, 35. O. Ruhle says that the 616 variant was an attempt to link Gaius Caesar (Caligula) to the beast out of the sea in Revelation 13. The numerical value of his name in Greek equals 616. Gerhard Kittel, ed. *The Theological Dictionary of the New Testament*, trans. Geoffrey W. Bromiley, vol. 1 (Grand Rapids: Eerdmans, 1964), 462–63.
4. Gentry, *The Beast of Revelation*, 53–54.

5. For a thorough discussion of the date of Revelation, see Mark Hitchcock, "The Stake in the Heart: The AD 95 Date of Revelation," in *The End Times Controversy* (Eugene, OR: Harvest House, 2003), 123–50. My full doctoral dissertation, "A Defense of the Domitianic Date of the Book of Revelation," defending the AD 95 date of Revelation can be accessed at pre-trib.org.
6. Robert L. Thomas, *Revelation 8-22: An Exegetical Commentary* (Chicago: Moody, 1995), 179–80.
7. Many preterists believe that a man named Gessius Florus, the Roman procurator or governor of Judea under Nero, was the false prophet referred to in Revelation 13:11-18. J. Stuart Russell, *The Parousia: The New Testament Doctrine of Our Lord's Second Coming* (1887; repr., Grand Rapids: Baker, 1999), 465–69; Kenneth L. Gentry Jr., *He Shall Have Dominion: A Postmillennial Eschatology* (Tyler, TX: Institute for Christian Economics, 1992), 410. Yet, neither Russell nor Gentry provides any historical evidence that Gessius Florus ever performed great signs and wonders, that he constructed an image of Nero, that he made the image speak, that he forced the mark of the Beast upon the populace, or that he executed those who failed to take the mark. Moreover, Josephus, the Jewish historian, mentions Gessius Florus in his writings but never mentions any activities by him that even remotely correspond to the prophecies of Revelation 13:11-18. If Florus did perform great signs and wonders or do any of the other things in Revelation 13, Josephus's failure to mention these stupendous facts is inexplicable. The inability to successfully name a historical person who fulfilled the role and activities of the false prophet in the Neronic era is a major stumbling block for the preterist view of the Beast.
8. David E. Aune, *Revelation 6–16*, Word Biblical Commentary, gen. ed. Bruce M. Metzger, vol. 52B (Nashville: Thomas Nelson, 1998), 771.
9. For a complete refutation of the view that Nero is the Beast of Revelation 13, see Andy Woods, "Revelation 13 and the First Beast," in *The End Times Controversy* (Eugene, OR: Harvest House, 2003), 237–50.
10. Irenaeus, who wrote in the late second century, suggested three names for the total 666: Evanthas, Lateinos, and Teitan (*Against Heresies* 5.30.3). But he never suggested Nero.
11. Simon J. Kistemaker, *Exposition of the Book of Revelation*, New Testament Commentary (Grand Rapids: Baker, 2001), 395. There may be evidence that some related Nero to the Beast of Revelation 13 in the sixth century AD, but even if this is true, that is still four hundred years after Revelation was written.
12. Thomas, *Revelation 8-22*, 185.
13. William F. Arndt and F. W. Gingrich, *A Greek-English Lexicon of the New Testament* (Chicago: University of Chicago Press, 1957), 876.
14. Thomas, *Revelation 8-22*, 181.
15. Hal Harless, "666: The Beast and His Mark in Revelation 13," *The Conservative Theological Journal* 7, no. 22 (December 2003): 342–46.
16. Henry M. Morris, *Revelation Record: A Scientific and Devotional Commentary on the Prophetic Book of the End of Times* (Carol Stream, IL: Tyndale, 1983), 255.
17. Dr. Arnold G. Fruchtenbaum, *The Footsteps of the Messiah: A Study of the Sequence of Prophetic Events*, rev. ed. (Tustin, CA: Ariel Publications, 2003), 255.
18. Ibid.
19. John F. Walvoord, *The Prophecy Knowledge Handbook: All the Prophecies of Scripture Explained in One Volume* (Wheaton, IL: SP Publications, 1990), 587.
20. M. R. DeHaan, *Studies in Revelation* (1946; repr., Grand Rapids: Kregel, 1998), 189.
21. Morris, *Revelation Record*, 256.
22. Ibid.

23. The word used for the seal of God on the foreheads of the saints in Revelation 7:3 is the Greek word *sphragizo*, which is used of the invisible seal of the Holy Spirit in the New Testament (2 Corinthians 1:22; Ephesians 1:13; 4:30). The word *mark* (*charagma*), on the other hand, refers to a visible mark, imprint, or etching. Therefore, while God's mark on His saints will be invisible, the Beast's mark will be visible.

CHAPTER 28: THE TWO WITNESSES

1. Material in this chapter was adapted from *The Complete Book of Bible Prophecy* (pp. 120–25).
2. David Jeremiah, *Escape the Coming Night: Messages from the Book of Revelation Study Guide*, vol. 2, 122.
3. John F. Walvoord, *The Revelation of Jesus Christ* (Chicago: Moody, 1966), 179–80.
4. Robert L. Thomas, *Revelation 8-22* (Chicago: Moody, 1995), 89.
5. Ray C. Stedman, *God's Final Word: Understanding Revelation* (Grand Rapids: Discovery House, 1991), 220.
6. Tim LaHaye, *Revelation Unveiled* (Grand Rapids: Zondervan, 1999), 188.
7. John Phillips, *Exploring Revelation* (Neptune, NJ: Loizeaux Brothers, 1991), 150.
8. Leon Wood, *The Bible and Future Events: An Introductory Survey of Last-Day Events* (Grand Rapids: Zondervan, 1973), 131–32. Robert Thomas makes a strong case for placing the ministry of the two witnesses in the last half of the Tribulation. See Thomas, *Revelation 8-22*, 84–86. Cf. John F. Walvoord, *Revelation*, rev. ed. (Chicago: Moody, 2011), 179–80.
9. Walvoord, *Revelation*, 179.
10. Paul N. Benware, *Understanding End Times Prophecy: A Comprehensive Approach* (Chicago: Moody, 1995), 254.

CHAPTER 29: SEVEN SOUNDING TRUMPETS AND SEVEN SUPER BOWLS

1. Charles R. Swindoll, *Insights on Revelation* (Grand Rapids: Zondervan, 2011), 136.
2. Ray C. Stedman, *God's Final Word: Understanding Revelation* (Grand Rapids: Discovery House, 1991), 194–95.
3. This material was adapted from *The Complete Book of Bible Prophecy* (pp. 209–210).
4. Swindoll, *Insights on Revelation*, 164.

CHAPTER 30: THE FALL OF BABYLON THE GREAT

1. Material in this chapter was adapted from The Complete Book of Bible Prophecy (pp. 96–100).
2. Charles R. Swindoll, *Insights on Revelation* (Grand Rapids: Zondervan, 2011), 228.
3. Charles H. Dyer, *The Rise of Babylon: Sign of the End Times* (Carol Stream, IL: Tyndale, 1991), 182.
4. Robert L. Thomas, *Revelation 8-22* (Chicago: Moody, 1995), 307.
5. Henry M. Morris, *Revelation Record: A Scientific and Devotional Commentary on the Prophetic Book of the End Times* (Carol Stream, IL: Tyndale, 1983), 348–49.
6. Charles H. Dyer, "The Identity of Babylon in Revelation 17–18," *Bibliotheca Sacra* 144 (October–December 1987): 441–43.
7. J. Vernon McGee, *Thru the Bible*, vol. 5 (Nashville: Thomas Nelson, 1983), 1,039.
8. Arnold G. Fruchtenbaum, *The Footsteps of the Messiah*, rev. ed. (Tustin, CA: Ariel Ministries, 2003), 237–38.

9. Thomas, *Revelation 8-22*, 282–83.
10. Swindoll, *Insights on Revelation*, 238.

CHAPTER 31: THE CAMPAIGN OF ARMAGEDDON

1. Adrian Rogers, *Unveiling the End Times in Our Time: The Triumph of the Lamb in Revelation* (Nashville: B&H, 2004), 222.
2. Daniel Schorr, "Reagan Recants: His Path from Armageddon to Detente," *Los Angeles Times*, January 3, 1988, articles.latimes.com/1988-01-03/opinion/op-32475_1_president-reagan.
3. "Reagan: Is Apocalypse Now?" *Atlanta Journal and Constitution*, October 29, 1983, www.ramsheadpress.com/messiah/PDF/CHAPTER26.pdf.
4. Billy Graham, Till Armageddon (Minneapolis: World Wide, 1981), 15.
5. Material in this chapter was adapted from *The Complete Book of Bible Prophecy* (pp. 73–76).

In Hebrew in Micah 2:12, the word "fold" is the word *Bozrah*, which means sheepfold. This passage predicts that someday Israel's king will lead his people from exile in Bozrah. The ancient city of Bozrah was located in the region of Mount Seir in Edom. The exact location of Bozrah is still disputed. It may be the present Arab village of Buseirah, or it may be the city known today as Petra. It seems best to identify the future city of refuge for the Jewish people as the rock city of Petra. As Arnold Fruchtenbaum notes, "Petra is located in a basin within Mount Seir, and is totally surrounded by mountains and cliffs. The only way in and out of the city is through a narrow passageway that extends for about a mile and can only be negotiated by foot or by horseback. This makes the city easy to defend, and its surrounding high cliffs give added meaning and confirmation to Isaiah 33:16. Only a few abreast can enter through this passage at any one time giving this city an even greater defensibility. The name *Bozrah* means 'sheepfold.' An ancient sheepfold had a narrow entrance so that the shepherd could count his sheep. Once inside the fold, the sheep had more room to move around. Petra is shaped like a giant sheepfold with its narrow passageway opening up to a spacious circle surrounded by cliffs." See Arnold G. Fruchtenbaum, *The Footsteps of the Messiah*, rev. ed. (Tustin, CA: Ariel Ministries, 2003), 296.

Also, the only nation in the Middle East that will escape the direct control of the Antichrist is the modern nation of Jordan. Daniel 11:41 says, "He will also enter the Beautiful Land, and many countries will fall; but these will be rescued out of his hand: Edom, Moab and the foremost of the sons of Ammon" (NASB). This makes the area of Petra, which lies in ancient Edom, a perfect place of refuge from the Antichrist during the Tribulation period.

6. The Scriptures say that the Lord will prepare a city of refuge for the Jewish remnant during the last half of the Tribulation. It will be a place prepared by God, which means it will be adequate as a place of refuge. This place is also consistently described as being in "the mountains" or "the wilderness" (Matthew 24:16; Revelation 12:6, 14, NASB). Therefore, this city must be prepared by God in advance, must be in the hills and in the wilderness. The city of Petra fits all of these criteria: it is adequate to hold what may be one million Jewish people; it is both in the hills and the wilderness; and it is accessible to the fleeing remnant. Therefore, putting all these points together, it is apparent that God will provide the fleeing Jewish remnant an accessible place of refuge in the wilderness and in the hills that will be like a sheepfold and that will be outside

the Antichrist's domain. The place that best fits the clues provided in Scripture is the magnificent rock city of Petra.

7. John Phillips, *Exploring Revelation: An Expository Commentary* (Grand Rapids: Kregel, 2001), 236.

CHAPTER 32: HERE COMES THE KING

1. Tim LaHaye and Jerry B. Jenkins, *Are We Living in the End Times?* (Carol Stream, IL: Tyndale, 1999), 221–22.
2. Material in this section was adapted from *The Complete Book of Bible Prophecy* (p. 211).
3. Material in this section was adapted from *The Complete Book of Bible Prophecy* (pp. 71–72).

CHAPTER 33: SEVENTY-FIVE DAYS TO GLORY

1. Leon J. Wood, *A Commentary on Daniel* (Grand Rapids: Zondervan, 1973), 327.
2. Ibid., 328–29.
3. John Phillips, *Exploring the Book of Daniel* (Grand Rapids: Kregel, 2004), 222–23.

PART 11: SATAN'S CHAIN AND THE SAINTS' REIGN

1. J. Dwight Pentecost, *Things to Come* (Grand Rapids: Zondervan, 1964), 476.
2. M. R. DeHaan, *The Great Society* (Radio Bible Class, 1965), 7–8.

CHAPTER 34: THE MILLENNIUM

1. Material from this chapter was adapted from *The Complete Book of Bible Prophecy* (pp. 28–34, 77, 80).
2. Charles C. Ryrie, *The Basis of the Premillennial Faith* (Neptune, NJ: Loizeaux Brothers, 1953), 145–46.
3. Loraine Boettner, *The Meaning of the Millennium: Four Views*, ed. Robert G. Clouse (Downers Grove, IL: InterVarsity Press, 1977), 117–18.
4. This section was adapted from *The Complete Book of Bible Prophecy* (pp. 35–36).
5. Kim Riddlebarger, *A Case for Amillennialism: Understanding the End Times* (Grand Rapids: Baker, 2003), 217.
6. Ibid., 217.
7. Grant R. Osborne, *Revelation* (Grand Rapids: Baker Academic, 2002), 702–3.
8. Harold W. Hoehner, "Evidence from Revelation 20," in *A Case for Premillennialism: A New Consensus*, gen. ed. Donald K. Campbell and Jeffrey L. Townsend (Chicago: Moody, 1992), 250.

CHAPTER 35: WHY THE MILLENNIUM?

1. These three points were adapted from *The Complete Book of Bible Prophecy* (pp. 80–81).
2. J. Dwight Pentecost, *Thy Kingdom Come: Tracing God's Kingdom Program and Covenant Promises throughout History* (Wheaton, IL: Victor Books, 1990), 316.
3. James Montgomery Boice, *The Last and Future World* (Grand Rapids: Zondervan, 1977), 27.
4. Adrian Rogers, *Unveiling the End Times in Our Time: The Triumph of the Lamb in Revelation* (Nashville: B&H, 2004), 181.

CHAPTER 36: WHEN THE WORLD IS TURNED RIGHT SIDE UP

1. Rick Ezell, "We Are Not Abandoned," *Jesus Christ Only*, www.jesuschristonly.com/illustrations/birth.html.

2. Charles R. Swindoll, *Insights on Revelation* (Grand Rapids: Zondervan, 2011), 258.
3. These ten points were adapted from *The Complete Book of Bible Prophecy* (pp. 78–79).
4. Ralph H. Alexander, "Ezekiel," in *The Expositor's Bible Commentary*, gen. ed. Frank E. Gaebelein, vol. 6 (Grand Rapids: Zondervan, 1986), 952.
5. Fruchtenbaum provides an extensive list of the differences between the Mosaic law and Ezekiel 40–48. Arnold G. Fruchtenbaum, *The Footsteps of the Messiah*, rev. ed. (Tustin, CA: Ariel Ministries, 2003), 462–64.
6. Ibid., 462.
7. Alexander, "Ezekiel," 950.
8. Mark F. Rooker, "Evidence from Ezekiel," in *A Case for Premillennialism: A New Consensus*, ed. Donald K. Campbell and Jeffrey L. Townsend (Chicago: Moody, 1992), 131–34; Alexander, "Ezekiel," 946–52; Fruchtenbaum, *The Footsteps of the Messiah*, 458–69; Randall Price, *The Coming Last Days Temple* (Eugene, OR: Harvest House, 1999), 533–57; Jerry M. Hullinger, "A Proposed Solution to the Problem of Animal Sacrifices in Ezekiel 40–48" (PhD dissertation, Dallas Theological Seminary, 1993); Hullinger, "The Problem of Animal Sacrifices in Ezekiel 40–48," *Bibliotheca Sacra* 152 (1995): 279–89; Thomas Ice, "Literal Sacrifices in the Millennium," *Pre-Trib Perspectives* 5 (2000), 1, 4–5; John C. Whitcomb, "Christ's Atonement and Animal Sacrifices in Israel," *Grace Theological Journal* 6 (1985): 201–21.
9. Hullinger, "The Problem of Animal Sacrifices," 288–89.

PART 12: THE SECOND COMING OF SATAN

1. Clarence Larkin, *The Book of Revelation* (New York: Cosimo, 2006), 199.
2. Joseph A. Seiss, *The Apocalypse: Lectures on the Book of Revelation* (New York: Cosimo, 2007), 462.

CHAPTER 37: SATAN'S LAST STAND

1. J. Vernon McGee, *Reveling Through Revelation*, 2 vols. (Pasadena, CA: Thru the Bible, 1974), 74–75.
2. J. Dwight Pentecost, *Things to Come* (Grand Rapids: Zondervan, 1958), 538.

PART 13: THE GREAT WHITE THRONE

1. Erwin Lutzer, *Your Eternal Reward: Triumph and Tears at the Judgment Seat of Christ* (Chicago: Moody, 1998), 164–65.

CHAPTER 38: JUDGMENT DAY

1. David Jeremiah, *Escape the Coming Night* (Dallas: Word Publishing, 1997), 236.
2. Erwin Lutzer, *Your Eternal Reward* (Chicago: Moody, 1998), 166.
3. Ibid., 167.
4. Jeremiah, *Escape the Coming Night*, 236.
5. Lutzer, *Your Eternal Reward*, 169.
6. John F. Walvoord, "Literal," in *Four Views on Hell*, gen. ed. William Crockett (Grand Rapids: Zondervan, 1996), 167.
7. These points were adapted from *The Complete Book of Prophecy* (pp. 218–19).
8. Lutzer, *One Minute After You Die*, 39.
9. Warren Wiersbe, *The Bible Exposition Commentary: New Testament*, vol. 2 (Wheaton, IL: Victor Books, 1989), 621.

PART 14: THE BEST IS YET TO COME

1. J. C. Ryle, *Heaven* (Great Britain: Christian Focus, 2000), 19–20, 23–24.

CHAPTER 39: NEW HEAVEN, NEW EARTH, NEW JERUSALEM

1. This story was taken from a pamphlet by J. R. Ecob, "The Story of Mr. Eternity" (The Herald of Hope, Inc., 2000).
2. These five points were adapted from Mark Hitchcock, *The Complete Book of Bible Prophecy* (Carol Stream, IL: Tyndale, 1999), 88–93.
3. Randy Alcorn provides an excellent case for the renovation view. Randy Alcorn, *Heaven* (Carol Stream, IL: Tyndale, 2004), 145–51.
4. John F. Walvoord, *Revelation*, ed. Mark Hitchcock and Philip E. Rawley, rev. ed. (Chicago: Moody, 2011), 317.
5. Charles R. Swindoll, *Insights on Revelation* (Grand Rapids: Zondervan, 2011), 271.
6. Ibid., 272.
7. Ibid., 273.
8. Steven J. Lawson, *Heaven Help Us!: Truths about Eternity That Will Help You Live Today* (Colorado Springs: NavPress, 1995), 148–49.
9. James M. Hamilton Jr., *Revelation: The Spirit Speaks to the Churches*, Preaching the Word, ed. R. Kent Hughes (Wheaton, IL: Crossway, 2012), 393.
10. Bruce Waltke and Cathi J. Fredricks, *Genesis: A Commentary* (Grand Rapids: Zondervan, 2001), 515.

Index

Scripture Index